Teaching Activities Manual for

The Catholic Youth Bible

Teaching Activities Manual for

The Catholic Youth Bible

Christine Schmertz Navarro
and contributing authors

Saint Mary's Press
Christian Brothers Publications
Winona, Minnesota

Contributing authors:

Kathleen Crawford Hodapp
Rick Keller-Scholz
Lars Lund

Genuine recycled paper with 10% post-consumer waste.
Printed with soy-based ink.

The publishing team included Shirley Kelter, development editor; Cheryl Drivdahl, copy editor; Lynn Dahdal, production editor; Hollace Storkel, typesetter; Cindi Ramm, cover designer; produced by the graphics division of Saint Mary's Press.

The acknowledgments continue on page 390.

Printed in the United States of America

Printing: 9 8 7 6 5 4 3 2

Year: 2008 07 06 05 04 03 02 01

ISBN 0-88489-560-2

Library of Congress Cataloging-in-Publication Data
Navarro, Christine Schmertz.
    Teaching activities manual for the Catholic youth Bible / Christine Schmertz Navarro and contributing authors.
        p. cm.
Includes bibliographical references.
    ISBN 0-88489-560-2 (pbk. : alk. paper)
    1. Bible—Study and teaching—Catholic Church. 2. Christian education of young people. I. Title.
    BS587 .N38 2000
    220'.071'2—dc21
                99-050758

Choose life so that you and your descendants may live, loving the LORD your God, obeying him, and holding fast to him. (Deut 30.19–20)

About the Author

Christine Schmertz Navarro taught high school theology for six years before taking time to stay home with her daughter, Francesca. She and her family live in Tacoma, Washington.

Contents

Introduction

Welcome to a new adventure in teaching the Bible to teenagers. We have designed this manual with the adventuresome teacher in mind—someone who has perhaps taught Scripture courses to high school students before. We assume that that someone is you.

You may have used conventional materials to teach the Scriptures, such as textbooks on the Bible, the Old Testament, or the New Testament. Maybe those were fine for a while, but now you are looking for something more—an approach that will take the Bible to a more personal level with students. You want your students to be more actively engaged in seeing how the Bible relates to their lives. You want them to be as excited as you are about discovering what God is saying to you and them through the Scriptures. And most of all, you want them to *read* the Bible, not just *read about* the Bible.

Okay. We have figured out that you are adventuresome, you love the Bible, and you love the kids you teach. What a great combination! Now we add to that mix *The Catholic Youth Bible,* the complete Bible for teenagers that intersperses the biblical text with over 650 lively, youth-friendly articles, pieces that draw teens into the biblical text itself to see how it speaks to them. Chances are you are already familiar with that resource, or you would not have picked up this manual. But in case you have not seen it, we will fill you in on some of the other features of *The Catholic Youth Bible,* or the *CYB,* as it is called in shorthand.

The articles in the *CYB* are tagged, for example, "Live It!" "Pray It!" "Did You Know?" "Introducing . . ." (focusing on important biblical people), and "Catholic Connections" (tracing the biblical roots of many Catholic beliefs and practices). Also featured are articles written from the perspectives of four different cultures: African American, Asian American, Hispanic and Latino American, and Native American.

The *CYB* also contains engaging section and book introductions, and includes nine full-color maps, eight reading plans, four special indexes, one full-color timeline of biblical events, and four pages of full-color photographs.

This manual serves the teacher who wants to use *The Catholic Youth Bible* as the primary text for a Scripture course. It contains the following items:
- learning activities for every book of the Bible, some applying to several books and many incorporating and extending the articles in the *CYB*
- eighteen student handouts
- lists of resources for teacher background and for ministry with teens (appendix A)
- a list of recommended audiovisuals (appendix B)
- ten prayer services (appendix C)
- two retreat outlines (appendix D)

For those who want to "move outside the box"—to go beyond the conventional textbook approach to teaching the Scriptures—the *CYB,* together with this manual, can provide just what is needed.

What Does This Manual Offer?

This manual is a resource for you to use in creating a course on the Bible. It is more like a cookbook of learning activities than a plan for structuring a course from *A* to *Z*. In other words, you can rely on your own creativity in laying out a course that addresses the needs and preferences of you and your students.

The learning activities in this manual are organized, as is the *CYB*, according to the sequence of the books of the Bible. But that organization need not be the structure of your course. You may not want to start at the beginning of this manual and do activities from every section, following the Bible book by book. You may prefer to select activities from this manual, including ones that extend the *CYB* articles, according to another course organization. Here are some possibilities:

■ Concentrate first on one biblical book or section of a book, not necessarily from the beginning of the Bible—for instance, one of the Gospels (Mark is the shortest) or Exodus, chapters 1–15 (the familiar story of Moses and the Israelites up through the escape from Egypt). This has the advantage of starting off the students with somewhat known material, and it also enables them to see one book or part of a book in total. Generally, Catholic students have been exposed to biblical passages in a mostly piecemeal fashion, as they are presented by the lectionary at Mass. Reading a whole book, or a significant portion of one, can shed new light on the old familiar passages. Then you might proceed to other selected books of the Bible as your semester's or year's schedule permits.

■ Follow the sequence used in our textbook *Written on Our Hearts: The Old Testament Story of God's Love,* by Mary Reed Newland (see appendix A). The approach taken there is to proceed through the Bible, not book by book, but in the order of salvation history, beginning with the "prehistory" in the first eleven chapters of Genesis. That has the advantage of following a rough chronology, to keep the Story straight.

■ Structure your course around selections from one of the first three indexes in the back of the *CYB*. The first index is of Bible passages on events, people, and teachings of Jesus; the second index relates Bible passages to each of the seven sacraments; and the third index points to Bible passages related to specific life and faith issues.

■ Use the suggested reading plans at the front of the *CYB* and structure a course following them, integrating the relevant articles from the *CYB* and the activities from this manual that address the passages in the reading plans. The students could even help to structure the course based on their own choice of reading plans as a group. The reading plans are as follows:
  1. "Reading the Bible with the Church" (the lectionary readings)
  2. "A Walk Through the Bible" (highlights of the Bible in chronological order)
  3. "Images of God"
  4. "Called by God" (people called to serve)
  5. "The Justice of God"
  6. "Sin and Salvation"
  7. "Why Do We Suffer?"
  8. "Women in the Bible"

■ Use the prayer services and retreats in appendices C and D of this manual at appropriate points in your course, and draw from the lists of print and audiovisual resources in appendices A and B to structure a course that fits the needs of your students.

Regardless of what approach you take to structuring your course, we believe this strongly: **It is crucial for students at the outset to get a broad picture of the whole Story of salvation history**, or at least a rough chronology of events. Later in this introduction, in the section "The First Step: A Sprint Through Salvation History," we offer a way to give them that overview.

What Do You Need in Addition to This Manual?

Background

As a cookbook, this manual offers you a smorgasbord of creative, engaging activities. It does not provide the in-depth background on the Bible that anyone teaching the Scriptures should have. You may already be a storehouse of such background knowledge from years of experience studying and teaching the Scriptures. If not, other excellent materials give that essential background, and full bibliographic information on a selection of those materials is included in appendix A.

We highly recommend having at hand an all-purpose study guide to the Bible. A scholarly work such as *The New Jerome Biblical Commentary,* edited by Raymond E. Brown, Joseph A. Fitzmyer, and Roland E. Murphy, would be helpful. But a less technical, more user-friendly guide will be a better aid for translating scholarly insights into lay, and especially teenage, terms.

For that purpose we recommend *The Catholic Bible: Personal Study Edition,* edited by Jean Marie Hiesberger. Besides the full text of the New American Bible, with its usual book introductions and footnotes, this edition has five hundred pages of excellent, easy-to-understand background on all the books of the Bible. Those pages include outlines; insightful articles; charts; a reading guide walk-through for each book; and for each book a feature called "At a Glance," which sums up briefly and well these crucial points: Who are the main players? What should I look for? When did this take place? Where did these events occur? Why was this book written? What is the story? (Note: Oxford University Press publishes another, more technical study guide, *The Catholic Study Bible,* edited by Donald Senior. This guide contains some material that overlaps that in *The Catholic Bible: Personal Study Edition.* For helping you teach high school students, *The Catholic Bible: Personal Study Edition* is preferred.)

Numerous other good resources on the Bible are available. You will need a good concordance to the version of the Bible you are using—for instance, *The Concise Concordance to the New Revised Standard Version,* edited by John R. Kohlenberger III (the *CYB* uses the NRSV). You will also need a good Bible dictionary: John L. McKenzie's *Dictionary of the Bible* is a classic that has held up extremely well; another excellent choice is *The HarperCollins Bible Dictionary,* edited by Paul J. Achtemeier.

For other background that can be translated into useful insights for the students, we recommend the highly readable *Responses to 101 Questions on the Bible,* by Raymond E. Brown (we are fortunate that such gifted scriptural scholars are able to write in down-to-earth language for the layperson). Another highly accessible book that can help you translate scholarly information into kid-friendly insights is *"And God Said What?" An Introduction to Biblical Literary Forms for Bible Lovers,* by Margaret Nutting Ralph. Anthony E. Gilles has written two little gems that give perspective on the Bible's development and context—*The People of the Book: The Story Behind the Old Testament* and *The People of the Way: The Story Behind the New Testament.* The four-page monthly *Scripture from Scratch* provides valuable, accessible background too.

Books that offer a kind of spirituality lens on the Bible can help you make your Scripture course much more nourishing for students' lives. Two by Richard Rohr and Joseph Martos offer a particularly accessible orientation to the spirituality of the Bible: *The Great Themes of Scripture: New Testament* and *The Great Themes of Scripture: Old Testament.* Two spiritually enriching books that highlight the justice themes throughout the Bible deserve special note: Joyce Hollyday's *Clothed with the Sun: Biblical Women, Social Justice, and Us* and Robert McAfee Brown's *Unexpected News: Reading the Bible with Third World Eyes.*

You may decide to supplement your course with textbooks like Mary Reed Newland's *Written on Our Hearts* (on the Old Testament) and Thomas Zanzig's *Jesus of History, Christ of Faith* (on the New Testament), even just to see how they present certain passages or deal with certain issues with a teenage audience.

You may weave into your classes the insights you gain into the history, context, theological intent, and so on, of a given book of the Bible. In the spirit of the learning processes advocated in this manual, those background insights and information should not be delivered as extensive lecture pieces (see the section "The Pedagogical Approach of This Manual" below). You may integrate your insights gained from background knowledge judiciously as they fit, simply in the course of introducing activities or commenting on the insights that students gain as they do the activities.

Art and Music Materials

Many of the activities in this manual tap into the artistic and musical creativity of the students. It will be beneficial to keep an ample supply of the following items in your classroom. The students can help provide these.

- construction paper
- poster board
- scissors
- glue
- markers, crayons, and colored pencils
- magazines and catalogs
- glitter, yarn, buttons, feathers, and other doodads
- small percussion instruments

The Pedagogical Approach of This Manual

The pairing of *The Catholic Youth Bible* with this manual of learning activities supposes that you, the teacher, will shape a unique vision for the course, selecting what books of the Bible to cover, in what sequence, and in what depth. As discussed in the preceding section, you will need to draw on your own background in the Scriptures and supplement that with whatever study guides or references are most useful to you.

To help the students understand the meaning of the Bible passages, encourage them to form the habit of writing down any questions they have or any terms or concepts with which they are unfamiliar, as they are reading. Discussions around their questions can precede or be integrated into the steps of the activities. In addition, there are certain activities, labeled "Exegetical Tools," that focus on different types of biblical criticism and introduce the use of various resources for exploring the Bible.

However, the approach of most of the activities in this manual is not primarily academic but invites the students to engage in a personal dialogue with the text of the Bible. Having an academic background will help you guide them in that engagement, but the students' focus will be less scholarly.

Let's return to the analogy of a cookbook we have been using for this manual. For the most part, in our cooking, we alternate between old favorites and new recipes to spice up our lives. In the same way, a veteran teacher can incorporate the new activities found in this manual with lesson plans from years past, tailoring the curriculum to meet the specific needs of the current students.

This is not a cookbook for total beginners; it does not take you step-by-step through the activities and tell you how to "cook." This book presumes that you have the background, the experience, and the knowledge of your students needed to use and adapt the activities as necessary.

The Power of the Scriptures in the Student–Teacher Relationship

This course rests on several important presuppositions about the Scriptures and the relationship between students and teachers. The first is that the Scriptures can speak powerfully to teenagers and their teachers about God and God's desires for their lives and world. The second is that God's word can speak to the needs, questions, and issues that are important to the students now. The third is that the teacher can not only discover ways in which God speaks through the Scriptures but also help the students discern, through careful listening, how God is communicating with them.

The Catholic Youth Bible and this manual of learning are based on the belief that God reaches out in love to teens through the Scriptures. During the tumultuous years of adolescence, God longs to offer peace, forgiveness, and affirmation. Jesus' model of living and teaching can speak powerfully in their lives.

Scriptural exegesis is a dialogue between the person who reads the Bible and the scriptural text. Each individual or group brings personal questions and concerns to the reading of the Scriptures, and this allows for many rich interpretations of the same passages. Marvelously, God works through this interchange to inspire, challenge, and express love for us. While human teachers may share scholarly interpretations of a passage with the students, the main teacher of this course is God. God speaks to the students, and the teacher facilitates that process and encourages reflection on its mystery. This teaching manual is invitational in nature rather than simply instructive.

The students can hear God speaking to them only when they come to God honestly from the reality of their own lives. This manual provides opportunities for them to reflect on the mysteries of the Scriptures in age-appropriate ways. And in the meantime, they will be educating *you* about who they are and what is important to them.

The manual asks you, as the teacher, to create opportunities for the scriptural text to speak to the students on a personal level, and then to invite the students to reflect on and share what each of them finds there. You must take a discerning role with the students. After they have engaged with the text, listen to their insights, and ask further questions to help them reflect on their own images of God and their own sense of God's invitation, message, and call to each one of them and to the Christian community now. Share your professional knowledge and teaching skills with the students, and then join them in being open to God's word, facilitating this exploration process for them.

The Value of Active Learning in Teaching the Scriptures

Traditionally, the Scriptures have been taught in the linguistic style that has characterized instruction in most disciplines. Reading the Bible, hearing lectures about its meaning, discussing questions related to the material, and writing reflections about its significance have been important ways that students have learned about the word of God. This manual's goal is to complement that style with an active learning approach to exploring the Scriptures. The activities share some of the following characteristics:

Each student must engage in the learning process. The activities in this manual invite *every* student to interact with the scriptural text personally. In addition, the variety of learning styles addressed by the activities can appeal to all students to varying degrees. Dramatic, artistic, and musical students can shine, as well as those whose skills are verbal. The extrovert and the introvert can find activities that interest them. And the process of active learning invites all students to expand their gifts in those different areas and their understanding of how various media can enhance learning in all of life.

The activities in this manual approach the Scriptures from the context of the students' lives. The activities attempt to answer the students' silent question, "Why should I bother reading the Bible or paying attention in class today?" The use of contemporary music, television, and other media as sources for reflection on the Bible helps the Scriptures' "credibility" with teens. The connection of the Scriptures to issues of emotional development, friendship, family, society and world, and personal future helps the students relate a piece of writing from two thousand years ago with what happens to them every day. You can help by narrowing and adapting the context of the activities as much as necessary to address the specific questions of your own students.

An active learning approach invites the students to examine the Scriptures and be open to their message at a deeper level. For instance, the students can explore biblical passages through art projects, role-plays, ethical scenarios, journal entries, musical themes, and other forms of expression. This invites the students to see both familiar and unfamiliar passages in a new light and to explore concepts in a new way. We, and our students, cannot simply look at a passage or issue from a one-dimensional perspective, but must delve more deeply into it and make new connections. An active learning approach encourages the students to explore the complexity and mystery of God's revelation in our world now.

The First Step: A Sprint Through Salvation History

Earlier, we said that students need to have an overview of salvation history, or at least a rough chronology of biblical events, so that they can appreciate certain passages or books of the Bible in the context of "the big Story." We recommended that before tackling specific books or passages, you lead an activity that will give them this crucial chronological, contextual background. Without that background, they may miss much of the fruit that this course holds out. We recommend facilitating a "sprint" through salvation history at the beginning of the course, even if you choose to structure the whole course according to the Story itself. That will help the young people to see the whole picture before examining the details.

Methods of Sprinting

If you can arrange for a two-hour block of time, consider giving the students an overview of biblical history through a wonderfully creative approach from the Horizons Program, a parish religious education program for senior high students published by Saint Mary's Press. Session 3 of the course *The Bible: Power and Promise,* by Brian Singer-Towns, offers an imaginative, engaging activity that literally takes the students on a journey through salvation history. Along the way they stop at various points to learn the Story by completing activities that they take turns presenting.

If you are limited to shorter class periods or want to do a simpler version of a biblical journey with your students, we recommend an approach like the one in the next section.

A Sample Sprint

Handout Intro–A

1. Give your students a copy of handout Intro–A, "A Sprint Through Salvation History." It divides the Story of salvation into eight sections or stages:
1. The founders and the Promise (Abraham and Sarah, and their descendants)
2. Moses, the Exodus, and the Sinai Covenant
3. The invasion of Canaan and the period of the Judges
4. The nation and the Temple (Saul, David, and Solomon)
5. The divided nation (Israel and Judah, and the kings and the prophets)
6. The Exile, the return to Judah, and the dispersion of the Jews
7. More domination by foreign powers (Greek and Roman)
8. Jesus as the Messiah of Israel (his life, death, and Resurrection) and the growth of the early church after Pentecost

Direct the students all to read the *entire* handout as homework or in class. As they read, they should follow along with the timeline of biblical history on pages 1542 to 1545 of the *CYB.* They should also consult the maps on pages 1535 to 1541 for locations.

2. Divide the class into eight groups, and assign each group one of the stages of the journey. Instruct the groups each to develop an artistic expression or symbol of their assigned stage, which they will present to the rest of the class at the next class period. Encourage the students to use their creativity. They may come up with a popular song that reminds them of what went on in that stage of salvation history. Or they may do a pantomime of, for instance, the escape from Egypt during the Exodus. They may create a visual—such as a painting, a drawing, or a collage. They may form a "human sculpture" to express a feeling or a theme from their assigned stage.

3. For the class period in which the journey takes place, if possible, set up eight stations in a large space such as a gym so that the students can actually move from place to place to get the feel of journeying. You might be able to use parts of the whole school, making for a pilgrimage-type procession from one place to another.

Gather the students and then lead them through the space you have arranged, stopping at each station in the journey to read the section of the handout about that stage of salvation history. At each station, tie the material from the handout in with the timeline and maps in the *CYB* to reinforce the chronology. Then invite the assigned group to present its work.

4. When you have completed the journey, gather back in the classroom. Go over the experience, clarify any questions about the sequence and events (referring again to the timeline), and discuss which symbols or artistic expressions were particularly helpful in getting across what was happening during the stages of salvation history.

Ready to Go!

Once you have taken the students through the basic events of salvation history, they will be ready to study the Bible with at least some sense of context. As you explore different books and passages of the Bible throughout the course, refer back to the basic narrative, with the accompanying timeline from the *CYB,* to situate the scriptural stories, prayers, prophecies, and so on, in their historical contexts. A resource such as *The Catholic Bible: Personal Study Edition,* edited by Jean Marie Hiesberger, can provide invaluable guidance to you as you help the students explore the scriptural books and passages.

"Teach Me Your Paths"

Teaching is always an adventure. When you are drawing out students to encounter God's word in their own lives, teaching may very well be the adventure of a lifetime. This course will be a growing, stretching experience for your students, and perhaps even more for you. After all, you cannot help others meet the living God without yourself meeting God in some pretty unexpected ways!

As you help the students explore the Bible through this course, let these words from Psalm 25 speak deeply in your heart as well as in your students' lives:

> To you, O Lord, I lift up my soul.
> O my God, in you I trust;
>> do not let me be put to shame;
>> do not let my enemies exult over me.
>
> . . . .
>
> Make me to know your ways, O Lord;
>> teach me your paths.
> Lead me in your truth, and teach me,
>> for you are the God of my salvation;
>> for you I wait all day long.

(Verses 1–5)

......► A Sprint Through Salvation History

The God revealed in the Old Testament is not aloof or distant from human affairs; this God acts within human history. The Story of God's actions and the people's responses over many centuries is called **salvation history.**

It will help to keep the big picture of that history in mind as we set out to discover the meaning of the Old Testament because the history and the Scriptures of ancient Israel were intertwined. . . . Do not be concerned about memorizing names and events at this point; they will come up again many times in this course. Instead, simply try to recognize the broad pattern of history.

First, referring to the timelines on pages [1542 to 1545 of the *CYB*], note the time period in which the biblical events happened. As you can see, humankind existed for many thousands of years before the biblical era; most of that time is called prehistory because no historical records of those ancient peoples exist. (The time period of the Creation and the earliest stories of humankind appearing in the Old Testament fall into the category of prehistory.) About 3000 [B.C.], history as we know it began, with the development of early forms of writing. The biblical period—from the beginnings of Israel as a people through the time of Jesus and the earliest years of the church—went from about 1850 [B.C.] until about [A.D.] 100 It lasted almost two thousand years. And that is about the same amount of time as has elapsed from the time of Jesus until today.

What follows is a brief overview of the events of the biblical period. You may also refer to the [maps on pages 1535 to 1541 of the *CYB*].

The Founders and the Promise

The history and the religion of the Israelites began with Abraham. Abraham was a wandering herdsman, or nomad, who lived in the region now called Iraq, around 1850 [B.C.] According to the Book of Genesis, God made an agreement with Abraham. God promised to make Abraham's descendants a blessing to the world and to give them the land of Canaan, later known as Palestine. The Promise, as this is called, was that Abraham's descendants would reveal the one God to the world. Christians believe that this Promise reached its fulfillment in the coming of Christ.

Abraham's descendants and their families inherited the Promise. Abraham, his son Isaac, and grandson Jacob would be called the patriarchs, or founders, of the Jewish faith. Their wives—Sarah, Rebekah, and Rachel—would be called the matriarchs.

The Exodus of the Israelites and the Covenant

At the close of the Book of Genesis, the descendants of Abraham are living in Egypt, having traveled there from Canaan in order to survive a famine. Yet as the Book of Exodus opens, we find them enslaved by the Egyptians. Practically nothing is known about the Israelites in Egypt from about 1700 to 1290 [B.C.]

Moses, the main character in the story of the Exodus, was one of the greatest religious leaders in history. About 1290 [B.C.], the understanding that one God was above all other gods came to Moses when God revealed God's name—Yahweh, meaning "I am the One who is always present." With God's power the Israelites, led by Moses, made a daring escape from Pharaoh's army through the sea—the Exodus—and were thus freed from slavery.

After a dramatic encounter between Moses and God on Mount Sinai, a covenant, or agreement, between Yahweh and the Israelites was confirmed. The Israelites' part of the Covenant was to keep the Ten Commandments, which God had presented to Moses. God's part was to make the Israelites "the people of God" and to be with them as long as they kept the Covenant. Once again God promised that they would be given the land of Canaan. But before they entered Canaan, they wandered for forty years in the desert as they learned to trust God's care for them.

Taking Over the Promised Land

After Moses' time the Israelites, led by Joshua, entered Canaan. Over the next centuries—from about 1250 to 1000 [B.C.]—they fought against the people who lived in that region. In these battles the Israelites were led by military leaders called judges. During this time the Israelites abandoned their nomadic ways for the more settled agricultural life that was native to the region.

The Nation and the Temple

Around 1000 [B.C.] Israel became recognized as a nation, with David as its anointed king and Jerusalem as its capital city. God made a promise to David that his royal line would endure forever. (Later Jews put their hopes in a descendant of David to save them from oppression.)

David's son Solomon built the Temple in Jerusalem, and it became the principal place of worship for the nation. As both a political and a religious capital, Jerusalem became a great and holy city.

The Kings and the Prophets

After Solomon's death in 922 [B.C.], the nation divided, with the kingdom of Israel in the north and the kingdom of Judah in the south. Heavy taxes and forced service in both kingdoms created hardships for the people. In addition, the kings often practiced idolatry—the worship of idols (images of other gods).

18

Prophets spoke out against both kingdoms' injustices to the people and infidelity to God. They questioned the behavior of the kings and called them and their people back to the Covenant. Yet the kingdoms continued to oppress the poor and worship pagan gods until eventually both kingdoms were crushed by powerful conquerors. The Assyrians obliterated the northern kingdom of Israel in 721 [B.C.] and took its people into exile. In 587 [B.C.] the Babylonians destroyed Judah, including the city of Jerusalem, and took its people to Babylon as captives.

The Babylonian Exile and the Jewish Disperson

While the people were exiled in Babylon, still other prophets encouraged them to repent of their sins and turn back to God. During this time the prophet known as Second Isaiah proclaimed that God was the one and only God. Monotheism, the belief in one God, was now the revelation of this people to the world, their blessing to the nations.

After fifty years in Babylon, the exiles were released from captivity by the conquering Persians and allowed to return home. Judah, no longer a politically independent kingdom, had become a district within the Persian Empire, and the returned exiles became known as Jews, from the word *Judah*. They rebuilt the Temple, and under Ezra and Nehemiah, they re-established the Law and restored Jerusalem. That city became the religious capital for the Jews who had resettled all over the world—that is, the Jews of the Dispersion.

During the exile the Jewish leaders had begun collecting and reflecting on their ancestral writings, forming the core of what would later become their Bible, known to Christians as the Old Testament.

More Oppressors

The Persian Empire was conquered in 330 [B.C.] by the armies of Alexander the Great, leader of the Greek Empire. This made the Greeks overlords of the Jews for nearly three hundred years, with the exception of a brief period of independence after a revolt led by the Maccabees family. The Greeks were followed by the Romans, who captured Jerusalem in 63 [B.C.] Although tolerant of other cultures and religions, the Roman Empire severely punished its subjects for revolts.

It was a dark time for the people of the Promise, who longed for release from oppression and for the day when all their hopes for a good and peaceful life would be fulfilled. Many Jews looked toward the coming of a messiah, one sent by God to save them; some expected this messiah to be from the family line of David.

It is at this point in the history of Israel that the Old Testament accounts end. . . .

Jesus, the Savior

Into a situation of defeat and darkness for the people of Israel, Jesus was born, one of the house, or family line, of David. Christians see Jesus as the long-awaited Messiah—the fulfillment of all God's promises to Israel and the Savior of the world. With his death and Resurrection, Jesus' followers recognized that he was the Son of God. The community of believers began to grow, first among Jews but later among Gentiles, or non-Jews. The story of Jesus and the growth of the early church is told in the New Testament.

(The material in this handout is quoted from *Written on Our Hearts: The Old Testament Story of God's Love,* by Mary Reed Newland, revised by Barbara Allaire [Winona, MN: Saint Mary's Press, 1999], pages 13–18. Copyright © 1999 by Saint Mary's Press. All rights reserved.)

Pentateuch

Genesis

Creation

Creative Presentations of the Creation Story
Genesis, chapters 1–2

The students make the first Genesis story come alive with their own creativity.

1. Call several students to read Gen 1.1—2.3 aloud.

2. Divide the class into seven groups. Assign a different day of Creation to each group and say something like this to the students:
    - Today each group is responsible for reading from Genesis the Bible passage associated with its assigned day of Creation and preparing a creative, nonverbal way to present that day to the other groups in our next class. You may use artwork, music, video, drama, rap, props, the environment of the classroom, costumes, and so on. Each presentation should run no longer than 4 minutes. The presentation should be respectful of the Scriptures, and may also be fun. Before the end of this class, each group will need to pass its ideas by me for approval and suggestions.

3. After the presentations are given at the next class, invite the students to discuss any insights or reflections that resulted from preparing or watching them.

Care for the Earth: Genesis
Genesis, chapter 1

Adapt the activity "Care for the Earth: Psalms," on page 120 of this manual, for use with Genesis, chapter 1.

Dominion over the Earth: Genesis
Genesis, chapter 1

The use of modern parallels challenges the students to think more carefully about the meaning of *dominion* in Gen 1.28–30.

1. Begin class by playing the song "Pass It On Down," by the country-and-western group Alabama, from the album *Pass It On Down* (BMG Music, 1990). That song encourages listeners to take care of the earth's environment so that future generations can enjoy the planet's resources. Provide the lyrics

on an overhead or computer projector, and discuss them after the song is played. Ask the students which ideas in the song are meaningful to them, are challenging to them, are disturbing, or speak some truth for them.

2. Give one student a set of keys. Say something like this to the student:
- I am going away for a month. I want you to take care of my house, my car, and my classroom while I am away. Use these keys as if they were your own. When I come back, I want to see my house, my car, and my classroom in the same condition in which I gave them to you.

Lead the students in a discussion about the various ways that request can be honored or dishonored.

3. Read Gen 1.28–30 aloud. Write two column headings on the board, "Stewardship" and "Ownership," and help the students brainstorm the differences between those concepts. Ask the students, "Which is more like the dominion given to the human beings in Genesis?" Remind them that only God owns the universe, and help them realize that the human dominion over the earth called for in the Scripture passage is one of stewardship, not ownership.

4. Divide the class into small groups. Instruct the groups each to brainstorm ways in which human beings are responsible and irresponsible stewards of creation today. Ask the groups to report their insights and resolutions back to the class.

5. Tell the students each to identify one way they are an irresponsible steward of creation and to write a reflection paper about that, including ideas for how they will commit to growing in responsibility for the gift of creation in that area.

Sin and Alienation

The Effect of Sin: Distance
Genesis, chapter 3

This activity invites the students to reflect on the effects of sin described in Genesis, chapter 3, and then to consider how sin in their own lives can distance them from God, themselves, others, and nature.

1. Ask five students to stand before the class and read aloud the parts for the characters in Genesis, chapter 3: narrator, serpent, woman, man, and God. Quietly direct the students who have the parts of the man and the woman to move farther from each other and from God as they read their lines.

2. After the reading, ask all the students what they observed about the characters. Then make the following comments in your own words:
- This story of disobedience to God shows how sin can affect our lives. Sin separates us from God and others, and from ourselves and nature. [Ask the students to explain this concept from the story.]

- Before they sin, the man and the woman in the story are in a harmonious relationship with all that is around them. After they sin, they think about themselves only, and they stop looking at God, each other, the world, and even their innermost selves.

3. Divide the class into four groups, labeling them "God," "Myself," "Other people," and "The natural world." Ask each group to come up with at least three things someone can do to create a distance between themselves and the entity identified by the group's label. Then tell the groups each to plan a brief pantomime that presents one of those actions and shows the separation that can occur. The groups should be creative and include all members in their presentation.

4. Invite each group in turn to present its pantomime, and ask the rest of the class to guess what it is portraying. Discuss the points that the groups bring out in the presentations. Conclude by saying this in your own words:
- God knew what the man and woman needed in order to be in harmony with the world around them. God knows what we need today as well. In the Scripture passage, sin is portrayed as the temptation to presume that we know better what we need than God does. Observing what brings us closer to or distances us from others, ourselves, God, and the world is a step toward learning what God wants for us.

Genesis in Hollywood
Genesis, chapter 3

Casting four biblical characters helps the students explore their own understanding of human nature, especially in light of temptation and weakness.

1. Divide the class into groups of four or five and ask them to read Genesis, chapter 3, with each person in the group assuming a different role: narrator, serpent, woman, man, and God.

2. Invite the students to imagine that they have been asked to cast the four main characters in the story (serpent, woman, man, and God) for a movie. Tell the groups to brainstorm about what actors they would like to play each character and then to discuss their selections.

3. With the entire class, take suggestions for each character, and write the suggestions on the board. Lead the students in a discussion of the following questions:
- What kind of personalities did you choose to represent each biblical figure and why?
- How does the selection of actors relate to temptation and sin?
- How was the serpent able to tempt the man and woman? Are some people better at tempting than others? Are some people more vulnerable to temptation? Are people more susceptible to temptation at some times than at others?
- What message does the story give about the nature of temptation and sin?

God Wants Our Best: Comfort and Challenge
Genesis, chapter 4

The students use the Cain and Abel story as an opportunity to think about the damage of comparing ourselves with others.

1. Assign several students to the characters in Gen 4.1–16 (narrator, Eve, the Lord, and Cain) and ask them to read the passage aloud to the class. Then invite those who read the parts of Cain and God to explain to the class (in character) how they felt in the story and why they did the things they did. Allow the class to ask the readers questions, and the readers to answer as their character might. For instance, the class might ask Cain how he felt about the choice God presented to him in Gen 4.6–7.

2. Continue the discussion with the class by raising these questions and observations in your own words:
   - Because God suggests that Cain's best will be accepted, what temptation lurks for Cain if he does not do his best? Does that exist for us, as well?
   - This story addresses our everyday lives. There are always people who appear more successful than us in some areas, and others who appear less successful. As in this biblical story, it is important that we focus on our own performance only and not evaluate ourselves based on other people's success. God simply wants us to try our best, and resist the temptation to compare ourselves with others and, even worse, to take out our frustration on others when we are feeling that we have not done our best or that our best isn't good enough.

3. Direct the students to work in pairs to come up with realistic modern Cain and Abel scenarios, asking some pairs to prepare feminine versions. Mention that the students may use sports, academics, parental approval, popularity, social life, and so on, in their examples. Invite them to share some of their stories with the class. Discuss the insights that arise.

Field of Dreams: Outrageous Requests
Genesis, chapters 6–9, 12

The movie *Field of Dreams* invites the students to reflect on God's outrageous requests and human beings' courageous responses.

1. Begin class by reading Gen 6.11—9.17 (the call of Noah) or Genesis, chapter 12 (the call of Abraham). Address any questions the students have about the content and biblical meaning of the story.

2. Show the students at least the first 40 minutes of the movie *Field of Dreams* (MCA/Universal, 1989, 106 min., rated PG), which gives a modern interpretation of Noah's and Abraham's courage to follow an unusual call. Consider playing the entire movie if you have time; though the first 40 minutes is enough to encourage reflection on this topic, the whole movie delivers several meaningful messages.

3. Ask the students to think of real modern people who, like the main character in the movie, have responded to God's outrageous requests. Offer a few examples of your own. Engage the students in a discussion on the following questions:

- What do their examples, the example from the movie, and the story from the Bible teach about trusting God?
- What do they teach about what God wants for us?

4. Put the students into small groups and ask each group to come up with an outrageous request that God might make to a group of four or five teens today. Explain that after writing that request down, each group should pass it on to another group, which will act out the teenagers' response to it, for the class. When all the groups have written a request and acted out a response, lead the class in a discussion about the following questions:

- How does God call young people?
- What are the risks and challenges of God's call?
- How does one learn to trust God?
- What are some ways that young people can make a difference in the world?

Variation. In step 3, instruct the students to find and share newspaper, magazine, or Internet stories about people who have responded to God's outrageous calls.

Abraham and Sarah's Family

Sarai's Journal
Genesis, chapter 12

This activity uses creative writing to draw the students into the story of Abram and Sarai, and allows them to experience the story from different perspectives.

1. Ask the students to read Gen 12.10–20 to themselves. Invite them to share their thoughts about the personal dynamics in the story and to explore why the major characters behave as they do.

2. Depending on the time available, either direct the students to write all three of the following reflections, or divide the class in thirds and assign a different perspective to each third:

- *Sarai's journal entry.* What does Sarai experience in Egypt? How does she feel about Abram?
- *God's journal entry.* How does God feel about Sarai, Abram, and Pharaoh throughout this story?
- *Abram's apology letter.* What might Abram say to Sarai to help her heal from her ordeal in Pharaoh's house?

3. When the students are done writing, gather them in small groups to compare their reflections. Then invite them to share the different perspectives of the story with the class.

4. As a personal reflection, have the students write in their journal, or on a piece of paper, about a time in their own life that resembled any aspect of this Genesis story. Ask them to write a prayer for God's healing from that situation.

Oral Tradition
Genesis

This activity employs a modified game of telephone to show the students that using oral tradition was a reliable way for the people of Israel to preserve the essence of their history.

1. Ask the students to note the detail in the Genesis accounts they have read, and explain that those stories were passed down by oral tradition before they were ever written down. Explain oral tradition and ask the following questions:

- What were the benefits and risks of oral tradition for the Jewish people?
- Would oral tradition be a successful way for us to keep track of information today? Why or why not?

2. Suggest that the class play a round of the telephone game to illustrate some of the risks of oral tradition. Whisper to one student a moderately complex sentence that has no particular meaning for the students, and ask that student to whisper it to the next, and so on, until the sentence has gone around the room. Do not allow the sentence to be repeated to any receiver.

When the sentence has made its round of the class, discuss its final form, which most likely will be quite different from the original. Note that often the message in the telephone game becomes garbled as it is passed on.

3. Play another round of telephone, this time beginning with a statement that will be valuable to the students, such as, "If we get this message right, there will be no homework tonight." If this too gets garbled, give a similar meaningful sentence and change the rules, allowing the sentence to be repeated to any receiver as often as necessary.

The students should be able to transmit the sentence successfully with this change. Point out that this sequence shows that oral tradition, in which meaningful stories are often repeated, was a successful means of preserving history for the people of Israel.

The Sacrifice of Children
Genesis, chapter 22

The students examine Abraham's willingness to sacrifice Isaac as an act of faith, and compare it with the unthinkable sacrifice of children that many adults participate in today.

1. Before this activity, from the library or Internet, gather several articles regarding children under age eighteen being "sacrificed" by adults in warfare, inhumane labor, or prostitution.

2. To begin this activity, read aloud Genesis, chapter 22 (the testing of Abraham). Emphasize that God is making it clear that God wants not Isaac's life—or any human life—but Abraham's faith.

3. Divide the class into groups of three or four. Give each group one of the articles you have gathered and a piece of newsprint. Direct the students to read, discuss, and summarize the article assigned to their group. Tell them to transfer to the newsprint the major pieces of information from the article (such as the country, the conditions under which the children live, the abuse, and the number of children involved.) Then ask each group to report its findings to the rest of the class.

4. Invite the students to share their thoughts and feelings on the situations they read and heard about. Ask if those situations help them imagine the pain of Abraham, who almost lost his child, and of countless parents who actually do lose children today. Also ask what they think they, as Christians, could do about the situations.

5. Tell the students about some human rights organizations, such as Amnesty International. Ask for volunteers to write letters on behalf of the children in the situations they have discussed, or make writing such letters a class project. (Most likely, all will want to write a letter.) The organizations may provide you with sample letters, addresses, and other information you need. Mail or e-mail the letters.

6. Take pictures, headlines, or key phrases or words from the articles the students read and create a collage with them, either on a bulletin board in the classroom or on poster board. Have each small group write a short prayer about the plight of the children, and read one prayer aloud each time the class meets—as a reminder for the students to keep those children's needs in their hearts and prayers.

Variation. In step 5, instead of having the students write letters, arrange for the class to sponsor a child through a relief organization.

Abraham and Trust
Genesis, chapters 12, 15–18, 22

Using a continuum to plot times that Abraham trusted God and times he mistrusted God, and reflecting on their own experiences, helps the students see that even the spiritual journey of a pioneer of faith in God shares some of the characteristics of their own spiritual journeys.

Handout **Gen–A**

1. Distribute handout Gen–A, "The Ups and Downs of Trust," to the students and review its directions with them. They might complete the handout during class or as a homework assignment.

2. After the students have completed the handout, set up a continuum along one wall of the classroom, designating one end "High," the middle "Average," and the other end "Low." For each Scripture reading about Abraham's life on the handout, call on a student to summarize it, then ask all the students to move to the spot on the continuum that matches what they graphed for it. Invite discussion after each reading, if you wish.

3. When all the readings about Abraham's life have been covered, lead a class discussion about the students' graphing of their own faith journeys. Talk about issues such as the following:

- In what ways does your own faith journey resemble Abraham's? In what ways does it differ?
- What made trusting easier or more challenging for Abraham? What makes trusting easier for you? When do you find it more difficult to trust?

Conclude the discussion with comments like these:

- All spiritual people, even biblical models of faith and saints, find it difficult to trust at times. But faith-filled people keep trying again, with God's help, even when their trust has been challenged. Knowing that there are similarities between ourselves and those people can reassure us that we can grow spiritually despite our doubts. It can also remind us that God has a call for us, like God did for Abraham.

Isaac and Rebekah's Family

Biblical Names
Genesis
"Sibling Rivalry," Gen 25.19–34, CYB

The students explore their own names to discover the significance of biblical names.

1. Read to the students the *CYB* article "Sibling Rivalry," which gives information about Jacob's name. Also consult a biblical dictionary (see appendix A) or other resource and talk about the meanings of the following names: Adam, Eve, Cain, Abel, Abraham, and Sarah. Offer the following explanation in your own words:

- Biblical names often reveal something about the identities of those called by God to fulfill a special mission. In fact, God often changed people's names to indicate that they had been called, such as when God changed Abram to Abraham, Sarai to Sarah, and Jacob to Israel.

2. Ask the students to research the meaning of their name and why they were given it. To help them get started, look up various students' names in a what-to-name-the-baby book from the library or a bookstore. Also invite the students to illustrate their name on paper or in some other art form, creatively conveying the name's meaning in the art. When they are done, provide an opportunity for them to share their work with the class.

Sibling Rivalry
Genesis, chapters 4, 25, 27, 29–30, 33, 37, 45
"Letting Go of the Past," Gen 33.1–17, CYB

This activity begins with a discussion of human stories of the Bible, to help the students see some of the tension present in relationships, as well as models of forgiveness.

1. Break the class into four groups. Ask each group to read one of the accounts of sibling rivalry listed below.
- Cain and Abel (Gen 4.1–16)
- Jacob and Esau (Gen 25.19–34; Genesis, chapter 27)
- Rachel and Leah (Gen 29.1—30.24)
- Joseph and his brothers (Genesis, chapter 37)

Encourage the students to discuss in their groups reasons for sibling rivalry and discord. Have each group prepare to act out for the class an example of sibling rivalry that someone in the group has experienced.

2. Allow the groups to present their examples of sibling rivalry. Then lead a class discussion of the particular challenges to forgiving hurts between family members.

3. For homework, instruct the students to read Genesis, chapter 33, in which Esau and Jacob reconcile, and Genesis, chapter 45, in which Joseph forgives his brothers. Assign a reflection paper in which the students describe a time they either forgave or were forgiven by a sibling, another relative, or a friend.

Jacob's Family

Joseph and the Amazing Technicolor Dreamcoat
Genesis, chapters 37–50
"Joseph," Gen 37.1—50.26, CYB

This exercise employs the lyrics and melodies of the Broadway musical *Joseph and the Amazing Technicolor Dreamcoat* to help the story of Joseph come alive for the students.

Each day that you examine the story of Joseph in class, play a song from *Joseph and the Amazing Technicolor Dreamcoat,* by Tim Rice and Andrew Lloyd Webber (PGD/Polygram, 1993), that correlates with the part of the story you cover. The song "Close Every Door" is especially nice for prayer, as it is reflective and speaks to Joseph's experience in jail and his need to rely on God.

Newsworthy Joseph
Genesis, chapters 37, 39–45

The students use the familiar format of news briefs to give one another a quick and entertaining overview of the Joseph stories.

1. Divide the class into five groups. Assign each group one of the following passages, and ask the groups to read their assigned passage as well as the chapter before and the chapter after it:
- Genesis, chapter 37 (Joseph's brothers become jealous, and Joseph mysteriously disappears.)
- Genesis, chapter 39 (Potiphar's wife accuses Joseph of assault, and Joseph goes to jail.)

- Genesis, chapters 40–41 (Joseph's dream interpretation gains him release from prison.)
- Genesis, chapter 42 (Joseph's brothers make their first journey to Egypt.)
- Genesis, chapters 43–45 (Joseph's brothers make a second trip to Egypt, and Joseph has a startling revelation.)

2. Ask the groups to present those sensational stories as brief newscasts, highlighting the important events, interviewing characters who were present, consulting authorities, and speculating about future developments. Mention that the use of humor, within reason, is fine. The groups could plan and rehearse their news briefs in one class period, obtain props at home, then present their skits in the following class period.

3. After the news briefs are shared, discuss the stories and characters with the class, noting any insights that came from the reading, preparation, or presentation. Help the students understand the purpose and meaning of the story of Joseph and his brothers.

Sex and Power in Genesis
Genesis, chapters 12, 34, 38–39
"No Way, Shechem!" Gen 34.1–31, CYB

The students examine and discuss examples of the abuse of sex and power in Genesis, in order to gain insight into similar situations today.

1. Read Genesis, chapter 34, with the class. Ask the students to identify which characters have more power, which have less, and why that is so (e.g., they might determine that Shechem is powerful because he is male and a prince). Then ask the students, "In the story, is power used for sex, or is sex used for power?"

2. Divide the class in thirds. As an in-class or homework assignment, tell each third of the class to read a different one of the stories listed below. Individually, in writing, the students should assess which biblical figures in their assigned story are more powerful and less powerful, and decide how sex and power are linked in the story. They should also reflect on the way they see sex and power in our modern society (have them provide specific examples), and share any insights about why those two human experiences are often seen together.
- Gen 12.10–20 (Sarai and Abram in Egypt)
- Genesis, chapter 38 (Judah and Tamar)
- Genesis, chapter 39 (Potiphar's wife and Joseph)

3. After the students have completed their reflections on the stories, on modern parallels, and on the relation between sex and power, invite them to share those reflections with the class. Then make the following points in your own words:
  - Sex and power are complicated issues, as can be seen in the various ways that they appear in the biblical stories. There are many loving ways to use power and sexuality [talk about those]. Both are gifts from God and are strong aspects of the human personality. Although it is tempting to use such forceful drives for selfishness, the message of the Gospels is to use all our gifts with respect for the dignity of other persons, in service, and in love.

Good Out of Evil
Genesis, chapter 45
"God's Master Plan," Gen 45.5–8, CYB

Reflection on the story of Joseph and other stories in Genesis invites the students to see the ways that God works in our lives, using even our human failings.

1. Read Gen 45.1–15 and discuss the way that good comes out of Joseph's mistreatment by his brothers. Ask the students, "How does Joseph see God's action in this event?"

2. Invite the students to identify in their own lives, or in the lives of people they know, similar situations in which human sin or selfishness caused difficulty, yet the end result was better than the original situation (e.g., a person was unjustly fired from a good job only to get a better one). Ask them each to write a short essay about one such event, answering these questions: "Do you see God's hand in this? Why or why not?" When the students have finished, invite them to share their reflections in a class discussion.

A Family Tree and a Review
Genesis
"Israel's Ancestry," at the end of Genesis, CYB

This activity asks the students to design a family tree beginning with Abraham, as a way to help them review stories at the end of Genesis.

1. Ask the students to use a piece of blank paper or poster board, and colored markers and pens, to create the family tree of Abraham, leaving space around each name for further writing or design. You may need to review with them how to lay out a family tree.

2. Tell the students to find and skim the stories in Genesis associated with each figure on the tree. Instruct them to add to the chart symbols, words, or small illustrations that will help them remember the stories.

● ● ● ● ● ● ● ● ● ● ● ● ● ▶ The Ups and Downs of Trust

Read or review the Bible stories about Abraham listed below. Then assess Abraham's level of trust in God in each account (high, medium, or low) and mark a dot at that level on the scale below the Bible cite. When you have assessed the trust level in all the accounts, connect the dots and make a graph. Below the graph, in a different color ink, write some important events in your own life and graph your own level of trust in God during those events. Compare the two graphs.

Abraham's life	Gen 12.1–9	Gen 12.10–20	Gen 15.1–6	Gen 16.1–6	Genesis, chapter 17	Gen 18.22–23	Gen 22.1–19
High							
Medium							
Low							

My own life							
High							
Medium							
Low							

Exodus

The Birth of Moses

An Oral and Visual Overview of Exodus
Exodus, chapters 1–14

A creative group project provides the students with a visual overview of God's liberation of the Israelites from slavery.

   1.   Divide the class into eight groups and assign each group one of these passages:
- Exodus, chapter 1
- Exodus, chapter 2
- Exodus, chapter 3
- Exodus, chapters 4–5
- Exodus, chapters 6–8
- Exodus, chapters 9–11
- Exodus, chapter 12
- Exodus, chapters 13–14

   2.   Ask the students, in their groups, to take turns reading and discussing their assigned passage. Suggest that to understand the context, they skim the passages before and after theirs. Once that is done, each member of the group should take on one of the following tasks. Every task in the list must be covered, and some tasks may be handled by more than one person.
- *Artist.* On a piece of poster board, draw a major event from the assigned passage.
- *Writer.* Write a one- to two-page paper summarizing the major events and themes of the passage as discussed by the group.
- *Presenter.* Prepare a 3- to 5-minute oral presentation describing the major events and themes of the passage.

   3.   When the students have completed their projects, arrange for them to share their work with the class, and discuss with them any insights or questions that arose in the preparation or sharing.

Midwives and Nonviolence
Exodus, chapter 1
"Saving Lives," Ex 1.15–22, CYB

The midwives' resistance to the Pharaoh's orders to kill infants in Exodus, chapter 1, models for the students nonviolence for the preservation of human life.

Direct the students to read Exodus, chapter 1, and the article "Saving Lives" from the *CYB*. Talk about the midwives' nonviolent approach toward Pharaoh's orders, exploring the personal courage necessary for such peaceful action by those women. Discuss the violent and nonviolent ways that people protest abortion today, listening to the comments and perspectives of the students.

Variations. Have the students research stories about protests against abortion (or other threats to human rights), finding examples of both violent and nonviolent approaches. Ask them, "What does the biblical story say about the proper way to respond to this destruction of human life (or other threat to human rights)?" Note that though violent protesters receive much media attention, most pro-life advocates (or other advocates of human rights) model the approach of the midwives.

If you have a Catholic pro-life organization in your parish, community, or diocese, invite a representative to speak with your class.

The Call of Moses

The activity "God's Call," on pages 148–149 of this manual, includes God's call to Moses, which is described in Exodus, chapters 3–4.

God's Self-Introduction
Exodus, chapter 3

God's self-introduction to Moses in Ex 3.6 invites the students to reflect on the people in their own lives who have shared something about God with them.

1. Tell the students to read Exodus, chapter 3, to themselves. Note that God assures Moses by telling him that he is listening to the God of his honored ancestors: Abraham, Isaac, and Jacob.

2. Direct the students to write a formal essay at home, describing three trustworthy people who have shared with them something appealing about God. The students should describe what is inviting about those individuals' relationship with God, and whether they themselves have encountered that God in the Scriptures, prayer, worship, or life events. They should include a cover page in which they portray the persons discussed in the essay through photography, symbols, or other creative means.

3. When their papers are done, invite the students to share with the class something about the people and relationships they described in them. Note any qualities of people and relationships that are commonly mentioned.

Delivery from the Egyptians

A Seder Meal
Exodus, chapter 12

This activity reveals that a communal celebration of an ancient Jewish feast has meaning for the students, as Christians, today.

    1. Read Ex 12.1–36 with the class. Then spend some time explaining and discussing the text of the ritual seder.
    Note: A good resource is "Celebrating a Christian Passover," by James Notebaart, in *The Holy Week Book,* by Eileen Elizabeth Freeman (San Jose, CA: Resource Publications, 1979), pages 76 to 79.

    2. Plan a seder meal for the class. Give the students various tasks such as food preparation, room decoration, cleanup, and preparation of prayers. Consider inviting other students, the families of your own students, or others to join the seder.

    3. During and after the seder, discuss the significance of the Passover for Jews and the relation of the Passover meal to the Christian Eucharist. You may wish to invite a Jewish person to join the class and share his or her experience of the Passover celebration.

The Exodus and Gospel Music
Exodus, chapters 14–15

The students relate the Song of Moses and the Israelites to music in the Gospel genre, and go on to explore that musical genre, which uses many Old Testament themes.

    1. Prepare for this activity by obtaining recordings and lyrics for some Gospel music about the Exodus and other Old Testament stories, such as that found in *Sister Thea: Songs of My People,* by Thea Bowman (Krystal Records, 1988).

    2. Have the students read Exodus, chapters 14–15. Define Gospel music and relate it to the Song of Moses in the reading. Then play some of the Gospel music you have obtained and distribute the lyrics you have obtained. Invite volunteers to perform some of the songs, or others they are familiar with, for the class.

    3. Discuss the following questions with the students:
- Why did Moses and the people want to sing when rescued by Pharaoh?
- In what ways does music allow us to appreciate biblical messages more deeply?

Moses Needed Support
Exodus, chapter 17
"Prayer in Support of Others," Ex 17.8–15, CYB

This activity reveals that Moses gave and needed support just as we do, and helps the students see that prayer is an important way to support others.

1. Read aloud with the class Ex 17.8–15 and the article "Prayer in Support of Others" from the *CYB*. Ask the students to think of people who support them in difficult times and others who may need support from them right now. Talk about praying as an important way that we can support others. Give the students some quiet time to pray for those who need their support and in thanksgiving for those who hold them up.

2. Pass out slips of paper and invite the students to write on them the names of people who need prayer support right now. Explain that the students should write each name on a separate slip and may use more than one slip. When they are done, collect the slips and place them in a bowl or jar in a prayer space in the room. Refer to them often when you pray as a class (you might lift up the bowl as you ask for God's love and mercy for those people). Keep a stack of paper slips and a pen or pencil by the bowl, so that students can add names at any time.

The Covenant at Mount Sinai

Covenants and Commandments
Exodus, chapters 19–20

An examination of the students' significant relationships sheds light on the covenant relationship between God and Israel.

1. Read Ex 19.1—20.21 and discuss the covenant relationship between God and the people of Israel. Present the following comments and questions in your own words:
   - The Israelites were familiar with political covenants that were treaties in which both parties had obligations to fulfill. The Covenant between God and Israel, though based on love, also asks something of both God and Israel. What does the Covenant require of each? How do the Covenant's requirements help to make the relationship between God and Israel successful? [Possibly review the covenants of Genesis, chapters 9 and 15, in order to examine similarities and differences between the Sinai Covenant and other covenants made with God.]

2. Divide the class into six groups and assign each group one of the following types of relationships:
   - parents and children
   - siblings

- boyfriends and girlfriends
- coaches and players
- teachers and students
- employers and employees

3. Instruct the groups each to list on paper the terms and conditions for their assigned relationship, in the form of commandments. Explain that, for example, a group might list the obligations parents have toward their children and the obligations children have toward their parents. Ask the groups each to prepare a skit that illustrates the importance of those commandments in everyday life.

4. After enjoying the students' performances, discuss how such covenants with others in their lives are relevant to the Covenant in the Scripture passage. Ask, "What are the similarities and differences between your own commandments and the Ten Commandments of God's Covenant with Israel?"

The Ten Commandments and Morality Plays
Exodus, chapter 20

The students use a Christian education technique from another era as an imaginative way to process the value of the Ten Commandments and to share the Commandments with the rest of the class.

1. Read Exodus, chapter 20, aloud with the students.

2. Divide the class into five groups and randomly assign two of the Ten Commandments to each group. Explain that each group is to prepare and present a morality play based on its assigned commandments. Give this simple explanation about morality plays in your own words:

- Morality plays were popular tools for teaching Christians how to lead good lives and avoid evil in the fifteenth and sixteenth centuries. The plays all had the same general plot: Good and evil competed for the human soul, and goodness always won out. The plays' characters included the Christian soul as well as personified vices and virtues. A morality play about the importance of honesty would feature a Christian considering a lie versus the truth. The other figures in the play would be Deceit and Honesty, in human form, who would try to convince the Christian to behave one way or the other, much like the familiar devil and angel on a person's shoulder.

Note that each play created by the students must feature a soul or souls struggling to keep the commandments, as well as personified virtues and vices, in a modern setting, competing for the soul. Mention that each student may play more than one part.

3. Allow the students adequate time to plan the plays, gather props at home, and perform the dramas. After the presentations, discuss the plays and the insights they give about the Commandments.

Living the Covenant

Prayer Styles: Guided Imagery—Would You Do It?
Exodus, chapter 22
"Would You Do It?" Ex 22.21–27, **CYB**

This exercise uses guided imagery to open the students' minds to the experience and feelings of privileged youth and homeless youth.

1. Read with the students Ex 22.21–27 and the article "Would You Do It?" from the *CYB*. Explain to the students what a guided imagery is. Ask the students to close their eyes, relax, and open their imagination. Lead the students in a guided imagery about the scene in the *CYB* article, from the perspective of each of the three young people in turn—first Dave, then Mike, and finally the homeless youth. Ask the students to imagine the sights, sounds, and smells of the scene as well as the thoughts and feelings of each young man.

2. Give the students some quiet time to write about the thoughts and feelings that arose during the guided imagery. Invite them to share their insights and answer these questions:
   - Why did Mike and Dave react differently?
   - What might you do in a similar situation? Why?

3. Discuss, as a class, the challenges of homelessness that face our society today. Ask these questions:
   - What are typical responses?
   - Who is responding as a Christian?

Variations. Invite to the class a speaker who works with homeless people, such as a volunteer from a Catholic Worker community.
Show the movie *Entertaining Angels* (Paulist Pictures, 1996, 112 min., rated PG-13), which is about Catholic Worker cofounders Dorothy Day and Peter Maurin.

Aaron, the Golden Calf, and Peer Pressure
Exodus, chapter 32
"Caught Up in the Moment," Ex 32.1–35, **CYB**

Aaron's willingness to please the Israelites by fashioning a golden calf in Exodus, chapter 32, invites a discussion of peer pressure today.

1. Direct the students to take turns reading aloud Exodus, chapter 32, and the *CYB* article "Caught Up in the Moment." Explain that the bull was an idol of Israel's pagan neighbors. Point out that the Israelites became impatient waiting for Moses' God to be revealed to them, so they turned to another god.

2. Discuss the following questions with the class:
   - Why did Aaron succumb to the Israelites' desire to make the golden calf?
   - Would he have done so if Moses had been present?

3. Divide the class, by interest, into the following categories:

- music
- art
- symbolism
- drama (role-play)
- any other media you think would fit your class and the topic of peer pressure

Subdivide large groups so that each group has no more than five students in it. Each group should first discuss what peer pressure is and how it works. Then it should devise a way to use its chosen medium to convey to the rest of the class its understanding of the dynamics of peer pressure.

4. Following the presentations and further discussion, conclude with a reading of Psalm 25 as a prayer to help the students deal with peer pressure.

Modern Idolatry
Exodus, chapter 32

A visual representation of modern idolatry gives the students insight into the appeal of the golden calf for the Israelites.

1. Have the students take turns reading Exodus, chapter 32, aloud, and explain that the bull was an idol of Israel's pagan neighbors.
Review Ex 20.1–6 and discuss the following statements and questions:
- Idolatry is the worship of false gods (those can be persons, places, or things).
- God is the only one who is worthy of the ultimate expression of human faith, hope, and love, because God is the creator of all things.
- What people, places, or things do people idolize today? In "worshiping" those false gods, people expect to find ultimate happiness and well-being. In reality, however, such idolatry brings only deep disappointment and frustration, because no creation is capable of giving what God alone can give—eternal life.

2. Gather the students in groups of no more than four to make collages of modern false gods. Distribute poster board, old newspapers and magazines, scissors, and glue for that purpose. The students should also individually write a short reflection about the allure of modern idols and then share their reflections, along with the collages, in a class discussion.

Seeing God in Hindsight
Exodus, chapter 33

Moses' ability to see God only after God's passing addresses a common spiritual experience: We often see that God was with us in a time of crisis only after the event is over. The students explore their experience of this in short essays and voluntary sharing.

1. Ask a student to read Ex 33.17–23, and say something like the following:

■ In some cases, we are not able to see God's presence while God is active and helping us through a difficulty, but later we can search and see God's hand in that experience. [Possibly use the poem "Footprints" (widely available from many sources) to help illustrate this.]

2. Give the students quiet time in class to write a short essay about a difficult time in their life. Suggest that they consider these questions:
■ Were you aware of God's presence during the struggle?
■ In looking back now, can you see God's presence in any aspect of that experience—circumstances, people, your own transformation?
Acknowledge that some students may still not see God's activity during that period.

3. When the students have completed their essays, invite any who are comfortable doing so to share their stories and discuss ways to recognize God's presence.

Building the Tabernacle

Creating a Prayer Space
Exodus, chapters 35–40

As the ancient Israelites created a sacred space for the tablets of the Ten Commandments, the students create a sacred space honoring the Bible in their classroom.

1. Review Exodus, chapters 35–40, with the students, highlighting various instructions regarding the housing of the Ten Commandment tablets (in the ark, the dwelling tent, etc.). Ask the students to identify the various reasons why God and the Israelites felt that it was important to set apart a special place for God's presence and word.

2. Divide the class into six small groups. Assign each of those groups the task of creating a classroom prayer space for use during one of the following periods of the school year:
■ Advent
■ Christmas
■ Ordinary Time (following the Christmas season)
■ Lent
■ Easter
■ Ordinary Time (continuing after the Easter season)
Lead the students to resources that will give them background on the liturgical year and the season they are assigned. Tell them to pay attention to colors, symbols, lectionary readings, and so on. Explain that they are free to use whatever material they need for the construction of their sacred space. Emphasize that the prayer space should in some way honor the Bible within the liturgical season.

3. The sacred space prepared by the students can be where the class prayer begins each day.

Wrap-up Reflection Paper:
"My Wanderings in the Desert of High School"
Exodus

The many experiences of the Sinai sojourn provide metaphors for the students to use in reflecting on the journey through adolescence.

1. Call the students to identify the kinds of experiences the Israelites had as they moved through the desert, and list them on the board. Your list might include these items:

- being lost
- worrying about many things
- grumbling about their conditions
- feeling frustration or gratitude toward God
- trusting in or doubting God
- worshiping false gods
- encountering strangers

Note that the sojourn in the desert was a time of transformation for the Israelites: they began as slaves, took on a nomadic lifestyle, and ended in the Promised Land as a free nation.

2. Assign the students a reflection paper in which they describe their "wanderings in the desert of high school," using the experiences of the Israelites as metaphors. Instruct the students to identify the various ways in which their high school journey is one of transformation. Suggest that, for example, they describe their condition as a first-year student and imagine their destination after graduation. Encourage them to record the various ways God has been with them on this journey.

As a cover page for the reflection, the students should map their own journey, imitating the journey of the Israelites. They may put mountains for hurdles or visually indicate times they felt as if they were moving in circles. They may use map 2, "The Exodus from Egypt," in the *CYB* as a model.

Leviticus

Law

Rules My Kids Will Have to Follow
Leviticus

Identifying reasonable rules that parents set for teenagers helps the students understand the rationale behind Leviticus's laws and provides an opportunity to browse Leviticus.

   1. Ask the students to imagine that it is thirty years in the future and that they are parents of high school students. On paper, the boys are to write down five rules their daughters have to obey, and the girls are to do the same for their sons. Instruct them to identify which rule is the most important. Then ask them to write down any rules given by parents today that do not make sense to them.

   2. Divide the class into groups of four to five according to gender. Explain that each group is to come to a consensus regarding a Top 5 set of rules for teenagers of the other gender, in order of importance, and record those on butcher paper or newsprint. When the groups are done, invite them to take turns explaining their findings to the rest of the class.

   3. Ask the students to identify why family rules, as well as consequences for noncompliance, are important. Then solicit some of the parental rules for teens that do not make sense to them, and allow some opportunity for them to speculate as to the rationale behind those rules.

   4. Have the students browse Leviticus and write down five laws that make sense to them and five that do not. In response to the laws that do not make sense, offer rationales drawn from a biblical commentary (see appendix A). Note that if parents' laws today can be a mystery, it is no surprise that even scholars have questions about some of the laws in Leviticus.

   5. Conclude by reading aloud the rewards of obedience to the Law in Lev 26.3–13.

The Sinai Café: Jewish Food Laws
Leviticus, chapter 11

This imaginative exercise allows the students to reflect on the dietary laws in Leviticus.

1. Ask several students to take turns reading Leviticus, chapter 11, aloud in class. Use a Bible dictionary (see appendix A) to explain any unfamiliar terms and creatures to the students.

2. Ask the students, in groups of four or five, to compose a creative menu for an imaginary pagan restaurant in Palestine. The menu offerings should come from the lists of creatures forbidden to Israelites of the time, and can be as ingenious as the students would like. For variety, direct different groups to cover different meals of the day, or different themes such as fast food, elegant dining, and so on. The students should decorate their menus using a variety of art supplies.

3. Arrange for the groups to share their menus, highlighting their favorite items. Then use comments and questions like the ones that follow to guide a class discussion:
- Scholars do not really know why some creatures were forbidden as food for the Israelites. What challenges might such dietary restrictions have presented to the Israelites who traveled among pagan tribes?
- [Explain something of the kosher dietary customs. Note that it is difficult to find establishments today that serve kosher food.] How can restaurants accommodate religious customs such as the strict kosher requirements for Orthodox Jews?

Note: The following resources provide helpful information about kosher dietary customs:
- *Jewish Literacy: The Most Important Things to Know About the Jewish Religion, Its People, and Its History,* by Joseph Telushkin (New York: William Morrow and Company, 1991)
- *The Kosher Companion: A Guide to Food, Cooking, Shopping, and Services,* by Trudy Garfunkel (Secaucus, NJ: Carol Publishing Group, 1997)
- *How to Run a Traditional Jewish Household,* by Blu Greenberg (New York: Simon and Schuster, 1983)

Israelite and U.S. Law—Reasonable?
Leviticus, chapter 19

Reflection on the demands of Israelite law challenges the students to think more closely about U.S. law.

1. Invite the students to take turns reading Leviticus, chapter 19, aloud to the class. Note that some of the laws in that passage differ significantly from those of our own legal system. Ask the students to name five interesting laws from the reading and write them on the board. Then ask for five U.S. laws that pertain especially to teenagers, and write those on the board.

2. Designate two places in the room as the "Reasonable" spot and the "Unreasonable" spot. As you read each biblical law from the board, ask the students to stand in the spot that reflects whether that law would be reasonable today. For each law, request that they explain their stance and speculate about the law's effectiveness for the Israelites. Then read out the U.S. laws and ask the students to choose a place to stand for each one. Also for each U.S. law, solicit explanations about the students' choices and ideas about the origins of the laws.

Modern Implications of the Jubilee Year
Leviticus, chapter 25
"7 x 7 + 1 = Jubilee!" Leviticus, chapter 25, CYB

An individual reflection and class discussion of the Jubilee year give the students an idea of the radical nature of observing such a practice.

    1. Direct the students to read Lev 25.8–12 and the *CYB* article "7 x 7 + 1 = Jubilee!" to themselves. Then ask them each to write down five things they would do to start fresh in the Jubilee year: one thing they would return to its original owner, one debt they would forgive, one new thing they would learn, one old habit they would break, and one new commitment they would make.

    2. Direct the students to form pairs and discuss the steps they would have to take to accomplish their goals for the Jubilee year.

    3. Gather the class and acknowledge that the Jubilee year encompasses all the types of new starts the students have been discussing. Talk about the "winners" and "losers" of the Jubilee year for the Israelites, the year's radical effects, and the emphasis it placed on divine rather than human ownership of land and property. Note that though the Israelites did not experience the same global economy as we do in the modern era, the logistics of the Jubilee year were still complex. Explain that Catholics continue to celebrate Jubilee years. Discuss modern parallels to ancient Jubilee celebrations and the implications of the Jubilee for our time.
    Note: For more information on the Jubilee, write to the National Conference of Catholic Bishops (NCCB), Secretariat for the Third Millennium and the Jubilee Year 2000, 3211 Fourth Street NE, Washington, DC 20017-1194; or explore the NCCB's Jubilee year Internet site at *http://www.nccbuscc.org/jubilee.*

    Variation. Assign the students to research and write reports about individuals and groups in the United States that advocate forgiving the debts of developing countries in light of Jubilee 2000.

Ritual

Prayer Styles: Communal Prayer—Ritual Atonement Service
Leviticus, chapter 16
"The Scapegoat," Lev 16.20–21, CYB

Though the modern notion of the scapegoat is somewhat negative, the traditional act of using a scapegoat to ritually experience God's forgiveness is positive. This activity leads the students to explore both traditions.

    1. Ask one student to read Lev 16.20–21 aloud for the class. Invite another to read the article "The Scapegoat" from the *CYB.* Discuss the modern meaning of a *scapegoat* and how a scapegoat artificially eases guilt about a wrongdoing. Note that the Israelite use of a scapegoat met the authentic human need to feel forgiveness for sins and freedom from the burden of guilt.

2. Place a basin, a pitcher of water, and towels in a central place in the classroom or prayer space. Use reflective music and soft lighting to create an environment for quiet prayer. Invite the students to ask God to show them a part of themselves that they need to let God's forgiveness touch. Explain that the class will now perform the following ritual to help the students let go of their guilt or shame:

- Each of you in turn will silently rise and go to the basin, keeping your need for forgiveness in mind. As a classmate washes your hands, you should allow God's forgiveness and healing to wash over you. After your hands are washed, you should wash the next student's hands. This ritual continues until all of you have come up and had your hands washed.

3. When the hand-washing ritual is completed, ask the students to join in reciting the Lord's Prayer.

Variation. Do the ritual washing in step 2 in the setting of a communal celebration of the sacrament of Reconciliation.

Family Holy Days
Leviticus, chapter 23

Identifying ways their families celebrate important events allows the students to see the value in the Israelites' rituals.

1. As homework, ask the students to identify a family celebration that is especially unifying in their family. On paper, they should describe the event, including information like when it occurs, who is present, how the celebration is carried out, and any special foods or rituals involved. They should bring their paper to the next class, along with some sort of symbol of the festivity, such as a picture or item used in it.

2. At the next class session, group the students by the type of celebration chosen—birthday, religious holiday, and so on. Ask the members of each group to compare and contrast traditions and to identify what aspects of their celebrations are unifying for their families.

3. Gather all the students to share insights from their small-group discussions. Then invite the students to take turns reading Leviticus, chapter 23, aloud. Ask them to explain how the holy days mentioned in that passage helped the Israelites develop a sense of unity with one another and with God.

Numbers

Human Dynamics of the Desert Journey

The Divisive Effects of Jealousy
Numbers, chapters 11–12

The students examine the familiar face of jealousy in the Bible in order to begin identifying some of jealousy's characteristics and effects.

1. Direct the students to read Num 11.26–30 and Numbers, chapter 12. Discuss the following questions:
- Why do the young man in Numbers, chapter 11, and Aaron and Miriam in chapter 12 feel jealous?
- What is jealousy? [Point out that jealousy springs from a desire to have what someone else possesses, whether that is affection, attention, or an object.]

2. Arrange the students in groups of four and instruct the groups each to write a jealousy scenario involving three teens. Each group should pass its finished narrative on to another group, which will make a skit out of it to share with the class. Three students in the second group should act the parts of the jealous teens, and the fourth should be a peer counselor who meets with them to work out the problem.

3. After the groups have performed their skits for the class, invite the students to share insights about the origins and effects of jealousy. Ask, "What advice would you give the young man in Numbers, chapter 11, or Aaron and Miriam in chapter 12?"

One Rash Moment
Numbers, chapter 20

Just like Moses and Aaron lost the Promised Land in an instant, many high school students lose their own dreams in seconds. This activity helps the students see that connection between the Old Testament and their own lives today.

1. Form groups of four to five, and ask the students to read aloud Num 20.1–13 in their groups. Offer the following reflections in your own words:
- Have you ever found yourself involved in something—a task, a relationship, a commitment—that used up all your energy and personal resources until it seemed like you had nothing left? Maybe that is how

Moses and Aaron felt when they reached Kā'desh. They had just lost their sister Miriam (verse 1), they had no food or water, and now the Israelites were getting hostile toward them.

■ No one is sure what Moses and Aaron did to show their lack of trust in God (verse 12). Maybe it was striking the rock twice; maybe it was losing their patience with the Israelites. Whatever it was, one rash moment brought life-changing consequences: Moses and Aaron would not enter the Promised Land.

2. Ask the groups each to think of five general situations in which junior high students might act rashly in response to a problem, need, or desire and suffer as a consequence. Have them write each situation on a separate slip of paper. Collect all the pieces of paper and look through the scenarios to screen out any that are in poor taste.

3. Set up some chairs in the front of the room. Allow each group to take a turn as a panel of older teens that makes recommendations to younger teens about how to avoid acting rashly. Read one or two selected scenarios aloud and ask the panel to comment about them. Then open the discussion to the rest of the class. Make general observations about the wisdom that the students share. Encourage them to discuss ways they deal with personal decisions that have serious consequences. Ask, "How might this wisdom have helped Moses and Aaron?"

Balaam: A Cartoonist's Perspective
Numbers, chapters 22–24

The students use political cartoons to reveal the imagery and humor in the story of Balak and Balaam.

1. Instruct the students to read Numbers, chapters 22–24, to themselves. Then ask them to summarize the plot for one another, and discuss with them the main points.

2. Bring in several current political cartoons and share them with the students. Mention that political cartoons often point out the weakness or foolishness in a political figure or situation. Ask the students to identify the political figures and situations found in the story from Numbers.

3. Tell the students that they are each to draw a single-frame political cartoon that addresses part of the story from Numbers; note that a verbal caption is optional. Add that the students should write a short paragraph on the other side of their paper, explaining how God works through that humorous biblical story. Provide the necessary art supplies and give the students time to work in class.

4. When the students have completed their assignment, invite them to share their cartoons and paragraphs or to post them in the classroom.

Jewish Holidays Come Alive
Numbers, chapters 28–29
"Other Jewish Feasts," Num 29.1–11, CYB

The Bible's description of ritual sacrifice in connection with the Jewish celebration of Yom Kippur invites the students to research the characteristics of modern Jewish holidays.

1. Ask the students to take turns reading Num 28.16—29.40 aloud. List the Jewish holidays from that passage on the board. Also ask someone to read the article "Other Jewish Feasts" from the *CYB*. Explain the following material to the students:
   - Before the destruction of the Jewish Temple in Jerusalem in A.D. 70, much of Jewish worship centered on sacrifice by priests in the Temple. After the fall of the Temple, Jewish worship changed significantly and so did the Jewish holidays.

2. Form small groups and ask them each to pick a different holiday from the list on the board. For homework, direct the groups each to research and prepare a presentation on their holiday, gathering information about customs and rituals. Explain that the groups are to report their findings to the class and also to engage the class in a hands-on experience of the holiday. Mention ideas such as preparing a traditional food, leading a short ritual, and bringing in items commonly associated with the tradition. Assign a day when the group presentations are due.
   Note: This is a great opportunity to use the Internet. Searches beginning with *Judaism* and continuing with the names of the individual holidays generally lead to good material.

3. On the day the presentations are due, invite the small groups to share with their classmates the information they have found and the experiences they have prepared.

Deuteronomy

Moses on Israel's History

Remembering the Holocaust
Deuteronomy, chapter 4

Deuteronomy 4.9 is on the wall before the eternal flame in the U.S. Holocaust Memorial Museum's Hall of Remembrance in Washington, D.C. That verse invites the students to discuss the necessity to remember the Holocaust.

Deuteronomy 4.9 may open or close a lesson plan about the Holocaust, particularly one that addresses the need to remember what happened in the past so as to prevent such events from recurring in our world. The U.S. Holocaust Memorial Museum's Education Department provides lesson plans and helpful guidance to teachers who wish to discuss the Holocaust. For information, write to the Education Department of the U.S. Holocaust Memorial Museum at 100 Raoul Wallenberg Place SW, Washington, DC 20024; or call the museum at 202-488-0400; or access the museum's web site at *http://www.ushmm.org.*

You might wish to show the students the movie *Schindler's List* (Amblin Entertainment, 1994, 197 min.). Be aware that that movie is rated R, and if necessary, obtain from parents and administrators the permission to show it.

Moses on Obedience to the Covenant

Deuteronomy: A Challenge to Do the Right Thing
Deuteronomy, chapter 6

The students discover that Moses urging the people to do what is right is a major theme for Deuteronomy and also emerges in popular music.

1. Ask the students to take turns reading Deuteronomy, chapter 6, aloud. Explain the following things to them in your own words:

- Moses' plea to the people to do what is right and follow God is a frequent theme of Deuteronomy.
- Deuteronomy 6.4–9 is an important proclamation of the Jewish faith known as the Shema. The Shema says that faithfulness to God alone leads to right action, whereas infidelity to God and loyalty to different gods or idols brings other wrongdoing.

2. As homework, instruct the students to select a tape or CD of a popular piece of music in which the songwriter urges people to choose the right thing and to stop doing wrong. Direct them to write down some or all of the lyrics,

and reflect in writing about the importance of the issue or issues raised in the song. Ask them to bring in their recording if they can.

3. Invite the students to share their songs and writings at the next class, choosing a few recordings to play for the class. Encourage the students to put the modern concerns expressed by the songs in the context of fidelity to God. Ask: "Could those problems be considered forms of modern idolatry? That is, are any of them examples of putting undue value on something other than God?"

Insiders and Outsiders
Deuteronomy, chapter 24
"The Poor, the Strangers, the Widows, and the Orphans," Deut 24.10–21,
  CYB

This activity invites the students to look at Israel's obligations to treat the outsider with care, and then act out their own view of insiders and outsiders and compare it with God's view as depicted in Deuteronomy.

1. Call the students to take turns reading Deut 24.10–21 out loud. Discuss the various laws listed in that passage, and point out that those laws repeatedly challenged Israel to include the outsiders of its day. Then ask a student to read aloud the article "The Poor, the Widows, and the Orphans" from the *CYB*.

2. Divide the class in two by some visible criteria such as hair or clothing color. Declare one half to be insiders and the other half to be outsiders. Ask the students to jot down some "feeling" adjectives they associate with their own group—for instance, an insider might feel *superior* and *safe,* whereas an outsider might feel *lonely.*

3. Form two concentric circles, with the insiders on the inside and the outsiders on the outside. Each insider should be partnered with an outsider; if you have an odd number of students, join the circle that is short. The partners should face each other and share adjectives that they feel describe each other's group—that is, perceptions that they hold of the other group. Then the circles should move in opposite directions so that each person in the outer circle exchanges perceptions with each person in the inner circle.

4. When everyone has gone around the circle, ask the students to write down some of the adjectives they heard in the circle and to reflect on the effects such labels have on people. Have them share those labels and insights with the class. Note that the only things separating insiders from outsiders are the groups' different points of view.

5. Note that like the Israelites, we have an obligation to include the outsider when we happen to be considered an insider. Direct the students to write a one-page reflection about their own experience of being an outsider or insider—or of placing another person or group in one of those positions.

Moses' Farewell

The Rewards of Obedience
Deuteronomy, chapter 28

The simple notions that obedience invites reward and disobedience brings punishment challenge the students to address the issue of obedience in their own lives.

1. Ask the students to take turns reading all or part of Deuteronomy, chapter 28. Write "Obedience = reward" and "Disobedience = punishment" on the board. Note that although the Bible passage portrays God as actively rewarding and punishing, much of the Pentateuch reveals that obedience to God's Law was itself a blessing, whereas disobedience was itself a curse.

2. Divide the class into four groups and assign each group one of the following topics:
- school
- home
- sports and other activities
- state law

Tell the groups each to find examples of opportunities for obedience and disobedience in their assigned area and to assess whether the simple equations on the board work in that area. Ask, "If not, what are other reasons people choose obedience or disobedience?"

3. Discuss the findings from step 2 as a class. Direct the students to choose some laws of the Catholic church, then ask these questions:
- Do you obey those laws because of reward and punishment or out of other motivations?
- Is your image of God similar to the one found in Deuteronomy?

Choose Life
Deuteronomy, chapter 30

This activity suggests that Moses' challenge to choose life has meaning to the teenager who at times also faces life-and-death choices.

1. Ask one student to read Deut 30.15–20 to the class. Point out the following items, in your own words:
- Moses offers the people a choice between life, prosperity, and blessing, and death, adversity, and curse. He basically puts forth two kinds of future: happy and unhappy.
- Moses' offer deals with more than physical life and death. He challenges people to make choices that lead to a full life with God and others, rather than decisions that stifle the human spirit and lead to isolation from God and others.
- Most people want happiness, yet many make deadly choices to obtain happiness. Those choices may threaten the physical, emotional, or spiritual health of oneself, others, or the natural world.

2. Form several small groups and pass out several popular magazines or newspapers to the groups. Ask the groups to look for mention of five "death" (ultimately self-destructive) choices and to write a brief description of each. Direct them to discuss what kind of happiness the people involved in those decisions were actually seeking, and to propose an alternative, life-giving choice that really would have led to the desired happiness. Note that life-giving choices often require more effort or self-discipline than do other choices.

3. Invite the groups to share their insights with the class. Identify any common characteristics of the different choices. Because life-giving choices are at times demanding, note that God's guidance and support was a key element of Moses' offer in the Bible passage read earlier.

Historical Books

Joshua

Entering the Promised Land

Unlikely Heroes
Joshua, chapter 2

Up to this point in the Old Testament books studied, all the biblical heroes have been flawed as well as gifted. The Bible challenges us to accept human limitations in heroes and to see the heroic possibilities within ourselves despite our failings. Rahab's unusual position as prostitute and biblical hero in Joshua, chapter 2, challenges the students' notion of what constitutes a hero.

1. Ask several students to read Joshua, chapter 2, assigning each a different character. Then call a student to read Mt 1.1–17. Point out that the prostitute Rahab has an important place in the story of entering the Promised Land and in the genealogy of Jesus.

2. Form small groups and have them discuss the attributes of modern superheroes, possibly showing a cartoon or movie clip to start the conversation. Invite the small groups to report the highlights of their discussion, and then ask these questions in your own words:
   - Do we expect human heroes to have the extraordinary personal qualities that we find in superheroes?
   - Why is it sometimes difficult to see the human failings of a person who is heroic?
   - How was Rahab a hero? How was she flawed?

3. Instruct the students to write a brief reflection about a time they unexpectedly found the hero in themselves or someone they know. Call volunteers to share their completed reflections with the class.

Prayer Styles: Sharing Personal Symbols—Memorial Stones
Joshua, chapter 4

Joshua used stones to express his people's experience of God. In this exercise, the students use symbols of their own choosing to express their high school experience.

1. Instruct the students to bring to the next class an item that symbolizes their experience of high school right now. That item should be something that they can comfortably explain to their classmates.

2. In the next class, tell some students to read Josh 4.1–14 aloud. Point out that the stones in that passage functioned as a memorial to the Israelites of an important event—the crossing of the Jordan River.

3. In a prayerful atmosphere, invite the students to take turns sharing their symbolic items, each explaining the meaning that her or his item has at this time in life. Instruct the students to build a pile of their symbols in a central place in the classroom, like the arrangement of stones at the Israelites' camping place. Then play some music for a quiet reflection time.

Conquest and Division of the Land

Exegetical Tools: What Is Exegesis?

This general introduction to exegesis lays the foundation for further opportunities to explore the biblical text through forms of biblical criticism and other scholarly resources.

Handout **Josh–A**

1. Make copies of handout Josh–A, "Exegetical Tools: What Is Exegesis?" one for each student, and cut each sheet in half along the broken line. Hand out the top half of the sheet and tell the students to follow the directions. After they have finished, allow them to share some of the conclusions that they have drawn from their reading.

2. Discuss the following issues in your own words:
- Reading any written material is, in some respects, like talking with another person. Both the reader and the text contribute something to the meaning of the words. What have we brought to the reading of the quote on the handout? [Point out some assumptions that the students may have held based on U.S. cultural values.]
- When we look at any written piece, there is much that we do not know. What don't we know about the author of the statement on the handout and about what she is saying?
- At first, we read things into an author's statements, in that we insert ourselves and our beliefs into the text. When we start asking questions of the text, we begin to allow the text to speak to us, giving it more attention. This process is called *exegesis,* meaning "a very close reading." This approach includes many different techniques that scholars use to understand what the biblical authors are really saying.

3. Pass out the bottom half of the handout and allow the students to read the statements on it. Ask the following questions:
- What new conclusions can you now draw?
- What further questions do you now have?
- What steps could you take to investigate the statement at the top of handout Josh–A further?

Point out that exegesis begins with an inquisitive mind. Note that as the course progresses, the students will be able to explore methods and resources available for pursuing some of their questions.

Exegetical Tools: Form Criticism—the Saga
Joshua, chapter 6

The students develop their understanding of the nature of a saga in order to appreciate the biblical authors' method of narrating the conquest of the Promised Land.

1. Write the following definition of a saga on the board:

A saga is a story, in historical form but with many elements (drama, foreshadowing, striking events) that resemble fiction. It is almost always concerned with heroic characters and the formative events of a people's history. (Jean Marie Hiesberger, ed., *The Catholic Bible*, p. 95)

2. Ask several students to read Joshua, chapter 6. Then discuss with the class how the story in that passage is like a saga.

3. Explain the following information to the students in your own words:
- One way of exploring the meaning of any text is to look at its form. Scholars call this approach to studying the Bible form criticism. By choosing a certain form of writing, an author gives the reader important clues about how to read the words.

4. Take out a newspaper and read first from a news brief, then from a comic strip, an obituary, an ad, and a list of sporting events scores. Ask the students what they expect to find in those different forms of writing. Point out that just by looking at the form of the writing, they learn a lot about the author's intent.

5. Help the students see why the saga is an appropriate form for the story in Joshua, chapter 6, and is more effective than a factual news account—which would certainly leave God out and minimize the importance of the event.

6. Direct the students each to take an important event in their own life from the last year, and write about it in a factual news brief style as well as in the genre of a saga. When they are done, allow the students to share some of their stories and observations.

Music and the Conquest of Jericho
Joshua, chapter 6

This activity facilitates an examination of the psychology of school athletics, in order to help the students imagine the power of Israel's methods for subduing Jericho.

1. Take the students to a school playing field or gym and ask them to recall an intense athletic competition with a rival school. Help the students recreate some of the events and feelings associated with that game.

2. Ask a student to read Josh 6.1–21 aloud to the class. Invite the students to identify the different tactics the Israelites used in bringing Jericho down.

3. Engage the students in a discussion as follows:

- Invite the students to imagine that their own school has adopted the Israelites' approach with Jericho for a big game, and have them verbally flesh out the scenario. Ask the students how the tactics they are describing might affect both teams and each team's fans.
- Lead the students to brainstorm tactics they have seen used by athletes and fans to psych themselves up against rivals and to intimidate opponents. Ask these questions:
  - Which of those tactics have been most effective?
  - Do some of those practices border on poor sportsmanship?
- Play or sing the school's fight song or alma mater, and discuss why it is sung at athletic events. Point out that it is reasonable to assume that the Israelites' marching and shouting brought the inhabitants of Jericho not only physical defeat but also psychological defeat.

The Twelve Tribes and the Cafeteria
Joshua, chapters 13–19

Although Israel's tribes were separate groups, their Covenant with God united them. In this exercise, the students reflect on what unites various groups in their school.

1. Explain to the students that in its early history, Israel was a loose confederation of twelve tribes that were united by the Covenant and came together for special feasts and in times of crisis.

2. Direct the students to sketch, on a sheet of blank paper, their eighth-grade cafeteria and how their eighth-grade class grouped for lunch, as best they can remember. Provide the following instructions in your own words:

- Consider whether your class had cliques. If it did, identify, in a respectful way, what gifts each group brought to the school, and write those on the other side of the sheet. Then identify and record the positive and negative characteristics of the cliques, and what common bonds or events united the groups into one community.

When the students are done writing, ask them to share their responses, cautioning them not to mention names or talk about a group disrespectfully.

3. Invite the students to reflect on the ways that their current high school class (that is, their whole grade level—first year, sophomore, junior, or senior) groups itself. If the students feel that their class is not united, ask them to suggest values and beliefs that could unite it. Then encourage the students to talk about the unity of their school as a whole. List ideas on the board; be sure to include values that are particular to a Catholic school.

4. Form small groups and instruct them to develop concrete action plans for using the ideas listed on the board to build school unity. When they are done, share the plans with the class, and choose one or several to implement.

•••••• ▶ Exegetical Tools: What Is Exegesis?

Read the following passage and write some conclusions you can draw about the speaker:

> After three weeks we decided to get married. He spent a night in our town with my uncle so he could pick me up in the morning. I stopped by the night before to make the arrangements. . . . I went straight to see my niece, who was like a sister to me. I told her I would need her the next morning. It took me about two hours to explain to her what was going on, but finally she understood and she agreed to go with me. I went home and had dinner with Mama. . . . I took the dress I wanted to wear with me and went back to my niece's house. (Virginia Lee Barnes and Janice Boddy, *Aman: The Story of a Somali Girl* [New York: Pantheon Books, 1994], pages 107–108. Copyright © 1994 by Aman and the Estate of Virginia Lee Barnes.)

Conclusions you can draw about the speaker:

_____

_____

_____

_____

_____

--✂

Read the following statements by the same speaker, and then write some observations about these thoughts and the previous statement:

> I remember I was thirteen years and seven months old when I was married. (Page 102)

> We had a great, great dinner, and then I asked her if I could spend the night over at my niece's because it was Ramadan and there would be feasting and reading of the Qur'an over there. (Page 108)

> In the car, about halfway back, I told him he had to give me some money. I wanted to go to Mogadishu. (Virginia Lee Barnes and Janice Boddy, *Aman: The Story of a Somali Girl* [New York: Pantheon Books, 1994], page 109. Copyright © 1994 by Aman and the Estate of Virginia Lee Barnes.)

Your observations about the thoughts listed here and about the previous statement:

_____

_____

_____

_____

_____

Judges

Israel's Need for Judges

Personal Idols: Reflections of God?
Judges, chapter 2

A look at role models fine-tunes the students' understanding of idolatry and of the power of public figures.

    1. To prepare for this activity, ask the students to bring in old newspapers and magazines that feature pictures of people whom children or teens, or both, idolize or look up to.

    2. To begin this activity, form small groups and ask them each to label a piece of butcher paper with three columns or areas: "Positive," "Positive and negative," and "Negative." Tell the groups to cut from the materials they brought in pictures of people who are positive role models, negative role models, or both—and to glue the pictures in the corresponding column or area on their paper. Note that they may also list public figures for whom there are no pictures. Add that they should then write on their poster some characteristics of each person pictured or listed—such as rich, athletic, selfish, and willing to serve.

    3. When the groups are done with their posters, gather the class and call several students to read Judges, chapter 2. Make the following comments in your own words:
- At the beginning of the reading, the Israelites have not kept their promise to break the altars of the Canaanites. The consequence of their broken promise is that they will struggle against the lure of pagan gods.
      We might not struggle with pagan gods, but we are affected by other idols. When we are unfaithful to God, we are apt to be lured to our idols—our other gods.

    4. Allow the groups to present their posters. Offer the following insights to the students in your own words as you help them distinguish between having a positive role model and being idolatrous:
- It is not idolatrous to look up to someone and pattern one's life after their positive qualities. People's lives can be sacramental in that they can reflect God to others.
- Being idolatrous means either putting someone before God or, more familiarly, blindly devoting oneself to someone.

    5. Invite a student to read Lk 12.48, and ask the class to consider whether fame carries a greater responsibility to be a positive role model.

Are We in Need of Judges?
Judges, chapters 2–3

Examining the Israelites' infidelity and need for judges helps the students discern if they seem to be moving away from or toward God.

1. Ask several students to read Judges, chapter 2, as an overview of the cycle of infidelity that repeats itself in the Book of Judges. Note that the Deuteronomic author of Judges saw the same pattern at work in Israelite history as was seen in Deuteronomy: "obedience equals reward" and "disobedience equals punishment."

2. Invite four students to stand in front of the class in a circle, each representing one of the four aspects of Israel's cycle of infidelity (listed below). Tell those students to prepare to read Judges, chapter 3, each one narrating the parts of the story that he or she represents.
- The Israelites disobey God.
- The Israelites suffer.
- The Israelites cry out to God.
- God sends a judge to deliver the Israelites.

3. While the readers are preparing, ask five different students to come forward. Assign one student the role of God and the other four the role of Israelites. Give these instructions to God and the Israelites in your own words:
- You are also to stand in front of the class. You are to listen to the four aspects of the cycle of infidelity as Judges, chapter 3, is read, and move closer to or farther from one another to indicate each aspect's effect on the covenant relationship. Keep in mind the image you are portraying and ask yourselves in each case, "Does God move away from the Israelites, or do the Israelites move away from God?"

4. Tell the rest of the class to read Judges, chapter 3, silently while it is read aloud, and to observe the movement of the students playing Israelites and God. After the reading, lead a discussion with the class, asking for the students' observations and including the following questions:
- Who suffers when someone disobeys God—God or the disobedient person? How?
- Does sin-related suffering exist because God moves away and punishes, or because people move away from God's blessings?
- Every person and institution moves toward and away from God. Where do you currently put your country, the church, your school, and yourself in the cycle of infidelity? Why? [Give the students time to jot down their ideas on that question, and then discuss their responses as a class.]

The Judges

Comic Strip Judges
Judges, chapters 3–4, 6–8, 11, 13–16

Although the biblical stories of the Old Testament judges are not all comical, their intriguing plots are good for comic strips and help give the students an overview of the Book of Judges.

    1. Direct the students to number off from 1 to 9 and then assign each of them the corresponding passage from the list below. Explain that each passage focuses on one or two judges from the tribes of ancient Israel.
1. Judges, chapter 3 (Othniel and Ehud)
2. Judges, chapter 4 (Deborah)
3. Judges, chapter 6 (Gideon)
4. Judges, chapters 7–8 (Gideon)
5. Judges, chapter 11 (Jephthah)
6. Judges, chapter 13 (Samson)
7. Judges, chapter 14 (Samson)
8. Judges, chapter 15 (Samson)
9. Judges, chapter 16 (Samson)

    2. Instruct the students to read their assigned passage and then use blank paper and colored markers or pencils to create a comic strip of it, covering the major events and adding some basic dialog where applicable. Tell them to write the name or names of the judge or judges from that passage at the top of the paper.

    3. Gather the students who reviewed the same passages in small groups to compare and contrast how they portrayed the judge or judges in that passage. Then invite each group to share with the class a few things about the judge or judges they studied.

    4. Spend a few minutes at the end of this activity passing around the comic strips, or display them in the classroom.

God's Use of Weakness: Samson
Judges, chapters 13–16
"Samson," near Judg 13.1, CYB

God's ability to use Samson's weaknesses for good reminds the students of God's power to transform our failings into God's purpose.

    1. Ask the students to jot down a time in their life when they made a mistake or fell short but found that it all worked out well anyway. You might want to give them the following examples:
■ Laura was late to pick up her friend, and the two missed the movie they had planned to see. But they ended up seeing a better and more inspiring movie later, and meanwhile they had time just to talk.

- Victor is a classic procrastinator, but somehow he always manages to squeeze his assignments in right at the last minute. Even though he (and sometimes those around him) suffers from stress, he usually gets A's and B's.

2. When the students are done writing, invite them to share some of their accounts. Then help them reflect on how God can bring good things out of our mistakes and weak points—or, perhaps more important, how God brings good *in spite of* our weaknesses. Emphasize that God's love and mercy are great and mysterious.

3. Ask a student to read the article "Samson" from the *CYB*. Note the three vows of nazirites:
- abstain from alcohol
- avoid contact with dead bodies
- refrain from cutting their hair

Divide the class into four groups and ask each group to read a different chapter from Judges, chapters 13–16. Tell the groups that as they read, they are to identify, in writing, Samson's virtues and his weaknesses, especially noting how he honored or dishonored his nazirite vows.

4. When the groups have finished their reading, ask them to share their findings with the class, and discuss how God ultimately worked through Samson's weaknesses to subdue the Philistines. Note that if Samson had been more virtuous in some areas, the same goals could have been accomplished but fewer people might have died. Point out that God works with our weaknesses but still wants us to be open to transformation.

Ruth

A Model of Loyalty and Goodness

Loyalty Lyrics
Ruth, chapter 1

Through Ruth's example of loyalty, this exercise invites the students to reflect on their own understanding of loyalty, using music and art.

1. Prepare for this exercise by directing the students each to find a song that talks about loyalty and to bring the lyrics and a recording of the song to class.

2. Begin this exercise by asking several students to read Ruth 1.1–18 aloud for the class. Discuss the different decisions that Naomi's daughters-in-law make. Comment on the story as follows, in your own words:
   - Ruth is under no obligation to leave her homeland and go to Israel with her mother-in-law. In fact, Naomi even encourages her to stay behind. Yet she goes. And by doing so, she finds a new life, and her loyalty is rewarded (as told in the rest of the Book of Ruth).
   - Ruth presents a striking contrast to Peter in the Gospels, who swore his loyalty to Jesus at the Last Supper but denied even knowing Jesus only a few hours later, when his own life was in danger.

   Help the students find one or more of the Gospel accounts of Peter's denial, using a concordance (see appendix A) or skimming the Gospels themselves. They should find and read the following passages:
- Mt 26.31–35,69–75
- Mk 14.26–31,66–72
- Lk 22.31–34,54–62
- Jn 13.36–38; 18.15–27
   Then continue your comments as follows:
   - Loyalty has a price, and it is not always easy to pay that price. Peter failed—although Jesus gave him the opportunity to redeem himself and still commissioned him to shepherd God's people (Jn 21.15–19). Ruth succeeded. Both Peter and Ruth are great biblical figures, and both, in their own way, teach us about loyalty.

3. Direct the students to take the words of Ruth 1.16, beginning with "Where you go, I will go," and some of the lyrics of their song, and to present them together in a work of art on a sheet of blank paper. Provide art supplies such as colored markers or pencils, magazines for cutting up, scissors, and glue. Play some of the students' songs in the background while they are working. When they are through, give them another sheet of paper and ask them to write a reflective essay about a personal experience of loyalty.

4. When the students are done with their creative reflections, invite them to share their artwork. Discuss the challenges and rewards of loyalty, and invite them to share their written reflections as examples.

God's Silent Presence
Ruth

As the students read and reflect on Ruth's story, they are led to recall experiences from their own lives that show how God is present and works through us even when God's voice is silent.

1. Invite the students to take turns reading the Book of Ruth aloud. Ask them to listen for the voice of God addressing one or more of the characters. Discuss the following questions with the students:
  - God is not a character in the Book of Ruth. Why is God's voice missing? Despite God's silence, God is present in the story of Ruth. How?
  - How does God act through the main characters?
  - How can a person be the voice of God by her or his actions? What are some specific examples of people doing that?

2. Ask the students to describe, in writing, an event in which someone's words or actions made God's presence very real to them.

The Domino Effect of Goodness
Ruth

This activity uses falling dominoes to help the students visualize the ripple effect of both good and evil actions.

1. Instruct the students to read the entire Book of Ruth. While they do so, line up a number of dominoes and leave one domino standing away from the others. When the students are done reading, communicate the following ideas in your own words:
  - In the rare situation that a human being is completely alone, a single act of good or evil affects only that person. [Knock down the single domino as you solicit from the students examples of that type of situation.]
  - More often, however, human actions affect others. A single good or evil action can set off a small or big chain reaction of good or evil. [Let a student volunteer knock over the first domino of the set you lined up, which will in turn knock the rest down.]
  - What is the meaning of the *domino effect?* What is an everyday example of that effect? What is a more serious example?
  - How did Naomi's selflessness toward her daughters-in-law set up a grace-filled domino effect? [As the students respond, portray that chain reaction in the form of a flowchart on the board.]

2. Ask the students to think of a personal example of the domino effect in the context of good or evil. Have them create a flowchart of that experience—similar in format to the one you drew on the board—and then share their reflections with the class.

HISTORICAL

Exegetical Tools: Historical Criticism in Ruth
Ruth

Some of the practices in the Book of Ruth invite questions that are addressed in the Bible's footnotes and in biblical dictionaries.

1. Prepare for this activity by collecting a variety of newspaper articles on current topics, one article for each student.

2. Begin this activity by telling the students to read the Book of Ruth and, as they read, to write down any questions that they have and any terms or concepts with which they are unfamiliar, such as the Levirate laws governing widows and remarriage.

3. When the students are done reading, solicit their questions and the unfamiliar terms and concepts they wrote down, and record those on the board. Explain that scholars use an exegetical tool called historical criticism when they try to answer questions about a passage by researching the historical circumstances of the time, such as political events, economic issues, or, as in this case, customs and traditions.

4. Illustrate the process of historical criticism in a modern context by giving the students the newspaper articles you brought in, and asking them to identify what a person two thousand years from now might have to research in order to understand those articles. Encourage the students to share their findings with the class.

5. Show the students how to use the footnotes and study articles in the Bible, and see if they are able to answer some of their own questions about the Book of Ruth.

6. Distribute copies of a biblical dictionary (see appendix A), or information about relevant passages in the Book of Ruth from one. Allow the students to skim the relevant dictionary passages, and then have them look up terms pertaining to Ruth.
Note: The single-volume *HarperCollins Bible Dictionary,* edited by Paul J. Achtemeier (see appendix A), has articles entitled "marriage," "widow," and "shoes."

7. Direct the students to create and perform some short skits presenting aspects of the Levirate law as it might be practiced today. Afterward, discuss some of the information and insights gained from this activity.

1 Samuel

Samuel the Prophet

Searching for Unconditional Love: Hannah and Elkanah
1 Samuel, chapter 1

The writing genre of the personals gives the students a fun tool for discussing the kind of life partnership many people seek.

1. Prepare for this exercise by screening and selecting a number of personal ads from a recent newspaper. Then begin the exercise by passing out those ads and allowing the students a few minutes to scan some. Ask the students to choose some examples, read them to the class, and talk about the kind of love each ad seeks.

2. Call a few students to read 1 Samuel, chapter 1, aloud to the class. Make these points in your own words:
- Childbearing was important to both men and women in Israelite society. Children were seen as gracious gifts from God, and having a large number of offspring was considered a divine blessing because the multiplication of descendants was part of God's Promise to Israel's ancestors.
- Elkanah's love for Hannah seems to be for who she is rather than for what she can do for him. That kind of love is called unconditional love.

As a class, write a personal ad for someone like Elkanah from Hannah, in order to identify some of the qualities of unconditional love.

3. Direct the students each to write a personal ad of their own, imagining that they are older, single, and ready to find a life partner who will love them for who they are. They should include both what they want someone to look for in them and what qualities they seek in someone else. When the students are done writing, invite them to share aspects of their personal ads as you conduct a discussion about important qualities of a strong marriage.

Divided Loyalties: Church and State
1 Samuel, chapter 8

This activity invites the students to explore the complexities of practicing faith in a political setting.

1. Ask the whole class to read 1 Sam 8.1–19, assigning the roles of narrator, some elders, God, Samuel, and the people. As the readers cite Samuel's different arguments for not having a king, and the people's opposing arguments for having a king, list those on the board. Ask the students to think of other reasonable arguments to support those positions, and add them to the appropriate lists.

2. Point out that at the heart of the issue of whether to have a king is the challenge of being faithful to God in the political sphere. Note that it is easy for rulers to forget God and abuse the people (Samuel's argument), and it is easier still for people to follow the visible leader than for them to trust in God (the people's argument). Offer the students this hypothetical example:

■ Theresa Chavez is a congresswoman who represents a half million people of various cultural, political, and religious backgrounds. Upon taking office, she pledged to represent those people fairly and accurately by voting on a variety of issues in a way that would best serve the needs of all her constituents.

Theresa is also a practicing Roman Catholic and is faced with a difficult challenge: Tomorrow she must vote for or against a bill that would make the government responsible for funding abortions for women with low incomes. Theresa personally shares the pro-life position of the church, but polls show that most people in her district are pro-choice.

3. Lead the students in a debate on the following question: "Should Theresa vote for or against that legislation?" Randomly divide the class into small groups. Assign half the groups the pro position (Theresa should set aside her religious beliefs and vote for the bill) and the other half the con position (Theresa should follow her religious beliefs and vote against the bill). Each group should develop five arguments for its assigned position.

4. Tell the students arguing the pro position to sit on the left side of the classroom, the students arguing the con position to sit on the right. Instruct the sides to turn their desks or chairs so that they face each other, with an aisle down the middle of the room. Allow each side to make opening arguments; after that, encourage the sides to rebut each other's statements. Moderate the debate in order to ensure a respectful and rational exchange of ideas.

5. After the debate, lead a class discussion that examines the difficulty of mixing politics with religion. See if any insights from the modern debate shed light on a reconciliation of the religion-versus-state debate of Samuel's time.

Seeing Others with God's Eyes
1 Samuel, chapter 16

Reflecting on the ways that they assess others prepares the students to process God's "unexpected" choice of David from among Jesse's sons.

1. Set up six stations in the classroom as follows:

■ *Station 1: A collage of faces.* Assemble a collage of ten faces that represent different sexes, ages, races, socioeconomic backgrounds, emotions, and so on. Number the faces 1 to 10. Post this instruction: "Select the three people in this collage that you think you might get along with, and write their numbers."

(This exercise is based on the activity "Who Would You Choose?" in *Get 'Em Talking,* by Mike Yaconelli and Scott Koenigsaecker, p. 93.)

■ *Station 2: My friend.* Set up several symbols of friendship, such as photos of friends and a friendship bracelet, ring, and pin. Post this instruction: "Write down the three qualities that you value most in your best friend."

- *Station 3: An advertisement or commercial.* Provide an example or two of a commercial or advertisement that is aimed at youth and is selling clothing or something else. Post this instruction: "How is this ad trying to improve your life?"
- *Station 4: Role models.* Give the names (and possibly pictures) of three inspirational figures with whom the students are familiar, such as Martin Luther King Jr., Mother Teresa, and a community or school figure. Post this instruction: "For each of these people, write a reason why he or she is a hero to many."
- *Station 5: My morning.* Display a box of cereal, a bowl, and a spoon (or some other symbols of a morning ritual). Post this instruction: "Write down three things you did this morning to get ready for school."
- *Station 6: My future spouse.* Set out a wedding portrait, perhaps of yourself or your parents, or of a famous couple that the students should recognize. Post this instruction: "Write down the top three things that you want your future spouse to like about you."

    Note: Some of the students may feel sure they do not desire marriage. Ask them to simply imagine finding one person or companion to spend the rest of their life with.

2. Divide the class into six small groups, and tell the students to bring a pen or pencil and a piece of paper with them as the groups rotate around the stations. They should number the paper from 1 to 6 (one number for each station), leaving after each number a sufficient amount of space for written responses.

Begin each small group at a different station. Allow the groups to spend 3 to 5 minutes at each station, giving a signal for them to move from one to another. Mention that each student should follow the set of instructions individually but move together with her or his group. Collect the papers at the end of the class.

3. After class, review the results of the station visits. At the next class, lead the students in a discussion about how we assess others and ourselves. Begin with the results for station 1. Share the top two responses, eliciting more information from the students about their choices. Help them see that our eyes gain some information about compatibility (age, mood, etc.), and our sight also limits us when it comes to getting to know another person.

Continue with the results for stations 2 and 4. Help the students see that what they value most in others are things that one cannot gain by looking at appearance only.

Then look at the results for stations 3 and 5. Discuss what the media tells the students they need to do in order to be accepted, and see if many of them indeed spend a good deal of time doing that. Help the students distinguish between a healthy pride in one's appearance and in flattering dress, and a fearful need to feel and look like an "acceptable person."

Last, talk about the responses for station 6, which can help the students see what they truly treasure in themselves and in significant relationships. Encourage them to share insights.

4. Ask a student to read 1 Sam 16.1–13, emphasizing verse 7. Note that though valuing appearance to some extent is natural, it is overemphasized in our society. We need to trust our inner sense, given to us by God, that inner qualities are a true measure of character, both in others and in ourselves.

Prayer Styles: Music and Prayer
1 Samuel, chapter 16

Just as Saul was soothed by David's music from the lyre, many of the students find music to be a source of comfort in tough times.

1. Start this activity with some reflective music and a quiet prayer. Then ask the students if the music during the prayer affected them and if so, how.

2. Have a student read 1 Sam 16.14–23 aloud. Invite the students to take a few moments and write a short paragraph answering the following questions:
   - When you are down or disturbed, what kind of music helps you? Are there specific songs or albums that you find particularly helpful?
   - How does that music affect you?
   - Do you listen to others playing or singing that music, or play it or sing it yourself?

3. Ask the students to talk about their music selections. Possibly gather a list of selections from the class to copy and distribute.

4. Follow up with a class period (or a portion of a class period) devoted to quiet reflection, allowing the students to bring in recorded music for meditation, or asking students to play their own instruments or sing. Near the end of the class, have the students write a one-page reflection about what they experienced, heard, thought, and felt during the class.

The Rise of David and the Downfall of King Saul

David and Goliath: "What Have I Done Now?"
1 Samuel, chapter 17
"Taking On Goliath," 1 Samuel, chapter 17, CYB

The students look for themselves in aspects of David's character as he takes on Goliath.

1. Assign the following roles for a dramatic reading of 1 Samuel, chapter 17: narrator, Goliath, Jesse, the Israelites, David, Eliab, Saul, and Abner. After the reading, ask the students to describe how David's attitude about Goliath developed.

2. Invite a student to read the article "Taking On Goliath" from the *CYB*. Tell the students to describe on paper one of the following events in their life:
   - a time when you were afraid to do something and either chose to be courageous or to back down
   - a time when you felt that you could not do something, but did it anyway
   - a time when your words got you into trouble

3. Form pairs and invite the students to share their responses with their partner. Consider sharing an example from your own life as well. Ask if God inspired any of the students' courageous actions as God did David's.

Saul and Jealousy: How Low Can You Go?
1 Samuel, chapters 18–19

This activity invites the students to reflect on how jealousy corrupted Saul, in order to help them recognize the damage that jealousy can cause in their own lives.

1. In preparation for this activity, ask the students to bring in an item that symbolizes jealousy for them. Give them an example: you might present a rotting apple and explain that jealousy eats away at a healthy person just like rot takes over a good apple.

2. To begin this activity, ask the students to share their symbols with the class. As they do so, note on the board characteristics of the symbols and ask questions for clarification.

Handout 1 Sam–A

3. Form small groups and ask them each to complete handout 1 Sam–A, "Jealousy: Saul and Teens Today," reviewing the instructions with them. After the groups have completed the handout, allow them to share their evaluations of Saul. Give the class some time to share examples of jealousy that are common in the lives of teenagers. Encourage the students to suggest healthy ways to deal with jealousy, and compare those to unhealthy ways.

Parents and Friends
1 Samuel, chapters 18–20
"Friends Forever," 1 Samuel, chapter 20, CYB

The students look at their own experiences with parents' reactions to friends, in order to gain some insight into the difficulties faced by David and Jonathan.

1. In the class before this activity, ask the students to read 1 Samuel, chapters 18–20, for homework.

2. Begin this activity by discussing with the students the major points of the assigned chapters. Have a student read the article "Friends Forever" from the *CYB* aloud to the class.

3. Divide the class into groups of four or five. Direct the groups each to come up with a skit involving a conflict between a teen and his or her parent or parents over a friendship of the teen's. The skit should have several acts:
   - The first act should show the teen and the friend relating.
   - The second act should feature the teen's parents discussing their fears about the friendship, or one parent thinking about those fears.
   - The third act should depict the parent or parents, the teen, and a counselor working out the situation. The counselor's advice to the family members should include spiritual aspects.

4. Invite the groups to take turns presenting their skits to the class. When all the skits have been presented, ask the students to identify any common themes that emerged in them, as well as insights gained by the students. Ask the students to ponder whether Saul would have been open to any negotiation about his son and David.

H
I
S
T
O
R
I
C
A
L

Saul and Suicide
1 Samuel, chapter 31
"Suicide Is Not an Answer," 1 Sam 31.1–7, CYB

A reading of the story of Saul's death by his own hand is an opportunity for the students to review the warning signs of suicide and resources available for those tempted to take their own life.

1. Ask a student to read 1 Sam 31.1–7 aloud, and another to read the article "Suicide Is Not an Answer" from the *CYB*.

2. Provide some current information on teen suicide prevention for the students, including signs that someone is feeling suicidal, responsible ways to help a friend in that condition, and phone numbers that the students can use to get help for themselves or others. Invite a school counselor or an outside speaker to address this sensitive, complex, and urgent topic.

3. Note that Saul seemed to have few real supporters throughout his downfall resulting in suicide. Even the biblical authors find little pity for him. Suggest that instead of harshly judging others or giving up on them, we should extend the gift of life by reaching out to people in pain as best we can and leading them to help.

••••••••••••► Jealousy: Saul and Teens Today

Jealousy is a very powerful and familiar human emotion. All people experience some level of jealousy. At times jealousy can be quite strong. Occasionally, jealousy leads a person to do dangerous or damaging things. Read 1 Samuel, chapters 18–19, and rate the following examples of Saul's jealousy of David as Normal, Strong, or Dangerous by checking the appropriate column. Then think of examples of Normal, Strong, and Dangerous jealousy that you observe in the lives of teens and write them out in the proper column. Conclude by giving advice to Saul and your peers about how to deal with jealousy.

Examples from the life of Saul	Normal jealousy	**Strong** jealousy	**Dangerous** jealousy
1 Sam 18.8–9			
1 Sam 18.10–11			
1 Sam 18.12–13			
1 Sam 18.17–19			
1 Sam 18.20–29			
1 Sam 19.8–10			
1 Sam 19.11–17			
Examples from the lives of teens today	Normal jealousy	**Strong** jealousy	**Dangerous** jealousy

What advice would you give to Saul to ease his jealousy? What helps teens deal successfully with jealousy?

2 Samuel

King David

Liturgical Dance and Movement
2 Samuel, chapter 6
"The Dance of Life," 2 Sam 6.12–19, CYB

David's joyful dance invites the students to discuss that form of worship and their experiences with it.

1. Prearrange to have a student in the class teach the class some popular dance steps. After the dance lesson, invite the students to reflect on social dancing and identify why it is fun and sometimes risky.

2. Invite another student to lead the class in a rendition of the wave or some other all-crowd movement used at sporting events, and discuss the value in such an activity.

3. Have one student read 2 Sam 6.12–19 aloud to the class, and another read the article "The Dance of Life" from the *CYB.*

4. Call a student to teach the class a sacred song involving ritual movement. If no one volunteers, teach a simple one yourself by rehearsing the actions and then performing them prayerfully. Ask the students to share their experiences with liturgical dance and movement, and have them compare and contrast liturgical movement with other forms of prayer.

5. Close by pointing out that liturgical dance and movement add another dimension to worship much like dancing does to a social event or the wave does to an athletic contest. Mention that when we focus on just ourselves, we might feel awkward, but when we let go of the self-consciousness and get involved in the dance and movement, we experience the worship more fully.

Variation. After step 4, show portions of the video *Glory Days* (St. Anthony Messenger Press, 1996, 120 min.), which features liturgical movement and dance, and ask for the students' reactions.

David's Wars
2 Samuel, chapter 8

David fought many battles at God's command. This exercise asks the students to examine the various battles people fight today.

1. Direct the students to answer these questions on a piece of paper:

- What battles have you fought or are you now fighting?
- What is worthwhile about them?
- What have you learned from them about yourself and others?
- Many U.S. citizens are waging a war on drugs. What are three other battles being fought in our society today?

2. Invite the students to share their answers to the last question, and list their ideas about societal battles on the board.

3. Ask a student to read 2 Samuel, chapter 8, to the class. Take a vote to find the five most important issues worth fighting for today. Tell the students each to decide which of those five topics they find most interesting, and then gather in a group with the others who do so. Direct the groups to discuss how God might expect us to battle against the opponents of their issue, like David fought the Philistines with God's help. Instruct the groups each to create an action plan for fighting for their issue. Note that the plan must be nonviolent.

4. Ask each group to share its action plan, and invite the class to discuss it.

Variation. After step 3, discuss how David got away with violence toward his enemies, and how sometimes in the Old Testament, even God is portrayed as violent, especially toward enemies. Compare that image of God to Jesus' image of a nonviolent, peace-loving God.

Note: Refer to biblical commentaries (see appendix A) to prepare for this discussion.

The Consequences of David's Sin

The Cost of Selfish Sexual Choices
2 Samuel, chapter 11

Learning about David's selfish behavior leads the students to reflect on the effects of a self-centered view of sexuality.

Note: The activity "Exegetical Tools: Source Criticism—the Chronicler," on page 90 of this manual, compares this passage to the Chronicler's version of the same time period.

1. Do a dramatic reading of 2 Samuel, chapter 11, assigning the following speaking roles: narrator, David, Bathsheba, Uriah, Joab, and the messenger.

2. Divide the class into four groups and assign each of the following scenarios to a different group. Tell each group to plan a short role-play for its scenario in order to identify who suffered from David's inability to control his lust.
- Uriah discusses his great marriage as he marches into battle.
- Bathsheba shares with a friend her grief about Uriah's death.
- Bathsheba and David converse at the dinner table after he has her husband killed.
- David overhears palace servants talking about what he has done to Bathsheba and Uriah.

3. Invite the groups to take turns performing their skits. Then discuss with the class the results of David's selfishness.

Integrity

2 Samuel, chapters 11–12
"Lust and Its Consequences," 2 Sam 11.1–5, CYB; *"The Power of a Good Story," 2 Sam 12.1–12*, CYB

The students use David's story and Nathan's parable as a discussion-starter about leaders and integrity.

1. Have several students read 2 Sam 11.1—12.15 aloud to the class, and another student read the articles "Lust and Its Consequences" and "The Power of a Good Story" from the *CYB*. Clarify the main events of the stories, making sure that the students understand the clever connection between the parable and David's sin. Ask the students to identify why the parable was much more effective than a straightforward accusation by Nathan in helping David see what he had done.

2. Assign the students each to interview a parent, a neighbor, or another adult about people the adult has worked for. The students should ask the interviewees if they have witnessed people in leadership (such as immediate supervisors or other managers) using power abusively, or if they have witnessed leaders acting with integrity. Tell the students to get specific examples—changing the names of people or workplaces to avoid identifying those involved—and write a report of the interview.

3. When the interviews and reports are done, ask the students to share some of their stories. Then place the students in groups of three or four. Direct the groups each to write a definition for integrity. Then tell them each to write a scenario in which a person is acting without integrity. Explain that the scenario should be from the life of a teenager and may be about school, work, family, baby-sitting, or dating, for instance.

4. When the groups have completed their writing, collect the scenarios and redistribute them so that each group receives one developed by another group—being careful not to reveal who gets whose. Now, instruct the groups each to create a parable, like Nathan's, that could be used to challenge the person who is acting without integrity in the scenario they just received.

5. When the parables are done, invite the groups to take turns reading their own to the class, and see if the groups are able to identify the parable that pertains to the scenario they wrote.

6. As a class, discuss ways that people in the stories could have acted differently, were they persons of integrity. Compare the definitions of integrity that the groups devised, and lead a discussion about what it means to live with integrity and to lead with integrity.

1 and 2 Kings

King Solomon

Parents' Guiding Words
1 Kings, chapter 2

This exercise uses interviews in which the students ask adults for words of wisdom as the starting point for a review of David's last words.

1. Invite a student to read 1 Kings 2.1–9 aloud to the class, and ask the class to identify the main points of David's speech to Solomon. Have the students evaluate whether David lived up to his words. For the next class, direct the students each to ask a parent or another adult they respect for a few words of wisdom about life.

2. At the next class, request that the students each transfer their interviewee's insights artistically onto a piece of construction paper, using colored markers or pencils and other art supplies. On the back of their paper, the students should write a one-paragraph reflection on those words.

3. When the reflections are done, invite the students to share their insights with the class, and encourage discussion. Help the students to relate this sharing to the previous class discussion about David's words to Solomon. Display some of the artwork.

Solomon's Request
1 Kings, chapter 3

In examining their own requests to God, the students evaluate Solomon's prayer for an understanding mind.

1. Ask the students to respond to this question in writing: "How would you answer if God said to you, 'Ask what I should give you' (1 Kings 3.5)?"

2. Invite the students to share some of the things they wrote. Then have a student read 1 Kings 3.1–15 aloud. Discuss Solomon's response to the same question and God's reaction to Solomon's prayer.

3. Direct the students each to identify a role in which they function as a leader—perhaps team captain, older sibling, or successful student. Tell them to write a brief prayer asking God for the kind of personal qualities that would make them more successful in that position.

Solomon and Modern Wisdom
1 Kings, chapter 3

The students develop and share modern skits to explore the wisdom of Solomon's decision in the famous story of his judgment of two women claiming to be one baby's mother.

1. Show a segment of a TV show where litigants bring their case before a judge. Choose a segment in which the judge is not given clear evidence and must come to a decision based on conflicting testimony from the plaintiff and the defendant. Then engage the students in a discussion about how the judge might have arrived at the judgment.

2. Ask several students to read 1 Kings 3.16–28 to the class. Point out that because Solomon is given no more evidence than the women's conflicting testimony, he has to find a clever way to discover who is the baby's mother.

3. Divide the class into small groups. Instruct the groups each to create a skit about a tough modern dilemma and to incorporate the kind of creative problem solving used by Solomon. Discuss each skit after it is presented to the class.

Variation. Invite a local judge to speak with the class and share her or his experiences, especially ones similar to the Bible story.

Solomon's Temple
1 Kings, chapter 7

Solomon's Temple was the center of the religious life of the ancient Israelites. A tour of a local parish church or cathedral is an excellent opportunity for the students to expand their understanding of and appreciation for such an assembly building as a focal point for Christian worship.

1. Call the students to take turns reading 1 Kings, chapter 7, aloud. Ask the class to explain why Solomon spared no expense building a structure to honor the ark of the Covenant. Help the students identify five reasons why people of faith build such structures.

2. Lead the students on a tour of a local parish church or, even better, the diocesan cathedral. Describe the various sacred items and symbols in the building, and explain how those help Catholics experience God's presence and how they deepen the communal bonds between the worshipers.

Variation. Invite someone to speak to the class about the process and costs of building, maintaining, and operating a church and the items in it (such as the organ and stained-glass windows), and the structure's history and meaning to the church community. Your guest might be a pastor, a parish staff member, or a member of a building or finance committee.

Prayer Styles: Guided Imagery—an Internal Holy Place
1 Kings, chapter 8
"Holy Places," 1 Kings 8.27–30, CYB

This activity presents a guided imagery to inspire the students to discover an internal place where they can meet God whenever they choose.

1. Take the students to a peaceful spot, or create a prayerful environment within the classroom through low lighting and quiet music. Direct the students to read to themselves 1 Kings 8.27–30 and the article "Holy Places" from the *CYB*.

2. Introduce or review the prayer style called guided imagery. In a reflective tone, ask the students to follow your instructions as you lead them through a guided imagery. Then present the following meditation in your own words, giving them time after each direction to process and absorb it:

- Close your eyes and relax each part of your body. [Name the toes, feet, calves, etc., all the way up to the head.] . . . Listen to your breathing—follow each inhale and exhale. . . . Let go of any concerns you have, and as stray thoughts come to you and distract you, let them float away like feathers or balloons. . . .

  Imagine yourself moving slowly, calmly to a place where you like to go to be alone. . . . Bring to mind the look, sounds, smells, and feel of this place. . . .

  Rest in this place for a while by yourself, then invite God to meet you here. . . . Ask if God has something to say to you. . . . What do you hear? . . . Is there something you want to ask of God? . . . How does God respond? . . .

  Say good-bye to God, leave this place where you have been alone with God, and return to the place where you were sitting with your class. Keep your eyes closed as you readjust to reality.

3. Give the students a minute or two of quiet to readjust to the class and process their prayer. Then ask if anyone would like to comment on what the prayer experience was like for them. Afterward, note that the students may go to this haven in their own heart to meet God whenever they want.

Variation. This activity may be adapted for use with another guided imagery, perhaps one selected especially for your particular class or situation. The series A Quiet Place Apart, by Jane E. Ayer (Winona, MN: Saint Mary's Press, 1993–1998), offers guided meditations based on Scripture themes. Each title in the series provides a leader's guide with directions and scripts, an audiocassette, and usually a CD.

The Splitting of the Kingdom

Solomon's Sins
1 Kings, chapters 9–11

Exploring Solomon's downfall helps the students consider how power corrupts in modern leadership as well.

Note: The activity "Exegetical Tools: Source Criticism—the Chronicler," on page 90 of this manual, compares this version of Solomon's sins to the Chronicler's treatment of the same subject.

1. To prepare for this exercise, have the students read 1 Kings, chapters 9–11, for homework.

2. Begin this exercise by forming small groups. Ask the groups to read Deut 17.14–20 and 1 Sam 8.10–18. They should then list the ways that Solomon violated guidelines for an Israelite king and fulfilled Samuel's warning about kings—based on the reading from 1 Kings.

3. Invite the groups to share their findings with the class. Lead a discussion of how and why Solomon changed from a wise and holy king into a corrupt and idolatrous tyrant.

4. Write the following statement on the board: "Power tends to corrupt and absolute power corrupts absolutely" (Lord Acton). Ask the students to agree or disagree with that statement and to reflect on its applicability in Solomon's reign. Invite the students to identify leaders today and assess how power affects their ability to rule and lead well.

Parents as Role Models
1 Kings, chapter 12

The students explore the issue of parents as role models, after reading about how Rehoboam follows Solomon's example as a harsh ruler.

1. Before class, create five signs with the following labels and place them in consecutive corners of the classroom (putting the first and last signs in the same corner):
- Zero years old (birth)
- Ten years old
- Twenty years old
- Thirty years old
- Forty years old

2. Begin this activity with a class discussion in which you help the students to define *role model* and to suggest characteristics of positive and negative role models. Write those characteristics on the board. Ask the students to identify specific role models, cultural or personal. List those role models on the board as well.

3. Ask a student to read 1 Kings 12.1–20 aloud and assess with the class whether Solomon was a positive role model for Rehoboam. Invite the students to share suggestions of concrete ways that parents can be positive role models.

4. Ask the students to imagine a timeline that extends around the room and that represents part of a human life span beginning at birth and continuing to age forty. Call their attention to the signs at the four corners of the room, each signifying a different age. Tell the students to position themselves around the room according to the way they answer this question: "On the average, at what age can people take full responsibility for their own actions and

not attribute their behavior to the kind of role models their parents are or were?" Assign the center of the room for people who respond "Never."

5. While the students are standing along the timeline, ask them to explain their choices. Help them see that though parents influence us greatly, with God's help, we need to take responsibility for our personal growth.

Kings and Prophets

Elijah Role-Plays
1 Kings, chapters 17–19, 21
"Elijah and Elisha," near 1 Kings 17.1, CYB

The students create skits around the last six chapters of 1 Kings as a way to understand the character Elijah.

Introduce the prophet Elijah by asking a student to read the article "Elijah and Elisha" from the *CYB*. Divide the class into small groups and ask the groups each to create and perform a short skit based on one of the following stories:
- 1 Kings, chapter 17 (Elijah and the widow)
- 1 Kings, chapter 18 (Elijah and the prophets of Baal)
- 1 Kings 19.1–18 (Elijah's encounter with God at Horeb)
- 1 Kings 21.1–18 (The seizure of Naboth's vineyard)

Passing On the Role of Prophet: Elisha and Christian Baptism
2 Kings, chapter 2

The students compare the experience of a Christian during Baptism to Elijah's transfer of prophetic power to Elisha.

1. Before class, obtain a baptismal candle—that is, a candle given to newly baptized children or adults. If you do not have one from a family member's Baptism, try borrowing one from a friend or ask a Catholic parish to supply one.

2. Begin this activity by calling several students to read 1 Kings 19.19–21 and 2 Kings 2.1–15 aloud to the class. Make the following point to the students in your own words:
- Elisha accepts Elijah's spirit of prophecy as well as Moses' leadership. The former is evident when Elijah throws his mantle over Elisha in 1 Kings, chapter 19, and the latter becomes apparent when Elisha parts the water like Elijah and Moses had done.

3. Distribute handout 2 Kings–A, "The Presentation of the Lighted Candle." Light the baptismal candle you brought, and have the students read the extracts from the handout aloud together. Then discuss these questions with the students:

Handout **2 Kings–A**

H I S T O R I C A L

- How is a newly baptized person's reception of this candle similar to Elisha's reception of Elijah's mantle?
- In what ways can baptized persons function as prophets in today's world? [Encourage the students to think of baptized persons from a variety of age-groups.]

Disposition and the Path Toward God
2 Kings, chapter 5

The disposition of various characters in 2 Kings, chapter 5, strengthened or weakened Naaman's ability to receive healing. The students learn that, similarly, one's chosen attitude helps one move toward or away from God.

Handout 2 Kings–B

1. Distribute handout 2 Kings–B, "Disposition and the Path Toward God," and ask the students to quietly complete the sentences in the first column. Assure the students that the handout will not be collected, so they may freely answer the questions.

2. Assign students to the different roles in 2 Kings, chapter 5: narrator, Naaman, girl serving Naaman's wife, king of Aram, king of Israel, Elisha, Naaman's servants, and Gehazi. Invite those students to read the chapter aloud for the class. Then ask all the students to fill in the second column of the handout chart, naming a character from that Scripture passage who fits each of the dispositions mentioned and citing the appropriate verse. Note that they may list the same character more than once.

3. When the students have completed column 2 of the handout, review their choices as a class, discussing conflicting assessments. Note that the story shows that God wanted Naaman's healing. Mention that some of the characters contributed to Naaman's healing and others threatened to block it. Ask the students to write "Helped" or "Hindered" in the third column of the handout, to indicate how each character in column 2 affected Naaman's healing.

4. Instruct the students to reflect on the sentences they completed on the handout and to indicate in the fourth column whether the different dispositions mentioned in the first column help or hinder their own relationship with God. Point out that our openness to God's grace varies, but if we know what dispositions help us to respond to God's invitation, we are more likely to be attentive to God's presence and open to receiving God's healing and other gifts.

A Report Card for Leaders
2 Kings, chapters 8–25
"Grading Kings," near 2 Kings 8.18, CYB

Because the students are familiar with receiving grades, a report card may be a fun way for them to assess the performance of leaders past and present.

Handout 2 Kings–C

1. Ask a student to read the *CYB* article "Grading Kings." Distribute handout 2 Kings–C, "Leadership Report Card," and review the instructions with the class. Give the students time to complete the handout individually.

2. Form small groups and ask the students to share with their group their evaluations and comments about the biblical kings and modern leaders. Direct the groups each to compile a list of characteristics that contribute to a leader's success or failure.

3. As a class, create a profile of the successful leader and another profile of the unsuccessful leader, and record those profiles on the board. Then ask, "If you had the power to create a national leader with three positive qualities and three negative qualities, which three qualities would you choose from each profile?" Help the class reach a consensus on that question.

Josiah: Inspirational Youth
2 Kings, chapters 22–23

Just as Josiah's discovery of the Law inspired the Israelites to renew their commitment to the Covenant, the leadership of youth today helps people of all ages dedicate themselves to important issues.

1. Form pairs and ask them to think of a symbol that represents how most people in U.S. society perceive young people. After a few minutes, invite the pairs to share and explain their symbol.

2. Call several students to read 2 Kings 22.1—23.3 aloud, assigning these character parts: narrator, Meshullam, Hilkiah, Shaphan, King Josiah, and Huldah. Point out that Josiah found the book of the Law when he was twenty-six years old. His own commitment to return to the Law inspired his people to do so also. Invite the students to share stories of young people who have inspired them.

3. Assign the students the task of investigating what kinds of service young people are involved in. Suggest that they use magazines, books, the Internet, and personal interviews as resources. Have them report their findings to the class.

4. Ask the students to promote young people as inspirational role models in society by submitting examples of youth service and leadership in your school to the local media or diocesan newspaper.

Exegetical Tools: Historical Criticism in 2 Kings
2 Kings, chapter 23

This activity asks the students to use biblical dictionaries to research the gods of Israel's neighbors, and then display their knowledge in artwork.

1. If necessary, familiarize the students with biblical dictionaries (see appendix A) and the practice of historical criticism (see the activity "Exegetical Tools: Historical Criticism in Ruth," on page 68 of this manual, for background on that topic).

2. Have several students read 2 Kings, chapter 23, aloud, and list on the board the foreign gods and practices mentioned.

3. Divide the class into groups and assign one or two of the listed gods to each group. Provide biblical dictionaries or information from the relevant pages of one, and direct the groups each to research their assigned god or gods. Afterward, for each god, they should draw on butcher paper or poster board a picture that reveals information about the god. They should include on the poster the name of the god, the country that worshiped the god, the Scripture citation in which the god is described, and a paragraph or list of key words describing the god.

Note: *The Eerdmans Bible Dictionary,* revised edition, edited by Allen C. Myers (Grand Rapids, MI: Eerdmans, 1987), has helpful articles on Baal, Asherah, Astarte (Ashtoreth,) Molech, and Chemosh. *The HarperCollins Bible Dictionary,* edited by Paul J. Achtemeier (see appendix A), also addresses several of those gods. The multivolume work *The Anchor Bible Dictionary,* edited by David Noel Freedman (New York: Doubleday, 1992), covers those gods in greater depth.

4. When the posters are done, display them in the classroom for easy reference as you read the rest of 2 Kings.

The Exile

Experiences of Exile
2 Kings, chapter 24

The description of the Israelites' Exile in 2 Kings, chapter 24, invites the students to examine modern examples of exile.

1. Ask one student to read 2 Kings, chapter 24, and another to read Psalm 137.

2. Assign the students to research modern examples of exile. Explain that they may study the recent history of their own cultural community (such as African American, Cuban American, Native American, or Japanese American) or another experience of exile.

Instead of asking the students to write a factual report, tell them to write several imaginary journal entries from a teenager in an exiled community. The entries may explain some of the historical circumstances of that experience as well as explore the emotional effect of leaving one's home. When the accounts are done, invite the students to share them and discuss common themes that emerge.

Read the following passages from the baptismal rites for children and adults. Note that Elisha's call by Elijah shares characteristics with a new Christian's call by Christ.

Number 100 from the Rite of Baptism for Children
Parents and godparent (or godparents), this light is entrusted to you to be kept burning brightly. This child of yours has been enlightened by Christ. He (she) is to walk always as a child of the light. May he (she) keep the flame of faith alive in his (her) heart. When the Lord comes, may he (she) go out to meet him with all the saints in the heavenly kingdom. (Page 404)

Number 230 from the Rite of Christian Initiation of Adults
You have been enlightened by Christ.
Walk always as children of the light
and keep the flame of faith alive in your hearts.
When the Lord comes, may you go out to meet him
with all the saints in the heavenly kingdom.

(*The Rites of the Catholic Church as Revised by Decree of the Second Vatican Ecumenical Council and Published by Authority of Pope Paul VI*, study edition, by the Catholic Church, English translation prepared by the International Commission on English in the Liturgy [New York: Pueblo Publishing Company, 1990], page 161. Copyright © 1976, 1983, 1988, 1990 by Pueblo Publishing Company.)

....▶ Disposition and the Path Toward God

Finish the sentences in column 1 from your own perspective, putting down the first thing that comes to your mind. Your teacher will explain how to fill out the rest of the chart.

My own disposition	The disposition of characters in 2 Kings, chapter 5	Did the character in column 2 help or hinder God's will?	Do my dispositions help or hinder God's will?
I suffer . . .	Suffering Character: Verse:		
I help . . .	Helping Character: Verse:		
I fear . . .	Fearing Character: Verse:		
I am confident . . .	Confident Character: Verse:		
I am arrogant . . .	Arrogant Character: Verse:		
I am grateful . . .	Grateful Character: Verse:		
I am generous . . .	Generous Character: Verse:		
I am selfless . . .	Selfless Character: Verse:		
I am greedy . . .	Greedy Character: Verse:		
I deceive . . .	Deceiving Character: Verse:		

Handout 2 Kings–B: Permission to reproduce this handout for classroom use is granted.

•••••••••••••••••••►Leadership Report Card

For each of the following biblical kings, read the Scripture passage listed and give the king a traditional letter grade (A to F). Then list three modern leaders and grade them as well. Write a comment about each leader in the space provided—either an affirmation for good work or a critique for areas that need improvement. Finally, answer the reflection question below the chart.

Grading period: Ancient Judah	Grading period: Present-day leaders
King Jehoram (2 Kings 8.16–24) Grade: Comments:	Name: Grade: Comments:
King Hezekiah (2 Kings, chapters 18–20) Grade: Comments:	Name: Grade: Comments:
King Manasseh (2 Kings 21.1–18) Grade: Comments:	Name: Grade: Comments:

In what ways does your assessment of current leaders resemble the assessment of Jewish leaders found in 2 Kings?

1 and 2 Chronicles

Exegetical Tools: Source Criticism—the Chronicler
2 Samuel, chapters 11–12; 1 Kings, chapter 11; 1 Chronicles, chapter 20;
*   2 Chronicles, chapter 9*
Introduction to 1 and 2 Chronicles, CYB

Exploring the richness of varying perspectives helps the students understand the presence of two historical views of the same biblical figures and events.

1. Explain the following points to the students in your own words:
■ Knowing the source of any kind of writing helps the reader understand the writing. Each author writes from a certain perspective and includes biases and opinions, whether by adding information, leaving it out, or presenting it in a certain way. Think of the different ways that politicians talk about the same issue! Biblical scholars take all this into consideration when they study the Bible using the approach that is called source criticism.

2. Choose a controversial event that most of the students have witnessed: a sporting event, election, change in school rules, or something else. Pick two perspectives for that event, such as those of the winners and the losers. Assign each viewpoint to half of the class, and tell the students to write a short account of the controversial event from their assigned viewpoint. When the students have completed their accounts, invite them to share their work, and note similarities and differences.

3. Instruct the students to compare the paired accounts from the Deuteronomic historian and the Chronicler in the following list. Discuss the differences between the accounts in each pair, and ask the students to identify how the two sources viewed the kings differently in each case.
■ 2 Samuel, chapters 11–12, and 1 Chronicles, chapter 20 [The Bathsheba incident is not included in 1 Chronicles.]
■ 1 Kings, chapter 11, and 2 Chr 9.29–31 [Solomon's worship of idols is left out by the Chronicler.]

4. Ask a student to read the introduction to 1 and 2 Chronicles from the *CYB*. Note that all of history, including that recorded in the Bible, is written from a certain perspective.

1 Chronicles

Prayer Styles: Ritual Prayer
1 Chronicles, chapter 16
"Ritual Prayer," 1 Chr 16.37–43, CYB

This exercise uses David's instructions for rituals honoring the ark of the Covenant to draw the students' attention to ritual prayer in the Catholic Tradition.

1. Call a student to read 1 Chr 16.37–43 and the article "Ritual Prayer" from the *CYB*.

2. Direct the students to quickly brainstorm examples of Catholic ritual prayer in four small groups, making a list of their ideas. Then ask representatives from the groups to take turns acting out the rituals as in the game of charades, so that the rest of the class can discover what the examples are. Write the names of the rituals on the board as they are discovered.

3. Lead a class discussion of the listed rituals, pointing out that many of them (such as genuflecting, using incense, making the sign of the cross, and praying the rosary) were easy to act out because they involve physical action as well as words. Ask, "Does physical activity heighten the power of a prayer ritual?" Plan to insert some active ritual the next time you pray as a class.

Mapping God's Presence
1 Chronicles, chapter 17
"Where Do We Place God?" 1 Chr 17.1–15, CYB

The issue of building a temple for God invites the students to reflect on where God dwells in their own lives.

1. Create a simple handout for the students, drawing and labeling a map with some local landmarks that teens frequent, such as the high school, a supermarket, a mall, and a church. Also create an overhead or computer transparency of that map, or draw it on the board.

2. Distribute the handout you have created. Tell the students to add to the map their house and any other places that are important to them. Then give the students a few minutes to put God on the map, indicating God's presence with a "G." Suggest that they also indicate places where they feel that God is more present or less present, if they wish; note that they may indicate such places with the markings "G+" and "G-."

3. Allow the students to share their sense of God's presence by adding their markings to the map you have reproduced on a transparency or on the board. Ask follow-up questions to help them articulate how God is present in those various places. Invite a student to read 1 Chr 17.1–15 and the article "Where Do We Place God?" from the *CYB* as part of this discussion. Ask, "How is God showing God's presence to us in those secular places just as God did to the people of Israel?"

2 Chronicles

Talents Gone Astray?
2 Chronicles, chapter 26

This activity asks the students to develop scenarios for an imaginary person, in order to help them understand that just as Uzziah allowed pride to get in the way of his service of God, we sometimes choose to use our talents for negative purposes.

1. Ask a student to read 2 Chr 26.16–21 aloud. Give the students some quiet time to make a short inventory of their talents. For each talent, they should write down one instance in which they used it with humility and another in which they used it with pride.

2. With the class, create an imaginary student. Name that student and select five talents or gifts for the student. Then divide the class into five groups, giving each group a different area of the student's life, such as home, school, friends, extracurricular activities, or work. Explain the assignment as follows:
   - Each group will develop and present scenarios for the student within its assigned area of life. In those scenarios, the student should face several decisions that call for using his or her talents with either humility or pride. The group should then describe whether the humble version of the student or the proud one is likable and why. Most likely, the groups will be attracted to aspects of both.

3. After the presentations, as a class, discuss the assessments of the groups and point out that our gifts and talents come from God and exist for the benefit of all people. Also emphasize the key understanding that humility leads people primarily to service, whereas pride leads them primarily to self-glorification.

Teen Tithing
2 Chronicles, chapter 31
"Giving the Best of the Best," 2 Chr 31.2–10, CYB

The students calculate a modern tithe in their own budget as a way to understand the generosity of the Israelites in supporting the priests.

1. Teach the students how to make a pie chart that describes how they spend their money, and ask them to prepare such a chart for the next class. Suggest that if a student does not regularly make or receive money, she or he create a hypothetical chart based on the typical income of a high school student. Ask the students to bring their calculators to the next class with their charts.

2. At the next class, invite the students to share ways in which they spend their money and to explore some of the values that they associate with money and its use.

3. Ask one student to read 2 Chr 31.2–10 and another to read the article "Giving the Best of the Best" from the *CYB*. Explain to the students what *tithe* and *sacrificial giving* mean:

- *Tithe* means "one-tenth." To tithe is to distribute one-tenth of our income to the church and to people who are poor as a concrete way to offer thanks and praise to God.
- *Sacrificial giving* means "giving more than might be comfortable for us"—that is, it should hurt a little. Perhaps giving away one-tenth of our income would be irresponsible or cause hardship; in that case, we are to give as much as we are able, including enough to make it a personal sacrifice. On the other hand, if we hardly notice giving away one-tenth of our income, we should increase our giving until we do notice it.
- In 2 Chr 31.5, Israel is giving its "first fruits." When we tithe, it is to be the first check we write or the first amount of money we spend—*not* what is left over. We give with a sense of trust that all our bills will get paid and all our needs will be taken care of. Our first earnings—our "first fruits"—shall go to God.
- We also give with a sincere commitment to the church and to those who are poor, as well as a belief that everyone's needs would be met if all believers faithfully tithed.

4. Instruct the students to remake their pie chart including a 10 percent tithe if they did not do so initially, and have them reflect in writing about how they would adjust their spending in order to give that percentage to the church and charity. When they have completed that task, talk about how money is used at parishes, and invite the students to share what charities they would contribute to. Discuss the challenges and rewards of sharing money that way. See if the budget trimming helped the students identify any priorities in their spending.

5. Assign the students to write a one-page essay about what they learned in this lesson. Suggest that they include ideas (and perhaps a commitment) on how they might practice tithing.

Variation. Invite a guest speaker to share about the effect of tithing in her or his life. If you do not know a person who is willing to talk about tithing, perhaps a local pastor could recommend someone. This kind of presentation serves as a powerful witness for young people.

Ezra and Nehemiah

Ezra

The Freedom to Be Oneself
Ezra, chapter 1

This exercise uses Cyrus's edict of freedom to the Jews as a starting point for a reflection on the freedom that is granted by others and the freedom we allow ourselves.

1. Call a student to read Ezra, chapter 1, aloud. Discuss with the class the importance of Cyrus's decision to let the Jews return home. Encourage the students to speculate about the changes in religious, economic, and political freedom that that brought. Ask, "What challenges might the Israelites have faced?" Emphasize that Cyrus's decree allowed them the freedom to express what was most important to them—their faith in God.

2. Direct the students to write their responses to the following questions:
- On a scale of 1 to 10, with 1 standing for "Not at all" and 10 standing for "Very," how free are you to be yourself with each of the following people: parents, teachers, peers of the same sex, and peers of the other sex?
- To what extent do others limit that freedom, and to what extent do you limit your own freedom? [Give the students examples of the difference to help them discern that.]
- [Preface this question with an explanation of the difference between freedom and license.] On a scale of 1 to 10, with 1 standing for "None" and 10 standing for "Very much," how much freedom to be themselves does your school allow students?

3. Form small groups and instruct them to discuss their answers to the preceding questions. Then invite them to summarize their ideas in a class discussion.

Mixed Marriages
Ezra, chapters 9–10
"Who Belongs, and Who Does Not?" Ezra, chapters 9–10, CYB

This activity uses Ezra's condemnation of interreligious marriage as the starting point for reflection on the challenges and richness of interfaith marriages.

1. Begin by offering a scenario and discussion opportunity such as this:
- Imagine that you have been asked to choose music for a social event. That event must feature music that you like and music that your par-

ents like. How do you go about doing that? What are the challenges and rewards of such a process?

Elicit reasons why such a process would be easier for some students than for others. For example, help the students realize that some of them may have musical tastes that are more similar to their parents', have more respect for their parents' musical interests, or possess better communication skills. Note that interfaith marriages can be rich or difficult for some of the same reasons.

    2. Ask several students to read Ezra, chapters 9–10, and the article "Who Belongs, and Who Does Not?" from the *CYB*. Point out that Ezra's stand against interfaith marriages reflects his fear that the very existence and identity of the Jewish people are at stake.

    3. Ask the students to brainstorm some of the ways that an interfaith marriage could deepen a couple's relationship and some ways that it could stretch it. Ask, "What personal qualities could really make a difference in such a relationship?" Invite the students to share examples of such relationships from their own experiences.

    Variations. Numbers 1633 to 1637 of the *Catechism* (see appendix A) speak concisely to the issue of mixed marriage and may be helpful for discussion.

    The movie *Fiddler on the Roof* (Mirisch Productions, 1971, 180 min., rated G) is a wonderful exploration of the benefits and limitations of requiring that people marry only others within their religious community. The story is also available as a play, musical scores for various instruments, and sound recordings. It might be fun to do a musical reading of all or parts of the script, with students singing and playing the music, or listening to or singing along with a sound recording. Discussion could be interspersed or saved to the end.

Nehemiah

A Social-Action Step
Nehemiah, chapter 1
"Nehemiah Prepares for Action," Nehemiah, chapter 1, CYB

Just as Nehemiah fasted in order to understand what action God called him to, the students deny themselves something in order to help themselves commit to social action.

    1. Ask one student to read Nehemiah, chapter 1, and another to read the article "Nehemiah Prepares for Action" from the *CYB*.

    2. Assign the students to engage in a short "fast" of their choice. Explain the assignment as follows, in your own words:
- Pick an issue that concerns you, and creatively deny yourself something in that area. For example, if you are concerned about the environment, your fasting could include denying yourself the convenience of throwing recyclable materials in the trash or of taking your own car instead of the bus. Write an account of your fasting experience as well as some reflection about your effort. Include a short prayer to God about the social issue involved.

Possibly incorporate the students' individual prayers into a class prayer.

The Process of Rebuilding
Nehemiah, chapter 2

The rebuilding of Jerusalem was a turning point in the development of Judaism. This exercise gives the students an opportunity to examine that event, as well as reflect on areas that need "rebuilding" in their own lives.

1. Direct the students to write about the following question: "What area in my life (what relationship, object, or situation) needs rebuilding?" Give some examples of symbolic rebuilding that might be required in a teenager's life. Note that many students' relationships with parents or siblings are in some state of disrepair.

2. After the students have finished writing, read Nehemiah, chapter 2, aloud and discuss it with the students, noting the following points in your own words:
    - Some officials ridiculed Nehemiah for his idea to rebuild the walls of Jerusalem, but Nehemiah felt God's presence with him.
    - In the New Testament, when the angel Gabriel tells Jesus' mother, Mary, that she will bear a son, she questions how that could be possible. The angel's response, "For nothing will be impossible with God" (Lk 1.37), applies also to rebuilding in our own lives, which may seem overwhelming.
    - The rebuilding of lives is God's work, and so God will do much of it if we have faith. Nehemiah's faith allowed him to propose the daunting task of rebuilding the walls of Jerusalem and to continue even in the face of ridicule.

3. Close with a time of quiet prayer for strength and trust in the areas that the students identified as needing rebuilding.

Tobit

Parenting and Marriage

Passing On One's Life Philosophy
Tobit, chapter 4

The students articulate some personal life philosophies after reading and discussing the words of wisdom Tobit passes on to his son.

    1. Ask several students to read Tobit, chapter 4, aloud to the class. Call the students to identify some of the main points in Tobit's philosophy-of-life speech to his son. Solicit the students' reactions to Tobit's ideas.

    2. Direct the students to write down five things from their own life philosophy that they would like to share with their children someday and why they have chosen those. After they have done that, tell them to pair with a student nearby and discuss their findings.

    3. Gather the students and ask them to mention one or two of their ideas. Encourage discussion about those. Then invite the students to identify what they can do to help ensure that their children take their ideas to heart.

Is There One Special Person for You?
Tobit, chapter 6

Raphael's words to Tobias "For she was set apart for you before the world was made" (Tob 6.18) invite the students to reflect on and discuss God's involvement in the vocation of Christian marriage.

    1. Ask several students to read Tobit, chapter 6, assigning the following roles: narrator, the angel Raphael, and the young man Tobias.

    2. Point out verse 18 of the Scripture passage to the students. Designate two spots in the classroom as "Agree" and "Disagree," and instruct the students to move to the place that reflects their response to this statement: "There is only one person in the world that God wants you to marry." Invite discussion about the students' reactions.

    3. Form small groups and ask them each to discuss the following questions:
- How might a person recognize that God is calling him or her to marriage or to another vocation?

- How can the church help couples discern whether their desire to marry is from God? Could a couple want to get married for reasons that conflict with God's desires for them?
- What are five specific things that the church could do to help teens and young adults who are dating learn to recognize how God calls them and what the church wants for them in Christian marriage?

4. As a class, discuss the students' responses to the questions in step 3.

Variations. Extend step 4 to familiarize the students with the procedures used by a Catholic parish that does an exceptional job with marriage preparation. Also, invite a priest, pastoral minister, or parishioner involved with marriage preparation to speak with the class.

Prayer and the Married Life
Tobit, chapter 8

Tobias and Sarah's prayer on their wedding night invites the students to discuss the role of prayer within the marriage relationship.

1. Form pairs, and ask them each to brainstorm the five most important characteristics of a successful marriage and to rank those in order of importance. When the pairs are done, invite them to share their ideas, writing them on the board. Then conduct a class vote to rank the pairs' suggestions in order of importance.

2. Call the students' attention to whatever importance they have placed on prayer within marriage (it may not even appear on the list). Ask them to offer a few reasons why prayer might be a significant addition to married life.

3. Have a student read Tob 8.1–8. Direct the students' attention to verse 7: "Grant . . . / . . . that we may grow old together." Ask the following questions in your own words:
- How many of you think that couples who pray together are more likely to stay close than those who do not?
- How could prayer help a man and woman in a marriage commitment? Do they need to pray together, or is praying separately just as good?
- Could prayer hurt a marriage?

4. Invite the students to imagine what they would say if someone they were dating asked to pray with them. Take some responses, and encourage the students to reflect on their comfort or discomfort with the issue. Ask, "Might you respond differently in ten years? Why or why not?"
Acknowledge that many teens might not feel comfortable praying with a date because praying with someone is an intimate gesture. Conclude by saying that marriage is an intimate human relationship and thus is an ideal place for prayer.

The Global View of Tobit

Prayer Styles: Shared Worship—Global Prayer
Tobit, chapter 13
"Hope for the Faithful," Tobit, chapter 13, CYB

This global prayer service resembles Tobit's prayer for Jerusalem in its wide scope.

    1. Prepare for this prayer service by finding newspaper stories, magazine articles, or information from the Internet about a variety of countries—as many countries as there are students in the class. Prepare copies of the materials for distribution to the students. Put a world map up in the classroom.

    2. Begin the prayer service by calling one student to read Tobit, chapter 13, and another to read the article "Hope for the Faithful" from the *CYB*.

    3. Pass out the information you have collected on different countries, and give the students some quiet time to read it and to write a short prayer of petition or thanksgiving for the people of the country assigned to them.

    4. Light a candle and then invite the students to come up one by one to the map you have posted. They should point out the location of their given country on the map, tell something about that country, and then read their prayer. The rest of the students should respond to each prayer, "Lord, hear our prayer," or another refrain.

    5. Close by having the students join hands and pray the Lord's Prayer together.

    (This activity comes from Sr. Mary Annette Dworshak, SNJM, Holy Names Academy, Seattle, Washington.)

Judith

A Role Model

Judith's Wisdom
Judith, chapter 8

Judith kept her head about her while everyone else was losing theirs. This activity examines Judith's courage and wisdom, and the application of both to modern crises.

1. Request several students to read Judith, chapter 8, aloud. Explain the passage in the context of the Book of Judith. Invite the students to identify some of Judith's words of wisdom and list them on the board. Ask the students to suggest modern situations in which those words of wisdom might be useful.

2. Assign the students each to pick a modern problem and to write a speech that Judith might give to the leaders who are dealing with it. Invite them to share their completed speeches with the class.

Judith as a Role Model
Judith, chapters 10–14

The students explore the virtues of faith, courage, leadership, and wisdom as they learn about Judith.

1. Call the students to do a dramatic reading of Judith, chapters 10–14. Assign the following roles: narrator, Uzziah and the two elders, Judith, the Assyrians, Holofernes, the servants, Bagoas, the people of Bethulia, and Achior. After the reading, discuss the intriguing story.

2. Divide the class into four groups and assign each group one of the following qualities:
- faith
- courage
- leadership
- wisdom

Instruct the groups each to find examples of their assigned quality in the passage from Judith, citing chapter and verse for each example. Once that is done, each group should identify several men and women today who exemplify that quality. When the groups are finished, ask them to report their findings to the class.

Leaders in the Church
Judith

This activity uses Judith's example of leadership to invite the students to research the role of women who have been religious leaders in the Catholic church.

1. After reading the Book of Judith, discuss what was remarkable about Judith's action. Encourage the students to think of questions that they would ask Judith if they had the chance, and write those on the board. Allow the class to suggest answers that Judith might have offered.

2. Lead the students to brainstorm the names of women who have taken leadership roles in the Catholic church and list them on the board. Supplement their list with other names you think of.

3. Assign the students to research some of those women in order to determine how the women might answer questions similar to those the students would like to ask of Judith. That research could be done individually, in pairs, or in groups. When it is completed, conduct a presentation of the information as a panel discussion, having the students speak for the woman they researched.

HISTORICAL

Esther

Destructive Biases

Vashti: A True Hero
Esther, chapter 1

Queen Vashti's refusal of an insulting request was a courageous act of self-respect in a culture that objectified women. The students explore her story and look beyond it to see how people in their own culture both use and respect others.

1. Have several students read Esther, chapter 1, aloud. Ask these questions:
   - What does the king's request reveal about his opinion of Vashti?
   - What does Vashti's response show about her view of herself?

2. Form groups and direct them to make mind maps around the words *person* and *object*. Explain that the words should be in the center of the page, and the groups should draw spokes out from the words and at the end of the spokes put adjectives and other words that they associate with the words. When the groups are done, invite them to share their responses. Synthesize their answers on the board. Sum up by saying the following things in your own words:
   - Though objects are to be used by people for their own purposes, persons deserve respect and human dignity. Unfortunately, we all become confused at times and use others instead of respecting them. We also sometimes allow others to use us.

3. Give the students a variety of popular magazines. Instruct them each to find five examples of ways that people use others, and five examples of ways that people respect others. Invite the students to share their findings.

4. Point out that Vashti was willing to sacrifice her status as queen rather than compromise her human dignity by allowing King Ahasuerus to use her. Note that her sense of personal integrity is a model for us to follow today.

Destruction of the Jews
Esther, chapter 3

An examination of pre-Christian anti-Semitism invites the students to discuss modern anti-Semitism

Ask several students to read Esther, chapter 3, aloud. Then lead a discussion as follows:

- Explain that following the Babylonian Exile, some Jews were living in lands outside of Israel, such as Persia. Add that they were known as the Diaspora, meaning "scattered abroad."
- Ask the students why they think Mordecai refused to bow down to Haman. Point out that a Jew's refusal to bow to the Persian ruler was punishable by death. Encourage the students to think of what they have seen people die for. Ask, "Is there any person or cause that you might consider dying for?"
- Note that as punishment, Haman sought to kill all the Jews living in Persia.
- Define anti-Semitism for the students and discuss various forms of it today.

Variations. Invite a rabbi to come to class to discuss anti-Semitism, or show the video *The Cross and the Star: Jews, Christians, and the Holocaust* (First Run Features, 1992, 52 min., not rated), which examines the history of the Christian persecution of Jews. The U.S. Holocaust Memorial Museum provides information on that subject: write to the Education Department of the U.S. Holocaust Memorial Museum, 100 Raoul Wallenberg Place SW, Washington, DC 20024; or call the museum at 202-488-0400; or access the museum's web site at *http://www.ushmm.org.*

Labeling
Esther, chapter 3
"Body Count," Esth 3.1–7, CYB

This activity helps the students to see that the labels they give others affect their actions toward those others just as Haman's labeling of Mordecai led to Haman's decision to destroy the Jews.

1. Ask one student to read Esth 3.1–7 and another to read the article "Body Count" from the *CYB.*

2. Draw an imaginary line down the middle of the room and divide the class into two groups. Give the students in each group an identifying sticker so that later everyone can easily recognize who belongs to which group (e.g., give each student in one group a yellow sticker, and each student in the other group a pink sticker). Offer the following explanation to the students in your own words:
   - As a group, you are going to create an impression of the other half of the class. You will randomly pick five characteristics that you want to attribute to the other group. The object of the exercise is for each group to convey its labels to the other group by nonverbal communication and indirect speech. For example, one group might assign the other group the characteristics violent and rich. The first group's members would then act afraid of those in the other group, and say things that imply that the other group is rich without actually stating so. Each group must try to guess what labels have been given it.

3. Give the groups some time to label each other and come up with some subtle strategies for communicating their labels. Then pair each student with a member of the other group. Give the pairs $2\frac{1}{2}$ minutes or so to talk about what they would normally discuss and slip the biases into their conversation. Then change the pairings and give the students another $2\frac{1}{2}$ minutes or so to engage in the same type of conversation with their new partner.

4. Allow the groups to regather and decide what labels the other group has given them. If either group does not discover all five labels given to it, let the other group offer further hints until the labels have all been identified.

5. Discuss the labeling experience and mention these and other insights gained from the activity:

- Other people can sense that we label them in positive or negative ways even if we never say so directly. [Ask the students how people sense that.] We must examine the labels we have given others, because they may be damaging and inaccurate.
- Labeling can be dangerous because vulnerable people may accept labels as the truth about themselves. Labeling can also lead to serious hurts such as it did in the Book of Esther, during the Holocaust, all around the world where there is ethnic conflict, and every day in a teenager's life.

Variation. In step 3, instead of pairing up all the students, pair up just one student from each group and invite the partners to carry on a conversation as the rest of the class observes. Then open the discussion to the class for questions or remarks that might give further clues as to the labels assigned by each group.

Purim

Esther and Purim
Esther, addition F

The Jewish feast of Purim celebrates the heroism of Esther, and because it is a joyous holiday, elements of it are fun to observe in class. The students re-create a celebration of Purim by researching the Book of Esther and Jewish sources.

Either assign the students the task of researching the feast of Purim and how it is celebrated today, or tell them about the feast yourself. Ask groups of students to bring in things that will make the feast come alive in the classroom, such as coins for a collection for people who are poor, costumes, pots and pans and anything else to make noise with, the texts of the blessings to be read, a scroll to represent the Torah, *hamantaschen* (poppy seed cookies), turkey meat, musical instruments, and party decorations. It would be fun to read the Book of Esther aloud with noisemakers if the students have not already heard the story. Some groups might even wish to hold a beauty contest, as is done in Tel Aviv, to choose Queen Esther among the women.

Note: The Internet is a helpful source of information for the feast of Purim. Also consider these books:

- *Jewish Literacy: The Most Important Things to Know About the Jewish Religion, Its People, and Its History,* by Joseph Telushkin (New York: William Morrow and Company, 1991)
- *Seasons of Our Joy: A Modern Guide to Jewish Holidays,* by Arthur Ocean Waskow (Boston: Beacon Press, 1990)

1 Maccabees

Nicknames
1 Maccabees, chapter 2

A brief presentation reveals that the names of Mattathias's sons all have special meaning and that the sons' nicknames capture something unique about them. The presentation is followed by a reflection on the significance of the students' own names and nicknames.

1. Ask a student to read 1 Macc 2.1–14 aloud to the class. Tell the students that the surnames of Mattathias's sons are said to mean, respectively, "Fortunate," "Burning," "Designated by Yahweh" (or "the Hammerer" or "Hammerhead"), "Awake," "Favorite." Review with the class each of the names and nicknames of Mattathias's sons. Ask the students why someone might assign those particular names to their children.

2. Request the students to discuss the significance of names and nicknames, explaining any historic meaning of their own first names and sharing examples of nicknames they have been given.

3. Suggest that as they read 1 Maccabees, the students reflect on whether the nickname Hammer is appropriate for Judas.

The Just War Theory
1 Maccabees, chapter 5
"A Just War," near 1 Macc 5.24, CYB

The students apply some of the criteria of the just war theory to Judas's campaigns.

1. Call a student to read the article "A Just War" from the *CYB*. Copy the criteria listed in the article onto the board in order, and number them 1 to 4. Then have the students read 1 Maccabees, chapter 5, aloud, asking them to find instances where a guideline was either followed or violated.

2. For each criterion listed on the board, assign two spots on either side of the classroom. Those spots will mark a continuum on which to measure examples of conflict. Label the spots for each criterion as follows:
- *Criterion 1.* "Exhausted" and "Not exhausted"
- *Criterion 2.* "Grave and certain" and "Not grave and certain"
- *Criterion 3.* "Successful" and "Unsuccessful"
- *Criterion 4.* "Greater evil produced" and "Equal or lesser evil produced"

For each criterion, give the students examples from modern warfare. For each example, ask the students to consider how well it meets the criterion for a just war and to stand at that point on the criterion's continuum. For instance, for the first criterion, begin with a series of question such as these:

- When the United States learned that Serbs were killing ethnic Albanians in Kosovo, should it have declared war on the Serbs? Did the Serbs' act of aggression justify a war? Were all means to avoid war exhausted?
- Instead of declaring war, the United States and other countries sent diplomats to Kosovo to address the problem. When those diplomatic efforts failed, should the United States have declared war? Would war have been justified then? Were all means to avoid war exhausted?
- When diplomatic efforts failed, the United States considered economic sanctions such as freezing Yugoslav assets held in U.S. banks. If those sanctions failed to stop the killing, would the United States be justified in declaring war on the Serbs? Would all means to avoid war be exhausted at that point?

Do this for all the criteria to help the students process the complexities of war.

3. Allow the students some quiet time to write a short reflection about the just war theory.

2 Maccabees

Martyrdom

2 Maccabees, chapter 7
"I Will Sacrifice Myself," 2 Maccabees, chapter 7, CYB

The edifying yet gruesome story of the martyrdom of seven brothers offers the students a good opportunity to examine the lives of other people who have died for their faith.

1. Ask several students to read 2 Maccabees, chapter 7, and the *CYB* article "I Will Sacrifice Myself." Make the following point in your own words:
   - In this story, God's people are once again faithful to the Covenant. This time, they are willing to die rather than violate a single law.

2. Guide the students in researching and giving reports on Christian martyrs, including canonized saints, such as Joan of Arc and Thomas Becket, and modern martyrs, such as Archbishop Oscar Romero. Help each student select a martyr to report on, put a 2-minute time limit on the reports, and invite the students to give them in the first person, with costumes and props.

Variations. There are a number of great films about Christian martyrs, including Joan of Arc and Thomas Becket (see appendix B). Those could be used by individual students for research, or shown for the class and discussed, or used in other creative ways.

The Feast of Hanukkah

2 Maccabees, chapter 10

The description of the first celebration of Hanukkah in 2 Maccabees invites the students to experience a hands-on celebration of the feast.

Call a student to read 2 Macc 10.1–9 aloud. Assign the students to research the customs and rituals associated with the Jewish feast of Hanukkah, or educate the students yourself about that holiday. Assign groups of students the task of bringing aspects of that celebration to life.

Note: The Internet is a good resource for information about Hanukkah. Also consider the books listed for the activity "Esther and Purim," on page 104 of this manual.

Wisdom and Poetry Books

Introduction to the Wisdom and Poetry Books

Wisdom Scripture Search and Artwork
Psalms, Proverbs, Ecclesiastes, Wisdom of Solomon, Sirach

This activity gives the students an overview of some of the wisdom literature.

1. Give each student a number from 1 to 5 and assign each number one of the following wisdom books:
- Psalms
- Proverbs
- Ecclesiastes
- Wisdom of Solomon
- Sirach

Direct the students to spend the next 20 minutes skimming the wisdom book that corresponds to their number, searching for "words of wisdom" that would serve as a good message for teenagers. They are to select one quote that is three to ten verses long for that purpose.

2. Provide construction paper, colored markers or pencils, rulers, magazines, scissors, and glue. Direct the students each to present their selected passage and its citation artistically on construction paper. Ask them to write a short paragraph explaining why that passage is appropriate for teens and to attach it to the back of the construction paper.

3. At the beginning of the next class, form five small groups, according to the books of wisdom assigned to the students. Invite the students to read and discuss their passages with the others in their group, then share some with the entire class.

Exegetical Tools: The Concordance and Wisdom Themes
Wisdom and poetry books

This activity introduces a biblical concordance while asking the students to examine an interesting issue in the wisdom literature and modern sources.

1. Introduce a biblical concordance (see appendix A for a recommended concordance). Show the students how to look up words and familiarize them with any codes that are specific to the concordance. Explain that concordances enable people to cross-reference words and phrases, locate specific verses, find out where the Bible treats certain subjects, and explore the meaning of words in different contexts.

2. Assign the students to research a topic of interest within the wisdom literature and then in several different modern contexts. Examples of topics often found in the wisdom literature are love, friendship, happiness, family relationships, and money. This project has four steps:

1. The students find six passages that speak about their chosen topic, in at least three different wisdom books. The concordance can help them find those passages. The students first use the word itself, such as *friendship,* and scan the list of passages under that term in the concordance, noting some passages to research. Not all the passages listed will use the word in the way that they want to pursue. If this effort does not give the students as many choices as they would like, they may then move on to other forms of the word, such as *friend* and *friends.* Synonyms are also good avenues for exploration, as are related terms.

2. The students find their topic addressed in three different modern media. Music lyrics, poetry, philosophy, cartoons, pictures, drawings, famous quotes, and passages from literature are good examples.

3. The students find an artistic way of presenting all this input together. Possibilities include creating a short book, poster collage, photo montage, sculpture, web page, small quilt or quilt square, or game.

4. The students write an essay discussing and evaluating the different biblical and modern views of their topic, and sharing their own reflections on the subject.

3. When the students have completed their projects, invite them to share their results in small groups, and then pick several to share with the whole class. Consider displaying the projects in the classroom.

Job

Job's Experience and Our Own

The Nature of Evil
Job, chapters 1–2
"Satan," Job 1.6—2.10, CYB

A discussion of Satan's role in Job's dilemma creates an opportunity for the students to explore the image of Satan and the way that evil works in the world.

    1. Divide the class into small groups. Ask the groups each to discuss their understanding of how evil works and to prepare a creative visual representation of evil for the next class. Give an example that reflects your own understanding of evil, and explain it. For instance, show the students a phone and give the following explanation:
- Evil is like a phone solicitation in some ways. Initially, the phone's ringing seems like something good, yet when one picks up the receiver anticipating the greeting of a friend, one encounters a stranger who wants to sell something. Evil is often deceptive in that at first, it seems like something good and rewarding, but on closer inspection, it demands a high price.

    2. In the next class, invite the groups to share their visual models of evil. Discuss the students' insights, asking follow-up questions to help the students articulate their ideas. Point out that now, evil is often associated with the devil or Satan, but historically, that was not always so.

    3. Call several students to read Job 1.6—2.7 and the article "Satan" from the *CYB* aloud to the class. Discuss Satan's role in Job's life and the historical development of Satan's association with evil. Sum up by saying that people understand the work of evil differently, and that the Bible shows us that God's goodness is stronger than evil.

Fair- and Foul-Weather Friends
Job, chapters 2, 4, 8, 16, 19, 42
"Being There," Job 2.11–13, CYB

The way that Job's friends interact with him during his ordeal invites the students to reflect on the nature of a strong friendship.

    1. Request one student to read Job 2.11–13 aloud and another to read the article "Being There" from the *CYB*. Point out that although Job's friends are initially simply present to Job, much of the Book of Job relates their debates with Job about what he did wrong.

2. Call several students to read the following passages aloud in order to get a sampling of the dialog between Job and his friends:

- Job 4.1–11 (Eliphaz and Job)
- Job 8.1–10 (Bildad and Job)
- Job 16.1–5 (Job and friends)
- Job 19.1–6 (Job and friends)

Invite the students to reflect on the way that the friends deal with Job in those passages. Point out that in Job 42.7–8, God reproves Job's friends for how they have treated him.

3. Encourage the students to share their understanding of what is a fair-weather friend. Point out that sometimes we encounter foul-weather friends—that is, people who become very helpful when we are in a crisis, only to move on when the excitement has passed. Neither is the type of friend that we can count on to be by our side through both good and bad times.

4. Ask the class to help create a tough scenario that a teen might face. After it has done so, divide the class into small groups and have them each brainstorm ways that someone could be a good friend to the person in crisis. Direct one group to do for the class a skit portraying a fair-weather friend's reaction to the situation, and a second group to do a skit portraying a foul-weather friend's actions. Have the remaining groups act out for the class the response of a reliable all-around friend.

5. Discuss insights that arise from the groups' performances, and help the students explore why people behave in various ways at different times. Close by asking the students how Job's experience of suffering might have been different with different friends.

Theological Questions in Job

Retribution Theology
Job
Introduction to Job, CYB

The students reflect on the theology of retribution by testing it in a modern context.

1. Direct the students to read the introduction to Job from the *CYB*. Explain the theology of retribution to the students, saying something like this:

- The theology of retribution is a familiar theme in the Old Testament. Within the theology of retribution, people believe that God blesses and rewards those who follow God's commandments faithfully, and punishes with suffering those who are not faithful to God. The Book of Job challenges that theology because Job is a just and good man to whom bad things happen.

2. Ask for a few examples of the theology of retribution from past reading of the Old Testament or from everyday life. You could begin the sharing with these two examples:

- The Israelites whine about their situation in the desert and are left to wander in the desert for forty years.

■ A woman is attentive to her elderly father, and when he dies, she inherits a greater portion of his estate than do her siblings.

Explain that the theology of retribution says that God has assessed the behavior of the Israelites and the woman, and punished or rewarded them accordingly.

3. Put the students in small groups and give each group some current newspapers and magazines. Instruct the students to leaf through the materials and find several examples of people who are suffering and of people who are experiencing blessings of various types. Ask them to see if the theology of retribution appears to apply in those cases. Then ask them to reflect on whether that theology makes sense in their own lives.

4. Invite the students to share with the class their findings from the articles they read. Help the students articulate their understanding of how God, good and evil actions, suffering, and blessing are connected. Ask the students to keep their own experience in mind as they read Job and the other wisdom and poetry books.

God on Trial
Job

The students role-play a trial in which God is indicted for the suffering they see around them.

1. Announce to the students that they will be participating in an important court case in which God is accused of causing the suffering in the world, particularly that related to natural disasters, disease, and accidents. If the students have read all of the Book of Job, they will see that this scenario is parallel to the one in that book. If they have not, direct them to read the introduction to Job from the *CYB,* and provide an overview of the story of Job.

2. Assign the following roles to some of the students: God, judge, defense attorney, prosecuting attorney, three witnesses for the prosecution, three witnesses for the defense, and any others who would help make the simulation realistic. Explain that the rest of the students will observe as jurors and cast the deciding vote regarding God's innocence or guilt.

3. Allow one class period for the attorneys and witnesses to set up their case. Assign to the rest of the class relevant passages from Job that can be used as background.

4. At the next class period, begin the court proceeding with brief opening arguments by both the prosecution and the defense, and continue it with testimony from both sets of witnesses. After closing arguments by the attorneys to the jury, have the jury deliberate in private and return to give its verdict.

5. Discuss the trial afterward with students, and ask them to draw comparisons between it and Job's encounter with God. Invite them to share any insights about God and suffering that have emerged.

6. Ask the students to brainstorm ideas of suffering in our world today. Then allow the students to choose one of two homework assignments:

- an essay for which they research one of the brainstormed situations and apply what they have learned about God and suffering
- a reflection paper on some aspect of suffering they have experienced

When the students have finished their homework assignments, engage the class in a discussion of their essays and reflections.

A Press Conference with God
Job, chapter 31

The students hold a "press conference" at which God invites them to ask questions much like Job did.

1. Tell the students to read Job, chapter 31, where Job questions why he suffers, because he has lived a just life. Explain to the students that Job's faith allows him to ask God life's tough questions.

2. Ask the students to imagine that God is available for a once-in-a-lifetime interview. Have them write down five questions for God on separate slips of paper. Invite them to share some of their questions with a neighboring student to see how another person would imagine God's response.

3. Conduct a "press conference" with God. Call student volunteers to take turns acting as God and answering questions respectfully. Direct the rest of the students to act as the press and ask their own questions of God. Allow discussion to arise naturally from the questions and responses.

Variation. If your class tends to be shy or quiet, and you think it may not respond well to the press conference format, use an interview format instead. In step 3, collect the students' questions, call volunteers to take turns acting as God, and interview God by reading the students' questions anonymously.

Psalms

Introduction to the Psalms

Modern Psalms
Psalms

The students review the various types of Psalms and create updated psalm translations or original psalms of their own.

1. Discuss the various types of Psalms with the students, looking up the following examples as a class:
- Psalm 8 (Praise)
- Psalm 22 (Lamentation)
- Psalm 73 (Wisdom)
- Psalm 92 (Thanksgiving)
- Psalm 101 (Royal)

2. Direct the students to translate any Psalm into modern language or ask them to create an original psalm patterned after one of the themes listed in step 1. The students should give their psalm a title, copy it onto construction paper, and present it artistically. Their creations may be used for class prayer in subsequent class periods.

Psalms and the Arts

Psalm Word Art
Psalms

This activity allows the students to meditate on the meaning of an individual psalm and then present the psalm creatively in symbolic art.

1. As homework before this activity, assign the students the task of looking through the Psalms and finding one that is meaningful to them.

2. Begin this activity by asking the students to think of an image that they associate with the psalm they chose. Consider mentioning that for example, the image of a shepherd or a shepherd's staff might come to mind when reading Psalm 23.

3. Distribute these art supplies: blank paper, colored markers or pencils, and rulers. Then tell the students to lightly sketch a simple outline of the image they thought of on a sheet of blank paper, and to write the words of the

117

psalm around the outline, using different colors. Caution them that they will need to do a little planning before starting so that they space out the words appropriately. While the students work, play reflective music. Ask the students to finish their pictures at home if the class time is not sufficient.

4. When all the students are done with their pictures, allow them to share their work and display it in the classroom.

Psalm Billboards
Psalms

The students select psalms with messages that are meaningful to teens, create a billboard that will convey the message well, and then decide where they would locate the billboard.

1. Invite the students to talk about billboards that they have seen locally or while traveling. Make the following points in your own words:
- Although billboards are most often used for product advertising, they also communicate other messages. Some ask people not to drink and drive, or request that people remember others in the community who are in need. Some religious organizations purchase billboard space for their messages.

2. Assign the students each one of the five books of the Psalms:
- *Book I.* Psalms 1–41
- *Book II.* Psalms 42–72
- *Book III.* Psalms 73–89
- *Book IV.* Psalms 90–106
- *Book V.* Psalms 107–150

Tell the students to read their assigned book and to look for a meaningful psalm from which they can select a few verses that have a message particularly relevant to teenagers.

3. Distribute sheets of blank paper and direct the students to use colored markers or pencils to sketch a billboard that conveys their psalm's message to teens. The billboard should somehow draw peoples' attention and invite them to process the meaning of the psalm.

4. When the students have finished sketching, instruct them to think of the best place to erect their billboard, pretending that there are no city, county, or state ordinances restricting them. Tell them to turn their billboard over and write on the back the location they have chosen. They should also explain, in writing, why the billboard's message will appeal to teens and why the chosen location would most effectively reach them.

5. Invite the students to share their completed work with the class.

WISDOM

Modern Music and the Psalms
Psalms

The students make connections between their music and the music of the ancient Israelites, the Psalms.

    1. Explain to the students that the Psalms were lyrics to liturgical music in ancient Israel. Review the various types of Psalms with students, looking up the following examples as a class:
- Psalm 19 (Praise)
- Psalm 80 (Lamentation)
- Psalm 128 (Wisdom)
- Psalm 30 (Thanksgiving)
- Psalm 110 (Royal)

    2. Tell the students to pick one of the types of Psalms listed in step 1 and find a modern song that has a similar theme. Ask them to bring to the next class the lyrics of the song and if possible a recording of the song.

    3. At the next class, instruct the students each to create a piece of art representing the lyrics they have chosen and some verses from a Psalm, giving the work an appropriate title such as "Thanksgiving" or "Lament." Explain that they may choose any Psalm that fits the topic of their lyrics. Provide a variety of art materials, and play some of the music the students brought in quietly as they work.

    4. Invite the students to share their completed artwork with the class, welcoming insights and questions. Display their pieces in the classroom or another part of the school.

Praying the Psalms
Psalms

This exercise allows the students to use the Psalms creatively in a class prayer service.

Divide the class into five groups, one for each day of the next week. Assign each group the psalm response for its day from the lectionary. Have each group design for the class a 15-minute prayer service that uses that psalm response. Encourage the groups to be creative and to plan an inviting prayer environment for the other students. Note that they should include at least one visual and one musical aspect in the service, and may also use other modes of expression.

    Note: See appendices A and B for resources filled with ideas for stories, skits, music, dance, personal reflection, and prayer.

WISDOM

Book I: Psalms 1–41

Dominion Over the Earth: Psalms
Psalm 8

Adapt the activity "Dominion over the Earth: Genesis," on pages 23–24 of this manual, for use with Psalm 8.

Care for the Earth: Psalms
Psalm 8

Psalm 8 may inspire the students to change their habits in order to help preserve the natural environment.

1. Help the students relax, then lead them through the following guided imagery, using your own words:
    - Visualize yourself in a favorite place. Perhaps you are on a beach, looking out at the ocean. Maybe you are in a city park, watching people. Perhaps you are high up on a mountain, looking out on vast horizons in every direction. Or maybe you are near home, in your own backyard. Wherever you are, be there for a moment. Take joy, with the psalmist, in knowing that the Creator of the universe cares for you, a mere mortal!

2. Call one or several students to read Psalm 8. Then continue with the following comments in your own words:
    - Psalm 8 marvels that God has made us partners in caring for creation. Human beings have not always done a good job of caring for the world. For instance, human greed and shortsightedness have led to the extinction of many plant and animal species. And we are at the brink of even worse global catastrophes. Let's remember the awesome responsibility God has given us, and keep the protection of the earth in our prayers.

3. Ask the students to reflect on, and perhaps write about, the following question: "What one habit might you develop or action might you take that would demonstrate respect and care for the earth?"

Variation. After the students read Psalm 8 in step 2, ask them to share their insights from the meditation and the reading. Then continue with your comments on our responsibility to protect the earth.

Book II: Psalms 42–72

Rejection and Faith
Psalm 42
"Randy's First Day of School," Psalm 42, CYB

Psalm 42 may give consolation during the tough times many teens face while trying to fit in. This activity helps the students explore why they reject others and what it feels like to be rejected.

1. Ask one student to read the *CYB* article "Randy's First Day of School" out loud, and another to read Psalm 42 to the class. Solicit some thoughts about Randy's story and about how helpful Psalm 42 might be in times of trouble.

2. Divide the class into three groups and, in your own words, pass on the following assignments to the groups:
   ▪ [To group 1] Imagine yourself in Randy's role. How do you feel about being overweight and about being teased for that at your old school? What do you feel as you walk into your new classroom?
   ▪ [To group 2] Imagine yourself in the role of the student who yells out a comment about Randy. What are you feeling as you shout, and what do you feel afterward?
   ▪ [To group 3] Imagine yourself as one of Randy's other new classmates. What are you feeling as Randy comes in the door? What is your reaction as the student shouts out?
Give the groups time to explore the suggestions you have assigned them.

3. Move the students into new groups of three, one from each of the groups formed in step 2. Ask the members of each new group to talk to one another from the perspective of their roles as Randy, the commenting student, and the onlooking class member. Have them imagine that the principal is there and is asking them to share their feelings and work through what happened to some sort of resolution.

4. Say something like the following to the students:
   ▪ All of us have parts of ourselves that make us feel insecure or vulnerable to ridicule from others. Some of us feel self-conscious about visible characteristics such as our appearance, others feel uncomfortable about invisible characteristics such as our personal history, our insecurities, or family issues.
   ▪ We may be tempted to ridicule others to bolster our own self-esteem, but it is important to see the similarities between ourselves and those who would be victims of our harsh words.
   ▪ To empathize means to imagine ourselves in the other person's position and then act as we would want others to.
   ▪ Unfortunately, we all experience Randy's position at times during our lives. When that happens, it is important to reach out to God, who sees us as we really are.

5. Request the students to read the last paragraph of the *CYB* article and write their reflections on it. You might want to lead the students through a prayer service in which they lift up their written reflections—their pains—to God.

For What Do You Thirst?
Psalm 63

Food and water and the Psalms come together to bring home to the students the experience of the soul's thirst for God.

1. Bring to class a large bag of extra-salty pretzels, a small bottle of water, a large pitcher of water, and paper cups, keeping the water and cups hidden.

Give the students each a pretzel and let them eat it. If there are enough pretzels, let them have seconds. As they eat, ask them if they are getting thirsty. Most likely, the answer will be a definite "Yes!" Then bring out the bottle of water, slowly open it, and begin to drink, telling them how refreshing the water is and how you wish you had enough to share with everyone.

2. Ask a student to read Psalm 63 aloud to the class. Then mention that the physical thirst they now experience is but a hint of the deeper thirst their souls have for God. Give them each a cup of water. Also mention that the relief that water gives to their thirst is but a hint of the relief that God's presence gives to their souls.

3. List the following categories on the board:
- physical
- emotional
- intellectual
- social
- spiritual

Tell the students to identify what a human being thirsts for in each category. Discuss their ideas with them.

4. Direct the students each to write a reflection in which they compare their high school years to a desert. Have them identify and describe the people and events that have served as oases. Ask them to explain how those people and events have helped quench the dryness in their soul. When they are done writing, invite them to share their reflections as they feel comfortable.

Book III: Psalms 73–89

Prayer Styles: The Jesuit Examen
Psalm 77
"The Big Picture," Psalm 77, CYB

The daily prayer exercise of the examen can help the students become more attentive to God's presence in their lives.

1. Create a prayerful atmosphere in the class, with soft lighting and reflective music, and arrange the students' seats in a circle if possible. Ask some students to read Psalm 77 and another to read the article "The Big Picture" from the *CYB.* Say something like this to the students:
- We are going to have a prayer experience based on an exercise called "The Examen," written by Saint Ignatius of Loyola in his guide *The Spiritual Exercises.*
- I am going to give you a few minutes of quiet time, and I want you to answer these questions:
  - For what experience in the last week am I most grateful? [Depending on the circumstances, you may choose to ask the students to reflect on a particular time period other than the last week: this day, this month, the past summer vacation, this school year, their high school career, etc.]
  - For what experience in the last week am I least grateful?
  [Write the two questions on the board.]

■ Afterward, I am going to ask that we go around the room and share something about those experiences. If the experiences for which you are most grateful and least grateful are too personal to share, also jot down for each question one experience that you are comfortable telling the class about.

2. Give the students time to respond to the questions on the board. Then begin the sharing portion of the prayer experience by offering your own response to the questions. After the students have also spoken, close the experience with a reading of Psalm 77.

Handout **Ps–A**

3. Distribute handout Ps–A, "The Jesuit Examen: A Simple Form," and read the description of the exercise with the students, discussing any questions that arise. Ask the students to experiment with the examen prayer style for a week. They should each day write down what they are most and least grateful for, and at the end of the week write a paragraph reflecting on the experience itself and noting any insights they have gained.

Consider not collecting and reading the papers. Instead, tell the students that the specific content of their written reflection may remain private, but they will be asked to share insights from it in a class discussion at the end of the week. If they know that their reflections will be private, the students can choose to be open and honest in them.

4. After a week, invite the students to share their general insights about the examen process.

Note: For further reading about the examen, consult Dennis Linn, Sheila Fabricant Linn, and Matthew Linn's *Sleeping with Bread: Holding What Gives You Life* (Mahwah, NJ: Paulist Press, 1995).

Book IV: Psalms 90–106

The Psalms and Liturgical Music
Psalm 91 and others

Psalm 91, the text for some familiar songs, invites the students to discuss and explore the relation between the Psalms and liturgical music.

1. Ask two students to read Psalm 91. Play or provide the lyrics for the song "On Eagle's Wings," by Michael Joncas, on the album *Come and Journey,* by David Haas, Marty Haugen, and Michael Joncas (GIA Publications, 1996), or "Blest Be the Lord," by Dan Schutte, on the album *A Dwelling Place,* a Saint Louis Jesuit collection (Oregon Catholic Press, 1991 [cassette] and 1998 [CD]), or both, and ask the students to look for the psalm's verses in those lyrics.

Note: Lyrics for both songs are provided in the hymnal *Gather Comprehensive,* edited by Robert J. Batastini and Michael A. Cymbala (Chicago: GIA Publications, 1994).

2. Provide the students with a Catholic hymnal such as *Gather Comprehensive* and direct them to look for songs that are based on the Psalms. (The *Gather* hymnal lists the Psalms in the index.) Have them compare the lyrics of those songs with the words of the psalms they reflect.

3. Invite the students to share the examples that they have found. They may be surprised that many familiar songs are connected with the Psalms. Note the importance of the Psalms in the Mass's liturgy of the word. Explain that one reason why many songs based on the Psalms are familiar is that they are often played between the first and second readings at Mass. Mention that the Psalms is the biblical book that is most regularly used in the Catholic Mass.

Book V: Psalms 107–150

A Personal Inventory
Psalm 115
"What Lasts?" Psalm 115, CYB

Psalm 115 invites the students to find value in life's important intangible experiences.

1. Ask two students to read Psalm 115. Say something such as this to the students:
- The author of this psalm is contrasting the ineffectiveness of tangible, visible gods like idols with the grandeur of the invisible but powerful God. [Define the terms *tangible* and *intangible*.] We today also value both tangible and intangible things. For example, we might value both our music collection and our friendships.
- Write down five tangible things that you value and five intangible things that you value. Imagine that those ten things are worth one hundred dollars together. How would you divide up the one hundred dollars to represent the value of each of the ten things? [Give the students time to do this.]

2. Explain that by assigning a monetary amount to each item, the students have also ranked the items. Direct each student to think of a situation in which he or she chose one of the top five items over the lower five in the last week. Invite the students to reflect, in writing, on whether they regularly find themselves choosing the most valuable items on their list.

3. Ask the students to share with the class their reflections on the ranking process and any insights that they have gained. Point out that relationships and powerful experiences are priceless, and we most often rank them as most precious. Finish by reading the article "What Lasts?" from the *CYB*.

"Wonderful Are Your Works"
Psalm 139
"The Sacredness of Life," Psalm 139, CYB

The students apply words of Psalm 139 directly to their own lives, so that they may refer to the psalm in the future for their own prayer.

1. Before this exercise, ask the students to bring in pictures of themselves that they can spare for an art project.

2. To begin this exercise, call several students to read Psalm 139. Write verse 13 on the board: "For it was you who formed my inward parts; / you knit me together in my mother's womb." Mention that Psalm 139 is a wonderful resource for the students because its words communicate God's unconditional love for each one of us. Ask another student to read the *CYB* article "The Sacredness of Life" to the class.

3. Invite the students' thoughts on the readings, being sensitive to the difficult nature of this discussion. Then assign the students to make a class collage using the pictures they brought in and the words of Ps 139.13–14.

4. Hold a meditative prayer service for the class, in which you read the verses of the psalm and invite the students to imagine themselves as the author of the psalm. Close by asking the students to share a prayer of thanksgiving for something about themselves.

Variation. In step 3, rather than assigning the students to create a class collage, have them make individual posters using their own pictures and the words of Ps 139.13–14.

W
I
S
D
O
M

•••••••► The Jesuit Examen: A Simple Form

Saint Ignatius of Loyola believed that daily experiences of faith, hope, joy, and love for which we are grateful are signs of God's presence, and that we should try to repeat and emphasize them. He further believed that experiences that regularly make us feel sad, hopeless, doubtful, and lonely may be areas in need of God's love and grace. To help us identify and reflect on both types of experiences, he created a prayer exercise called the examen, which he described in his guide *The Spiritual Exercises.* This handout presents a simple form of the exercise that is a prayerful means of reviewing your day, week, year, and so on. It can be done alone or with others.

1. Before going to sleep, quiet yourself and imagine God's love for you.

2. Together with God, look over your day and ask yourself this pair of questions:
   - For what experience today am I most grateful?
   - For what experience today am I least grateful?

   Also reflect on these questions if you wish to:
   - When today did I give and receive the most love? When today did I give and receive the least love?
   - When today did I feel the most alive? When today did I feel the most drained of life?
   - When today did I have the greatest sense of belonging to myself, others, God, and the universe? When today did I have the least sense of belonging?
   - When today was I happiest? When today was I saddest?
   - What was today's high point? What was today's low point?

3. Thank God for the whole day and especially the part that made you feel grateful. Ask God's help for dealing with difficult experiences.

(This information about the examen comes from Dennis Linn, Sheila Fabricant Linn, and Matthew Linn, SJ, *Sleeping with Bread: Holding What Gives You Life* [Mahwah, NJ: Paulist Press, 1995], copyright © 1995 by Dennis Linn, Sheila Fabricant Linn, and The Wisconsin Province of the Society of Jesus; and from *The Spiritual Exercises of St. Ignatius: Based on Studies in the Language of the Autograph,* translated by Louis J. Puhl, SJ [Chicago: Loyola University Press, 1951], pages 142–143, copyright © 1951 by The Newman Press. The questions are adapted from *Sleeping with Bread,* pages 6–7.)

Handout Ps–A: Permission to reproduce this handout for classroom use is granted.

Proverbs

The Value of Wisdom

Prayer Styles: Guided Imagery—My Future
Proverbs, chapter 3
"Your Future," Prov 3.5–8, CYB

A guided imagery in which the students envision themselves as older adults helps them identify their hopes and God's desires for their future.

1. Invite a student to read Prov 3.5–8, and point out that God wants to help us make good decisions in the present and for the future.

2. Ask the students to bring to mind two career choices they have considered. Tell them to keep those in mind as they enter into the following guided imagery. If necessary, explain that prayer style.

3. Create a prayerful and meditative atmosphere for the students. Step by step, invite them to close their eyes, relax different parts of their body, and let go of cares and concerns. Then ask them to create the following situation in their mind, giving adequate pauses for them to allow the images to surface:
    - Imagine that you are being transported into the future. . . . Watch the years flow by. . . . Picture yourself as a seventy-year-old man or woman at home on a sunny Saturday afternoon. . . . What are the sights, sounds, and smells of your home? . . . What are you feeling? . . . Are you alone or with others? . . .

        Reflect on your talents and interests; which ones are most important to you? . . .

        Recall the two career options you thought of back in class during high school. . . . Imagine how your life would have been had you chosen the first career. . . . What feelings and thoughts emerge as you picture this? . . . [Allow a longer pause here.]

        Now, think about how your life would have been if you had pursued the second career. . . . What thoughts and feelings emerge from this reflection? . . . [Longer pause]

        Invite God to be present with you. . . . What thoughts does God share about this experience? . . . [Longer pause]

        Take your leave of God . . . and feel yourself transported back to the present.

4. Allow the students a few moments to come back to the present, and then give them a short time to write in their journal about their experience. Ask them to make observations about themselves as an older person and to note any insights they gained about their potential careers. If the students did not connect with this meditation, allow them to write about their struggles with it.

W
I
S
D
O
M

5. When the students are done writing, invite them to share any insights they gained from the activity, and ask follow-up questions if they seem appropriate. Call a student to read the article "Your Future" from the *CYB* in closing, and encourage the students to include God in their decisions about the future.

Wisdom and Folly
Proverbs, chapter 9

The students create skits reflecting the characteristics of the wise person and the scoffer, mentioned in Proverbs, chapter 9.

1. Have several students read Proverbs, chapter 9. Ask the class to compare the characteristics of the wise person and the scoffer and list them on the board.

2. Divide the class into groups of four or five. Direct the groups each to create a scenario in which a person must make a choice to act wisely or foolishly. The skit should feature two endings: one reflecting the foolish choice and one the wise choice. Possible skit topics are prom night, a ski trip, finals week, and curfew.

3. As soon as the groups are prepared, direct one group to perform its skit with the foolish ending. Invite the rest of the class to suggest a wise ending for the skit, and then have the group perform the skit with the wise ending that it has prepared. Engage the class in a discussion about the differences between the two versions of the skit, and ask the students to share insights about the experience of wisdom and foolishness in the lives of teenagers. Then invite the remaining groups to perform their skits, following the same procedure for each group.

Wisdom for Teens

Temperance
Proverbs, chapter 23

The students explore the issues of socializing, alcohol use, and their relationships with their parents.

1. Ask a student to read Prov 23.29–35 aloud. Have the students identify the effects of drinking that are mentioned in that passage and list them on the board.

2. Explain that you would like the students to indicate their answers to a series of questions by moving to the corresponding part of the classroom. Identify one end of the room as "0 percent," the other end as "100 percent," one area of the room as "Yes," and another area as "No." Then ask the students questions such as the ones that follow, in order to elicit their attitudes about drinking practices. After the students move to the part of the room that reflects their answer, invite discussion about those practices and attitudes.

- What percentage of the students in this school drink alcohol?
- Of those students, what percentage regularly drink to the point of intoxication?
- Is it socially acceptable for a student not to drink and still have fun at parties?
- Do some parents allow their children to drink alcohol?
- What percentage of parents forbid their high school students to drink?

3. Divide the class into five groups. Tell the groups that their task is to plan a workshop for parents called "Teenage Social Life: What Teens Wish Their Parents Knew." Assign each group the responsibility for planning an hour-long workshop session about one of the following topics:
- why people drink
- curfews
- peer pressure
- alcohol-free activities
- drinking and driving

Direct the groups each to outline the points they would like to cover and to create an activity of some sort in which the parents can participate. Give them class time to do this planning.

4. Invite the groups to take turns presenting their seminars, with the other students playing the role of the parents. Ask follow-up questions when appropriate, allowing for discussion. Elicit from the students what they most want to communicate to their parents and what they really feel they need from their parents during their high school years.

5. After all the groups have made their presentations, instruct the students each to write a short paragraph about ways in which they might better communicate their own needs to their parents or guardians.

Variation. In steps 4 and 5, arrange for the students to give the seminar for their parents, the school, or the community at large. Conduct the follow-up discussion as a conclusion to the seminar. If parents (or other adults) are invited to the seminar, include follow-up questions aimed at them—like, "What do you most want to communicate to your children (or children in general) about the topics of this gathering?"

Bumper Stickers, Etcetera
Proverbs

The students pick a passage from Proverbs that they think is particularly meaningful and then draw a sample bumper sticker or other item that conveys its message.

1. Tell the students to look through the Book of Proverbs and find a proverb that they think is insightful, wise, or funny. Consider giving Prov 5.12–14 as an example, as it extols the importance of listening to teachers.

2. Invite the students to suggest ways that wisdom is visually shared with others in our culture: on bumper stickers, inspirational posters, tea bags, T-shirts, bookmarks, and so forth. Direct the students each to draw one such item with their chosen proverb on it. On the back of the drawing, they should

write a short paragraph explaining why the proverb appeals to them and why they chose that item to express it.

3. Call the students to share their work when they are done.

Ecclesiastes

Evaluating Ecclesiastes' Message in the Modern Day

The Lure of Advertising
Ecclesiastes, chapter 1
"New and Improved!" Eccl 1.1–11, CYB

This activity helps the students examine what makes advertising compelling. It points out that advertising's frequent claim that something is "new and improved" contradicts the values in Ecclesiastes, chapter 1.

1. Provide enough popular magazines so that each student has one. Direct the students to look through the ads in their magazine, answering the following questions on a piece of paper:
   - Which is my favorite ad and why?
   - Which five advertised items would I consider buying and why?
   - What are five techniques that advertisers use to get me to buy their products?

2. Conduct a class discussion about the magazine ads, inviting the students to share their answers to and insights from the questions in step 1.

3. Invite one student to read Eccl 1.1–11 and another to read the article "New and Improved!" from the *CYB*. Call the students to apply the insights offered in the article to some of the magazine advertisements they found. Then invite them to share with the class their reflections about the following questions:
   - Does the advertising industry thrive on a person's low self-esteem or unhappiness?
   - Does the industry try to make us feel inadequate?
   - In what ways are we susceptible to its efforts?
   - How can we be less vulnerable to advertising?

"What Time Is It in My Life?"
Ecclesiastes, chapter 3

This reflection activity challenges the students to explore the connection between Ecclesiastes and their life.

1. Ask a student to read Eccl 3.1–8 aloud, and discuss the passage with the students.

2. Direct the students each to write on a piece of paper the heading "It is time for me to . . ." They should then read the statements from the Bible

passage and for each, jot down the option that they find most appropriate for this time in their life. For example, for verse 3, they should jot down "kill" or "heal."

3. When the students have finished their list, have them write a reflection paper entitled "What Time Is It in My Life?" The first half of the paper should describe the most important thing that they should be doing at this time, and the second half should discuss the most important thing they should refrain from doing. The paper should include examples that help explain why they chose those two things as most important.

4. After the students complete their papers, invite them to share general or specific insights from their reflections with the class, if they feel comfortable doing so.

Song of Solomon

Sexuality and Love

Sexuality and Television
Song of Solomon
Introduction to Song of Solomon, CYB

Reflecting on the relation between sex and love in the media helps the students process the integration of sex and love in the Song of Solomon.

1. A week before you conduct this activity, direct the students to watch a TV situation comedy or drama that depicts the relation between sex and love. After viewing the program, they should write a reflection about it, entitled "Sex and Love on [the TV show title]." The students should address the following points in their paper:
- the sexual themes explored in the show
- the way that love is portrayed in the show
- the relation between sex and love as it is portrayed in the show
- whether the show is typical of the media's view of sexuality and love
- whether the show's portrayal of sex and love supports or conflicts with their own ideas about a healthy balance between sex and love

The students will use the insights they gain from preparing that reflection in a class discussion on the topic of sex and love in their society.

In addition, have the students suggest a half-hour situation comedy or drama for the class to watch as a whole. Either tape this second TV show yourself or ask a student to tape it for you.

2. Begin this activity by watching the taped TV show as a class, and allow discussion around the same issues the students addressed in their papers.

3. Conclude this activity by asking a student to read the introduction to the Song of Solomon from the *CYB.* Suggest that the students compare the societal and biblical views of sexuality and love as they read the Song of Solomon.

Love Songs
Song of Solomon, chapter 2

This exercise helps the students distinguish between popular songs that integrate love and sexuality in a healthy way, and popular songs that objectify people.

1. Ask a student to read Song 2.8–17, and direct the students to notice how affectionately and respectfully the author speaks of the beloved. Point

out that the passion found in the Song of Solomon exists between two people who are committed to each other, and thus is a good model of love and sexuality.

Note that love and passion are favorite subjects of songwriters but are not always presented together. Explain that sometimes, songs portray the object of passion as just that—an object rather than a person. Discuss the difference between treating someone as an object and treating someone as a person.

2. As homework, ask half the students each to find a contemporary song that speaks of both passion and love in the respectful way found in the Song of Solomon. Have them copy the relevant lyrics and then write a short reflection about why that song is a good model of a healthy relation between passionate sexuality and love.

Direct the other half of the class each to find a contemporary song that portrays passion and love in a way that is disrespectful of people, that objectifies people. Have them copy the relevant lyrics and write a short reflection about why that song is not a good model of a healthy relation between passionate sexuality and love.

3. In the next class, allow the students to share the lyrics they have found, and write common insights on the board. Focusing on the songs with a positive message, suggest that though the songs themselves may not speak of marriage, the students can perhaps imagine the respectful and passionate love they describe as existing in a committed marriage. Help the students brainstorm why a marriage is the most powerful and rewarding environment in which to have a sexual relationship.

Variation. At the end of step 1, instead of conducting a discussion about the difference between treating someone as an object and treating someone as a person, help the students make mind maps for the words *person* and *object,* as described in the activity "Vashti: A True Hero," on page 102 of this manual.

Wisdom of Solomon

The Nature of Wisdom

Wisdom and Virtue
Wisdom of Solomon, chapters 4, 8

The Wisdom of Solomon praises virtue and invites the students to examine the cardinal and theological virtues.

    1. Call a student to read Wis 8.7. Explain that prudence, justice, fortitude, and temperance are known as the cardinal virtues both in classic philosophy and in Roman Catholicism. Also explain that the theological virtues are faith, hope, and charity. Help the students understand those terms by referring to a dictionary or to the *Catechism,* numbers 1803 to 1829, which define and describe them.

    Ask a second student to read Wis 4.1–3, where the author praises the importance of the virtues.

    2. Divide the class into seven groups and assign each group a different cardinal or theological virtue. Explain the assignment as follows, in your own words:

- Each group should prepare a short skit that shares both the value of its virtue and the challenges to keeping the virtue in a modern, everyday scenario. One student in the group should creatively dress like the virtue, and others may enhance the performance by dressing as a corresponding vice or by providing other props. Everyone who can should bring in costumes and props, and I will add to the collection as well.

Announce that the groups will present their skits in the next class, and give them time to prepare.

    3. At the next class, after the groups have all presented their skits, discuss with the class the insights that come out of the skits, and the need for virtues in our modern day.

The Qualities of Wisdom
Wisdom of Solomon, chapter 7

This exercise helps the students understand the meaning of the characteristics assigned to wisdom.

    1. Request a student to read Wis 7.22–23 aloud for the class.

    2. Divide the class into groups of five and give each group a dictionary. Instruct the groups to look up all the characteristics of wisdom mentioned in

the Bible passage and define them. Explain that one member of the group should write down the characteristics, the group should offer definitions or look them up as necessary, and the recorder should write the definitions down as well.

Then ask the groups each to narrate an actual event, using as many of the words they have identified as possible, in the order they appear in the Bible verses. Give them an example such as this:

- My *intelligent* sister invited me to a movie after *holy* Mass on Sunday. That film was *unique* in *manifold* ways. After a *subtle* hint from our father, we realized that the only way to become *mobile* was to take the bus. I would like to say that the windows were *clear* and the ride was *unpolluted*, but . . .

3. After the groups have shared their definitions and narratives with the class, ask the students to close their eyes while you read the characteristics in Wis 7.22–23 slowly out loud, allowing them to imagine a being who possesses all those characteristics. Then invite the students to describe their impressions of that being named Wisdom.

God's Presence in Our Own History

God-in-My-Life Timeline
Wisdom of Solomon
"Supernatural Resources," Wis 19.22, CYB

Creating a timeline helps the students see that through the ups and downs of their past, God has been present.

1. Write the following verse from Wisdom of Solomon on the board: "For in everything, O Lord, you have exalted and glorified your people, / and you have not neglected to help them at all times and in all places" (19.22). Ask a student to read the article "Supernatural Resources" from the *CYB*.

2. Tell the students to look back over their life and make a list of the important events that they recall. The students themselves should determine what events to include, but you might mention some of the following occasions to help get them going:

- achievements
- firsts (day at middle school, time driving, etc.)
- births of siblings
- moves
- divorces and marriages of parents
- deaths
- new activities
- vacations
- illnesses
- meeting and losing friends

Direct the students to mark the really positive or joyful experiences with an up arrow (↑) and the difficult experiences with a down arrow (↓↑), leaving the fairly neutral experiences unmarked.

3. Instruct the students to draw a timeline of their life using the squares of a sidewalk, the markings on a ruler, or some other visual symbols. They are to plot their life events along this creative timeline, indicating its ups and downs. For each event, they should also indicate with words or a picture how God was present. For instance, God could have been present in the joy of positive events, and through friends or prayer in negative ones.

Determine whether the students would feel comfortable doing this activity in class or would find it more meaningful doing it at home in private. Be aware that this project invites a careful reading by you, affirmation of the students' personal journeys, and possibly some personal commentary or discussion with individual students.

4. When the students have completed their timelines, allow them to share with the class the experiences they have recorded and their insights about the activity, as the comfort level and atmosphere of the class allow.

(This activity was inspired by one by Joan Hourigan, Holy Names Academy, Seattle, Washington.)

Sirach

Sirach on Our Treatment of Others

Purposeful Acts of Kindness
Sirach, chapter 3

This activity introduces the idea of random acts of kindness through a reading from Sirach, and helps the students explore a campaign for furthering that concept today.

1. Ask a student to read Sir 3.17–19. Familiarize the students with the "random acts of kindness and senseless acts of beauty" campaign, and possibly read some examples from the book *Random Acts of Kindness,* by the editors of Conari Press (Berkeley, CA: Conari Press, 1993). Here are a few ideas you could share with them:

   - The "random acts of kindness and senseless acts of beauty" campaign began when a man got tired of all the media coverage about random acts of violence and senseless acts of destruction. He decided to start a campaign to change the nation's preoccupation with violence and destruction.
   - It was an easy campaign; he just encouraged people to do simple, random, anonymous acts of kindness or beauty without looking for a reward or a pat on the back. Before long, stories were circulating about people doing acts of kindness and beauty for no reason other than the goodness of their hearts. A boy shoveled the walk of an elderly person without asking the person beforehand or even telling the person afterward. Just before the holidays, someone left a basket full of food and presents on the steps of a young couple struggling to make ends meet.
   - It takes a humble heart to do a random act of kindess or beauty. It takes heeding the advice that Sir 3.17 gives: "My child, perform your tasks with humility."

2. Assign the students to perform at least one act of kindness or beauty of their choice over the next few days, and to write a short account of that act.

3. After a few days, invite the students to share their stories with the class and to reflect on the ease or difficulty of their acts as well as on how those acts affected both themselves and the others involved. Ask the students what might happen if each of them performed such an act daily and if more people did so.

Point out that because the acts they have reported on were assigned for homework, they do not qualify as random. Note that really, acts of kindness and beauty should never be random; the Christian message requires that we do such acts and that they be purposeful, sensible, and in the spirit of humility mentioned in Sirach.

4. Post the students' accounts of their acts in the room or create a small book of them.

Choose Your Friends Wisely
Sirach, chapters 6, 9, 37

The choice of friends, a recurring theme in the wisdom literature, can have numerous consequences, both positive and negative. This activity invites the students to learn about qualities of friendship from the perspective of an older person looking back on life.

1. Ask several students to read Sir 6.5–17; 9.10; 37.1–6 aloud. Have the students identify Ben Sira's main points about the qualities of good friends and unreliable friends.

2. Assign the students to interview an adult who is thirty-five years or older. They are to use these interview questions:
- Who is your best friend? How long have you been friends?
- What qualities make this person a good friend?
- What is your favorite memory with your best friend?
- What is the biggest challenge that you and your friend have had to overcome together?
- What advice do you have for a young person, about what to look for in a good friend?
  Tell the students to write a summary of their interview and a short reflection about the content of the interview and the interview process.

3. When the students have completed their interviews and writings, invite them to share with the class some of the adults' wisdom as well as their own insights. Ask, "Does Ben Sira share thoughts about friendship that are similar to our own?"

Sexism Reversal
Sirach, chapters 25–26

To our modern ears, some of the descriptions of women throughout the wisdom literature might seem sexist against women. This activity asks the students to rewrite passages from Sirach with equally absurd comments about men, as a humorous way of dealing with a sensitive topic.

1. Ask several students to read Sir 25.13—26.18. Note that the author of Sirach wrote those passages in a patriarchal culture that had very different standards for men and women. Mention that though some of the statements in those passages are more blatantly stereotypical than we usually encounter today, stereotypes of both men and women still exist.

2. Divide the class into five groups and give each group one of the following passages:
- Sir 25.13–19
- Sir 25.20–26
- Sir 26.1–9

- Sir 26.10–12
- Sir 26.13–18

Explain that each group should rewrite its passage as if it were criticizing or praising a man (rather than a woman), using the same kind of style, using similar types of language, and drawing parallels as much as possible.

3. When the groups are done, call them together to read the whole passage with its new twist. Then invite discussion, asking follow-up questions of comments that are made. Encourage the students to talk about their experience of transposing the text and to comment on the prevalence of sexual stereotypes today. Ask, "Why is it sometimes comfortable to use stereotypes, even though they are inaccurate?"

Gossip: Causes and Effects
Sirach, chapters 19, 28
"Just Walk Away," Sir 28.12–18, CYB

Role-plays help the students examine the attraction of gossip as well as how gossip affects all parties involved.

1. Invite several students to read these Bible passages about gossip: Sir 19.4–17; 28.12–18. Help the students to define gossip and slander, and have them point out the observations made about both in the passages just read. Ask some follow-up questions such as, "When might it be a sin not to reveal a conversation?" (see 19.8) and "Why might someone hate you when they see you gossiping?" (see 19.9). Then call a student to read the article "Just Walk Away" from the *CYB*.

2. Divide the class into groups of five. Instruct the groups each to prepare a short role-play that addresses the following questions through a gossip or slander situation that might be familiar to teens:
- Why do people gossip?
- How can gossip injure the person who is gossiped about?
- How can gossip hurt the person who gossips?
- Is some discussion of other people's affairs legitimate? If so, how do you draw the line between that kind of talk and damaging gossip?

3. After each group has presented its role-play, ask follow-up questions and invite discussion about the effects of gossip. Affirm the students' own wisdom about an age-old problem.

Applying Sirach's Wisdom

Exegetical Tools:
Using a Concordance for the Sirach Challenge
Sirach

Some students pose questions about several different topics and then ask other students to look for answers to those questions in Sirach. A biblical concordance can aid in this search.

1. Divide the class into groups. Assign each group a topic that is covered in Sirach, such as one of these:

- treating parents properly
- handling wealth
- friendship
- speaking wisely
- parenting

Tell the groups each to come up with five questions about their topic, such as, "Should children always respect their parents?" Explain that each group should then pass its questions to another group so that all the groups end up with new questions. Add that the groups are to try to find verses in Sirach that answer their new questions, writing out the appropriate verses. Note that not all questions can be answered in Sirach, but this exercise should help the students to become familiar with the author's view of the subjects covered in the book.

2. Introduce a biblical concordance that covers Sirach (see appendix A for a recommended concordance). If the concordance you are using lists Sirach in the Apocrypha, point that out, explaining what the Apocrypha is. If necessary, explain or review how to use a concordance (refer to the activity "Exegetical Tools: The Concordance and Wisdom Themes," on pages 111–112 of this manual, for a discussion of that tool).

Provide enough copies of the concordance, or enough copies of the relevant pages from it, for each group. Direct the groups each to search for the answers to their questions in the concordance. Suggest that they look up other words in addition to the main terms—so, for questions pertaining to wealth, they might look up *rich* and *money* in order to find potentially relevant passages.

3. After most of the groups have exhausted Ben Sira's wisdom on the assigned subjects, invite them to share Ben Sira's answers to their questions. Ask the students to decide whether Ben Sira's wisdom is still relevant today.

Personal Wisdom

Sirach Discussion-Starters
Sirach

This exercise invites the students to discuss the advice in Sirach and to decide how wise that advice is.

1. Divide the class into five groups and assign each group one of the following seven passages from Sirach:

- Sir 4.20–28 (Self-esteem)
- Sir 6.5–17; 9.10 (Friendship)
- Sir 21.19–21 (Education)
- Sir 23.13 (Foul language)
- Sir 30.7–13 (Parenting)
- Sir 40.1–11 (The human condition)
- Sir 41.1–4 (Death)

Direct the groups each to read and discuss their passage. After 10 minutes, give the groups each a piece of butcher paper, and ask them to list the main points made by Sirach on their topic and then five of their own thoughts that arose from their conversation.

2. Depending on the time and the students' interest, either invite the groups to simply present a summary of their conversation by sharing their main ideas, or ask the students to initiate and conduct a class discussion on some or all of the topics. If you choose the latter option, call for volunteers to lead the discussion by coming forward, bringing up ideas and possible areas of disagreement, and then calling on the other students in order to engage them in conversation.

3. Direct the students to rank Ben Sira's wisdom on a scale from 1 to 5, with 1 standing for "Not wise at all" and 5 standing for "Very wise." This can be done by calling for a show of hands or by directing the students to stand along a continuum marked by five spots in the classroom. Wrap up the exercise by inviting the students to explain their opinions of Sirach.

Cartoons from Sirach
Sirach

Many sayings from Sirach provide or suggest images or ideas that the students can express well in a single-frame cartoon.

1. Bring in examples of single-frame cartoons from the newspaper and pass them around to show the students how the picture refers to the caption.

2. Allow the students to find a short phrase or verse in Sirach that lends itself to such a cartoon. Here are some possibilities:
- Sir 5.15
- Sir 7.3
- Sir 11.25
- Sir 14.5
- Sir 21.19,21
- Sir 30.14
- Sir 33.5
- Sir 33.6
- Sir 41.19

Supply blank paper and colored markers or pencils. Give the students time to draw and color their cartoons in class.

3. When the students are done, invite them to share their cartoons with the class. Display the cartoons in the classroom.

A Personal Wisdom Book
Wisdom and poetry books

After reading the wisdom literature, the students have a chance to express the wisdom that they have gained in their own lives.

Explain that in this exercise, the students will each put together a short book that shares their own insights about life and the world. The book should be neatly written or typed on blank paper, and should include some sort of illustration or design elements.

You might ask the students to pick between five and ten personal insights that they can phrase in one or two sentences, and then present those words of wisdom as they choose. Or you might direct the students to pattern their own words of wisdom after the different genres or topics that they have found in the wisdom literature. With this approach, they could include the following items:

- *For Job.* A paragraph answering the question What is the relation between God and suffering?
- *For Psalms.* A psalm of praise, thanksgiving, lament, or petition (The students may consult the introduction to the Psalms in the *CYB* for descriptions and examples.)
- *For Proverbs.* Several proverbs that reflect the students' own experience
- *For Ecclesiastes.* A paragraph answering the question Is there anything new under the sun? (see Eccl 1.9)
- *For Song of Solomon.* A short love poem (This can be passionate but should be "rated PG.")
- *For Wisdom of Solomon.* Several verses describing wisdom such as those found in Wis 6.12–25
- *For Sirach.* Some words of wisdom about other topics

(This activity is based on one created by Christine Sullivan, Holy Names Academy, Seattle, Washington.)

W
I
S
D
O
M

Prophets

Isaiah

First Isaiah

Swords into Plowshares
Isaiah, chapter 2
"Swords into Plowshares," Isa 2.1–5, CYB

The students link the message of peacemaking from Isaiah with teachings of nonviolence from Jesus and apply them to conflicts the students face.

1. Tell the students to read Isa 2.1–5 aloud. Explain the historical context for the passage, including a definition of *plowshares.*

2. Pass out slips of paper and ask the students to write down examples of realistic conflicts that could be resolved either peacefully or with violence. Explain that a violent resolution does not always involve physical injury but can in some cases cause emotional, property, or other damage. Collect the examples when the students are done writing.

3. Create an invisible continuum across the classroom, designating one end "Swords" (violence) and the other end "Plowshares" (peace). Then read the students' conflict examples aloud to the class. As you read each scenario, ask the students to stand on the continuum at the place that reflects their initial sense of how to solve the situation. For each example, invite discussion about different solutions.

4. Form small groups and direct them each to find in the Gospels a passage that reflects the words or actions of Jesus regarding violence or nonviolence. Invite each group to report its findings to the class, and in light of its insights, reopen the discussion on the students' scenarios of conflict.

5. Call a student to read the article "Swords into Plowshares" from the *CYB*. Instruct the students each to write a short essay addressing the questions posed in the article.

Exegetical Tools: Historical Criticism and the Biblical Dictionary—the Prophets' World
Isaiah, chapters 3, 5, 13, 34, 43; Ezekiel, chapter 16; Daniel, chapter 3

Through the writings of Isaiah and other prophets, the students explore and present three elements of the prophets' world: fashion, music, and animals.

1. Introduce or review the research process called historical criticism (see the activity "Exegetical Tools: Historical Criticism in Ruth," on page 68 of this manual).

2. Divide the class into three groups representing fashion, music, and animals, and assign the groups to read the following passages from the Prophets:

- *Fashion.* Isa 3.18–26, Ezek 16.9–14, Dan 3.21
- *Music.* Isa 5.11–12, Dan 3.5
- *Animals.* Isa 13.21; 34.14; 43.20

Tell the groups each to list terms related to their topic as they read, and to then research those terms. Pass out copies of a Bible dictionary, or information from the relevant pages of one, for the groups to use in their study. The articles under the following terms, and others, in a biblical dictionary should have pertinent information that the students can use: "jewelry," "dress," "music," and "wilderness."

3. Direct the groups each to create a visual presentation about their subject. The students may dress up, bring in musical instruments, or draw or find pictures. Encourage creativity.

4. Give the groups time in class to prepare and give their presentations. Then review the verses surrounding their assigned passages from Isaiah, Ezekiel, and Daniel, to see if the students can gain a richer understanding of the prophets' writings.

The Prophets' Emergency Broadcasting System
Isaiah, chapters 3–4

This activity uses Isaiah's blunt warnings to the daughters of Zion to encourage the students to see the dangers in materialism.

1. Ask the students to define materialism, and lead them to discuss how the media promote materialism.

2. Form groups of three. Direct the groups each to list three to five dangers of materialism and then share those with the class.

3. Read the warning from Isa 3.16—4.1 aloud in a dramatic way. Discuss with the students why Isaiah needed to be so straightforward in addressing the social injustice in the lives of the people. Ask how Isaiah might reach out to those who are enslaved by materialism today.

4. Instruct the students to stay in the same groups and design a message for the PEBS—Prophets' Emergency Broadcasting System. Explain that each group's message will interrupt regularly scheduled programming, and the group may decide whether it will play on the radio or television. As soon as the groups are done, invite them to present their messages in class and to discuss the insights that they share.

God's Call
Isaiah, chapter 6; Exodus, chapters 3–4; Amos, chapter 3; Jeremiah,
*   chapter 1; Luke, chapter 1*
"Here I Am, Lord!" Isa 6.1–13, CYB

Role-plays of different biblical calls invite the students to reflect on how their experiences are similar to those biblical ones.

1. Ask one student to read Isa 6.1–13 and another to read the article "Here I Am, Lord!" from the *CYB*.

2. Divide the class into five groups and assign each group one of the biblical calls mentioned in the article, including Isaiah's. Direct the groups to read the Bible passage for their call that is listed in the article, extending the reading for Moses' call to Ex 3.1—4.17. Ask the groups each to prepare a role-play for their call, complete with props. They should identify the biblical pattern mentioned in the article for their prophet.

3. After the groups have presented their role-plays, point out that the objections put forth by each biblical hero are not unusual. Write the following statements on the board:
- "I don't know what to say, so . . ." (Moses)
- "What will people think if I . . ."(Samuel)
- "I am not good enough to . . ." (Isaiah)
- "I am too young to . . ." (Jeremiah)
- "There is no way that this can happen, so . . ." (Mary)
Help the groups to brainstorm realistic sentence-endings that reflect typical excuses for teens and adults. Note that human insecurity and false humility can really get in the way of following God's call.

Artistic Interpretations of the Messianic Promise
Isaiah, chapter 9

Giving color, shape, and form to the messianic promise in Isaiah, chapter 9, helps the students appreciate the beauty of the language and imagery in Isaiah.

1. Playing soft music in the background, read Isa 9.2–7 to the class meditatively.

2. Have the students silently reread the passage in their Bible, and then ask them to identify the key images in the passage.

3. Divide the class into six groups, and randomly and secretly assign each group a different verse from the passage to illustrate. Provide large sheets of paper, and colored markers or pencils, or paints. Instruct the students not to tell the other groups which verse they have been assigned.

4. When the groups have completed their illustrations, collect the papers and display them in no particular order. Tell the students you will read the Scripture passage again, and you would like to see if they can identify which illustration matches each verse.

5. After your reading, give the small groups the opportunity to explain their drawings and to share any reflections that the artwork inspired.

PROPHETS

Gifts–of–the–Holy Spirit Charades
Isaiah, chapter 11

Several students silently act out the different gifts of the Holy Spirit, which are introduced in Isaiah.

1. Divide the class into two groups. Select three students in each group, and secretly assign each of them a different one of the following six gifts of the Holy Spirit mentioned in Isa 11.2–3. Do not assign any student the gift of piety, which is also mentioned in the reading (see "fear of the Lord," verse 2).
- wisdom
- understanding
- counsel
- fortitude ("might," verse 2)
- knowledge
- wonder and awe ("fear of the Lord," verse 3)

2. Using the gestures and rules for the game of charades, present the word *piety* to the students and ask them to guess it. Recruit a student to record the time it took the students to make the correct guess.

3. Allow the designated students time for preparing to present their gifts to their group as a charade. Challenge each group to beat your time and to guess its charades the fastest. Then time the groups as they play out their charades. When both groups are done, congratulate the winner.

4. Ask several students to read Isa 11.1–9 aloud for the class. Discuss the qualities of the messianic king in depth, and the role of the Holy Spirit's gifts in the sacrament of Confirmation.

Lambs and Wolves
Isaiah, chapter 11
"Lions and Lambs," Isa 11.6–9, CYB

Using the message and imagery that Isaiah presents, the students identify oppressive relationships in our society and suggest constructive paths toward harmony.

1. Call several students to read Isa 11.1–9 aloud to the class and another student to read the article "Lions and Lambs" from the *CYB.*

2. Draw the students' attention to the different pairs of creatures presented in Isa 11.6–9. Ask the students to identify the traditional roles that those creatures play together and to note the peaceful scenes pictured in the passage.

3. Put two columns on the board, one labeled "Wolf" and the other "Lamb," to represent the strong and the vulnerable. Form pairs of students, and instruct the pairs each to come up with at least three modern human parallels of the oppressive relationship between the wolf and the lamb. After a few minutes, ask for examples to put in each column on the board.

4. Form groups of four. Direct the groups each to adopt one of the pairs listed on the board and to draw up a plan that reflects Isaiah's hope for that pair. The groups should identify five steps the "wolf" could take to treat the "lamb" justly, or five steps that the lamb might take to demand justice from the wolf.

Second Isaiah

A Job Recommendation: Jesus as Suffering Servant
Isaiah, chapters 42, 49–50, 52–53
"The Servant Songs," Isa 42.1–7, CYB

This activity helps the students find ways that Jesus' life and ministry resemble those of the suffering servant in Isaiah.

1. Ask a student to read the article "The Servant Songs" from the *CYB*. Call several other students to read aloud the passages mentioned in the article. As the students read the verses, help the class compile a job description for the suffering servant, listing the main characteristics of that person on the board.

2. Form small groups and ask each group to think of aspects of Jesus' life that match the job description on the board. Allow the groups to look through the New Testament for ideas. Direct the groups each to compose a recommendation for Jesus as if Jesus were applying for the job of suffering servant, using examples from the New Testament for support.

3. Invite the groups to share aspects of their completed recommendations that show parallels between Jesus' life and the prophecies in Isaiah.

Isaiah, Music, and Prayer
Isaiah
"Be Not Afraid," Isa 43.1–5, CYB

The students gain a deeper awareness of the beautiful messages within the Book of Isaiah as they prepare short prayer experiences from music inspired by the prophet.

1. To prepare for this activity, obtain a recording or copy of the song "Be Not Afraid," from the album *Spirit and Soul,* by Tom Prin (Even Par Records, 1997), and copies of a collection of Catholic liturgical music such as *Gather Comprehensive,* edited by Robert J. Batastini and Michael A. Cymbala (Chicago: GIA Publications, 1994), or *Glory and Praise,* revised edition, by North American Liturgy Resources and GIA Publications (Phoenix, AZ: North American Liturgy Resources and GIA Publications, 1994).

2. To begin this activity, ask one student to read Isa 43.1–5 aloud, and another to read the article "Be Not Afraid" from the *CYB*.

3. Play or sing the song "Be Not Afraid" for the students and help them to find the biblical verses within the song.

4. Divide the class into groups, and give each group one of your copies of a collection of Catholic liturgical music. Demonstrate how the students can find music inspired by Isaiah in the index.

5. Instruct the groups each to plan for the class a short prayer experience incorporating a liturgical song based on a passage from Isaiah, the related verses from Isaiah, and some other creative element such as a popular piece of music with a similar theme. The prayer service should be no longer than 10 minutes.

6. Invite the groups to take turns leading the rest of the class in worship over the next several weeks.

Prayer Styles: Mantra and Choral Reading
Isaiah, chapter 43

This activity allows the students to reflect on the comforting words and presence of God by composing a prayer using the text from Isaiah, chapter 43.

1. Introduce the mantra as a form of prayer as follows, using your own words:
- A mantra is a repeated word or phrase often used in Eastern traditions for centering prayer and meditation. The word or phrase is said slowly and quietly so that the person can focus on the word, blocking out other stimuli. The effect is rhythmic and comforting.

2. Read the first verse of Isaiah, chapter 43, aloud. Repeat, "Do not fear, for I have redeemed you; / I have called you by name, you are mine." Ask the students to reflect on the feelings, thoughts, and memories that that phrase evokes in them, and write those in a journal or on a piece of paper.

3. Form groups of four, and direct them each to compose a prayer that uses the phrase from Isa 43.1 as a mantra repeated softly behind it.

4. Arrange for each group to lead the class in prayer one day during the next week or two. In each case, have one or two students read the verses their group composed, and the rest of the class members close their eyes and softly, reverently repeat the mantra throughout the prayer. Encourage the use of background music during the prayers.

Third Isaiah

The Mission to the Oppressed
Isaiah, chapter 61

To understand the concrete significance of the prophet Isaiah's mission, the students explore ways that people today can "bring good news to the oppressed" (Isa 61.1).

1. Ask a student to read Isa 61.1–4 aloud. Review the different tasks of the prophet by calling the students to give modern examples of people who fit these categories:

- oppressed
- brokenhearted
- captive
- imprisoned
- mourning

2. Divide the class into five groups and assign each group one of the categories listed in step 1. Tell the groups to think of concrete ways that people today could follow the lead of the prophet. Provide large sheets of paper and colored markers or pens, and have the groups make posters that invite other people to action. An example for the first task of the prophet is a poster displaying the slogan "Bring good news to the oppressed—raise the minimum wage!"

3. Invite the groups to share their posters and insights with the class. Encourage related discussion.

Images of God in Isaiah
Isaiah

This activity guides the students in a look at the different ways that the Book of Isaiah portrays God.

Handout **Isa–A**

1. Cut handout Isa–A, "Images of God in Isaiah," into separate slips of paper, each containing a citation from Isaiah. Pass around a container with the slips of paper and ask each student to pick one. Direct the students to look up their citation in the Bible and write the passage on the slip of paper.

2. Say something such as this to the students:

- Sometimes, Christians perceive that the God of the New Testament is a loving, caring God in contrast with the violent and angry God in the Old Testament. It is true that the Old Testament authors portray God's anger and frustration with the people, but they also present God's love for the people and desire that the people will love in return.

3. Form an invisible continuum across the classroom. Label one end of the continuum "Angry God" and the other "Loving God." Ask the students to line up along the continuum according to the image of God presented on their slip of paper. They should rank themselves so that the person with the most loving image is at one end and the person with the angriest image is at the other.

4. Once the students are lined up, ask them to take turns reading their passages, beginning with the most angry and ending with the most loving. Then lead the students to discuss why one Old Testament book offers such a variety of imagery of God, and to share their reactions to the images read aloud.

P
R
O
P
H
E
T
S

Isa 8.13	Isa 41.10
Isa 8.14	Isa 43.25
Isa 10.18	Isa 44.24
Isa 12.2	Isa 45.7
Isa 13.9	Isa 47.3
Isa 24.1	Isa 49.15
Isa 25.1	Isa 51.12
Isa 25.8	Isa 54.10
Isa 26.4	Isa 55.8–9
Isa 30.18	Isa 62.5
Isa 40.1	Isa 64.8
Isa 40.11	Isa 65.17
Isa 40.28	Isa 66.13

Jeremiah

Jeremiah's Call

Split Screen Calling
Jeremiah, chapter 1
"Who, Me?" Jer 1.4–10, CYB

Dramatic readings of the passage of Jeremiah's call help the students see the similarities between themselves and the young prophet.

Note: The activity "God's Call," on pages 148–149 of this manual, includes God's call to Jeremiah.

1. Instruct the students to read Jer 1.4–10 silently. Call one student to read aloud the article "Who, Me?" from the *CYB.*

2. Divide the class into two groups. One group should prepare a reading of the Scripture text as is, with the entire group taking the part of the narrator and separate people playing God and Jeremiah.

The other group is to plan a modern version of the Scripture passage, with Jeremiah as Jeremy, a teen in today's world. Its version should be true to the Scripture text, matching it line for line, but in the vernacular of modern teens. That group should also use choral reading for the narrator and single voices for God and Jeremy.

3. After enough preparation, direct one group to the left side of the room and the other to the right side. Have the groups present their readings one verse at a time, alternating left to right. Advise the students to stay in character throughout the presentation.

4. Invite the students to discuss the nature of God's call to Jeremiah and the ways that God could be calling young people today.

Prophecy and the Modern World

Life Games
Jeremiah, chapters 2–6
"Jeremiah," near Jer 2.20, CYB

The students create a board game that incorporates the kinds of choices that Jeremiah discusses in chapters 2–6.

1. Call several students to read Jeremiah, chapter 2, aloud and another student to read the article "Jeremiah" from the *CYB*. Help the students identify the poor choices that Jeremiah mentions in the chapter.

2. Divide the class into groups of four or five. Direct the groups each to design a board game that addresses decision making and incorporates sources of true life (i.e., life-giving decisions and choices, as opposed to destructive ones), worthwhile and worthless goals, and so on. They should draw a rough sketch of the board, make some sample cards, draw game pieces, and choose a targeted age-group. The groups should also write a brief description of the game, and a summary of the objectives and rules.

3. When the groups are ready, invite them to present their games. Discuss the insights about decision making and goals that arise.

Variations. If time allows, let the groups complete their board games and play them in steps 2 and 3. You might also provide art supplies and a collection of small objects for use as game pieces, to help the students make their games more realistic.

Host a game party for the students' families or middle schoolers or older people, setting up the finished games at different tables and providing beverages and snacks. Direct the students to guide the games, and help them lead brief discussions afterward.

Donate the games to a program for families, middle schoolers, or older people.

True Peace
Jeremiah, chapter 6

Jeremiah's critique of false peace invites the students to reflect on the nature of true peace.

1. Have one student read Jer 6.13–15. Note that in that passage, Jeremiah points out that those who are unjust claim that there is peace while they are exploiting the vulnerable.

2. Challenge the students to reflect on their understanding of the qualities of true peace. After giving them some time to brainstorm, ask them each to formulate their thoughts about peace into five sentences. Tell the students to word those sentences so that their first letters form the word *peace*. Direct the students to write their sentences on blank paper so that the word *peace* is readable, and allow them to decorate their paper as they wish with symbols and illustrations, using colored markers or pencils.

3. Invite the students to share their sentences, and allow discussion to arise from those insights.

Advertising: False Prophecy
Jeremiah, chapter 14

The students examine different ads to see the similarity between advertising's claim that all will be well if one buys a particular product or service, and the claim of the false prophets in Jeremiah.

1. Prepare for this exercise by videotaping some television ads to use as examples for the class.

2. Begin this exercise by asking a student to read Jer 14.13–16 aloud to the class. Say something such as this to the students:
   - It is important to see that Jeremiah rejects the false prophets' message of peace and hope because it is not from God. He explains that the people listen to the false prophets because their message is appealing. Advertisers also offer appealing, easy solutions to difficult problems through the products and services they promote.

Prompt the students to give examples of advertisers doing that.

3. Show your taped examples of television advertising to the class and encourage the students to identify what human needs the products are claiming to meet. Help the students distinguish ads that use human fear to sell items (such as beauty aids and insurance). Lead the students to brainstorm truer means of addressing those needs. Discuss whether faith in God might be another means of meeting them.

The Shape of Our Relationship with God
Jeremiah, chapter 18

This activity invites the students to mold a piece of clay into a shape that reflects who they are in their current relationship with God.

1. Ask one student to read Jer 18.1–11 aloud to the class. Offer the following thoughts to the class in your own words:
   - If you've ever turned clay on a potter's wheel, you know it's not easy. The clay seems to have a mind of its own and pushes and pulls itself in directions the potter does not intend for it to go. But if a work of clay doesn't turn out, the potter can always smash it down and start over—again and again.
   - Jeremiah reminds the Israelites and us that we are like clay in God's hands. God creates us and has a vision of who we will become, and God wants to form us and mold us toward that potential. But we tend to push and pull ourselves in other directions, often reworking ourselves into "another vessel" (verse 4) than we were created to be. The more we allow the potter—God—to shape us, the more we become the vessel God intended or created us to be.

2. Invite the students to close their eyes, and lead them through a short guided imagery about the potter working with clay. Begin this meditation by rereading Jer 18.1–4 to them and giving them cues to help them imagine the sights and smells of a workshop. Then encourage them to envision themselves

as the clay being molded by the potter's hand. Finally, ask the students to reflect quietly on this question: "Into what shape does the potter mold the lump of clay?"

3. Give the students each some clay and ask them to mold the image they saw during the meditation. Play some reflective music while the students work.

4. Assign the students to write a reflection about this experience and to share their thoughts with the class as they are comfortable.

Variation. In step 3, instead of directing the students to mold an image out of clay, ask them to sketch the image on paper.

God Responds to Jeremiah's Despair
Jeremiah, chapter 20

The students use what they know of God to imagine how God might respond to someone in crisis, like Jeremiah.

1. Read Jer 20.7–18 to the students in a dramatic way with sorrowful music in the background. Discuss with the students the multitude of feelings in the passage. Note that God does not respond to Jeremiah's lonely cry. Ask the students why God is unresponsive.

2. Assign groups to write a response to Jeremiah from God, each using one of the following forms:
- a personal letter
- a videotaped message
- a singing telegram
- a poem
- a gift and a thoughtful card
- a telephone counseling hot line

3. Arrange for the groups to present their responses in class. Discuss which response would be most comforting to Jeremiah.

4. Direct the students each to write a reflection about a time they felt God responding to their sadness or despair.

Jeremiah and Jesus

The Lives of Jeremiah and Jesus
Jeremiah

This activity asks the students to match Old Testament and New Testament verses that reveal a similarity between the lives of Jeremiah and Jesus.

Handout **Jer–A**

1. Pass out copies of handout Jer–A, "Jeremiah and Jesus Match," to the students. Review the instructions and address any questions. Give the students time to work on the handout individually or in pairs.

2. After the students have completed their work, ask them to share their answers about parallels between Jeremiah and Jesus. Invite them to discuss any similarities they have observed between Jesus and other prophets.

▶ Jeremiah and Jesus Match

Jeremiah and Jesus shared some common experiences during their lifetimes. Look up the following passages for those two men. Decide which experience from column 2 is discussed in each passage, and put the proper letter in the space.

JEREMIAH	Common experiences	JESUS
1. Jer 12.6 ____	a. Both are touched by God in the womb of their mother.	1. Lk 4.16–29 ____
2. Jer 31.31–34 ____	b. Both are rejected by friends from home.	2. Lk 22.20 ____
3. Jer 37.17–21 ____	c. Both mourn about the condition of their homeland.	3. Lk 19.28,41–44 ____
4. Jer 8.18–22 ____	d. Both refer to the Temple as a "den of robbers."	4. Jn 3.1–21 ____
5. Jer 1.5 ____	e. Both are consulted fearfully and secretly by believers.	5. Lk 1.26–38 ____
6. Jer 7.11 ____	f. Both speak of the New Covenant.	6. Mt 21.12–13 ____

Reflection Question

Was Jesus a prophet? Why or why not?

Lamentations

Poetic Expressions of Grief

Exegetical Tools:
Form Criticism—Lamentations and Acrostic Poetry
Lamentations
Introduction to Lamentations, CYB

The students learn about and imitate the form of poetry used in Lamentations.

1. Ask several students to read Lamentations, chapter 1, aloud to the class, or allow the students some quiet time to skim the book. Then have one student read the introduction to Lamentations from the *CYB*.

2. Review the exegetical tool called form criticism, or introduce the students to that tool if you have not already covered it (see the activity "Exegetical Tools: Form Criticism—the Saga," on page 59 of this manual, for background).

3. Note the form of writing in Lamentations, offering the following information in your own words:
- This book is a lament presented in the form of an acrostic poem based on the Hebrew alphabet—that is, it is written in sets of twenty-two verses, each starting with a different letter of the Hebrew alphabet, which also has twenty-two letters. In Hebrew, the lines were written in alphabetical order, although that is not evident in the English translation. The poems were probably written in that form because they were community prayers, and matching them to the alphabet made them easier for people to remember.

4. Engage the students in a discussion about why the Book of Lamentations is included in the Bible. Ask if they can think of other examples where grief, frustration, and anger are expressed in prayer, like they are in the laments.

5. Invite the students to remember a time when they felt angry with God, abandoned, or generally sad about the way things were. Direct them to write a lament expressing those feelings as if they were going through the experience right now. Encourage them to capture the language and style they see in Lamentations. Challenge them to form their lament as an acrostic poem.

6. Call the students to share aspects of their completed laments or to comment on the process of writing them.

Music and Grieving
Lamentations
"Growing Through Loss," near the end of Lamentations, CYB

The students use the laments of Israel to help them reflect on music's power to express grief and bring healing.

1. After reading some selected passages about loss from Lamentations, ask a student to read the article "Growing Through Loss" from the *CYB*.

2. As homework for the next class, instruct the students each to find a piece of music that is in the style of a lament or sounds like a lament. The music may have sorrowful lyrics, use a grieving theme, or express the student's own sadness. Have the students write down some of the lyrics or a description of the music, and then reflect in writing on the particular way that the music helps people to communicate sorrow. Also request that they bring in a recording of the music.

3. At the next class, play some of the pieces the students bring in. Lead a discussion about ways that people grieve and heal from sorrow.

Baruch

Culture Clash

Modern Value Conflicts
Baruch, chapter 4
"Stand Up!" Bar 4.17–19, CYB

Using a television show as an example of modern U.S. values, the students evaluate the complementarity and tension between U.S. and Christian values.

1. To prepare for this activity, tape a TV show that deals with U.S. values and bring the tape to class (see step 3).

2. To begin this activity, call several students to take turns reading Bar 4.1–29 aloud to the class. Ask another student to read the article "Stand Up!" from the *CYB*.

Handout **Bar–A**

3. Pass out copies of handout Bar–A, "Christianity and the Media." Go over the handout instructions with the class. Help the students suggest important Christian values, and lead the class to vote for the most important five. Then show the tape of a TV show that you have brought in, and give the students time to complete the handout.

4. After the students have completed the handout, allow them to share the results from their charts, and invite further observations about the media and Christian values. Ask questions about television and value formation, challenging the students to think about how they might teach values and handle television with their own kids someday.

Variation. Instead of showing a tape of a TV show, ask the students to take their handout home, select a TV show and watch it, and complete the handout. Give the students a week to complete the assignment, then gather the class to discuss the students' findings.

··············► Christianity and the Media

Baruch shows that the Jews experienced some conflicts between their own beliefs and the values that they encountered in other cultures while in exile. U.S. Christians sometimes find their beliefs supported by their culture and other times find their values in opposition to their culture. As a class, choose five values that you believe are central to Christianity and list them in the chart below. Then watch a television drama or situation comedy to see how one aspect of U.S. culture reflects U.S. values. Name and describe the show in the spaces provided above the chart, assess the TV show's treatment of each listed Christian value by marking the appropriate box in the chart, and write a short reflection about the show in the space provided below the chart.

Name of TV show:

Date and time watched:

Short plot summary:

Five important Christian values	Treatment of the five important Christian values in the TV show				
	Strongly supported	Supported	Treated neutrally or not addressed	Opposed	Strongly opposed
1.					
2.					
3.					
4.					
5.					

Overall, to what extent did this show support or oppose Christian values? Why?

Ezekiel

Ezekiel's Visions

The Living Creature Sketch
Ezekiel, chapter 1

This activity invites the student to sketch living creatures in order to gain a sense of creation's awe inspiring presence.

1. Divide the class into small groups and give each group a large sheet of paper. Each group should then read Ezek 1.1–21 and use colored markers or pencils to draw the living creatures described in the passage.

2. Invite the groups to share their posters with one another. Allow the class to vote on the poster that most closely resembles the description. Call a student to read Ezek 1.22–28 aloud, and then ask the students to consider how they might react if confronted with such a sight.

Multimedia Visions
Ezekiel, chapters 1–3, 8–11, 40, 43, 47

The students acquire an understanding of the power of Ezekiel's visions by presenting some of those visions to their peers using music and visual props.

1. Divide the class into four groups and assign each group one of these passages:
- Ezek 1.4—3.15
- Ezekiel, chapters 8–11
- Ezekiel, chapters 40, 43
- Ezek 47.1–12

Direct the students to take turns reading their passage in their group. Also present the following instructions in your own words:
- The groups will then prepare to give multimedia presentations of the visions presented in their passages. Each group is to present its vision to the class by summarizing it or reading parts of it, with some background music and some sort of visual aid to help make it come alive. It may add other creative twists such as skits, or interactive activities that involve the rest of the class. It should also submit a short paragraph that explains why it chose to present the vision as it did.

Give the groups one or more days to prepare their presentations and explanations.

2. After the presentations, discuss the Bible passages and the students' interpretations of them.

Ezekiel's Symbolic Actions

Modern Street Theater
Ezekiel, chapters 4–5, 12, 24
"Street Theater," Ezek 4.1—5.4, CYB

This activity invites the students to pattern an assessment of current problems after Ezekiel's symbolic actions, by creating symbolic actions of their own for the modern day.

1. Introduce the kinds of symbolic actions that Ezekiel performed, by reading the article "Street Theater" from the *CYB*. Select some of the following Scripture passages for the students to read aloud:
- Ezek 4.1–3
- Ezek 4.4–17
- Ezekiel, chapter 5
- Ezek 12.1–6
- Ezek 24.15–17

Explain the significance of the actions in those passages by referring to the footnotes in a study edition of the Bible or by consulting a biblical commentary (see appendix A).

2. Divide the class into small groups. Ask the groups each to choose a modern political or social problem that concerns them. Have them create a symbolic action that describes the problem itself or the possible consequences if the situation does not improve. Note that they should emphasize gestures over speaking and use few props.

3. After each group has performed its action, allow the other students to guess what problem the group is addressing. Then invite the group to explain why it chose to portray the problem as it did. Discuss any insights that arise.

4. When all the groups have performed and discussed their actions, urge the students to think about how they could most successfully convey their group's message of concern today. Note that in Ezekiel's day, many of the people to whom the prophet was speaking actually passed by him and saw his street theater, whereas today, people generally pick up messages in very different ways. Ask, "How might God suggest that a modern Ezekiel convey a message like the one that concerns your group?"

Imaging Jealousy
Ezekiel, chapter 8

Drawing what comes to mind when Ezekiel describes the image of jealousy helps the students refine their understanding of jealousy.

1. Prepare for this activity by asking the students to bring in a collection of junk like old tools, utensils, small appliances, clothing, packing materials, and so on. Contribute to the collection yourself, and also supply heavy wire and duct tape.

2. Call a student to read Ezek 8.1–6. Distribute blank paper and instruct the students each to sketch a sculpture that represents what they think Ezekiel's image of jealousy would look like. Have them explain their image on the back of the paper.

3. Invite the students to share their sketches and thoughts about jealousy. Briefly discuss the nature of jealousy.

4. Help the class choose one of the students' sketches, create a composite of several sketches, or come up with an entirely new idea, and create a jealousy sculpture using the materials provided by the students and you. Display the completed sculpture in the room or elsewhere in the school, perhaps with an appropriate label.

Fashion

The activity "Exegetical Tools: Historical Criticism and the Biblical Dictionary—the Prophets' World," on pages 147–148 of this manual, includes an exploration of fashion as it is presented in Ezekiel, chapter 16.

Oracles of Restoration

Prayer Styles:
Guided Imagery—Entering the Scene of the Dry Bones
Ezekiel, chapter 37
"Bone Dry," Ezekiel, chapter 37, CYB

Imagining themselves in the scene of Ezekiel's dry bones helps the students to see how God is calling them to life.

1. Ask a student to read the article "Bone Dry" from the *CYB*.

2. Offer the following explanation in your own words:
- One way to meditate on the Bible is to imagine oneself in a biblical scene. I would like to guide you through an experience of that prayer form as I read Ezek 37.1–14. I will read the passage slowly twice, and I will ask you to imagine yourself first as Ezekiel and then as one of the skeletons that is brought to life. As I read, close your eyes and use your imagination to create the scene, surrounding yourself with the sights and smells and other things that I tell about. At the end, I will give you a few moments of quiet time to think and write about your experience.

3. Proceed with the guided imagery, reminding the students to imagine themselves as Ezekiel during the first reading and as a skeleton during the second. To prepare them for the second reading, ask the students to bring to mind some aspect of their situation that feels lifeless right now: a relationship, a school or extracurricular activity, or whatever. As the bones come to life, invite the students to imagine life coming into that area of their situation as well. Make sure to read the passage slowly and to pause at appropriate intervals to allow the students time to imagine the scene. Give them a few moments at the end to process the meditation, as well as some time to write about it.

4. Invite the students to share their experience of imagining themselves in a biblical scene and any insights they gained, if they feel comfortable doing so.

Visions of the Temple

Biblical Measurements
Ezekiel, chapter 40

This activity asks the students to look up the modern equivalents of biblical measurements for weight, capacity, and length and then to find everyday objects that correspond to those units.

1. Call a student to read Ezek 40.1–16. Ask the students to identify unfamiliar units of measure in that passage, notably a long cubit, a cubit, and a handbreadth in verse 5.

2. Explain that a long cubit is one cubit plus one handbreadth, a cubit is the length of a person's arm from the tip of the middle finger to the elbow, and a handbreadth is the width of four fingers. Direct several students to use those units to measure an object in your room, such as the chalkboard or your desk. Speculate about some of the accuracy issues those units of measure may have raised.

3. Divide the class into six groups and assign two groups to each of the categories of Hebrew measurements listed below.
- *Length.* cubit, span, handbreadth, finger
- *Liquid capacity.* measure or cor, bath, hin, kab, log
- *Weight.* talent, mina, shekel
Tell the groups each to look up their assigned units of measure in one of these resources:
- a standard dictionary
- *The New Oxford Annotated Bible with the Apocryphal/Deuterocanonical Books,* new revised standard version, edited by Bruce M. Metzger and Roland E. Murphy (New York: Oxford University Press, 1994), pages 424 to 425
- a biblical dictionary (see appendix A), under the term "weights and measurements"
- a list of the assigned measurements that you have created for them
Be aware that all sources may not concur on the measurements, and ask the students to list the sources they used.

4. Instruct the students to find everyday objects at home that correspond to the units of measure assigned to their group. You might provide examples such as these: a handbreadth is about the height of a standard egg carton, a hin is about a gallon of milk, and a mina is equivalent to five sticks of butter. Suggest that the students be creative yet find items that their peers will recognize. Direct them to bring the objects, or sketches or photos of them, to the next class.

5. At the next class, give the groups each a strip of poster board and ask them to write on it the equivalency for their item: for example, 1 hin = 1 gallon. Then call the groups to share their items and labels, and invite the students to take some measurements with the units they have been studying.

Daniel

Fashion and Animals

The activity "Exegetical Tools: Historical Criticism and the Biblical Dictionary—the Prophets' World," on pages 147–148 of this manual, includes an exploration of fashion and animals as they are presented in Daniel, chapter 3.

Daniel at the Babylonian Court

Exegetical Tools: The Concordance and Dreams
Daniel, chapter 4

Nebuchadnezzar's second dream in Daniel invites the students to find examples of the way dreams appear throughout the Bible and to discuss God's use of dreams to communicate with human beings.

1. Ask several students to take turns reading Daniel, chapter 4, aloud. Discuss the dream described in that chapter, and Daniel's interpretation of it.

2. If necessary, explain or review how to use a concordance (refer to the activity "Exegetical Tools: The Concordance and Wisdom Themes," on pages 111–112 of this manual, for a discussion of that tool). Then divide the class into four groups and provide each group with a concordance or information from the relevant pages of a concordance. Direct the students to look up "dream," and also other forms of the word, such as "dreamed."

3. Assign each group one of the following areas of the Bible:
- Genesis, chapters 1–20
- Genesis, chapters 28–32
- Genesis, chapters 37–50
- Matthew, chapters 1–2

Ask the groups to look through their assigned area of the Bible, and locate and read the passages that speak of dreams. Tell the groups to prepare to share with the rest of the class what they find out about God's use of dreams.

4. Invite the groups to present their findings. Ask the students if they have learned anything from their own dream life. Pose the question, "Could God have spoken to you through a dream?"

Variation. Assign the students to keep a dream journal for a week or two, and to record in it as much as they can remember about their dreams. After they awaken from each dream, they should write a paragraph or two about what it might mean, what the symbols in it could be pointing to, and how God might be speaking to them through it. Refer the students to books on

Christian interpretations of dreams, such as the ones listed below, or include information from such books in an in-class discussion.
- *God, Dreams, and Revelation: A Christian Interpretation of Dreams,* by Morton T. Kelsey (Minneapolis: Augsburg, 1991)
- *The Unconscious Christian: Images of God in Dreams,* by James A. Hall (New York: Paulist Press, 1993)

Daniel Theater
Daniel, chapters 3, 5–6

Several interesting stories in the Book of Daniel lend themselves to skits that the students do as an overview of that book.

   1. Divide the class into three groups in proportion to the number of characters listed for each passage below. Assign each group one of these passages. Direct the groups to prepare a skit based on their passage and featuring the characters listed for it.
- *Daniel, chapter 3.* two narrators, a herald, Chaldeans, Nebuchadnezzar, Shadrach, Meshach, Abednego, Azariah, and counselors
- *Daniel, chapter 5.* two narrators, a human hand, King Belshazzar, the king's wise men, the queen, and Daniel
- *Daniel, chapter 6.* two narrators, presidents and satraps, Daniel, and King Darius (You may want to refer the students to a Bible dictionary for a definition of the term *satraps.*)

   2. After the students have performed their skits, ask them to identify similarities between the stories. Discuss these questions:
- What messages do the stories give about God, the Persian rulers, and devout Jews?
- How might the stories give hope to Jews experiencing persecution?

Encountering God in Highs and Lows
Daniel, chapter 4
"King Nebuchadnezzar's Conversion," Daniel, chapter 4, CYB

Though tough times such as those experienced by Nebuchadnezzar are often graced by a sense of God's closeness, God is just as close in moments of joy and goodness. This activity encourages the students to write about both types of experiences.

   1. Call several students to read Daniel, chapter 4, aloud to the class, and give some relevant background about Nebuchadnezzar. Invite another student to read the article "King Nebuchadnezzar's Conversion" from the *CYB.*

   2. Say something such as this to the students:
- Most of us have experienced a deeper need for God during tough times. God is always with us, in joyful times and in difficult moments. I want you to write about two experiences of God's presence in your life, one in a difficult time and one in a positive time.

Give the students examples of such experiences and help expand their sense of God's presence beyond church and personal prayer. Then assign a day for their reflections to be brought to class.

3. On the day that the reflections are due, ask the students to think of three or more adjectives that describe their experience of God. Depending on the comfort level of the class, either invite the students to share something about their experiences or call them to volunteer one adjective they associate with the presence of God. Ask follow-up questions when appropriate to help them reflect more deeply.

4. Close by thanking the students for their witnessing. Point out that God is present to us in many ways, and that reflecting on our experiences of God's presence makes us more attentive to that presence.

Daniel's Visions

Exegetical Tools:
Form Criticism and the Biblical Commentary
Daniel, chapters 7–12
"Apocalyptic Literature," Daniel, chapters 7–10, CYB

This activity gives the students practice in using a biblical commentary and teaches them about apocalyptic literature, using some of the symbolism in the Book of Daniel.

1. Invite a student to read aloud the article "Apocalyptic Literature" from the *CYB*.

2. If necessary, introduce or review the research process called form criticism (see the activity "Exegetical Tools: Form Criticism—the Saga," on page 59 of this manual, for background). Then divide the class into small groups and assign each group one or more chapters from Daniel, chapters 7–12. Direct the groups each to list the symbols they find in their assigned passage.

3. Guide the groups in using a biblical commentary to understand the symbols they have identified (see appendix A for recommended biblical commentaries). Suggest that they jot notes as they research the symbols, and invite them to share their findings when they are all done.

Resurrection Meaning
Daniel, chapter 12
"Resurrection," Dan 12.1–3, CYB

Resurrection is rarely mentioned in the Old Testament. Daniel's reference to it is an opportunity for the students to reflect on its meaning.

1. Ask one student to read Dan 12.1–3 and another to read the article "Resurrection" from the *CYB*. Point out that much of the Old Testament does not speak of resurrection.

2. Direct the students each to create a word map to begin thinking about the significance of life after death. They should write the word "resurrection" in the center of a piece of paper and then jot around it any other words they associate with it.

3. Encourage the students to use that brainstorming to formulate a brief answer to the question, "How does belief in resurrection affect the way I think about this life and about death?" After giving them several minutes to write about that, tell them to discuss their answer with another student.

4. Conclude by conducting a class discussion about resurrection.

Hosea

Hosea's Marriage

Personal Metaphors
Hosea, chapter 1
Introduction to Hosea, CYB

The metaphor of the prophet Hosea's marriage standing for God's relationship with Israel invites the students to think of experiences from their own lives that help them understand God.

1. Call two students to read Hosea, chapter 1, aloud to the class. Have another student read the introduction to Hosea from the *CYB.*

2. Say something such as this to the students:
   - God's request that Hosea use his marriage as a symbol of God's relationship with Israel may seem unusual, but such a use of metaphor and symbolism is common. In fact, relying on symbolism and metaphor is the only way that human beings can discuss God. We must use familiar images and terms to talk about the God we cannot see.
Help the students identify some symbols and metaphors in everyday and religious discourse, in order to be sure they understand the terms.

3. Tell the students to think of a metaphor that gives them some insight about their relationship with God. Have them describe that metaphor in writing or by illustration.

4. Invite the students to share their metaphors as they feel comfortable. Discuss the many different ways that a relationship with God can be imagined.

The Message of Hosea

Hosea Cards
Hosea, chapters 11, 14

By writing cards of invitation, forgiveness, and encouragement, the students become familiar with the gentle love and prodding of the prophet Hosea.

1. Divide the class into four groups. Assign each group one of the following passages:
- Hos 11.1–4
- Hos 14.1–2

- Hos 14.4–7
- Hos 14.8–9

Instruct the groups each to create a greeting card using the language and message of their passage from Hosea. Give each group a large piece of paper for its card, so that all the students in the group can be involved in the design and so that others in the class will be able to see the finished product easily when it is displayed. Also provide colored markers or pencils and other art supplies needed for this work.

2. Invite the groups to share their finished cards with the class and discuss each card's message.

Joel

Repent and Be Saved

A Lenten Project
Joel, chapter 2
"Ash Wednesday," Joel 2.12–18, CYB

A class decision to contribute financially to a charitable organization helps the students integrate prayer, fasting, and almsgiving during Lent.

1. Request one student to read Joel 2.12–18 aloud and another to read the article "Ash Wednesday" from the *CYB*. Say something such as this to the students:
   - Catholics are invited every year to pray, fast, and give alms during Lent. It is important to see that the three activities are connected.
   - Jesus echoes the message of the prophets in saying that those with plenty are responsible for the suffering of those who are oppressed. Thus, we are called to give alms to people who are poor.
   - Fasting challenges us to detach ourselves from possessions and become more generous with our gifts.
   - Prayer sustains us while we fast and prompts us to be selfless.

2. Invite the class to participate in a Lenten project that involves making a contribution to a charity. Assign the class to research charitable organizations and select one.
   Then provide the following instructions in your own words.
   - Think of something that prevents you from being generous with time or money—such as buying fast food, going to movies, watching television, or shopping for clothes—and fast from that activity at some level throughout Lent. Calculate how much money or time you will save through that fasting, and give that amount of money or time to the charitable organization the class chose. Keep a prayer and reflection journal throughout the experience.

3. Collect the students' money on a regular basis throughout Lent, and make regular contributions to the charity chosen by the class. Also help the students carry out their commitments of time to the charity. During Holy Week, revisit Joel, chapter 2, in a short prayer service that honors the spiritual growth of the students as well as the human need for continued conversion. Invite the students to share reflections about the process of giving.

Variations. Instead of selecting a class charity and arranging for the students to give it their time or money in steps 2 and 3, suggest that each student individually identify some need and address it. For example, they might know a neighbor, family member, friend, or organization that could use their generous help for a period of time. This activity may not fall during the season of Lent. If it does not, consider adapting it for the current time.

175

Amos

Amos's Call

The activity "God's Call," on pages 148–149 of this manual, includes God's call to Amos, which is described in Amos, chapter 3.

Amos's Condemnation

Status-of-Society Images
Amos, chapters 7–9

Just as God showed Amos the health of his society through images, the students present an image that captures a positive or negative aspect of their society.

    1. Invite several students to read Am 7.1–9; 8.1–3; 9.1–4 aloud to the class. Help the students understand the significance of the various visions described in those passages.

    2. For homework, tell the students to think of an image that captures an element of their society today. Allow them to bring in an object from home that expresses their insights or to illustrate the image on a piece of paper.

    3. When the students have finished their homework, give them time in class to share and explain their objects or pictures, and note some of their observations on the board. Ask them, "What is helpful about the use of images in this exercise and in the Book of Amos?"

    Variation. In step 2, arrange a field trip to an art show or gallery or museum and direct the students to choose from the collection there a work of art that captures an element of their society today. Instruct the students to photograph the work (with permission and with no flash), sketch it, or purchase a postcard or print of it. Arrange for the class to discuss the objects in a meeting room at the facility or later in the classroom.

Power Simulation: Amos
Amos, chapter 8
"Stand Up and Be Counted!" Am 8.4–8, CYB

A classroom simulation of the power struggle presented in Amos, chapter 8, stimulates a discussion about the need for those who are powerful to act on behalf of those who are powerless.

Adapt the activity "Power Simulation: Micah," on page 181 of this manual, for use with Amos, chapter 8, and the article "Stand Up and Be Counted!"

Standing Up for the Poor
Amos, chapter 8
"Stand Up and Be Counted!" Am 8.4–8, CYB

This activity allows the students, in the presence of a guest lecturer, to reflect on and voice some of their feelings, questions, and struggles about those who are poor.

1. Invite an advocate and worker for people who are poor to speak to the class. Begin the activity by telling the students to read Am 8.4–8 and the *CYB* article "Stand Up and Be Counted!" to themselves. Then ask the guest to share experiences, learnings, struggles, joys, and so on. Encourage the students to ask questions.

2. Assign for homework a one-page reflection addressing the following questions:
    - What was your reaction to the speaker?
    - Which story, statement, or insight from the speaker made a strong impression on you? Why?
    - What about this presentation and discussion challenged you?

3. Invite the students to share their reflections in the next class.

Variations. Find out from the speaker if there is some kind of project the class can do to help the people or organization that the speaker represents. Help the class carry out such a project, ensuring that the students feel ownership of the work they do on behalf of those who are poor.
Arrange a field trip to a local service agency or to a local service historical site like the Hull House in Chicago.

P
R
O
P
H
E
T
S

Obadiah

Sin and Vengeance

The Consequences of Sin
Obadiah
"What Goes Around," Obadiah, verse 15, CYB

The Book of Obadiah invites the students to discuss the consequences of sinning and the issue of vengeance.

1. Prepare for this activity by finding a news story, clip from a recent movie, or song that talks about vengeance (see step 4).

2. Begin this activity by asking several students to take turns reading the Book of Obadiah aloud. Then invite one student to read the article "What Goes Around" from the *CYB*.

3. Designate one place in the classroom "Agree" and another place "Disagree." Then ask the students each to move to the spot that reflects their opinion about this statement: "What goes around comes around." While the students remain in the place they have chosen, conduct an informal debate. Invite the students to give concrete examples that support their view of the statement. Acting as a devil's advocate, challenge the students in order to help them refine their positions. Allow them to change places if they wish.

4. Direct the students to return to their seats, and begin a discussion of the issue of vengeance by providing the news story, movie clip, or song that you found. Encourage the students to talk about whether vengeance is an acceptable attitude in modern culture. Ask them if it is ever acceptable to take revenge on someone who has sinned, and if so, when. Allow the students to discuss and debate those questions.

Ask the students if they know or can find Bible passages that state Jesus' opinion about treating those who have wronged us. They might suggest these:
- Mt 5.21–26
- Mt 5.43–48
- Mt 18.23–35
- Lk 6.27–36
- Lk 15.11–32
- Lk 23.34
- Jn 8.1–11

Continue the discussion, incorporating Jesus' perspective.

5. Conclude by saying something such as this:
- Though sin sometimes appears to have no visible punishment, it always damages the sinner internally. Though the desire for revenge may seem natural, Jesus is clear that forgiveness is the way to approach someone who wrongs us. God alone distributes justice for human actions.

178

Jonah

Jonah and the Fish

Service Learning: Jonah and Other Children's Stories
Jonah and other passages

The story of Jonah is one of the many biblical stories that can easily be told at a child's level. This activity gives the students the opportunity to make short biblical storybooks to share with younger children.

1. In preparation for this activity, contact a local Catholic grade school or parish religious education coordinator. Find a K–3 teacher who includes Bible stories in his or her teaching and is interested in helping your class with a service learning project. Ask the teacher to select some biblical stories that your students can turn into books and then read with the younger children.

Direct the students to read the Book of Jonah at home. Also ask the students to bring in art supplies, or provide those yourself. Collect several examples of simple children's books to share with the students.

2. Begin this activity by discussing the main parts of the story of Jonah with the students. Share the examples of children's books that you brought in, pointing out the simple language and concepts as well as the pictures. Talk about the elementary school class you will be working with and discuss its needs and abilities. Ask students who have young brothers and sisters to contribute insights and ideas. Brainstorm with the students about how the Book of Jonah might be presented as a children's book.

3. Share the list of biblical stories from the grade-school teacher and give every student a story. Distribute blank paper to the students and allow them to begin their stories in class, giving them adequate time at home to complete their writing. Challenge them to add illustrations and design elements to enhance their stories.

4. At a later date, arrange for the students to take a field trip to read their stories one-on-one or in small groups with the younger students. Give the books as gifts to the children's class.

5. Afterward, ask the students to write a short reflection about the process of writing the stories and reading them with the children. During class, allow the students to share their experiences of service.

Variations. If time does not allow for the process of writing and illustrating stories, arrange for the students to go to an elementary class and read selected Bible stories that have already been published.

Help the students to create web pages with their stories, or to scan their finished books and put them in web pages.

Jonah and the Assyrians

Our Perception of Foreign Nations
Jonah

This activity helps the students see that Jonah's lack of faith in the Assyrians is similar to modern people's biased views of people of other countries.

1. Prepare for this activity by obtaining enough world maps or globes for several small groups to use, one large map for the class to refer to, and several pads of self-stick notes.

2. Begin this activity by calling several students to take turns reading the Book of Jonah aloud to the class. Discuss the story, focusing on Jonah's attitude toward the people of Nineveh.

3. Divide the class into small groups. Allow each group to look at one of the world maps or globes you have obtained. Hang the large map in the front of the class. Give the groups each five self-stick notes and ask them to write on each note an assumption about another country or its people commonly shared by people in the United States.

After a short period of time, call a spokesperson from each group to come up to the large map and stick the group's notes onto the appropriate countries while reading the notes out loud. Ask follow-up questions about the labels, inviting the students to speculate about the origins of the assumptions presented.

4. When all the groups have shared their labels, discuss the reasons for stereotypes and the dangers of biases. Note that the people of Nineveh were more responsive to God than was God's prophet Jonah. Invite the students to volunteer some positive characteristics for several of the countries that were given negative labels on the map. Then ask the students to look at stereotypes about cultural groups in their own country and to suggest some ways to improve those stereotypes.

Micah

The Plea for Conversion

Power Simulation: Micah
Micah, chapter 3

A classroom simulation of the power struggle presented in Mic 3.5 stimulates a discussion about the need for those who are powerful to act on behalf of those who are powerless.

1. Prepare two items for this exercise:
- Develop a simulation that is similar to the story in Mic 3.5, in which the powerful claim to know what the powerless need. For instance, you, the powerful teacher, could decide that the powerless students do not need any type of review or guidance for a test.
- Gather several news articles about powerful people making decisions for vulnerable people, and make enough copies of them for all the students.

2. Start this exercise with the prepared simulation and a related discussion. For example, allow the students to voice their frustrations as you play the role of the powerful teacher who knows better what they need than they do themselves. Note the students' vulnerability in this situation and the way you have taken advantage of it. Ask them to give examples of similarly abusive situations in society.

3. Call a student to read Mic 3.5, and pass out the copies of news articles you have prepared. Direct the students to read the articles and to discuss them, first in small groups and then with the rest of the class. Ask, "What changes might Micah suggest in the contemporary situations covered by the articles?"

Micah's Call for a Return to God
Micah, chapter 4

Using gesture and mime, the students express the power of Micah's words and his call for repentance.

1. Have the students read Mic 4.1–4 together. Ask them to notice the strong verbs and images in the writing.

2. Divide the class into groups of four or five. Instruct the groups each to create a presentation of the passage using gesture and mime. Explain that the presentation should be choreographed and done with a narrator. Encourage sweeping arm movements and motion. Allow instrumental music to be played in the background. (Either supply music for the presentations or, if the gestures

181

and mimes are presented in the next class session, invite the students to bring in music to accompany their work.)

3. Invite the groups to share their completed presentations with the class. Allow discussion to arise from the gestures and mimes.

Turning Swords into Plowshares
Micah, chapter 4

This activity calls the students to portray visually the presence of swords and plowshares in our modern world.

1. Ask several students to read Mic 4.1–7 aloud.

2. Divide the class into groups of three or four, and give each group a piece of poster board or butcher paper, an assortment of old magazines and newspapers, scissors, glue, and other art supplies. Instruct the groups each to make a collage on the swords-and-plowshares theme. Suggest that they paste violent "sword" pictures and headlines on one side of their poster, and peaceful "plowshare" items on the other. Mention that forming their collage into the shapes of a sword and a plowshare is one way to capture a symbolic image.

3. When the groups are done, discuss with them their choices of pictures, headlines, and articles for each side of their poster. Then display the posters in the classroom.

PROPHETS

Nahum

Confusing God Imagery

Our Personal God Image
Nahum, chapter 2
"Images of God," Nahum 2.10—3.3, CYB

Nahum's contradictory descriptions of God invite the students to reflect on their own conflicting images of God.

1. Ask several students to take turns reading excerpts from Nahum, chapter 2, and another student to read the article "Images of God" from the *CYB*. Discuss both the violent and reassuring images of God portrayed in the Scripture passage, and review how those contrasting images are explained in the *CYB* article.

2. Tell the students to write "God" in the center of a blank piece of paper. Give them several quiet minutes and have them fill up the page with at least fifteen adjectives that describe their personal experience of God. Explain that those words may reflect either a positive or negative sense of God.

3. Direct the students to identify the three words on their page that best describe God for them. Instruct the students to circle any pairs of words that are antonyms, such as *"close"* and *"distant,"* or *"judging"* and *"forgiving."* Tell them that on the other side of the page, they should write sentences that explain their understanding or experience of those contradictions.

4. When the students are done writing, invite them to share with a partner some insights from this exercise. Then conduct a class discussion about God, honoring and listening to the students' experiences and inviting comments from everyone.

Habakkuk

Perplexing Questions

Our Challenge and God's Response
Habakkuk, chapter 1

The students find numerous examples of violence and trouble in society, to echo Habakkuk's words, and then attempt to formulate God's answers to the questions those examples raise.

1. Ask a student to read Hab 1.1–4 aloud to the class. Say something such as this to the students:
   - If we turn on the local or national news every evening, we can witness "destruction and violence." I am going to ask you to identify issues that trouble you in the same way that the issues of Habakkuk's time upset him.

2. Divide the class into groups and hand each group a piece of poster board or butcher paper, colored markers or pencils, an assortment of recent newspapers and magazines that may be cut up, scissors, and glue. Have the groups write all or part of Hab 1.1–5 on the paper and then cut out headlines that illustrate the passage in the modern day. As they are working, they should focus on any questions for God that come to mind, and write them on a separate sheet of paper.

3. Near the end of the class period or the next day in class, invite the students to share their posters and their questions. Discuss the questions and ask the students to formulate possible responses from God.

Zephaniah

A Message of Woe and Hope

Ideal-World Videos: Zephaniah
Zephaniah, chapter 3

The students use short video skits to portray the way the modern world has accomplished the vision of the ideal time described in Zephaniah, chapter 3.

Adapt the activity "Ideal-World Videos: Zechariah," on page 189 of this manual, for use with Zephaniah, chapter 3.

Signs of Hope: Zephaniah
Zephaniah, chapter 3

Though the vision of an ideal time portrayed in Zephaniah, chapter 3, has not been fully realized, the students provide concrete examples of ways it is being accomplished.

    1. Have several students take turns reading Zephaniah, chapter 3. On the board, list the characteristics of the day described in that passage.

    2. For homework, ask the students each to find a physical object that illustrates one or more of the qualities of that ideal time and to bring it to class. The object may be a newspaper article, a picture, an account of an actual event written by the student, or any other creative item.

    3. Invite the students to share with the class the items that they have found. Discuss those items and other signs of hope witnessed by the students.

Haggai

Building the Community

Building the Catholic Parish: A Modern Call
Haggai, chapter 1
"God at the Center," Haggai, chapter 1, CYB

By making calculations based on an actual parish budget, the students try to understand the modern implications of Haggai's call to contribute to the rebuilding of the Temple.

    1. In preparation for this activity, ask a local parish for a copy of its yearly financial statement. Meet with the business manager to discuss the way that the spending breaks down, so that you can pass that information on accurately to the students. Find out the number of families in the parish, the various sources of income for the parish, the average donation per household, and other pertinent information. With permission, make copies of the financial statement for the students or compile the salient data for them on your own. Invite the business manager to visit the classroom as an expert when you are doing this activity.

    2. Begin this activity by asking two students to take turns reading Haggai, chapter 1, aloud. Then invite another student to read the article "God at the Center" from the *CYB* to the class. Discuss the people's sense that they cannot afford to contribute more to the Temple, and God's response. Note the similarity between that biblical outlook and the perspective that some Catholics have toward their own parishes today. If a parish business manager is present, invite her or him to share insights on that.

    3. Distribute copies of the financial statement you have obtained or the financial data you have compiled. Direct the students each to create two pie charts. One should reflect the parish income, and the other the parish expenses.

    When the students have finished their charts, ask them to calculate what they think would be the average donation per household; then match their calculations with the information given to you by the business manager. Discuss the process of tithing and help the students speculate about the percentage of income each household is contributing.

    4. Instruct the students to write a short reflection about the realities of running a parish and their sense of the worth of the parish services. Then discuss with the students related issues that arise from their reflections, such as the value of parish life and the importance of sharing financially with the community.

5. Have the students calculate a tithe for their own weekly income. Ask if they would be willing to commit that much money to their church. Tell them to write their reflections about that and their reasons for giving or not giving to their church. Assure them that they need not mention figures or describe their income in their reflection.

Zechariah

Different Ways of Seeing Things

Picturing Zechariah's Visions
Zechariah, chapters 1–6

This activity invites the students to reflect on the visions of Zechariah by portraying them in art.

1. Using a Bible commentary (see appendix A), give background on Zechariah—who he is, why he is considered a prophet, who he is addressing, and so on. Then divide the class into eight groups, assign each group a different vision of Zechariah, and instruct one student from each group to read the vision aloud for the others in the group. The passages for the eight visions are as follows:
- Zech 1.7–17
- Zech 1.18–21
- Zech 2.1–5
- Zechariah, chapter 3
- Zechariah, chapter 4
- Zech 5.1–4
- Zech 5.5–11
- Zech 6.1–8

2. Allow the groups each to discuss the possible meaning of their assigned vision. Provide information from a biblical commentary to aid their discussion.

3. Give each student a sheet of blank paper and colored markers or pencils. Tell the students each to draw the vision their group was assigned as best they understand it. They may either portray the vision literally or incorporate some of the symbolism they have learned.

4. Have the students share their portrayals first with the others in their group and then with the rest of the class. Allow discussion to arise naturally.

Signs of Hope: Zechariah
Zechariah, chapter 8

The students provide concrete examples of ways the world will look when God returns.

Adapt the activity "Signs of Hope: Zephaniah," on page 185 of this manual, for use with Zechariah, chapter 8.

Ideal-World Videos: Zechariah
Zechariah, chapter 8

The students use short video skits to portray the way the modern world will look when God returns.

1. Call several students to take turns reading Zechariah, chapter 8, aloud to the class. Help the students identify characteristics of the ideal world of which the prophet speaks.

2. Allow the students to create groups of four or five. Ensure that each group has access to a video camera, either from the school or from the families of the students.

Direct the groups each to select an area of life that they would like to portray in its actual form and in its ideal form. Provide examples such as the school lunchroom, a carpool, and the school locker room, and let the students propose their own. Ensure that each group selects a different area.

3. Tell the groups each to make a short video portraying the way things really are in their selected area of life, and then the same scene in the ideal world, where all people follow God's will in their attitudes and actions. Allow for the humor that will naturally arise through exaggeration, and so on, in the pieces.

4. Arrange a video day, on which the class presents its videos. Discuss issues that arise from the videos and suggest reasons why the world does not appear more ideal. Many of the ideal portrayals may seem dull and plastic, without conflict. Challenge the students to reflect about whether that really reflects God's influence.

Malachi

The Need for Justice

Charades: Is That Any Way to Treat a Friend . . . or God?
Malachi, chapter 1

Drawing parallels between how they treat their friends and how they treat God allows the students to assess their sense of God as friend.

1. Divide the class into two groups. Assign one group the topic of a relationship with a close friend, and the other group the topic of a relationship with God. Have each group come up with ten adjectives that describe a strong relationship of its assigned type. Then ask the groups each to narrow their adjective list down to a Top 5.

2. Invite each group to perform charades for the other group as an entertaining way of sharing its Top 5 characteristics. Write the adjectives on the board as they are identified, and note similarities and differences.

3. Depending on the type of response by the students, challenge them to think a bit about God as friend, by drawing parallels between human friendship and a relationship with God. These are some examples, and many others will work:
    - What would happen if you were supposed to meet a friend and did not show up? (This is analogous to skipping church.)
    - What might happen to a friendship if you never called? (This is analogous to lapses in prayer.)
    - What would happen if you never did what your friend asked you to? (This is analogous to not following biblical commandments or norms.)

4. Call a student to read Mal 1.6–14. Help the class see that the Israelites took God's friendship for granted as we often do today, treating human beings with greater respect than they treated God. Request the students to discuss in pairs why people tend to let God down. Then conduct a class discussion, summarizing the students' insights.

The Minimum Wage: A Living Wage?
Malachi, chapter 3

This real-life activity shows the students that God's anger may be leveled at those who suggest that the minimum wage can support a family.

1. Ask a student to read Mal 3.1–12. Draw the class's attention to verse 5, in which God judges those who oppress people by giving them unjust wages.

2. Assign the following project to the students, to be done individually:

- Create a family of four—two parents and two children under the age of eighteen.
- Name each person in the family and assign ages to the children.
- Presume that the family lives in your area and that one or both parents have minimum wage jobs. [Tell the students the current minimum wage and help them find realistic jobs for the adults, picking a location for the jobs as well. Use local newspaper ads as a resource.]
- Calculate the parents' usable income for a month, based on the number of hours worked, the wage, taxes, and Social Security deductions. [Assist the class with this; the more that you share about tax brackets, and so on, the more realistic this will be.]
- Calculate a monthly budget for the family, based on its real needs. Include a real rent with a real address (drawn from newspaper, Internet, or other sources,) transportation expenses that reflect the distance between home and work (including car payment, insurance, gas, and tolls, or public transportation fees), child care, health insurance, life insurance, utilities, food, clothes, and other expenses. [The students should consult their parents about food costs and other matters, to get a realistic sense of those expenses.]
- Assess the difference between the wages of the parents and their expenses.
- Decide where to cut the budget if necessary or how to use any surplus money.
- Write a short reflection about the budgeting process.

(Consider putting these instructions in a handout, especially if you are working with young high school students.)

3. Discuss the students' findings in class.

Variation. Invite the students to pursue the issue of a just wage by contacting local groups that lobby for fair wages or by writing local political leaders about that issue.

Gospels
and the Acts of the Apostles

Matthew

Jesus in the Gospels
Matthew, Mark, Luke, John

The students use modern media to explore similarities and differences between the Gospel stories of Jesus' life.

1. Offer the following background information in your own words:
   - The four Gospels are accounts of the life and teachings of Jesus, as interpreted by their different authors.
   - Three of the Gospels—Matthew, Mark, and Luke—follow the same basic outline and present events in the same basic order. Those are called the synoptic Gospels. The fourth Gospel, John, does not follow the same outline and contains long reflections about who Jesus is.
   - Studying the four Gospels together gives us a clearer, deeper picture of Jesus and his ministry than we can gain through any one of the Gospels separately.

2. Divide the class into four groups and assign each group a different one of the four Gospels. Explain that the groups will each read their assigned Gospel and present it to the class using a dramatic medium chosen by the group. Provide the groups with media choices such as these, inviting their additions:
   - videotape
   - photo album
   - newspaper or news magazine
   - book
   - play
   - TV news program or news magazine program, either live or on tape
   - web page
   - dramatic reading

   Tell the students that their presentations are to last about 10 minutes and should involve all members of their group. Encourage them to use props, costumes, music, and so on. Give them a week or more to prepare the presentations; you may want to time their performances to follow your last lesson on the Gospels.

3. Direct the students to take notes while watching the performances of other groups, jotting down the major events and topics covered by the presentations. When all the groups have performed, lead the class in a discussion of the similarities and differences between the Gospel stories, recording major points on the board as they are covered.

Variation. In step 3, rather than allowing the groups each to choose their own medium, help the class to agree on one medium to be used by all the groups. This option might offer an easier comparison of the Gospels.

An Overview of Matthew

Mathematical Equations for Matthew
Matthew

This activity provides an overview of the Gospel of Matthew by challenging the students to solve and create mathematical equations using various facts from the Gospel.

   1. Explain to the students that this activity is designed to familiarize them with the Gospel of Matthew. Mention that it asks them to solve and create some mathematical equations based on the Gospel.

   2. Write the following examples on the board and ask the students to use their Bible to find the answers. Invite the students to share their findings.
■ Add the number of gifts from the Wise Men to the number of parables found in Matthew, chapter 13, and then multiply the result by the number of blind men healed in Mt 20.29–34. $[(3 + 7) \times 2 = 20]$
■ Solve for the number of healings in Mt 9.1–34 to the power of 2, multiplied by the number of people Jesus feeds in Matthew, chapter 15, and divided by the number of people fed in Matthew, chapter 14. $[6^2 \times 4{,}000 \div 5{,}000 = 28.8]$

   3. Divide the class into groups of four. Challenge the groups each to come up with five equations of their own, ranging from very simple to extremely challenging. Give out an index card for each equation, and ask that the equation appear on the front and the answer or explanation on the back.

   4. Invite the groups to exchange their completed equation cards and solve the problems. Afterward, call the students to share some of their initial impressions of Matthew's Gospel.

Responses to the Birth of Jesus

See the activity "Christmas Carols and the Two Infancy Narratives," on page 222 of this manual, for a comparison of the infancy narratives in Matthew and Luke.

Singing Telegrams
Matthew, chapters 1–2

This activity invites the students to work together to compose singing telegrams based on passages in Matthew's infancy narrative.

   1. Direct the students to read Matthew, chapters 1–2. Discuss the role of a messenger in the passage, by noting the different messages delivered by angels.

   2. Form small groups. Instruct the groups each to compose and rehearse a singing telegram based on one of these Scripture passages:
■ Mt 1.18–24   ■ Mt 2.1–15   ■ Mt 2.16–23

Explain that the groups are to include the scriptural dialog and then creatively embellish their telegram in keeping with the mood of the selection. Add that they may tape their telegram or perform it live, and that they may use props or costumes.

3. After the groups have shared their telegrams with the class, discuss their presentations as a way of delving more deeply into the Gospel passages portrayed.

The Visit of the Wise Men
Matthew, chapter 2

An examination of the Wise Men's visit to the baby Jesus helps the students to reflect on the gifts that God has given them.

1. Ask a student to read Mt 2.1–12 aloud. Discuss the significance of that story in Matthew's infancy narrative. The students might use a biblical commentary to explore the symbolism of the Wise Men's gifts (see appendix A for recommended commentaries; see the activity "Exegetical Tools: Form Criticism and the Biblical Commentary," on page 171 of this manual, for an example of how to use biblical commentaries).

2. For the next class, have the students each bring three objects that symbolize the personal gifts that God has given them to make the world a better place. For example, a rock could symbolize a person's strength or loyalty, a lightbulb might symbolize cheerfulness or optimism, and eyeglasses could symbolize insight or intuitiveness.

3. At the next class, create a prayerful atmosphere and invite the students to present and discuss their symbols. Point out that the birth of Jesus prompted the Wise Men to share their gifts. Request the students to identify what inspires them to share their own gifts.

Epiphany Celebrations
Matthew, chapter 2
"Jesus Brought the Good News of Salvation to People of All Races!"
 Mt 2.1–12, CYB

Studying the biblical visit of the Wise Men allows the students to explore the various ways that the Epiphany is celebrated around the world.

1. Ask one student to read Mt 2.1–12 aloud to the class and another to read the article "Jesus Brought the Good News of Salvation to People of All Races!" from the *CYB*. Call the students to share the ways that Epiphany is celebrated in their own families. Inquire if anyone knows how Epiphany is celebrated in other cultures or regions of the world.

2. Divide the class into several groups and direct them each to research a different culture and its celebration of Epiphany. Note that good information for such a search is available on the Internet and also may be found in a school

media center or community library. Also mention that France, Italy, Greece, and Latin American countries have special practices associated with Epiphany.

Assign the groups to bring an element of their researched celebration into the classroom through food, costume, story, or other means, and to use that as a way to share their research.

3. Set aside ample class time to enjoy the fruits of the students' research, and conclude with discussion as appropriate.

Jesus' Emergence into Public Life

Visual Baptism Presentations
Matthew, chapter 3

This exercise allows the students to present creative interpretations of Matthew, chapter 3, and compare their results.

1. Direct the students to read Matthew, chapter 3, to themselves. Urge them to be attentive to any aspects of the story that stand out for them. Consider suggesting that they read it a few times to ensure that they understand the entire story.

2. As a homework assignment, instruct the students to present the story from the reading in a visual way with an artistic medium, such as blocks, clay, collage, sand, beads, wood, or metal. Encourage them to give shape, form, and color to the story as a whole or to the part that emerged for them in a special way. Encourage the students to trust their intuition as ideas emerge.

3. Invite the students to share their completed artistic interpretations and explain their choice of medium. Note how the various readings of the passage enrich everyone's understanding.

The Temptation in the Desert
Matthew, chapter 4
"Jesus' Temptations, My Temptations," Mt 4.1–11, CYB

This exercise helps the students make connections between the temptations Jesus faced in the desert and the temptations that they face in their own lives.

1. Ask a student to read Mt 4.1–11 aloud. Invite the students to suggest the lifelong struggles that the temptations in the reading may have symbolized for Jesus. Then have a student read the article "Jesus' Temptations, My Temptations" from the *CYB,* and discuss that interpretation of the passage.

2. Prompt the students to propose a variety of everyday situations that might present temptations to teenagers. Encourage them to suggest scenarios from school, activities, social life, work, and family life.

3. Divide the class into small groups and assign each group one of the proposed situations. Tell the groups each to create and perform a skit in which a young person or persons face three temptations. Explain that just as Jesus drew on the Scriptures as a defense against temptation, the teen or teens in the skit should find a way to resist temptation.

4. After the skits have been performed, discuss the themes that arise from them. With the students, examine the nature of temptation and resistance as well as the role that those experiences play in one's spiritual life.

The Sermon on the Mount

Tunes from the Sermon on the Mount
Matthew, chapters 5–7

The students take sayings from the Sermon on the Mount and put them to the tunes of popular songs, to help themselves remember messages from the Gospels.

1. Ask several students to read the Sermon on the Mount, Mt 5.1—7.27, out loud.

2. Form pairs, and instruct the pairs each to pick from the reading five to seven sayings that seem particularly important in living out the values of Jesus.
Direct the pairs to put their sayings to music. Explain that they are to select a popular song whose tune will showcase the verses. Note that they should feel free to adapt the biblical language to fit with the melody as long as they are faithful to the meaning of the scripture. Mention that the song they create must include a refrain that everyone can sing along with.

3. Invite the pairs to share their songs with the class. Ask them to discuss their choice of verses and music.

Beatitudes Charades
Matthew, chapter 5

The students play charades with the Beatitudes, challenging one another to find the wisdom taught by those declarations.

1. Prepare for this activity by writing each part of the eight Beatitudes on a separate index card. (One part begins "Blessed are," and the other part begins "for.") Shuffle the cards and put them facedown in a pile. Also write on the board the phrases "Blessed are" and "for," for the students' reference in step 3.

2. Begin this activity by asking the students to read Mt 5.1–12 silently. Give the students a general introduction to the Beatitudes and the Sermon on the Mount.

3. Divide the class into two teams and point out your pile of Beatitude cards. Ask a representative from the first team to choose a card from the pile. Explain that that student should then perform the phrase on the card as a charade for his or her team to guess. Draw the students' attention to the phrases "Blessed are" and "for" on the board, and mention that the performer does not need to include those phrases in the charade.

Once the first team has guessed its phrase, call a representative from the second team to act out a card. Continue in this manner until the teams have gone through the whole pile of cards.

4. Review the Beatitudes in order by pairing up the students who acted out their parts. Discuss the message of the Beatitudes and the personal interpretations made by the students through the charades.

Variation. If you care to introduce some competition, assign a student to record the length of each charade in step 3, and then acknowledge the team with the lowest overall time.

Prayer Styles: Meditative Repetition—the Lord's Prayer
Matthew, chapter 6
"A Lord's Prayer Reflection," Mt 6.5–15, CYB

A meditative recitation of the Lord's Prayer helps the students experience the prayer more personally.

1. Ask two students to take turns reading Mt 6.1–14 aloud to the class. Discuss the simple, direct qualities of the Lord's Prayer in light of Jesus' other teaching about prayer in that passage.

2. Call another student to read the article "A Lord's Prayer Reflection" from the *CYB*. Encourage the students to think about the words of the prayer. Mention that both focusing on the words of the Lord's Prayer and allowing those words to enter our heart in a meditative manner deepen our understanding of the prayer.

3. Create a quiet, relaxed atmosphere for the students. Invite them to close their eyes, and lead them in a repetitive reading of the Lord's Prayer. Read the prayer slowly, allowing the students to repeat each word slowly to themselves. Discourage them from thinking about the words. Tell them to rather let the words wash over them, hearing them with their heart.

4. Encourage the students to share any insights from the prayer or reactions to the style of prayer used. Note that they may enter more deeply into any traditional prayer by using repetitive prayer. Explain that they may repeat one phrase of the prayer rather than just one word, repeat the whole prayer many times, or repeat one word or syllable of the prayer for each step they take while walking.

Treasure Boxes
Matthew, chapter 6

The students decorate boxes, fill them with symbols of their treasures, and reflect on the meaning those treasures have in their lives.

1. Read Mt 6.19–21 to the students. Then ask them to reflect on the use of the word *treasure* as they listen quietly to the passage, and read it again.

2. Give the students some quiet time to make a list of their own treasures. Tell them they will be designing a box filled with some of the treasures on their list, or with symbols of those treasures. Ask the students to bring from home a box that can be decorated, items for decorating the box, and personal treasures or symbols of them.

3. When the students return with their treasure box materials, furnish paint, construction paper, ribbon, fake jewels, glue, and other art supplies. Instruct the students to decorate their boxes and place their treasures inside them.

4. Direct the students each to write a reflection describing what their treasures reveal about their heart (verse 20) or other insights they gained from this activity, in light of the Gospel passage.

5. After the boxes and reflections are completed, conduct a short prayer experience centered on the Scripture passage. Offer a blessing over the boxes during the prayer time. Invite the students to share some of the treasures in their boxes if they wish.

What Does It Mean to Be Judgmental?
Matthew, chapter 7

This activity encourages the students to think about when they need to judge others less and when they may need to step in and confront others.

1. Before class, prepare eight scenarios that might cause a teen to judge or confront a peer. Your examples should include clear-cut situations (such as a serious crime), straightforward but challenging situations (such as drinking and driving), and situations that some students will not take too seriously (such as lying to parents and cheating on homework). For each situation, identify four possible responses that reflect the following types:
- a live-and-let-live attitude
- a concern but no action
- a highly judgmental reaction
- a direct confrontation based on care and honesty

2. To begin this activity, call one student to read Mt 7.1–5 aloud to the class. Invite the students to discuss how they define a judgmental attitude. Offer the following points in your own words:
- Jesus reminds us that the temptation to point out the faults of others while ignoring our own faults is hypocritical.
- Does that mean we should never be concerned with the behavior of others? Is Jesus saying, "Live and let live," reflecting an attitude common in our culture today? Not at all.
- It is sometimes necessary for followers of Christ to stand up and confront sinful situations—to say: "This action or attitude is wrong and is hurting others. I cannot remain silent in the face of this sin."

3. Read to the students the situations you prepared before class, beginning with a clear-cut situation and moving to the most ambiguous situation. After reading the first situation, point out four spots in the room that correspond to the four responses you have prepared, and direct the students to stand closest to the spot indicating the response that they might make. Ask

them to explain their responses, and allow them to respectfully question persons in other locations. At the end of the discussion, instruct the students to vote, by a show of hands, on whether it would be wrong to tell a friend that the action is wrong. Record the vote on the board and jot down some of the insights shared. Continue in this manner for all the situations you have prepared.

4. After completing the scenarios, invite the students to make general observations about how to apply Jesus' teaching to their everyday lives. Then ask, "Given Jesus' behavior and overall message in the Gospel, would he agree with your guidelines for expressing judgment?"

Jesus' Miraculous Touch

Mapping Miracles
Matthew, chapters 13–17

The students trace Jesus' route throughout Palestine, noting where he performed miracles and identifying the miracles with symbols or pictures on a map.

1. In preparation for this activity, ask the students to read Mt 13.53—17.27. Have them make a list of the places Jesus travels in those passages, including the citation for each place (for reference) and the miracles that occur in each place.

Handout Mt–A

2. To begin this activity, pass out handout Mt–A, "A Map of First–Century Palestine." Tell the students to refer to their list of places and miracles, and to use lines and arrows to show Jesus' route in the region. Then ask the students to mark each place Jesus performed a miracle, by drawing a small symbol or picture that depicts the miracle.

3. Invite the students to share their completed maps. Discuss anything of interest about Jesus' travels and ask the students to share their favorite miracles.

Rap Songs on the Feeding of Five Thousand
Matthew, chapter 14

Creating a rap about the miracle of the loaves and fish helps the students focus on the story and its meaning.

1. Divide the class into groups of four or five. Direct the students to read Mt 14.13–21 in their groups, and then ask the groups each to compose a short rap song about the passage. Tell the students that they should emphasize the words and phrases that have the greatest meaning.

2. When the groups are ready, invite them to take turns performing their rap songs. While each group is performing, encourage everyone else to keep the rhythm of the song with various sounds. After all the students have performed, discuss which words and phrases were emphasized in the songs and

why. Help the students discover how the different interpretations of the songs deepen the meaning of the passage for them.

The Reign of God

Exegetical Tools:
Form Criticism—Contemporary Parables of the Reign of God
Matthew, chapter 13
"The Kingdom Is Like . . . ," Mt 13.10–53, CYB

Imitating Jesus' use of parables allows the students to illustrate the nature of the Reign of God.

    1. Before this activity, prepare a grab bag that contains everyday items such as a comb, button, safety pin, fork, watch, magnet, paper clip, battery, thumbtack, bandage, screwdriver, self-stick note, postage stamp, and scissors. Provide a different item for each student in the class.

    2. Begin this activity by asking several students to read Mt 13.10–53 aloud to the class. Invite another student to read the article "The Kingdom Is Like . . ." from the *CYB*. Review the parables from the passage, asking the students to identify the common, everyday elements within them and to evaluate how each element is similar to a quality of the Reign, or Kingdom, of God.

    3. Pass around the grab bag you have prepared. Tell the students each to select an item and then write a parable that compares that item to the Reign of God.

    4. Invite the students to share some of their finished parables. Ask them to reflect on why teaching through parables may have been particularly effective for Jesus' audience and may be for us today as well.

The Greatest Sale
Matthew, chapter 13

The students think about what is most important to them when they draw the treasure for which they would sell everything.

    1. Call a student to read Mt 13.44–45 aloud to the class. Tell the students to imagine that a local store is selling something for which they would give everything. Have them create a drawing that reflects the item's qualities, both tangible and intangible.

    2. Invite the students to share some of the qualities of the items they have drawn. Note the similarities and differences between their items and the life offered by Jesus in the Gospels.

    3. Ask the students to take a few minutes to write down why people refuse the life God offers through Jesus, and then invite them to discuss their thoughts on that issue.

Our Image in Jesus' Eyes
Matthew, chapter 16
"Peter the Rock," Mt 16.13–20, **CYB**

Jesus' reference to Peter as a rock invites the students to ask Jesus what image he might use to describe them.

1. Bring a rock to class to use as an illustration. Also prepare a brief guided imagery that puts the students in the place of Peter in the first half of the Bible passage for this activity. In the meditation, the students should answer the question "But who do you say that I am?" (Mt 16.13). Then they should listen for the name that Jesus gives them in return.

2. Ask one student to read Mt 16.13–23 aloud to the class and another to read the article "Peter the Rock" from the *CYB*. Discuss why Jesus chose the image of a rock to portray Peter in verses 13–20, despite Peter's apparent lack of faith in verses 21–23. Pass around the rock you brought to class, and ask the students to suggest the qualities of a rock that could translate into human characteristics. Point out that though Peter did not always live up to his name's meaning—"rock"—Jesus probably gave him that name because he could see Peter's best self.

3. Introduce or review the prayer style called guided imagery. Ask the students each to think of an object that describes themselves as a spiritual person. Then lead the students through the guided imagery you have prepared.

4. Invite the students to reflect on the title that they used to describe Jesus in the guided imagery, as well as Jesus' name for them. Emphasize these points:
   - God views us much differently than we see ourselves. Often when we look at ourselves, we are distracted by the effects of sin and weakness in our lives. God sees the best that we are, values us for that beauty, embraces us in our imperfection, and calls us to live as our best selves with confidence.

Children and the Reign of God

ABC Books
Matthew, chapters 13–18
"Parables," Mt 13.10, **CYB**

This activity helps the students see that whereas Jesus found parables effective for communicating with his audience, they can use a different storytelling form to present Jesus' teachings to children today.

1. Direct the students to read Matthew, chapters 13–18, in preparation for this activity. Bring in writing and art supplies for the students to use in creating ABC books in step 3.

2. Open this activity by inviting a student to read the article "Parables" from the *CYB*. Highlight several parables from the Scripture passage that the students read before this class, and invite them to reflect on how effective parables were for Jesus' audience. Explain the following points in your own words:

- ABC books are an effective way to share information with children to-day. ABC books use letters of the alphabet to create a story or to emphasize key points of a story. For example, an ABC book might say, *"C is for the crowds that gathered to listen to Jesus' stories,"* or *"D is for the disciples, who were Jesus' special friends."*

3. Divide the class into groups of four. Have the members of each group collaborate on an ABC book that shares important parts of Matthew, chapters 13–18, in a way that is understandable and fun for children. Note that each letter of the alphabet should communicate a full biblical idea rather than just an isolated element—for example, the letter *W* might be represented by Jesus walking on water, not by water alone. Explain that the students should list the chapter and verse that inspires each letter.

4. Arrange for the books to be assembled, illustrated, and shared in class. After the sharing, lead the students to discuss any reflections they have about the project. Consider donating the finished books to a Sunday school class or reading them to a group of elementary school children as a nice way to pass on the knowledge gained by the students in this activity.

Becoming Like Children
Matthew, chapter 18

Comparing their experience of life today with that of their childhood helps the students see what kind of attitude Jesus invites us to have.

1. Prepare for this activity by creating a childhood play environment for the students, with puzzles, bubbles, trucks, and other items of interest to a young child. Bring enough objects for all the students and place them in an open area in the classroom.

2. Begin this activity by inviting the students to spend 15 minutes or so playing with the toys you have set out. Then ask the students to share their reflections about the playtime, addressing these questions:
- What did you like about the toys?
- What memories did the toys bring back?

3. Invite the students to share adjectives that describe the worldview of young children and list those on the board. (You may need to explain the meaning of *worldview*.) Ask the students to contrast the worldview of children with that of teens and then adults.

4. Direct a student to read Mt 18.1–5 aloud to the class. Call the students to use their prior observations from this activity to explore why we must become like children in order to enter the kingdom of heaven, or Reign of God. Discuss the challenges that that conversion presents to older people.

Prayer Styles: Guided Imagery—Jesus and the Children
Matthew, chapter 19

The students experience the open arms of Jesus while picturing themselves as children approaching Jesus.

1. Introduce or review the prayer style called guided imagery. Dim the lights in the room and play soft instrumental music in the background. Urge the students to get comfortable and concentrate on their breathing. Tell the students to remember a photograph of themselves at age five or six. Create a picture by speaking of the sights, smells, and sounds of a beautiful day in ancient Palestine, and have them place themselves in that picture, as a child. Then, speaking quietly, lead the students in a prayerful visualization of Mt 19.13–15. Keep your voice soft and rhythmic.

Direct the students to picture Jesus and to identify how inviting he is compared with the other adults in the passage you just read. Help the students feel Jesus' desire to touch them and hold them, in spite of the disciples' stern remarks. Recall Jesus' invitation, "Let the little children come to me, and do not stop them" (Mt 19.13). Invite the students to listen to their own inner response as they sit with Jesus.

2. Afterward, instruct the students to write in their journal about their meditation experience. Also invite them to share their thoughts with the class.

Jesus' Passion

Skits of Comforting Friendship
Matthew, chapter 26
"Jesus' Imperfect Friends," Mt 26.36–45, CYB

This activity challenges the students to create skits in which Peter, James, and John do *not* fall asleep on Jesus in the Garden of Gethsemane. The skits explore what those Apostles could have said or done to comfort Jesus in his difficult time.

1. Ask one student to read Mt 26.36–46 aloud and another to read the article "Jesus' Imperfect Friends" from the *CYB*. Discuss how Jesus was let down by his friends when he was really counting on them.

2. Form small groups. Have the students discuss in their groups what Jesus' friends could have done differently to comfort and support Jesus. Direct the groups each to prepare a skit for the scene in Gethsemane, focusing on ways that Jesus' friends could have been there for him. Explain that the students should give voices and facial expressions to the friends and to Jesus. Ask each group to finish its skit with the refrain of a song that summarizes what kind of friendship Jesus needed at that moment.

3. Invite the groups to share their skits with the class. Discuss the insights that emerge about Jesus' experience in Gethsemane and about the nature of true friendship.

Journal Entries from the Passion
Matthew, chapters 26–27

Writing journal entries from the perspective of different characters in the Passion story allows the students to reflect on why people reacted to Jesus as differently as they did.

Handout Mt–B

1. Cut a copy of handout Mt–B, "Characters in Matthew's Passion Narrative," into slips of paper representing the various characters of Matthew's Passion account. Give each student a slip of paper. If you have a large group, you may assign the characters with an asterisk to two or more students.

2. Invite several students to read Matthew, chapters 26–27, aloud to the class. Tell the students to pay close attention to the experience of their assigned character in the story, and to reread all pertinent passages silently afterward. Note that the citation on their slip refers to the first mention of their character in the passage from Matthew.

3. Direct the students each to write, from the perspective of their character, a short journal entry in which they share their thoughts and feelings about the encounter with Jesus. Challenge them to visualize the sights, sounds, energy, and emotions of the scene as well as to enter into the role of their character, in order to create an authentic-sounding entry.

4. Call the students to share some of their journal entries with the class. Then ask the students to group themselves according to the following descriptions of their characters:
- people who saw Jesus as a threat
- neutral people who happened to be involved with Jesus
- people who loved and supported Jesus

Ask the students to explain to their group why their character fit the group's description.

5. Call representatives from each group to introduce their characters and explain characteristics that are common among the people in their group. Ask the students questions to help them see more similarities and differences between the various characters. For example:
- Why did some seemingly neutral people actually turn toward Jesus?
- Were all Jesus' supporters faithful throughout?

Discuss the students' responses.

The Paschal Mystery

Personal Reflection: The Paschal Mystery
Matthew, chapters 27–28

After reflecting on the transformation that occurs for Jesus and his followers between his death and his Resurrection, the students identify the stages inherent in a personal experience of the paschal mystery.

1. Ask several students to read Mt 27.45—28.20 to the class. Say something such as this to the students:

- These chapters in Matthew tell us of the paschal mystery, the miracle of life triumphing over suffering and death through Jesus' Resurrection. As Christians, we celebrate our sharing in that promise of eternal life, and we know that suffering and death in our own lives have meaning and will lead to greater life.
- Jesus' followers had several experiences on their journey from death to new life. First, they watched in terror as Jesus was arrested in the Garden of Gethsemane and was beaten and tortured by his enemies. Next, they grieved Jesus' gruesome death. Then they waited through the next days, feeling lost and empty and confused. Finally, Jesus rose from the dead, and the disciples felt joy and new life again.
- Your assignment is to write a reflection about the paschal mystery in your own life as experienced in a small or big event. Each of you is living through a stage of the paschal mystery right now. Some of you may be experiencing Good Friday—you are dying to something, and the resurrection seems a long way off. Others of you may be experiencing a Holy Saturday period—your struggle or loss is in the past, but you are uncertain and waiting, hoping for new life. Still others of you may be feeling that you have encountered resurrection—you have discovered a sense of new life where you once found suffering. It is also common to feel like you are in more than one stage at a time. You are to write about the paschal mystery in connection with your whole life or with one stage of your life.

Help the students draw parallels between the Gospel account of the paschal mystery, the Easter events, and their own lives, by giving examples and answering questions. Recognize that the students have had varied life experiences, and try to help all of them find a way to connect with this assignment. Note that the students need not have had a traumatic life event in order to do this project. Mention that they will turn in their reflections and you will read them and comment on them.

2. Give the students adequate time to complete their reflection essays. Spend time writing comments to the students while reading their essays. Invite the students to share their reflections as the classroom environment permits.

(This activity was contributed by Sr. Jane O'Brien, ANG, Georgetown Visitation Preparatory School, Washington, D.C.)

The Resurrection of Jesus

See the activity "Resurrection Talk Show: A Comparison of the Gospel Accounts," on pages 241–242 of this manual, for an exploration of Jesus' Resurrection.

.........▶ A Map of First-Century Palestine

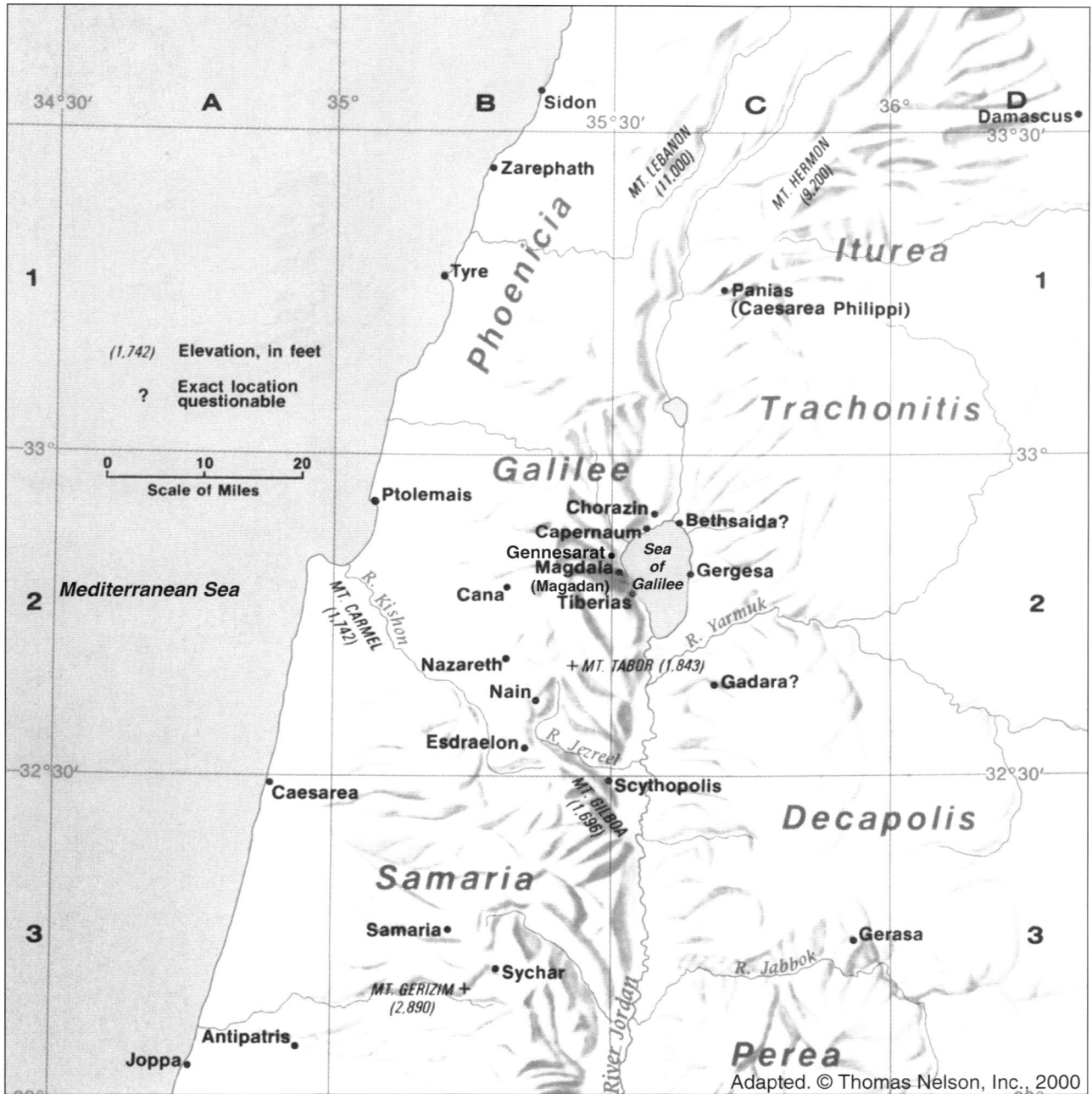

A map of first-century Palestine showing the Mediterranean Sea, Galilee, Samaria, Decapolis, Perea, Phoenicia, Iturea, Trachonitis, and numerous cities including Sidon, Zarephath, Tyre, Damascus, Panias (Caesarea Philippi), Ptolemais, Chorazin, Capernaum, Bethsaida?, Gennesarat, Magdala (Magadan), Gergesa, Cana, Tiberias, Nazareth, Nain, Gadara?, Esdraelon, Caesarea, Scythopolis, Samaria, Gerasa, Sychar, Antipatris, Joppa. Also shown: Sea of Galilee, MT. LEBANON (11,000), MT. HERMON (9,200), MT. CARMEL (1,742), MT. TABOR (1,843), MT. GILBOA (1,696), MT. GERIZIM (2,890), R. Kishon, R. Yarmuk, R. Jezreel, R. Jabbok, River Jordan.

(1,742) Elevation, in feet
? Exact location questionable

0 10 20 Scale of Miles

Adapted. © Thomas Nelson, Inc., 2000

*According to a footnote for Mt 15.39 in *The New Oxford Annotated Bible with the Apocryphal/Deuterocanonical Books,* new revised standard version, edited by Bruce M. Metzger and Roland E. Murphy (New York: Oxford University Press, 1994), the site of Magadan is not known for certain but was apparently on the west side of the Sea of Galilee.

Caiaphas (26.3)	Barabbas (27.16)
A woman with ointment (26.7)	Pilate's wife (27.19)
Judas Iscariot (26.14)	A member of the crowd (27.20)*
The man who owns the house used for Jesus' Passover with the Apostles (26.18)	A soldier (27.27)*
Peter (26.33)	Simon of Cyrene (27.32)
A son of Zebedee (26.37)*	A bandit (27.38)*
A person with a sword or club (26.47)*	A passerby (27.39)*
The high priest's slave who lost an ear (26.51)	A bystander with wine (27.48)
Jesus' follower who cuts off the slave's ear (26.51)	A person to whom a risen saint appears (27.53)*
A scribe (26.57)*	The centurion (27.54)
An elder (26.57)*	Mary Magdalene (27.56)
A false witness (26.60)*	Mary the mother of James and Joseph (27.56)
Pilate (27.2)	The mother of the sons of Zebedee (27.56)

Mark

The Call of the Disciples

Wanted: Modern Disciples
Mark, chapter 1

This exercise invites the students to create want ads for modern disciples, in order to identify the role of disciples now and during Jesus' time.

    1. Bring to class some pages from the classified section of a newspaper. Open this exercise by reading Mk 1.16–20 aloud, emphasizing the word *immediately*. Ask the students to reflect on Jesus' words and how he must have said them in order for the four men to leave their nets immediately and follow him.

    2. Form small groups and ask the students to discuss in them what kinds of want ads or employment notices today would get that kind of immediate response. To encourage their thinking, pass out the newspaper pages you brought to class.

    3. Divide the class into small groups and direct the groups each to design a catchy, influential ad for recruiting modern disciples of Jesus. Explain that they should choose a medium—newspaper, billboard, computer, radio, or television—and then create the script or design. Provide art supplies as needed, and give the groups time to work on their ads in class.

    4. Invite the groups to present their finished ads to the class. Discuss the students' sense of what is attractive about Jesus' message.

Prayer Styles: Guided Imagery—Jesus in My House
Mark, chapter 2
"Getting Personal," Mk 2.13–17, CYB

Jesus' presence at Levi's home invites the students to imagine what would transpire if Jesus were to drop by their own home for dinner.

    1. Call one student to read Mk 2.13–17 aloud to the class and another to read the article "Getting Personal" from the *CYB*.

    2. Introduce or review the prayer style called guided imagery. Invite the students to prepare for a guided imagery by closing their eyes and using deep breathing to relax. Create a meditative atmosphere in the class by dimming the lights and possibly playing some reflective music.
    Help the students imagine that Jesus is visiting their home, using some of the following cues and questions in your own words. Give plenty of time after each cue or question to allow the students to imagine reactions and dialog.

- Envision yourself at home with your family; bring to mind familiar sounds, sights, and smells. . . . What is everyone doing? . . . The doorbell rings, and it is Jesus. . . . How do the people in your family react upon seeing Jesus? . . . What does he look like? . . . What do different family members say when he arrives? . . . Does he stay for a meal? . . . What is the conversation like? . . . What does Jesus say to you personally? . . . Do other people, such as neighbors, friends, and relatives, get involved? . . .

Close the meditation by inviting the students to imagine Jesus taking leave of their home and family.

3. At the end of the prayer experience, allow the students some quiet time to reflect. Then invite the students to share their thoughts on the meditation as they feel comfortable. Ask some questions about what they imagined, such as these:

- What was Jesus like?
- How did he interact with your family?
- How did others react to him?

Allow for discussion as it arises.

Stories and Miracles of Jesus

The Sower's Theater
Mark, chapter 4

The students act out the parable of the sower as a way of applying its meaning to their lives.

1. Form groups of four, and ask the students to read the parable of the sower, Mk 4.1–20, in their groups.

2. Tell the groups each to plan a skit in which they portray the four types of seed and soil in the parable. The students should act out all the items in the story, animate and inanimate, such as the seed, ground, and weeds.

3. After viewing the presentations as a class, discuss the symbolism of the seeds and soil and the relevance of the parable to everyday life. Give the students some time to reflect on the process of becoming "good soil" ourselves so that God's "seed" can "bear fruit" in our own lives.

4. Assign the students to write an essay describing the obstacles that would be encountered by a sower of God's seed today.

Flipbook Miracles
Mark, chapters 4–8

The students create flipbooks to become familiar with the miracles in Mark's Gospel.

GOSPELS

1. Prepare for this activity by obtaining a small flipbook to use for a sample, or making one yourself as described in step 2.

2. Begin this activity by assigning one of the following ten miracles to each student:
- Calming of the storm (Mk 4.35–41)
- Healing of the demoniac (Mk 5.1–20)
- Healing of Jairus's daughter (Mk 5.21–43)
- Healing of the woman with hemorrhages (Mk 5.24–34)
- Feeding of the five thousand (Mk 6.30–44)
- Walking on water (Mk 6.47–52)
- Healing of the Syrophoenician's daughter (Mk 7.24–30)
- Healing of the deaf man (Mk 7.31–37)
- Feeding of the four thousand (Mk 8.1–10)
- Healing of the blind man (Mk 8.22–26)

Instruct the students each to create a small flipbook of their assigned miracle, using unlined paper, scissors, and a stapler. Explain that flipbooks are small books of pictures that are like the frames of a motion picture, so that when one flips through the book, the figures in the book appear to move. Show the students the example you obtained or created for this activity.

Note that the students' books should each be about thirty pages long. Mention that stick figures are acceptable, but caution the students to make sure the action moves smoothly from picture to picture. Direct the students to put their name on their book.

3. After the students have finished their books, collect them and then pass them out randomly. See if the students can follow the story action of each miracle. Have the students each view several miracle flipbooks before returning them to their illustrators.

4. Help the students explore the nature and power of the miracles by discussing the following questions with them:
- What allows each miracle to take place?
- What does each miracle story teach, and how?
- What might happen next to the person or persons affected by each miracle? Why?

Scrapbooks on Healing
Mark, chapters 5, 7–8

The students create scrapbook pages for persons who were healed by Jesus, with those pages showing how the persons' lives were forever changed.

1. Prepare for this class by bringing items that might be found in a scrapbook: programs and tickets from plays and concerts, greeting cards, photos, pressed flowers, graduation cap tassels, and so on. Ask the students to bring in such items as well. Also bring in a blank scrapbook whose pages can be removed, or provide sheets of blank paper and supplies for binding them into a book.

2. Ask a student to read Mk 5.25–34 aloud. Discuss the transformation that Jesus' healing brought to the sick woman's life in that passage. Make the following points to your class in your own words:

- Notice how this woman initially reacts to Jesus—almost as though he were a magician. That is, she does not call out to him in any way, but wants to benefit anonymously from his power.
- Jesus, knowing that someone has reached out to him in faith, is not satisfied with that kind of relationship. He turns his gaze into the crowd pressing all around him, determined to find the woman.

3. Divide the class into six groups and assign each group one of the following passages:

- Mk 5.1–20 (Healing of the demoniac)
- Mk 5.21–43 (Healing of Jairus's daughter)
- Mk 5.24–34 (Healing of the woman with hemorrhages)
- Mk 7.24–30 (Healing of the Syrophoenician's daughter)
- Mk 7.31–37 (Healing of the deaf man)
- Mk 8.22–26 (Healing of the blind man)

Ask the students to read their selection silently and then discuss in their group the following questions about what might have happened to the main character after his or her healing encounter with Jesus:

- What did the person first say? How must he or she have felt?
- How did Jesus respond to the person? What did he do and say?
- What was the first thing that the person might have done after being healed?
- How did the families of the healed person react?
- What might the person who was healed think about that event five or ten years down the road?
- What kind of faith do you think the healed person had?

4. Tell the groups each to make several scrapbook pages with pictures, memories, and keepsakes that communicate the healing and transformation that took place as a result of their assigned miracle. Make available the scrapbook items that have been brought in by you and the students, and distribute the blank scrapbook pages or papers, as well as colored markers or pencils and other necessary supplies. Allow the groups enough class time to complete their pages.

5. Direct the students each to write, on a separate sheet of paper, a reflection based on the following questions:

- How would you describe your faith in Jesus? Is it strictly an impersonal affair? Is Jesus your "divine magician," who will make things right if you ask him?
- Jesus offers us healing and salvation, and wants us to receive them in a real and personal friendship with him. Do you believe that Jesus has the power to change your life? Will you let yourself be open to a personal friendship with Jesus?

6. Invite the students to share their scrapbook pages with the class, and discuss their insights and reflections. Emphasize the radical difference that Jesus' healings made in the troubled people's lives. Ask the students whether they believe that a relationship with Jesus can bring such transformation today. After the discussion, put the scrapbook pages together and display the book for classroom use.

The Invitation to Know and Believe in Jesus

Images of Jesus
Mark, chapter 8

This activity asks the students to reflect on how they perceive the identity of Jesus, by assessing their reactions to different visual portrayals of Jesus.

1. In preparation for this activity, ask the students to bring in a variety of visual representations of Jesus. Note that those might come from textbooks, holy cards, and illustrated Bibles. Refer to page 1549 in the *CYB,* which features many cultural images of Jesus. Gather some images yourself.

Note: An interesting examination of historically popular images of Jesus can be found in *The Illustrated Jesus Through the Centuries,* by Jaroslav Jan Pelikan (New Haven, CT: Yale University Press, 1997).

2. Begin this activity by spreading out the images of Jesus that have been brought in, and giving the students some time to look at them. Ask the students to respond in writing to the following questions:
   - Select three images that you like. How do those three images express your understanding of Jesus?
   - Pick one image of Jesus that you do not understand or care for. Why is that image of Jesus hard to relate to?

3. Invite the students to share some of their reactions with the class and note their insights on the board. Then ask several students to read Mark, chapter 8, aloud. Engage the class in a discussion about the various images of Jesus presented in that chapter of Mark. Include the following questions:
   - How does Jesus identify himself?
   - How do Jesus' followers identify him?
   - How might the Apostles' various perceptions of Jesus' identity have affected the way they related to him?

Help My Unbelief
Mark, chapter 9
"I Believe; Help My Unbelief!" Mk 9.14–29, CYB

The father of the boy healed in Mk 9.14–29 articulates an experience with which the students can likely identify—that of believing in Jesus at the same time that they disbelieve.

1. Ask one student to read Mk 9.14–29 aloud to the class and another to read the article "I Believe; Help My Unbelief!" from the *CYB.* Note that like the father in the story, we can experience both belief and doubt, even at the same moment.

2. Direct the students each to draw two areas on a blank sheet of paper, labeling one "Belief" and the other "Unbelief." They should feel free to design those areas to represent the experience of faith and doubt. They are then to illustrate, within the appropriate area, experiences from their own life that have inspired belief and unbelief.

3. Invite the students to share examples of belief and unbelief with another student and then with the entire class. Note the following points in your own words:

- People—including the Apostles—commonly have both an abundance and a lack of faith. Jesus responds to the faith of the man in the story and heals the man's son accordingly. God not only is the object of our faith, but also sustains our belief.

The Rich Man's Journal Entry and Letter to Jesus
Mark, chapter 10

The students write a journal entry that reflects how the rich man in Mark, chapter 10, feels after getting home from listening to Jesus. They also write a letter to Jesus from the man's perspective.

1. Assign each of three students one of the character parts from Mark 10.17–22: narrator, rich man, and Jesus. Have the three students read that passage aloud to the class.

2. Playing quiet music in the background, ask the students each to write a journal entry from the perspective of the rich man returning home.

3. Invite the students to share their finished journal entries in small groups. Have the groups each compose a letter that the rich man might have written to Jesus a week after his encounter with Jesus.

4. Call two students to read Mk 10.23–31 aloud to the class. Encourage the groups to discuss their letters in light of Jesus' teaching about possessions.

Jesus' Teaching

Jesus' Comments on Our Society
Mark, chapter 11

This activity invites the students to reflect about how Jesus might react to some institutions in their culture today.

1. In preparation for this activity, create a handout that consists of a map of your area, featuring major institutions with which the students are familiar. Include some of the following places or items: the students' houses, the high school, a shopping center, a movie theater, a church, a restaurant, a beauty salon, a sports stadium, and a popular hangout. Leave room near each institution for the students to write or draw a brief response in step 2. (A similar map is suggested for the activity "Mapping God's Presence," on page 91 of this manual. If you created a map for that activity, you might want to use the same one for this activity. Or, for variety, you might prefer to develop a new map, featuring different institutions.) Make enough copies of the map for all the students.

2. Begin this activity by asking a student to read Mk 11.15–19 aloud to the class. Explain the context of Jesus' anger in that passage. Then distribute copies of the map you created. Tell the students that for each place on the map, they are to imagine how Jesus would react to what goes on there and then, near that place on the map, write down what Jesus might say about it or draw a symbol portraying his attitude toward it.

3. When the students are done writing and drawing, direct them each to share their responses with two other students. Then invite them to share their responses with the class as the basis for a discussion about the values that do or do not exist in the various institutions identified on the map.

Answered Prayer
Mark, chapter 11
"Unanswered Prayer," Mk 11.24, **CYB**

Jesus' statement that our prayers will be answered challenges the students to reflect on their own understanding of the way that God responds to prayer.

1. Request one student to read Mk 11.20–24 aloud to the class and another to read the article "Unanswered Prayer" from the *CYB*.

2. Designate three spots in the room "Agree," "Disagree," and "Neutral." Direct the students to respond to the following statements by moving to the appropriate spot in the room. After each statement, allow the students to explain their positions, encouraging them to refer to concrete examples that have inspired their opinions. Consider polling the students in a similar fashion throughout the discussion as provocative points are raised.
- God answers all our prayers.
- God answers all our prayers if we believe that God is doing so.

3. Have the students re-examine Mk 11.24 and reflect on the interesting wording of Jesus' statement. Discuss what Jesus' teaching means for a Christian's faith and prayer life.

The Greatest Commandments Artwork
Mark, chapter 12

An artistic portrayal of the first two commandments helps the students to reflect more deeply on the meaning of the Commandments.

1. Ask a student to read Mk 12.28–34 aloud to the class. Instruct the students to reflect on the meaning of Mk 12.29–31 and then interpret that passage artistically. Give them a lot of room to be creative. Distribute art supplies such as blank paper, colored markers or pencils, old magazines, scissors, and glue, to help them express themselves.

2. Invite the students to share their finished artwork as a springboard for discussion about the Commandments.

GOSPELS

"Keep Awake!" Jingles
Mark, chapter 13

The students reinforce the Scripture message "Keep awake!" by using it to create catchy radio jingles for different audiences and time periods.

1. Read Mk 13.32–37 dramatically for the class. Discuss the message "Keep awake" in the context of the Scripture passage. Ask these questions:
    ■ What was Jesus saying to his disciples?
    ■ How could Jesus get that message to his many disciples today?

2. Form small groups and direct them to prepare radio jingles with Jesus' message. Assign each group a different time of day, type of station, and type of show for airing the message—such as news, morning commute, country music, afternoon, alternative rock, evening, oldies, Friday rush hour, and late-night talk. Note that for all the groups, the message will be the same: "Keep alert, for you do not know when the time will come."

3. When the groups are all ready, lead them in sharing and discussing their messages.

Jesus' Passion and Death

Stained-Glass Windows for the Passion
Mark, chapters 14–15

This activity helps the students understand and personalize Jesus' Passion by portraying its events symbolically in a design for a stained-glass window.

1. Divide Mark, chapters 14–15, among several students and ask them to read those chapters aloud for the class. Note that those chapters cover Jesus' Passion—that is, his sufferings between the Last Supper and his death. Encourage the students to reflect on the Passion story by thinking about its sights, sounds, tastes, smells, and textures. Ask the students these questions:
    ■ What one event from the story sticks out in your mind? Why?
    ■ How do your senses respond to that event?

2. Distribute blank paper and colored markers or pencils, and have the students give shape, color, and form to that one event. Next, direct the students to share their papers in groups of four. Then invite the students to share comments about the artwork with the class.

3. Say something such as the following to the students in your own words:
    ■ Imagine that your group is a designing team for the J. C. Stained-Glass Company. Saint Mark's, a small parish, has commissioned you to design a new stained–glass window for its church. The parish wishes to base the window on the Passion narrative in Mark's Gospel, and it wants a symbolic portrayal as opposed to a literal illustration. Work on this assignment with your group. You may discuss possible designs by refer-

ring to your earlier individual sketches. The completed group design should be put on a large piece of poster board.

Distribute poster board and give the students sufficient time to work on their group design.

4. Allow the groups to share their finished designs with the class. When the presentations are completed, give out a sheet of blank paper to each student, ask the students to switch roles and now pretend they are the parishioners of Saint Mark's, and solicit their vote on the design that they like the best. Ask them also to write one paragraph explaining their choice.

Variations. Instead of having the groups execute their designs on poster board in step 3, arrange for them to paint their ideas in tempera on the classroom windows or some other windows in the school. Or provide colored cellophane or tissue paper and invite the groups each to cut out their design, create a "lead" frame from heavy black or gray paper, and mount their design in an assigned window.

The Stations of the Cross
Mark, chapters 14–15

This activity asks the students to reflect more deeply on Jesus' sufferings by building their own wooden representation of Mark's Passion account.

Note: This project is labor-intensive for the teacher and the students.

1. In preparation for this activity, ask the students to read Mk 14.22—15.47 and to bring in casual clothes or smocks so that they can work comfortably on a large art project. Also decide which of the following materials you will bring and which to assign to the students, and ensure that all the necessary items are available for the activity:

- hammers
- thin wood molding
- pieces of wood in different sizes (The students could contribute scrap wood as small as toothpicks and popsicle sticks.)
- pieces of fabric, construction paper, and so on
- small nails
- a jigsaw
- glue guns
- sandpaper
- colored markers
- paint
- 4-by-6-inch index cards

Consider asking for adult volunteers to assist in the use of the various tools for this project. Also, you may want to obtain parental permission for this activity.

2. Begin this activity by explaining the tradition of praying the stations of the cross, and ask the students to share their experiences with that kind of prayer. Offer some examples, if you wish.

3. Divide Mark's Passion story into the following fourteen sections, assigning one or more students to each section:

- Mk 14.22–25
- Mk 14.32–42
- Mk 14.43–52
- Mk 14.53–65
- Mk 14.66–72

- Mk 15.1–5
- Mk 15.6–15
- Mk 15.16–20
- Mk 15.21–22
- Mk 15.23–27

- Mk 15.29–32
- Mk 15.33–39
- Mk 15.40–41
- Mk 15.42–47

Explain that those passages correspond to the various stations of the cross. After reading their assigned section, the students are to sketch some ideas for a work of art that illustrates the corresponding station of the cross. Their finished work will be made of pieces of wood set in a frame and should incorporate the following guidelines:

- The finished work must include a cross but must not simply be a cross or series of crosses.
- A part of the Scripture passage used for the piece (chapter, verses, and words) should be written on the front side of the piece somewhere.

Explain that to execute their design, the students will first construct a square frame by gluing or nailing 1-foot pieces of thin wood molding together. They will then cut (and color, if they wish) wood pieces that form a 1-foot-square design. They may use fabric or colored paper as part of their design if they want to. Finally, they will either glue or nail their design together and set it into the frame, or glue or nail their design piece by piece into the frame.

Allow the students time to complete their stations of the cross, and provide guidance and assistance as necessary.

4. After the students have completed the building part of the project, pass out index cards. Have the students write on their card a description of their piece's meaning for them, noting how they designed the piece. They should then affix the card to the back of the project.

5. When the students have completed their individual stations of the cross, display the stations according to the order of the text. Review the story, piece by piece, noting the way hopelessness and hope are intermingled all the way through Mark's Passion account. Focus on the symbolism of the cross throughout.

6. After class, the finished display could be used in a prayer service or put up somewhere in the school. It could even be donated to a chapel or a mission church, especially if it turns out well.

Jesus' Resurrection

See the activity "Resurrection Talk Show: A Comparison of the Gospel Accounts," on pages 241–242 of this manual, for an exploration of Jesus' Resurrection.

Luke

Mary's Call

The activity "God's Call," on pages 148–149 of this manual, includes God's call to Mary, which is described in Luke, chapter 1.

Jesus' Early Years

Prayer Styles:
Recitation—the Liturgy of the Hours and the Marian Prayers
Luke, chapter 1
"The Magnificat, the Prayer of the Poor!" Lk 1.39–56, CYB;
   "The Benedictus," Lk 1.46–80, CYB

This activity prepares the students to lead prayer experiences using the liturgy of the hours and various prayers about Mary, after learning about the Magnificat and the Benedictus.

1. Before this activity, prepare one handout that gives a general explanation of the liturgy of the hours and another that includes Marian prayers such as the Hail Mary, Hail Holy Queen, Memorare, Angelus, and rosary. Also consider bringing in other resources that refer to or contain Marian prayers.

2. Ask several students to read Luke, chapter 1, aloud to the class. Stop to discuss the Magnificat (verses 46–55) and the Benedictus (verses 68–79), referring to the handout and the articles about those prayers in the *CYB.* Talk with the students about recited prayer and about the important role that type of prayer has played in the Catholic church.

3. Divide the class into small groups to lead the liturgy of hours and various Marian prayers over the next several weeks, using the handouts and other resources you have provided. Give one group the text of lauds for a specific day and one group the text of vespers for another day, and designate certain groups to lead the class in the other prayers on other days. Encourage the groups to reflect on their assigned traditional prayer, and ask them to provide for the class other prayers, music, ritual, and art that complement and explore its meaning.

Variation. To take this activity another step, direct the students to interview parents, grandparents, elderly parishioners, and so forth, for whom the traditional prayers have been an important part of their practice of Catholicism. Tell the students to explore with their interviewees what the prayers mean to them, how they learned the prayers, how the prayers have become part of their spiritual life, and so on.

Christmas Carols and the Two Infancy Narratives
Luke, chapters 1–2; Matthew, chapters 1–2

The students identify aspects of Matthew's and Luke's infancy narratives that have been woven into popular Christmas carols.

1. In preparation for this activity, direct the students to read Mt 1.18—2.23 and Luke, chapters 1–2, jotting down the similarities and differences between those accounts of Jesus' birth.

Obtain copies of the lyrics for a dozen or so Christmas carols with biblical themes, such as these:
- "Silent Night"
- "The First Noel"
- "Angels We Have Heard on High"
- "What Child Is This?"
- "Joy to the World"
- "We Three Kings of Orient Are"
- "O Come, All Ye Faithful"
- "Hark! the Herald Angels Sing"
- "O Little Town of Bethlehem"
- "O Holy Night"
- "It Came upon the Midnight Clear"
- "Away in a Manger"

2. Divide the class into groups and give each group the lyrics for several Christmas carols to review. The students should assess whether different verses of each song echo Luke's or Matthew's version of the infancy narrative. They should also note how much of the song is not based directly on the Scriptures. They might want to use different-colored markers or highlighters to mark the different versions.

3. After the groups have completed their review, ask them to share their findings with the rest of the class. Help the students reflect on possible reasons why the Gospel versions differ and why the two versions are often mixed together into one account. Ask these questions:
   - Which Gospel version is most commonly used?
   - Which version touches you most deeply?

Diaries of the Holy Family
Luke, chapter 2
"The Holy Family," Lk 2.41–52, CYB

This exercise invites the students to write diary entries from the perspectives of Mary, Joseph, and Jesus upon returning home from Jerusalem.

1. Direct the students to read Lk 2.41–52 and the article "The Holy Family" from the *CYB*.

2. Ask the students to share with the class a time when they and their parents had different perspectives on something that happened. Discuss how perceptions are the reality of the individual.

3. Divide the class into three equal parts. Ask one third to write a journal entry from Mary's perspective after she returns home from Jerusalem. Have the second third write from Joseph's point of view, and the last third write from Jesus' viewpoint. Play soft music in the background as the students write.

4. Invite the students to share entries from the different perspectives. Ask them if the misunderstanding in the Bible passage sheds any light on their own conflicts with parents.

Jesus Calls the Apostles

Explaining One's Call
Luke, chapters 4–6

Creating skits that portray the Apostles' process of letting others know that they will now be following Jesus helps the students explore the power and challenge of Jesus' call.

1. Divide the class into six groups. Assign the groups each a scenario from the list below, and ask them to read the corresponding verses from the Bible.
- Simon and his mother-in-law (Lk 4.38–39) and possibly other family members (Lk 5.1–11)
- John and James and their father, Zebedee (Lk 5.1–11)
- Levi (Matthew) and his Roman tax collector superiors (Lk 5.27–32)
- Simon the Zealot and his Zealot party members (Lk 6.12–16)
- James and his father, Alphaeus (Lk 6.12–16)
- Any of the other Apostles and a friend (Lk 6.12–16)
    Give the groups the following instructions in your own words:
    - Imagine that you are the Apostle or Apostles in your assigned scenario. Create a skit in which you describe to the other characters in the scenario the day Jesus called you, your reaction to Jesus' invitation, and your choice to follow Jesus. You may include in the skit any other characters that might enhance it. If you do not find enough information provided in the Scripture passage, you may guess at how the scenario went.

2. After the skits have been performed, invite the students to discuss the nature of Jesus' call by focusing on questions such as these:
    - How does Jesus call people today? What responses might people make to his call and why?
    - What makes you want to follow Jesus? What holds you back from doing so?

Jesus Teaches and Prays

Advertising the Good News
Luke, chapter 6

The students use popular ad slogans or jingles to communicate the messages of Luke's Sermon on the Plain.

1. Prepare for this activity by having the students bring popular magazines to class.

2. Begin this activity by asking the students to read Lk 6.17–49 to themselves. Then review the passage with the students, inviting them to list Jesus' main points and writing those on the board.

3. Form pairs and direct them to think of several advertising slogans or jingles that they can adapt to the messages that Jesus puts forth in the Bible passage. Suggest that they page through the magazines they have brought, to find ideas. Explain that each student should then pick one slogan or jingle and portray it artistically on blank paper, using colored markers or pencils.

4. Invite the students to share their completed artwork with the class. Discuss this question: "Does the use of advertising to communicate Jesus' message shed any light on the practice of advertising or on the nature of Jesus' message?"

Prayer and Life
Luke, chapter 6

An examination of the relation between Jesus' prayer and his ministry invites the students to reflect on prayer's effects on daily living and to interview adults who pray.

1. Call a student to read Lk 6.6–16 aloud to the class. Note the parts of the passage that precede and follow verse 12, and have the students reflect about why prayer might have been important for Jesus at the time.

2. Form pairs and direct them to skim Luke's Gospel and find other times when Jesus prayed. Discuss with them the role that prayer played in Jesus' life. Give them the opportunity to raise questions about prayer. List their questions on the board.

3. As a class, choose from the list on the board five questions that every student will ask an adult over age thirty, in an interview about prayer experiences. Then direct the students each to choose five more questions from the list or write down others that come to mind. Tell the students each to use their list of ten questions to interview an adult outside of class. Note that the adults need only answer the questions with which they feel comfortable.

4. After the students have completed their interviews, have them each write a paper that summarizes their interview and then reflects on the adult's input and the student's own experiences of prayer.

5. Invite the students to share some aspects of their interviews and papers with the class, and allow discussion to arise from the sharing. Ask, "What similarities can you see between Jesus' need for prayer and your own?"

Artwork from Luke's Gospel
Luke, chapters 6, 8, 11, 13

Jesus' parables in Luke's Gospel are visual and lend themselves to artistic portrayal. This activity allows the students to express their understanding of the parables by creating a piece of art.

1. Ask the students to read these parables of Jesus' and to notice the images that strike them:
- Lk 6.43–45
- Lk 6.46–49
- Lk 8.16–18
- Lk 11.33–36
- Lk 13.6–9
- Lk 13.18–19
- Lk 13.22–30

2. Direct the students to portray an aspect of one of those parables artistically on blank paper, using colored markers or pencils. Mention that they may use pictures, symbols, or arrangements of some of the parable's verses. Allow the students to choose their aspect, but see that all the parables are covered.

3. When the students have completed their artwork, tell them to group with the others who chose the same parable, in order to compare interpretations. Then invite the groups to share their insights and artwork with the rest of the class.

Miraculous Events

Musical Mime: The Calming of the Storm
Luke, chapter 8

This exercise invites the students to work in groups on a musical mime of the calming of the storm.

1. Discuss with the students the power of body language. Note that nonverbal messages often speak more loudly than verbal ones.

2. Form groups and ask them each to develop a musical mime for Lk 8.22–25. Explain that music should be used in the background and props may be added for effect.

3. Invite the groups to present their mimes to the class. After all the mimes have been performed, discuss what was effective in them and invite the students to share new dimensions of the stories that emerged from them.

Modern Miracles
Luke, chapter 9

This activity asks the students to open themselves to accept God's power and work together to share food and companionship with people in need, as Jesus did when he was on earth.

1. Read Lk 9.10–17 aloud with the students. Make the following points in your own words:
   - Though Jesus is no longer among us performing miracles, God continues to work miracles in and through us every day. We can see the power of God's miracles when people work together to accomplish God's will.

2. Raise the issue of hunger in the students' own community, and connect it to the hunger of the crowd in the Gospel reading. Guide the students to brainstorm creative ways that they could gather others to bring food to those who need it. Help them choose one of their ideas, develop a plan for implementing the idea, and carry out the plan. For example, they might host a talent show or variety show, collect gifts of food as the price of admission, and donate the food to the local food shelf. Or they might host a soup supper for older people or homeless people, incorporating a movie or some other form of entertainment and each bringing a can of food to add to the pot.

3. After the students perform their service, gather them for a brief discussion. Invite their observations and feelings from the experience. Try to respond to their questions and concerns. Emphasize the idea that God works through people to bring about modern miracles. Note the power of pulling together, and how much people can do when they share their gifts and talents. Conclude with a prayer asking God to help you and the students always remain open to doing God's work.

Transfiguration Pamphlets
Luke, chapter 9

This exercise brings Jesus' Transfiguration to the students on a personal level as they draw on their own experiences to write advice for others who are in painful situations.

1. Ask a student to read Lk 9.28–36 aloud to the class. Invite the students to share about a time in their life when things were too good to be true or when they felt on top of the world.
Discuss how Peter, John, and James must have felt that way too. Note that one moment they were basking in the presence of Moses, Elijah, and Jesus, and the next moment they were alone.

2. Form small groups and direct them each to develop a pamphlet that is filled with advice on how to handle letdowns after tremendous highs. Tell the groups to create their pamphlet on blank paper and fold it in thirds. Encourage them to decorate it and to include quotes, tips, stories, and pictures.

3. Pass the completed pamphlets around the class as a discussion-starter about Jesus and the Apostles' experience of coming down the mountain.

Love of God and Neighbor

Finger Puppet Theater: The Good Samaritan and Lk 10.29
Luke, chapter 10
"Discrimination in Jesus' Time," Lk 10.25–37, CYB

The students use finger puppets to explore the different elements of the good Samaritan story.

1. Have the students read the parable of the good Samaritan, Lk 10.25–37, to themselves. Offer the class some background about the Samaritans.

2. Call two volunteers to "act out" the parable of the good Samaritan using just their hands on a desktop in front of the class. Explain that they can make their fingers "walk," "carry," and so on, and they are to tell the story verbally as they are acting it out.

3. After the finger play, invite discussion on the meaning of the story and the effect of the story on Jesus' listeners. Ask a student to read the article "Discrimination in Jesus' Time" from the *CYB* aloud to the class.

4. Pair off the students, and invite the pairs each to translate the parable into our own time and to prepare their own finger puppet parable. Suggest that they create simple desktop props or sets if they want to enhance their presentation.

5. Invite the pairs to share their parables. Discuss the insights that the performances reveal. Ask the students to reflect on their own willingness to take on the role of good Samaritan.

Personality Sketches: Martha and Mary
Luke, chapter 10

The students explore the personality differences between Mary and Martha, and project how the women's personality traits play out in modern situations.

1. Tell the students to read Lk 10.38–42 individually, then write several paragraphs comparing and contrasting the two sisters.

2. Discuss the major difference between the women in the Bible passage: Mary is a busy, task-oriented, active person; Martha is a contemplative listener. Ask which of the two Jesus seems to sympathize with and why.

3. Divide the class into groups of four or five. Ask each group to imagine a contemporary real-life situation that Mary and Martha might face differently, and to create a skit about it. Suggest situations such as the following:
- dealing with a friend's crisis
- problem solving with a spouse
- caring for a tired child
- planning a group prayer experience

Consider asking the students also to read Jn 11.1–53, the raising of Lazarus, to flesh out their character study of Martha and Mary.

4. Invite the groups to present their skits in turn. After each skit, lead a discussion about the specific strengths and weaknesses each personality type brings to the situation.

5. When the skits have all been performed and discussed, acknowledge that Jesus favored Mary's style in this story, and ask if Martha's personality might have shone in other Gospel situations, had she been present.

Clowning with the Rich Fool
Luke, chapter 12
"The Greed Trap," Lk 12.13–21, CYB

Creating a clown show or mime based on the story of the rich fool helps the students explore the concept of greed.

1. Direct the students to recall their experiences with clowns. Ask these questions:
   - What makes a "good" clown?
   - Why are clowns popular?

2. Read Lk 12.13–21, the story of the rich fool, together with the class. Afterward, read the article "The Greed Trap" from the *CYB*.

3. As a class, discuss how the rich fool could be presented as a clown. Solicit the students' responses to these questions:
   - What would he look like? Why?
   - How would he act? Why?
   Also discuss the concept of greed and ask the students to come up with ways that miming or clowning could get that idea across.

4. Form small groups and direct them each to create a miming or clowning routine that tells the moral of the parable of the rich fool in a modern context. Encourage the use of whiteface, costumes, and props because they will add to the skit. Mention that the act may have humorous parts but must also make a point.

5. Arrange for the groups to present their acts to the class, and invite observations about the skits' messages.

Prayer Styles: Mindfulness
Luke, chapter 12
"The Anxiety Trap," Lk 12.22–31, CYB

Exploring the Buddhist practice of mindfulness helps the students focus on the blessings of the moment rather than on their fears for the future.

1. To begin this activity, ask one student to read Lk 12.22–31 aloud to the class and another to read the article "The Anxiety Trap" from the *CYB*.

Handout Lk–A

2. Pass out handout Lk–A, "The Practice of Mindfulness," to the students and go over the quotes on it, making sure the students understand the concept of mindfulness.

GOSPELS

3. Give the students some practice in mindfulness by having them relax and focus only on their breathing, encouraging them to let go of distractions.

4. Read the exercise from handout Lk–A with the students. Give the students sufficient time to complete the two experiments of mindfulness at home and to write about their experiences and record their reflections. If they struggle with the exercise, note that mastering the technique of mindfulness can take months or even years of practice.

Variation. Invite a guest speaker—perhaps a practicing Buddhist—to the class to address the topic of mindfulness in step 3. Also consider inviting someone who practices the form of meditation called centering prayer to share her or his experience with the class. It would be interesting for the students to hear the two perspectives.

Cuisine and Puzzles in Luke

Exegetical Tools: Historical Criticism—Foods in Luke's Gospel
Luke

This activity invites the students to bring in foods mentioned in Luke, in order to understand the place that food had in Jesus' culture and to appreciate the references to food made in that Gospel.

1. Ask a student to read Lk 13.6–9 aloud to the class. Note the central role of the fig in the story.

2. Direct the students to do a Scripture search of Luke to find where other foods or ingredients are mentioned. They should list the chapter and verse in which they find each reference. When they are done, lead the class in compiling a master list of all the references found by the students. The students should find olive oil, yeast, wheat, fish, bread, grapes, salt, and "mint and rue and herbs" (11.42).

3. Provide the students with information about other foods that were common during Jesus' lifetime in Palestine. Add those foods and corresponding Bible cites to the master list compiled by the class.
Note: Good sources are the articles "food" and "bread" in *The HarperCollins Bible Dictionary,* edited by Paul J. Achtemeier (see appendix A).

4. Plan a day for the students to bring in foods that Jesus and his friends may have eaten. On that day, look at the class's master list of Bible references to foods, and talk about the significance of the items on it. Ask the students to discuss the following questions:
- What does the kind of food used in a culture and how that food is shared tell us about what the culture values? What do the foods used by Jesus and his friends tell us about Jesus' world?
- What are the different ways that food is shared in our multicultural United States? What do the foods that are shared tell us about our culture?

G
O
S
P
E
L
S

Puzzles and Jumbles in Luke
Luke, chapters 8–20

This activity challenges the students to create word jumbles and crossword puzzles based on chapters 8–20 of Luke, and can serve as a review of the Gospel of Luke.

1. Divide chapters 8–20 of Luke into four or five equal parts. Then divide the class into a corresponding number of groups and assign each group one of those sections. Instruct the groups each to create a series of word jumbles or a crossword puzzle that highlights important points and characters in its assigned section. Give some examples of word jumbles, such as tols eeshp (lost sheep) and chir nma dna saalruz (rich man and Lazarus).

2. Pass the completed puzzles and jumbles from group to group and challenge the groups to solve them, or make overhead or computer transparencies of them and solve them as a class in a game show fashion. Invite the students to highlight important concepts about the relevant biblical material as they solve the puzzles and jumbles.

Service to Others

See the activity "Skits: Social Rules in the Reign of God," on pages 239–240 of this manual, for an exploration of the way that Jesus promotes the reversal of social roles in Luke, chapter 14.

Conversion of Heart

The Challenge of Forgiveness
Luke, chapter 15

The students develop role-plays that explore the realities of forgiveness and love experienced by the prodigal son's family after his return.

1. Call a student to read Lk 15.1–10 aloud to the class. Then assign the following roles to four students: Jesus, younger son, father, and older son. Ask those four students to read verses 11–32 aloud to the class.

2. Discuss the story of the prodigal son in light of Lk 15.1–2, noting the parallels between the older son and the Pharisees, the younger son and the sinners, and the father and God. Emphasize God's tremendous desire to love and forgive shown in this difficult human situation.

3. Invite the students to reflect on the challenge of human forgiveness. Divide the class into six groups and assign each of the following relationships from the story of the prodigal son to two groups:
- father and younger son
- father and older son
- younger son and older son

Ask the individuals within the groups each to write a journal entry from the perspective of one of the characters in their assigned relationship or of God in that relationship, basing it on the events of the story and their sense of what challenges lie ahead as the characters try to live together as a family. The group members should divide up the characters among themselves and then share what they wrote with one another.

4. Direct the groups each to prepare a skit portraying a casual encounter between their two human characters a week after the return of the prodigal son. Explain that the skit should reflect some of the emotions expressed in the journal entries and the challenge of trying to move forward as a family in light of the divisions of the past. Add that the skits should also reflect on how God might be a part of the reconciliation process.

5. After the groups present their skits, allow the insights from the presentations to become the basis for a discussion about the process of forgiveness. Ask, "Why is it sometimes most difficult yet most important to forgive within families?"

Interpretive Skits: Zacchaeus
Luke, chapter 19

The students create skits that portray Zacchaeus describing his conversion experience to his wife and friends.

1. Request a student to read Lk 19.1–10 aloud to the class. Review the role of the tax collector with the students to help explain the story.

2. Divide the class into small groups and ask the students to imagine the personalities of Zacchaeus, his wife, his family, and his friends. Direct the groups each to create a short skit that portrays Zacchaeus telling his wife why he decided to give half of his possessions to the poor. The groups should embellish the skit by adding children, friends, neighbors, and so on, to it.

3. After enjoying the presentations, discuss the ways that the groups chose to portray the various characters. Help the students to explore how a drastic conversion like Zacchaeus's would affect a person today and that person's marriage, family, and social circle. Ask, "Does Jesus still inspire such change two thousand years after Zacchaeus?"

The Passion, Death, and Resurrection of Jesus

See the activity "Resurrection Talk Show: A Comparison of the Gospel Accounts," on pages 241–242 of this manual, for an exploration of Jesus' Resurrection.

The *Palestinian Times:* The Good News Edition
Luke, chapters 19–24

Creating a four-page newspaper that features the teachings, events, and people from the last week of Jesus' life helps the students understand and remember those things.

Handout Lk–B

1. In preparation for this activity, have the students read Lk 19.29—24.53 for homework.

2. To begin this activity, divide the class into small groups. Give the groups copies of handout Lk–B, "The *Palestinian Times:* The Good News Edition," and go over the directions with them. Provide expectations about the format and quality of the assignment.

3. Give the groups some time in class to work on this project. Consider providing some biblical tools such as a concordance, biblical dictionary, biblical commentary, and biblical atlas to assist the students.

4. On the day that the project is due, invite the groups to share their newspapers with the class. Then encourage the students to reflect on their experiences with this journalism project. Ask, "What insights did this approach give you about the Passion and death of Jesus?"

Signs of God's Presence
Luke, chapter 24
"Jesus Is with Us!" Lk 24.13–35, CYB

Reflecting on Jesus' appearance to his followers on the road to Emmaus invites the students to identify God's presence in their everyday lives.

1. Ask several students to take the roles of narrator, Jesus, Cleopas, and Cleopas's companion for a reading of Lk 24.13–35. Call another student to read the article "Jesus Is with Us!" from the *CYB*.

2. Discuss the meaning of the word *sign*. Note that a sign points to the presence of something greater than itself. For instance, a road sign indicates something that might have gone unnoticed or identifies a street, college, or whatever.
Ask the students to identify the signs of Jesus that his two companions notice on the road to Emmaus. Also ask them to identify the signs that Tim observes at Mass in the *CYB* article. List both sets of signs on the board. Note that though those signs were not equivalent to God, they helped people recognize God's presence.

3. Form small groups and have the students think of signs of God's presence from their own experience. Ask the groups each to make "road signs" that portray those indicators that God is present. Supply appropriate art materials, such as construction paper, colored markers or pencils, scissors, and glue.

4. Invite the groups to share their completed signs with the class and discuss what helps us be attentive to such signs in our lives. Afterward, display the signs in the classroom or around the school, or both.

⋯⋯⋯⋯⋯► The Practice of Mindfulness

While washing the dishes one should only be washing the dishes, which means that while washing the dishes one should be completely aware of the fact that one is washing the dishes. At first glance, that might seem a little silly: why put so much stress on a simple thing? But that's precisely the point. The fact that I am standing there and washing these bowls is a wondrous reality. I'm being completely myself, following my breath, conscious of my presence, and conscious of my thoughts and actions. There's no way I can be tossed around mindlessly like a bottle slapped here and there on the waves. (Pages 3–4)

If while washing dishes, we think only of the cup of tea that awaits us, thus hurrying to get the dishes out of the way as if they were a nuisance, then we are not "washing the dishes to wash the dishes." What's more, we are not alive during the time we are washing the dishes. In fact we are completely incapable of realizing the miracle of life while standing at the sink. If we can't wash the dishes, the chances are we won't be able to drink our tea either. While drinking the cup of tea, we will only be thinking of other things, barely aware of the cup in our hands. Thus we are sucked away into the future—and we are incapable of actually living one minute of life. (Thich Nhat Hanh, *The Miracle of Mindfulness: A Manual on Meditation,* revised edition, translated by Mobi Ho [Boston: Beacon Press, 1987], pages 4–5. Copyright © 1975, 1976 by Thich Nhat Hanh. Preface and English translation copyright © 1975, 1976, 1987 by Mobi Ho.)

Exercise

In two fifteen-minute blocks, explore the Buddhist practice of mindfulness by completely focusing on the activity that you are doing—riding the bus, eating, listening to music, running, or whatever. Be sensitive to the sights, sounds, smells, and feel of the activity. Then, in the spaces below, describe your experiences and reflect on the values, challenges, and results of this exercise.

■ My description of the first experience:

■ My description of the second experience:

■ My reflections on the value and challenges of mindfulness:

■ How mindfulness might help people become more aware of the good things in their lives and be less anxious:

·············▶ The *Palestinian Times:* The Good News Edition

Read Lk 19.28—24.53 and any other materials provided by your teacher. Using those sources, create a four-page newspaper that includes the following nine items. For each item, cite the chapters and verses from Luke, and the titles and page numbers of other sources that supplied information.

1. **Feature article.** Using major headlines, create a main story around the torture, death, and Resurrection of Jesus (Luke, chapters 22–24).

2. **Letters to the editor.** Write reactions to the news that Jesus rose from the dead, from the positions of two of the following characters:
   - a male or female disciple of Jesus
   - Pontius Pilate
   - a Pharisee, Sadducee, chief priest, or scribe
   - a Zealot

3. **Interview.** Choose one of the following passages and report an interview with the main character or characters. The interview should have at least four questions and answers.
   - Simon Peter's betrayal and forgiveness (Lk 22.31–34,54–62)
   - Joseph of Arimathea and the burial of Jesus (Lk 23.50–56)
   - The Roman soldier at the cross (Lk 23.44–49)
   - The disciples walking to Emmaus (Lk 24.13–35)

4. **Financial article.** Create a finance question-and-answer article based on at least two of the following passages:
   - Lk 19.45–47
   - Lk 20.20–26
   - Lk 21.1–4

5. **Guest editorials.** Write a guest editorial by Jesus entitled "Why I Don't Get Along with the Pharisees, Sadducees, Chief Priests, and Scribes," and then a rebuttal by one of those groups, entitled "Why We Don't Get Along with Jesus." For background, use two of the following passages in which Jesus and the Pharisees or Sadducees are arguing. Under each headline, give the corresponding side's view of the issue and related feelings.
   - Lk 19.45–48
   - Lk 20.1–8
   - Lk 20.9–19
   - Lk 20.27–40
   - Lk 20.45–47

6. **Horoscope.** List Jesus' predictions about the future, which can be found in these and other passages:
   - Lk 19.41–44
   - Lk 21.5–6
   - Lk 21.7–19
   - Lk 21.20–24
   - Lk 21.25–28
   - Lk 21.29–33

7. **Picture.** Provide one picture that relates to one of the news items listed above, and write a caption for the picture.

8. **Advertisement.** Create one advertisement for an item related to something in Luke, chapters 19–24.

9. **One additional article.** Create an article for a section such as weather, gardening, kids, comics, puzzles, sports, or want ads.

John

Who Is This Jesus?

Diagram of the Beginning
John, chapter 1
"The 'Cosmic Christ,'" Jn 1.1–18, CYB

A visual presentation of the prologue to John's Gospel helps the students explore the meaning of that complex passage.

   1. Invite a student to read Jn 1.1–18 aloud to the class. Ask another student to read the article "The 'Cosmic Christ'" from the *CYB*.

   2. Direct the students each to diagram several verses from the reading. The students should feel free to present the verses in any way that helps them understand the relationships described. They may portray the verses with symbols only, use key words and symbols, or write out the verses in a way that helps map their meaning. The students should list any questions that emerge for them about the passage.

   3. After a designated time, invite the students to share their visual interpretations of the passage by putting some of them on the board and discussing any questions that emerge.

John the Baptist: The Musical
John, chapters 1–2

This exercise invites the students to tell the stories of John, chapters 1–2, through musical dialog in the Broadway tradition.

   1. Show the students a video clip from the movie version of a good Broadway musical, such as one of these:
   - *Evita* (Paulist Pictures, 1996, 112 min., rated PG-13)
   - *Fiddler on the Roof* (Mirisch Productions, 1971, 180 min., rated G)
   - *Godspell* (Columbia Pictures, 1973, 102 min., rated G)
   - *West Side Story* (United Artists, 1961, 151 min., not rated)
Discuss with the students the roles of the music, movement, and dialog in telling the story.

   2. Divide the class into four groups and assign each group one of these passages:
   - Jn 1.19–28
   - Jn 1.35–51
   - Jn 2.1–12
   - Jn 2.13–25

Direct the groups to prepare to tell their passage musically, either in person or on videotape. Explain that in the preparation process, they should focus on the story line first and then add music, dance, and movement. Encourage them to sing the dialog. (Sometimes, telling the groups all to use music with a common thread, such as Christmas songs or fifties or sixties pieces, works well.)

3. After the groups present their musicals, lead a class discussion of the new perspectives of the Scripture passages that arose from the use of music and movement.

Variation. Invite a drama teacher or drama student to join the class and offer perspectives on the points covered in step 1.

In step 1, obtain a script, score, and sound recording for one of the musicals mentioned, and lead the students through a dramatic musical reading of part of the work.

"I Am" Mobile
John, chapters 5, 6, 8, 10–11, 14–15
"'I Am' Sayings of Jesus," John 5.16–18, CYB

The students construct a mobile illustrating the various ways that Jesus describes himself in John's Gospel.

1. Before this activity, make a frame for a mobile out of wood or wire, and gather cardboard, scissors, colored markers or pencils, string and other materials for finishing the mobile.

2. Begin this activity by asking a student to read the article "'I Am' Sayings of Jesus" from the *CYB*. Direct the students to form pairs and to read John, chapters 5, 6, 8, 10–11, and 14–15, with their partners, listing the different "I Am" statements that Jesus makes.

3. Show the students the mobile frame you have made, and ask them to finish the mobile. Instruct one or two students to cut the letters of the phrase "I Am" out of heavy cardboard. That will be the top of the mobile. Have the students in their pairs draw on cardboard the images that Jesus describes in the reading, and attach them to the mobile.

Then invite the students to prepare cardboard pieces with other related phrases or images of Jesus, and hang them from the "I Am" images, so that the mobile has several layers. You also might want to invite the students to suggest their own endings for the "I Am" sentence-starter, and hang them as another layer.

4. Talk about the different images presented in the completed mobile, and introduce or review the characteristics of metaphors. Discuss how metaphors are powerful ways for us to gain insights into the nature of God.

The Bread of Life: Breads from Around the World
John, chapter 6
"The Eucharist," John, chapter 6, CYB

This activity invites the students to reflect on the symbolism of bread, the miracle of the loaves, and Jesus' statement "I am the bread of life" (Jn 6.35).

1. Have a student read the article "The Eucharist" from the *CYB* to the class.

2. Tell the students that you would like them to bring breads from around the world into class on a designated day. Ask the students to brainstorm a variety of breads that they might bring, and list their responses on the board. Invite them to suggest breads that reflect their cultural heritage or family traditions, and then fill in the list with breads from societies not represented in the class.
Tell the students to choose a partner, and ask each pair of students to bring one type of bread and an appropriate spread or other complementary food. Mention that any research they do on the foods would be a bonus.
Note: Providing some recipes for different breads would be helpful. The Internet is a rich resource for international recipes.

3. On the designated day, provide drinks and give the students free time to sample the different foods and visit with one another. Then invite them to share some of the breads' stories. They might tell something about their family, about the culture's use of the bread, or even about how they came to bake or buy their particular loaf.
The students will probably have a good time while the tasting is going on. Note that, and help them see that bread provides an important time for people to connect with one another, in addition to being the backbone of many cultures' diets.

4. The next day in class, invite the students to take turns reading John, chapter 6. Address the story of the multiplication of loaves and fish, and Jesus' discussion of his role as the bread of life, examining both in light of the class's experience and reflections about bread the previous day. Remind the students that bread is the backbone of many cultures' diets. Invite them to see the central role that Jesus is claiming in our lives with the statement of his role. Note that he not only nourishes us physically but also is the center of our community building.

Jesus' Miracles and Teachings

Gospel Role-Plays
John, chapters 2, 4–5, 8–9

A number of the longer stories in John's Gospel lend themselves nicely to role-plays that help the students understand and remember those stories. The role-plays may be performed together as an overview of chapters 2, 4–5, and 8–9, or separately as the passages are discussed individually.

1. Divide the class into groups of five or more, and assign each group a passage with the same number of characters from the list below. Ask the groups to read their assigned passage and discuss its meaning. Then invite them each to prepare a short skit that narrates their passage and explores its meaning. Note that they may need to provide some extra dialog or props, or both.

- *Jn 2.1–11 (The wedding at Cana).* narrator, Mary, Jesus, servants, chief steward, and bridegroom
- *Jn 4.7–42 (The Samaritan woman at the well).* narrator, Samaritan woman, Jesus, two or more disciples, and two or more Samaritans from the city
- *Jn 5.1–18 (The healing of a man on the Sabbath).* narrator, ill man, Jesus, and two or more Jews
- *Jn 8.2–11 (The woman caught in adultery).* narrator, Jesus, crowd, one or more Scribes, one or more Pharisees, and adulteress
- *John, chapter 9 (The man born blind).* narrator, Jesus, blind man, two or more disciples, two or more neighbors, two or more Pharisees and Jews, and blind man's mother and father

2. After each skit is performed, invite the actors and audience to reflect on the message and interpretation of the story.

Prayer Styles: Guided Imagery—Throwing Stones
John, chapter 8
"Divine Compassion," Jn 8.2–11, CYB

This activity reviews the biblical story of the woman caught in adultery and then engages the students in a hands-on guided imagery in which they act out a similar movement from judgment and anger to empathy and forgiveness.

1. Prepare for this activity by collecting enough rocks for all the students in the class. Pile them in the space where the students will be. If possible, arrange to take the students outside for this activity.

2. Begin this activity by asking one student to read Jn 8.2–11 aloud to the class and another to read the article "Divine Compassion" from the *CYB*.

3. Introduce or review the prayer style called guided imagery. Give the following instructions to the students in your own words, pausing frequently to allow them sufficient time to follow your cues:

- Please follow my directions as we go through a guided imagery. I will ask you to start and stop moving throughout.

    Imagine the face of a person with whom you feel angry or whom you judge as wrong or bad.

    Imagine that you have had an encounter with this person with whom you are angry. . . . You are so angry that in your frustration, you feel like you could hurl a rock at the person.

    START. Begin to move slowly toward the pile of rocks. . . . Look for a rock. Which one will you choose? Why?

    STOP. Hold this posture and consider the rocks and their power.

    START. Reach for a rock, pick it up, and slowly stand up.

    STOP. Feel the rock's weight. How angry would you have to be to actually throw this rock hard at someone?

    START. Slowly begin to move into a throwing position.

    STOP. Jesus says, "Let anyone among you who is without sin be the first to throw a stone at her" (Jn 8.7). Sense how tense you feel, ready to release. Picture the person you are angry with curled up on the ground, and Jesus standing right in front of him or her. Jesus again says, "The one without sin may cast the first stone." You still do not move. You become aware of the number of rocks poised in the air all around you. What if the rocks were aimed at you? The weight in your hand is your own dislike for the person you are picturing. It is your pain to bear. Jesus says it again: "The one without sin may cast the first stone."

START. You slowly bring your arm down and drop the stone.

STOP. What have you released?

4. Give the students some quiet time to reflect about this meditation or write about it in their journal. Invite them to share any insights that they feel comfortable contributing. Close the discussion by talking about our needing Jesus' healing presence in order to release our anger and move toward forgiveness.

Good Shepherd Cartoons
John, chapter 10
"Jesus, the Good Shepherd," John 10.1–18, CYB

Creating cartoon strips that feature the sheep in Jesus' flock helps the students explore the idea of Jesus as the good shepherd.

1. Bring in various samples of popular cartoons, such as "Calvin and Hobbes," "Peanuts," "The Far Side," "Ziggy," and "Cathy." Pass them around and ask the students to assess what makes a good cartoon.

2. Explain to the students that they will be creating cartoon strips based on the sheep and good shepherd images found in John's Gospel. Tell the students to keep that in mind and listen carefully as you read Jn 10.1–18. After your reading, ask a student to read aloud the background information on shepherding found in the article "Jesus, the Good Shepherd" in the *CYB*.

3. Divide the class into groups. Discuss the cartoon assignment in terms of audience and tone. Tell the groups each to create a cartoon strip for children, for office calendars, or for those with a keen sense of humor. Tell the students that creating cartoons involves more than art: it requires ideas, layout, and character (or sheep) development as well. Provide blank paper and other art supplies for this project.

4. Share the groups' completed cartoons with the class by hanging them up in the room. Make observations connecting the images in the cartoons to Jesus' relationship with his followers, and use those observations as a basis for a discussion of Jesus as the good shepherd.

Skits: Social Rules in the Reign of God
John, chapter 13; Luke, chapter 14
"Jesus Models Service to Others," John 13.1–17, CYB

The way that Jesus promotes the reversal of social roles challenges the students to use modern social expectations to express the radical message of the Reign of God.

1. Request one student to read Jn 13.1–17 aloud to the class and another to read the article "Jesus Models Service to Others" from the *CYB*. Discuss the surprising social reversal that Jesus advocates in the Scripture reading. Ask volunteers to read Lk 14.7–24, and contrast the social recommendations that Jesus makes in that passage with the social conventions that would normally be followed.

2. Divide the class into groups. Direct the groups each to identify a commonly accepted social practice and adapt it to communicate something of Jesus' message. Invite them to prepare a two-part skit that portrays the expectations in modern society and then the expectations of the Reign of God. Ask the groups to explain their skits to you before presenting them, for your approval.

3. Following the skit presentations, note the values that were portrayed in each one, highlighting the different paths held up by society and by the Gospels.

Jesus' Farewell Discourse

Farewell Discourse Cards
John, chapters 14–17

The students read the scriptural account of Jesus' farewell discourse and create greeting cards from verses in that passage.

1. In preparation for this activity, ask the students to read Jesus' farewell discourse, John, chapters 14–17. Also ensure that white drawing paper, colored markers or pencils, and watercolor paints are available.

2. Begin this activity by giving the students white drawing paper and asking them to design a greeting card that is based on a verse or verses from the Scripture reading. The card may simply feature the verse or verses, or have a theme such as encouragement, inspiration, sympathy, or congratulations. The students may illustrate the card and add other text as appropriate.

3. Ask the students to share their completed cards or display them, and to reflect on the timelessness and meaning of Jesus' words. Invite them to send the cards to people who might appreciate receiving a comforting message.

The Passion Narrative
John, chapters 18–19

The students explore John's narrative of Jesus' Passion.

Several activities from the Passion narratives in the synoptic Gospels can easily be adapted to enrich the reading of John's Passion account:
- "Skits of Comforting Friendship," on page 206 of this manual
- "Journal Entries from the Passion," on page 207

- "Stained-Glass Windows for the Passion," on pages 218–219
- "The Stations of the Cross," on pages 219–220
- "The *Palestinian Times:* The Good News Edition," on page 232
- "Signs of God's Presence," on page 232

The Resurrection

Resurrection Talk Show: A Comparison of the Gospel Accounts
John, chapters 20–21; Matthew, chapter 28; Mark, chapter 16; Luke, chapter 24

A "talk show" with questions from a live audience allows the students to address the four different Gospel accounts of the Resurrection and the nature of the risen Jesus.

1. Have the students prepare for this activity by reading John, chapters 20–21, Matthew, chapter 28, Mark, chapter 16, and Luke, chapter 24.

2. Divide the class into nine groups for two talk show episodes. The first episode will cover initial experiences of and reactions to the Resurrection and will feature groups assigned to these readings:
- Jn 20.1–18
- Mt 28.1–10
- Mk 16.1–8
- Lk 24.1–12

The second episode will cover post-Resurrection encounters with the risen Jesus and will include groups assigned to these readings:
- Jn 20.19–29
- Jn 21.1–23
- Mt 28.16–20
- Lk 24.13–35
- Lk 24.36–43

Let the students know that you will act as the host of the show.

3. Direct the groups each to read their assigned passage and to prepare to play the roles in that reading. Mention that the students need to imagine what it was like to experience the Resurrection and then reflect on how it affected the lives of those involved.

4. Stage the first talk show episode, with you interviewing the students playing the characters from the first set of Scripture readings, and the students assigned to the second set of readings serving as the audience. Solicit the various versions of what happened at the tomb, and allow the audience to ask questions about the event. Encourage discussion about the variety of accounts, the nature of the risen Jesus, the power of the Resurrection on the people's lives, and so on.

In this episode, there will likely be more than one Mary Magdalene, Peter, and so on, each representing a different account. Challenge the students to think about how the differences in accounts emerged. Help them to understand this by having them consider a powerful experience in their own lives and the different ways that people present could describe it.

Host the second episode of the talk show in a similar fashion, inviting related questions and discussion.

5. Given the variety of accounts, help the students arrive at the basic version of what happened at the tomb and the essence of an encounter with the resurrected Jesus.

Dear Jesus Letters and Answers to Doubts
John, chapter 20

The students create a list of questions and then collaborate on letters that ask Jesus to address the doubts and questions of teens.

1. Direct the students to reflect quietly and prayerfully on Jn 20.19–29. With quiet music playing, ask them each to make a list of their questions and doubts surrounding Jesus.

2. Form small groups, and encourage the students to share with their group some of their questions and doubts. Each group should then address several of those questions in the format of a Dear Abby letter to Jesus.

3. Instruct the groups each to pass their letter to another group, which should formulate the answer it thinks Jesus would give. Each letter, along with its answer, should then be returned to the group that wrote it.

4. Invite each group to present the questions it addressed and the responses to those questions. Carefully listen to both questions and answers. Help the students to be attentive to the hopes and concerns that they express through their questions and responses, and to the image of Jesus that they present.

Prayer Styles: Guided Imagery—Do You Love Me?
John, chapter 21

A guided imagery of Peter's encounter with Jesus on the shore of the Sea of Tiberias helps the students enter into their own experience of the risen Jesus.

1. Call several students to read Jn 21.1–23 aloud to the class.

2. Introduce or review the nature of a guided imagery with the students, and settle the students into a reflective mind-set. Then guide the students in a meditation based on Jn 21.15–17, using the following steps and your own imagination:
- Create a quiet mood with some music or a simple exercise of having the students attend to their breathing for several counts, or both.
- Place the students in the Bible scene, on the beach, bringing to their minds the sights, sounds, smells, and feel of the setting.
- Tell the rest of the story meditatively, allowing sufficient time for the students to imagine the people and the things being said. When Jesus speaks to Peter, invite the students to imagine Jesus asking them the same questions. Allow the students time to reflect on their own responses. Give them time to dialog with Jesus personally at the end of the story.

- Wrap up the meditation by asking the students to take leave of Jesus and to return to the classroom or space you are in.

   3. Give the students time to reflect on the experience in writing. Then discuss the story, asking the students to reflect on why Jesus asks Peter the same question repeatedly. Invite them to contribute any insights or reflections they are comfortable sharing.

The Good News of Our Class
John, chapter 21
"The Gospel According to . . . ," Jn 21.24–25, CYB

Reflecting on the final sentence of John's Gospel helps the students consider the ways that they see Jesus bringing good news to the world today.

   1. Ask one student to read Jn 21.24–25 and another to read the article "The Gospel According to . . ." from the *CYB*.

   2. Invite the students to reflect on one way that they have seen Jesus working in the world today. Note that they may choose an experience from their own lives or the lives of friends or family, or look to the larger society and world for a sign of Jesus' good news.

   3. As homework for the next class, request the students to bring in a visual representation of the good news they have reflected on, accompanied by a brief, typed account of their reflection. Note that they will be contributing both items to a class collage or bulletin board.

   4. In the next class, invite the students to share their visual representations and written accounts with one another informally or in the context of a prayer experience.

   5. Create a collage or bulletin board with the students' visual and written contributions. The presentation could have a title such as "The Good News According to Second Period."

Acts

Introduction to the Acts of the Apostles

Acts of the Apostles Comic Book: An Overview
Acts of the Apostles
Introduction to Acts, CYB

The students create a comic book version of the Acts of the Apostles in order to get an overview of its story line.

1. Before this activity, prepare 8½-by-11-inch pieces of paper with a border that defines where the students should illustrate their cartoons and also allows the cartoons to be bound together in a book. The top, right side, and bottom of the page might have a 1-inch border, and the left side a 1½-inch border.

2. Begin this activity by inviting a student to read the introduction to Acts from the *CYB* aloud to the class.

3. Divide the class into groups of two or three and divide the chapters from Acts equally among the groups. Then hand each student a sheet of the bordered paper you have prepared, distribute colored markers or pens, and give these instructions in your own words:
- Each group should read its assigned chapters, then outline the major events and concepts of those chapters and identify the most important events that occur within them.
- Every member of the group should next make a one-page cartoon with several panels. Depending on the nature of the assigned chapters, you may make several panels that each depict an event, or use several panels to retell a longer, more important, or more detailed story. The panels should be drawn within the designated border of the sheet of paper I just gave you, and should include captions that describe the event and cite the relevant chapter and verse. Despite the cartoon form of this activity, humor is not a necessary or desired characteristic for every story.

4. After collecting the finished cartoons, copy them and make books to distribute for a quick look at the Acts of the Apostles. Go over the cartoons with the students, filling in the missing story lines as you go along.

Variation. In step 4, instead of copying the cartoons and binding the copies together in books, make computer or overhead transparencies of the cartoons and share them with the class in that form. If you choose this option, you may simply distribute blank sheets of paper for the cartoons, rather than preparing sheets with printed borders.

Jesus' Ascension

Filming the Ascension
Acts of the Apostles, chapter 1

The students plan a movie scene depicting the Ascension, as a way of reflecting on that event.

    1. Direct the students to read Acts 1.1–14 silently.

    2. Divide the class into groups of four or five. Ask the students to imagine that they are in charge of shooting a movie about the Acts of the Apostles. Explain that their current project is to plan the scene portraying the Ascension of Jesus, Acts 1.6–11. Note that each group should do these things:
- Describe the location for the shoot. (The students should think of a place in the United States that might most closely resemble Palestine.)
- Select actors, costumes, and stage directions—covering all the lines and nonverbal actions presented in the Scripture reading.
- List props and describe sets, explaining how to portray Jesus' departure literally or symbolically.
- Choose music as background for the scene.

    3. Invite the groups to share their finished plans for the scene. Elicit their reflections, based on their plans, about the power of the Ascension for Jesus' followers. Also help them recognize what their choices in life reveal about their perception of Jesus and his followers, miraculous events, personal transformation, and so on.

A Decision-Making Simulation
Acts of the Apostles, chapter 1

This activity helps the students explore the pros and cons of making decisions using three approaches: voting, consensus, and prayerful discernment. They begin this exploration with a simulation of the approach used by Jesus' followers to select the twelfth Apostle.

    1. Conduct a simulation of the discernment process used by the Apostles in Acts of the Apostles, chapter 1, as follows: Gather all the students into a circle and describe to them a class decision that you would usually present for their vote or make yourself—such as the date of a test, the due date for an assignment, or what to do about low test grades. Present two options to the students and ask them to pray with you about the best decision. Lead them in this process in the following way:
- Say: "Lord, you know the heart of everyone here in this circle. Show us which one of the two options you have chosen . . ."
- Assign a short stick to one decision and a long stick to the other. Align one end of the sticks and hide the other end, so the two sticks appear to be the same length. Then present the two sticks to a student and ask the student to choose one. Announce that the decision assigned to the chosen stick is the one the class will follow.
- Discuss with the students whether the decision is the best one and what part they think God had in it.

2. Read Acts 1.12–26 together in class. Discuss with the students why another disciple was needed and note the process used for selecting him. Discuss the virtues and limitations of that decision-making approach.

3. Discuss with the class these three different ways that people make decisions in groups:
- voting (majority decision)
- consensus (mutual agreement)
- prayerful discernment (prayer for God's guidance)

Divide the class into three groups and assign each group to one of those three decision-making methods. Announce a real issue faced by the class or school, and ask the groups each to plan a way to conduct their assigned decision-making process for that issue.

4. Have each group lead the class in reaching a decision using its assigned process. Compare the outcomes and discuss which method is most effective and why. Help the students see how the three different approaches are better suited to some settings than others.

5. To explore the issue of decision making further, ask the students to research the different ways that it is handled in their parishes.

Exegetical Tools:
The Concordance—a Study of the Holy Spirit
Acts of the Apostles
"Pentecost," Acts 2.1–13, CYB

Finding the many references to the Holy Spirit in Acts allows the students to look at the varied manifestations of the Spirit.

1. Invite several students to read Acts of the Apostles, chapter 2, and the article "Pentecost" from the *CYB* aloud to the class. Discuss the powerful effects of the Spirit's presence in the Scripture account.

2. Divide the class into five groups and assign each group one of the following sections of the Bible:
- Acts of the Apostles, chapters 1–4
- Acts of the Apostles, chapters 5–8
- Acts of the Apostles, chapters 9–11
- Acts of the Apostles, chapters 13, 15–16, 19
- Acts of the Apostles, chapters 20–21, 23, 28

Ask the groups each to find references to the Holy Spirit in their assigned chapters and to write down the qualities and powers of the Holy Spirit. Explain that the groups should then devise a creative way of presenting the Spirit's characteristics, such as through a short résumé, job description, advertisement, or commercial.

3. Invite the groups to share their presentations. As they do so, create a master list of the Spirit's qualities on the board. Then review with the students the seven gifts of the Holy Spirit and the fruits of the Holy Spirit (see *Catechism,* nos. 1830–1832), and match those with the characteristics found in Acts.

4. Ask the students to write a short reflection about a time that they experienced the Holy Spirit or experienced some of the gifts or fruits of the Spirit. Invite the students to share their stories as they are comfortable.

5. Conclude by pointing out that it was by powerful lived experience that the early church first recognized the activity of the Spirit as the presence of God.

Living Models of the Trinity
Acts of the Apostles, chapter 2

The students create life-size models of the Trinity as a way of reflecting on the nature of God.

1. Allow the students to form groups of four and tell them to read Acts of the Apostles, chapter 2, in their groups.

2. Discuss the description of Pentecost given in the reading. Point out the following things in your own words:

- At Pentecost, Jesus' followers experienced the fullness of the Trinity. As Jews, they had experienced God the father from their earliest years. Then they met Jesus and experienced him as God through his life, death, and Resurrection. Now, they also experienced the divine presence of the Spirit. The Trinity is a mystery that Christians have tried to explain for centuries.

3. Direct the students, in their groups, to develop a model of the Trinity, using their own bodies to represent the "threeness" and "oneness" of God. Explain that the model should reflect something of the nature of the three persons of the Trinity as well as their relationship with one another. Note that the fourth member of each group should describe the model to the rest of the class.

4. Invite the groups to present their models. After the presentations, ask questions to help the students reflect on their understanding of God. Summarize the insights about the Trinity that emerge.

Variations. To promote further discussion, in step 3, direct the groups to add to their model a human and address the question "How do human beings relate to God as Trinity?"

To explore another avenue of reflection, in step 4, conduct a discussion about how the belief in God as Trinity affects the way that Christians relate with one another in everyday life.

G
O
S
P
E
L
S

The Christian Life

Christian Community: A Model
Acts of the Apostles, chapters 2, 4
"Christian Community," Acts 2.43–47, CYB

Looking at some of the realities of living in Christian community helps the students appreciate the challenges and blessings of that type of lifestyle.

1. Prepare for this activity by familiarizing yourself with some current examples of communal living, whether Christian or secular.
Note: Searches on the Internet using terms such as *co-housing* and *intentional community* will turn up many sites. Adding *Christian* to the searches will narrow them.

2. Begin this activity by asking a student to read Acts 2.43–47 and 4.32–37 aloud to the class. Have another student read the article "Christian Community" from the *CYB.*

3. With the help of the students, create a profile of a small Christian community composed of four couples and their children. Decide on details such as the number and ages of the children, professions of the adults, and names. Ask the students to identify some of the issues a Christian community might face.

4. Invite the students to group themselves according to those with artistic or design gifts, logical or organizational skills, and relational or spiritual interests (you may prefer to form the groups yourself). Assign the following tasks to the groups:
- *Group 1: artistic or design gifts.* Design a large home that would house the hypothetical Christian community: discuss the families' needs for privacy and community, and then sketch a floor plan.
- *Group 2: logical or organizational skills.* Discuss economic and decision-making realities for the families; outline, in writing, the ways that they would share resources and the processes they would use for making decisions that would affect the whole group.
- *Group 3: relational or spiritual interests.* Talk about the ways that the community would consciously promote Christian values and close relationships between its members; explore how the community would experience prayer and nurture spirituality, as well as the overall lifestyle, parenting choices, and so forth, of the community. Write a summary of the discussion.
Instruct the groups to make computer or overhead transparencies of their proposals and ideas, to present to the class.

5. After the groups have explained their ideas to one another, invite the students to reflect about the lifestyle they have described. Lead the class in a discussion about what is attractive and unattractive in that kind of Christian living. Help them to brainstorm ways that single-family households can create a greater Christian community. Remind them that God can give people the grace to work through some of the challenges presented by a Christian community model for living.

Variations. To explore this topic further, have the students find and share stories from the New Testament about early Christians and the challenges they faced.

Invite a guest speaker who is living in an intentional Christian community to share her or his experience with the class.

Stewardship: Time-and-Talents Pie Charts
Acts of the Apostles, chapter 4
"Stewardship," Acts 4.32–37, CYB

This exercise challenges the students to reflect on the way that they use their time and talents, by diagramming two pie charts.

  1. Ask one student to read Acts 4.32–37 and another to read the article "Stewardship" from the *CYB*. Invite the students' reactions about the lifestyle portrayed in the passage from Acts.

  2. Direct the students each to make a pie chart that reflects how they use their time in an average week, according to categories such as sleeping, eating, studying, participating in extracurricular activities, working, being with family, being alone, and being with friends. Explain that for each category, the students should list both the talents or gifts they are using during that time, and whether that activity is primarily for themselves, others, or a combination. You might give an example, such as this: "When I am with friends, I give the gifts of my good listening skills and my sense of humor. In return, I receive support and fun, so this activity is both for me and for others."

  3. Instruct the students to make a second pie chart that reflects the percentage of time that they spend on themselves and others, dividing that chart into the categories family, friends, community, and so on. Note that the percentages should be approximations, although the students should use their basic math skills for a certain degree of accuracy. Add that they should include in the pie chart the talents that they regularly employ.

  4. Tell the students to write a short reflection about the discoveries they have made about their use of time and talents in light of the passage from Acts. Though some will be surprised at how much they focus on themselves, others will be equally surprised at how much time they spend for the good of others.
  Tell the students that though God calls Christians to give of themselves at all times in life, the high school years tend to be heavy on receiving in preparation for a lifetime of service through career, family, and relationships.

Student Discipleship on Trial
Acts of the Apostles, chapter 5
"Pop Quiz," Acts 5.27–39, CYB

This activity allows the students to both defend and prosecute discipleship in their school's student body.

  1. Ask several students to read aloud Acts 5.12–42 and the article "Pop Quiz" from the *CYB*. Discuss the reasons why the Jewish leadership feels threatened. Also discuss the leaders' request of the Apostles, and the response the Apostles give.

2. Brainstorm with the class some examples of what it means for teenagers to live the Gospel. Tell the students that they will now run a mock trial in which the student body of their school is charged with being disciples of Jesus. Note that a guilty verdict would mean that the student body, for the most part, lives up to the Christian message; a not-guilty verdict would mean that the student body, for the most part, does not live up to the Gospel. Assign the following roles:

- judge
- bailiff
- prosecuting attorney or attorneys
- defense attorney or attorneys
- three witnesses for the prosecution, who will give testimony that supports the discipleship of the student body
- three witnesses for the defense, who will give testimony that calls into question the student body's discipleship
- a jury made up of the remaining students

Explain that the trial will follow this sequence: After a call to order, the judge explains the criteria for judging the innocence or guilt of the student body. The prosecution and defense give opening statements and then question and cross-examine the witnesses. The attorneys then present final arguments before the jury deliberates and decides.

3. Allow time for the students to prepare, then hold the trial. Afterward, discuss the outcome of the trial and the arguments made throughout.

Note the reactions of the Apostles in Acts 5.29–32 and 5.40–42, and compare them with the reasons that the student body might have for being attracted to a Christian lifestyle or resisting such a lifestyle. Ask, "Where might Gamaliel's wisdom be used in some aspects of church or society today?"

The Amazing Works of the Spirit

Newspaper Headlines: Miraculous Events in Acts
Acts of the Apostles, chapters 5, 9–10, 12–14, 16, 19–20

The students create newspaper headlines and lead stories surrounding the amazing events in Acts.

1. Bring to class some examples of newspaper headlines and lead stories, especially those that present sensational information.

2. Divide the class into pairs, and assign one or more of these eleven stories to each pair of students, making sure all the stories are covered:
- Acts 5.1–11 (Ananias and Sapphira)
- Acts 9.36–43 (Tabitha)
- Acts of the Apostles, chapter 10 (Cornelius)
- Acts 12.1–19 (Peter's escape)
- Acts 12.20–23 (Herod's death)
- Acts 13.1–12 (The blinding of a false prophet)
- Acts 14.8–20 (The healing of a lame man)
- Acts 16.16–18 (The calling out of a girl's divination spirit)
- Acts 16.19–40 (Paul and Silas's release from prison in Philippi)

- Acts 19.11–20 (Paul's miracles)
- Acts 20.7–12 (The boy who fell three floors)

Pass out the examples of newspaper headlines and lead stories that you brought to class. Ask the students to note the way that the headlines are phrased and the style used in the stories.

Tell the pairs of students to read their assigned story from Acts and then design a newspaper headline with a corresponding article and picture. Mention that the pairs may include witness interviews or other pieces to add to the authentic feel of the report. Note that the report should be typed.

3. When the reports are ready, allow the pairs to summarize their stories for the class and pass around their articles for everyone to review. Discuss the following questions with the students:

- What do these amazing events say about the nature of early Christianity?
- Do such events happen today because of the work of the Spirit?

Jerusalem Live!
Acts of the Apostles, chapters 7–8

The students prepare a live television broadcast from Jerusalem at the scenes of Stephen's martyrdom and Saul's persecution.

1. Divide the class into groups and read Acts 6.8—8.3 together. Tell the students that they should collaborate in their groups to create a live television program based on the events in the reading. Give some examples of current news shows as models. Explain that the students' programs should include live reporting as well as interviews with Stephen's family, his friends, and Saul.

2. Invite the groups to perform their news programs in class, and discuss the insights that emerge in the interviews and narration of events. Ask the students to note parallels between Stephen's death and Jesus' Crucifixion.

Saul Timelines: Charting a Spiritual Journey
Acts of the Apostles, chapters 8–13
"Saint Paul," Acts 8.1–3, CYB

The students create a timeline that follows Saul from his days of being a persecutor of Christians to his conversion and early preaching.

1. To prepare for this activity, assign the students to read Acts 7.54—13.52 beforehand. Ask the students to bring in large colored markers or provide them yourself. Also provide butcher paper or continuous-feed computer paper.

2. To begin this activity, ask a student to read the article "Saint Paul" from the *CYB*.

3. Divide the class into groups and give each group a long strip of butcher paper or computer paper. Then offer the following instructions in your own words:

- Each group is to create a timeline that traces Saul's spiritual growth from the days he ordered persecutions of Christians, through his conversion experience, and into his early preaching for Christianity. The timeline should be similar to a line graph and should chart the ups and downs of the key events of Saul's life as portrayed in Acts of the Apostles, chapters 8–13. Feel free to enhance the timeline with a theme. The graph should be colorful and may also include different symbols or illustrations.

4. Have each group hang its completed timeline up in the classroom or the hall. Discuss Saul's unusual journey toward Jesus, noting similarities and differences between the timelines. Invite the students to share their reflections about Paul's conversion. Ask, "What does Paul's transformation say about our own potential for conversion?"

Spiritual Sight
Acts of the Apostles, chapter 9
"Conversion," Acts 9.1–19, CYB

Experiences with blindness help the students see that conversions such as Paul's often occur when our regular vision is obscured and we are invited to see with the eyes of faith.

1. Bring in enough blindfolds for half the class, as well as a bright light, water for Baptism, and other items for the role-play in step 2.

2. Begin this activity by assigning the students to the following characters for a role-play of Acts 9.1–22: narrator, Saul, voice of Jesus, people traveling with Saul, Ananias, disciples, and people in the synagogue. Encourage the students to enhance the role-play with the use of a blindfold, bright light, water for Baptism, and other items you have provided.

3. After the performance, emphasize the stages of Saul's conversion by presenting the following points in your own words:
- First, Saul could see physically but was spiritually blind to Jesus' message and in fact misconstrued it completely.
- Then he was physically blinded while receiving spiritual sight.
- Finally, both his physical and spiritual sight were restored.

4. Provide blindfolds for half the class, and pair each blindfolded student up with a nonblindfolded student. Direct the nonblindfolded students to lead their blindfolded partners on a faith walk around the classroom. Then have the pairs alternate leaders, switching blindfolds. (If you are able to do this in a larger area of the school, it will be more interesting.)

5. Invite the students to reflect on their experiences of leading and being led, of being able to see and not being able to see. Ask what it was like to be dependent on another and forced to trust that that person would be careful.

6. Conclude by leading a discussion about conversion as a change of heart rather than a switch to another religious tradition. Point out these ideas in your own words:
- Many people can hear God's voice more clearly when some sort of blindness forces them to negotiate their life in a new way. Illness, loss,

suffering, and new situations make it difficult for us to see where we are going and force us to reach out to others or God in ways we might not when we feel self-assured on our familiar path. Reflect on that phenomenon in your own life or in the lives of others.

Variation. There are excellent contemporary movies that portray conversion in a religious or secular way. Here are two examples:
- *Groundhog Day* (Columbia Pictures, 1993, 101 min., rated PG)
- *Patch Adams* (Universal Studios, 1998, 109 min., rated PG-13)

Bringing such movies to the students' minds, choosing clips from them and showing the clips to the students, or viewing a whole movie with the students can be a powerful way of illustrating the reality that the students discover in this activity. The use of such movies may be added to the activity following the conclusion in step 6.

Paul's Travels

Acts of the Apostles Floor Map
Acts of the Apostles, chapters 12–28

This activity invites the students to experience Paul's journeys by re-creating them on a large map.

Handout **Acts–A**

1. In preparation for this activity, create a large map of the eastern and central area of the Mediterranean Sea at the time of Paul. The map will be placed on the floor and should be big enough to be seen well by the students as they gather around it. Refer to handout Acts–A, "Paul's Missionary Journeys," and sketch the map freehand on several pieces of butcher paper or newsprint taped together. Or make a transparency of the handout, project it onto butcher paper or newsprint taped to the wall, and trace the map. Consider providing small figurines to symbolize groups of people and events, as well as yarn and either tacks or tape to indicate the routes taken by Paul.

2. Place the map you have created on the floor and gather the class around the map. Then read the story of Paul's missionary journeys aloud from Acts of the Apostles, chapters 12–28. If you have provided figurines, yarn, and tacks or tape, urge the students to help you place them on the map as you read.

Variations. If circumstances do not permit the creation of a large map, make copies of the handout so that the students can follow Paul's journeys individually on a smaller scale as you read the passage. Or make an overhead or computer transparency of the map and project it during your reading.

Instead of working with the whole class together in step 2, divide it into small groups and assign part of the Scripture reading to each group. Pass out copies of handout Acts–A. Direct the groups each to trace on their map the portion of Paul's journey covered in their assigned passage, and to prepare a summary of that portion of the journey. When all the groups are ready, invite them to present their portions of the journey in chronological order, with each group marking its portion of the route on the large floor map and presenting its summary to the class.

The Council of Jerusalem

Discernment and the Council of Jerusalem
Acts of the Apostles, chapter 15
"Unity in Faith and Love," Acts 15.1–35, CYB

Tracing the discernment process used at the Council of Jerusalem leads the students to use aspects of the process to assess issues facing their church and society today.

1. Invite several students to read Acts 15.1–35 aloud to the class. Ask another to read the article "Unity in Faith and Love" from the *CYB.*

2. Divide the class into small groups. Ask the groups each to skim Acts of the Apostles, chapters 10–15, and trace the origins of the Gentile controversy and the background for its resolution, notably in 10.1—11.18. When they are done, discuss the divisive issues that faced the early church, and list them on the board.

3. Ask the students to suggest church issues or societal issues that are divisive today, and then assign one issue to each small group. Tell each group to summarize the main points put forth by the opposing sides of the issue, and then to write a plan for resolving the issue. Either tell the students to research the issue, or suggest that they simply pool their existing knowledge. Discuss with them various conflict resolution skills such as listening, negotiating, cooperating, compromising, and agreeing to disagree. Suggest that they incorporate some of those skills in their plan.

4. Conclude by asking the students to identify similarities between the conflicts faced by the Council of Jerusalem and those faced by the Catholic church today. Ask, "How do the dramatic changes in the church (size, diversity, etc.) make resolving the conflicts it faces more difficult and, at the same time, possibly more necessary?"

Variation. The assessment in step 3 could instead be handled in a class discussion.

►Paul's Missionary Journeys

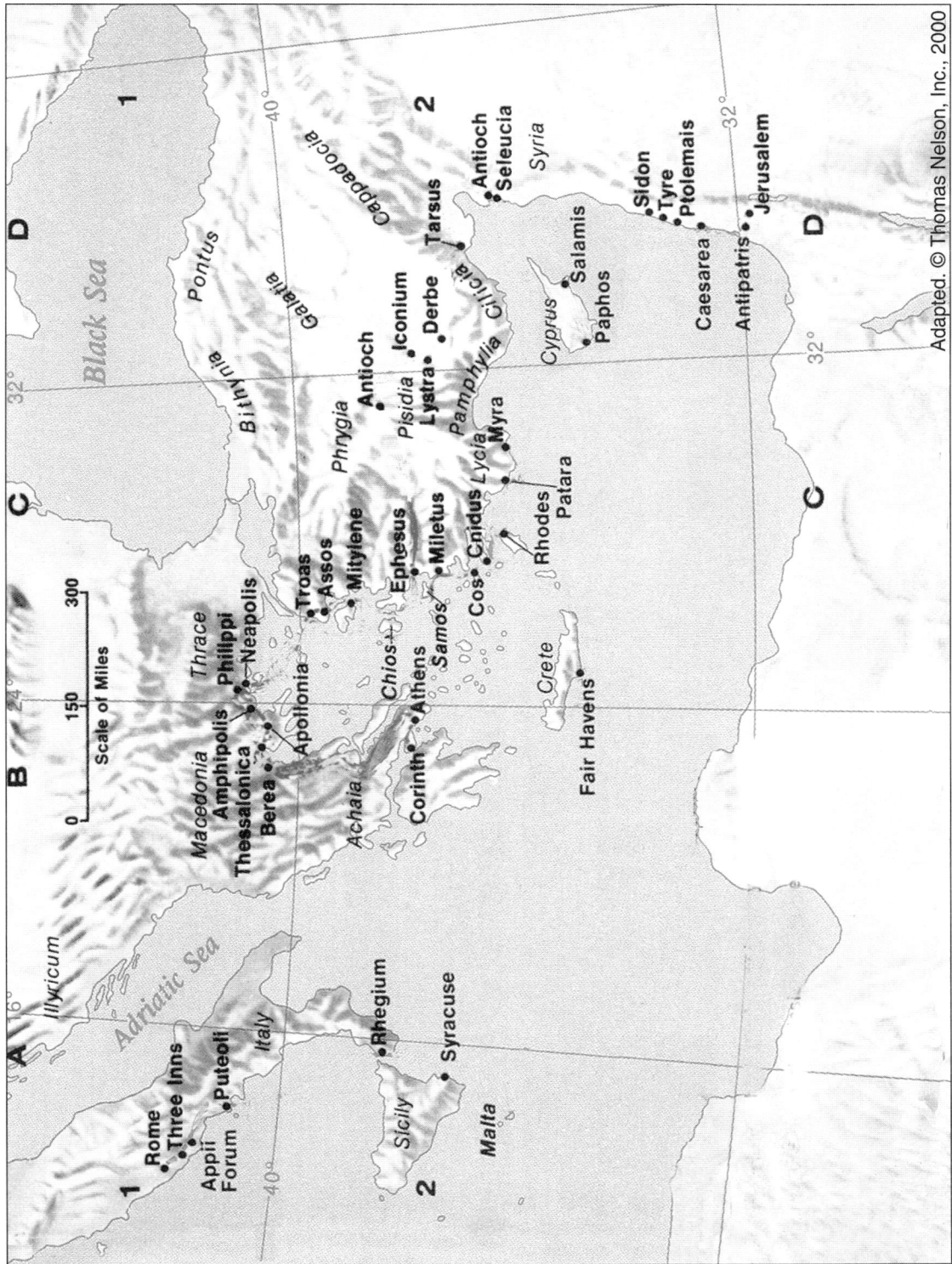

Adapted. © Thomas Nelson, Inc., 2000

Letters and Revelation

Introduction to the Letters Attributed to Paul

Exegetical Tools:
Form Criticism—the Letters and Paul's Message
Romans, 1 and 2 Corinthians, Galatians, Ephesians, Philippians, Colossians, 1 and 2 Thessalonians, 1 and 2 Timothy, Titus, Philemon, Hebrews

Exploring the nature of letters helps the students to understand more deeply the message and method of the New Testament letters attributed to Paul.

1. If the students are unfamiliar with form criticism, introduce that scholarly approach by referring to "Exegetical Tools: Form Criticism—the Saga," on page 59 of this manual.

Handout **Rom–A**

2. Distribute handout Rom–A, "Contemporary Letters," to the students, and tell them to read the letters on it and answer the questions. Review the questions with them when they are done.

3. Give the students the following pieces of information about the authors and recipients of the letters on the handout, and then direct them to reread the letters with this new information:
- Pete's mother is wealthy, as is Pete.
- Pete is on the university varsity baseball team.
- Alicia is in a competitive graduate school program.
- Randall refers to Sue Randall, a top-notch professor in that program.

Ask the students to note the assumptions that they made initially about the letters, and the different interpretations suggested by the new information.

4. Make the following points to the students in your own words:
- When reading other people's letters, we never know as much as their authors and recipients do. A letter is intended for a specific audience and addresses information relevant to the author and recipient. Letters often do not explain themselves completely because much is already understood between those two parties. Often, the author never intends for anyone but the recipient to read the letter.
- Given the many years separating us from the scriptural letters traditionally said to be written by Paul, the translation of those letters from Greek to English, and the letter format itself, we may feel like we cannot make sense of those writings at all or use them in our lives.
- Though it is healthy to be careful about interpreting Paul and his followers, it is important to realize that the more we know about them and about the people to whom they wrote, the better we can interpret what they were saying. Once we have an understanding of what they were talking about in their own time, we then can allow that information to shed light on issues that are relevant to our own lives today.

5. As you move through the letters attributed to Paul, remind the students of the importance of reading the background provided in the book introductions and articles of the *CYB*.

Packing for Paul's Journeys

Romans, 1 and 2 Corinthians, Galatians, Ephesians, Philippians, Colossians, 1 and 2 Thessalonians, 1 and 2 Timothy, Titus, Philemon, Hebrews

This activity asks the students to prepare travel kits for Paul as they learn about some of the challenges that he faced during his journeys.

1. Introduce the traveling Paul by reviewing map 7, "Paul's First and Second Journeys," and map 8, "Paul's Third and Fourth Journeys," in the *CYB*. Point out that Paul often mentions his journeys in the letters to his followers.

Handout **Rom–B**

2. Pass out copies of handout Rom–B, "The Nature of Paul's Travels," and invite various students to read the excerpts from it aloud. Discuss some of the challenges that Paul faced in his travels.

3. Divide the class into groups of four. Instruct the groups each to use the material from the handout and other information they know about Paul, to come up with ten modern items that they would give to Paul to ease his journey. Those should be things he could carry while walking—not a car or a plane ticket. The groups should bring at least five of the actual items to the next class, and pictures that they have found or drawn of the other items.

4. In the next class, invite the groups to present their items to everyone. Then help the students to review the last quote from the handout, being sure to assist with the vocabulary. Ask, "How might Paul's use of the modern conveniences you have presented have changed his ability to communicate the Christian message and the nature of the message itself?"

LETTERS

Romans

The Human Struggle

The Face of Hypocrisy
Romans, chapter 2

This exercise encourages the students to explore the nature of hypocrisy by drawing faces that portray that phenomenon.

1. Consider introducing this exercise by creating a simulation of hypocrisy. For example, take a class rule that you generally enforce, break it with seeming nonchalance, and see how the students react. If they protest, pretend that it is not inconsistent for you to have done this, and so on. Elicit the meaning of the word hypocrisy from this process. Ask the students why it would bother them for you to be hypocritical.

2. Invite several students to read Rom 2.1–24 aloud, and help the students understand the different issues discussed there. Note that Paul is asking people to practice what they preach.

3. Direct the students each to create a visual presentation of hypocrisy, using colored markers or pencils and other art supplies. Mention that a hypocritical person is often referred to as being two-faced, so portraying the concept in the context of a face is a good place to begin. Suggest that the students put song lyrics, parts of the passage from Romans, or memorable quotes in their visual presentation.

4. Use the completed pieces of art to prompt a discussion on hypocrisy. Point out that we are all guilty of being hypocritical at times, and that the real evil in hypocrisy is the effect that it has on others. Emphasize that when we are hypocritical, we betray the trust that others have in us.

The Wages of Sin
Romans, chapter 6
"In Christ, We Receive New Life!" Rom 6.1–23, CYB

This simulation uses poker chips as wages for sin, contrasting those wages with the gift of eternal life.

1. Before this activity, obtain blue, red, and white plastic poker chips, or make some from colored poster board or construction paper.

2. Begin this activity by asking a student to read Rom 6.12–23 aloud to the class.

3. Put the students into small groups; provide each group with a pile of blue, red, and white poker chips; and say the following things to the students in your own words:

- What kinds of actions are sinful? Let's compare sin to an employee's work, and assign various sinful actions different values and wages. The poker chips I just gave you represent different values for the sinful actions. Blue is for the worst type of sin, red is for lesser types of sin, and white is for the least serious type of sin. All sinful actions can be assigned a chip value as well as a total number of chips (up to five). In your groups, brainstorm a list of fifteen sinful actions, assign a chip value and number to each action, and then line up all the actions from the least sinful to the most sinful.

Give the groups time to finish their assignment.

4. Invite the groups to share their completed sin assessments, noting similarities and discrepancies between the groups' assigned values for similar sins.

5. Lead the students in a discussion of the Scripture passage, using these or similar questions:

- What does it mean to say that the "wages of sin is death" (Rom 6.23)?
- Is that the truth even for single-white-chip sins? If so, why?
- Could we make up a similar list of wages for good deeds? Why or why not?
- Would the "wages for good deeds" be enough to offset the "wages of sin"? In other words, would "good deed wages" save us from death? [Ask for several examples of good deeds that might counteract some bad deeds.]
- What does it mean to say, "But the free gift of God is eternal life" (verse 23)?
- How is a gift different from a wage?
- Why does eternal life have to be a gift?
- If eternal life is not a wage but a gift, how does it offset the "poker chips of death" we all collect?
- How might human beings naturally respond to being given such a gift?

6. Invite the students to read the article "In Christ, We Receive New Life!" from the *CYB* and then have them reread Rom 6.12–23 to deepen their understanding of Paul's complex argument.

A Window to the Inner War
Romans, chapter 7
"Our Inner Struggles," Rom 7.20, CYB

Using Romans, chapter 7, and a contemporary musical interpretation, the students create a visual presentation of the inner conflict described by Paul.

1. For this activity, consider using the song "In the Light," by DC Talk, on the album *Jesus Freak* (Emd/Chordant, 1995). Also obtain permission to paint the windows of your classroom or of the lunchroom or of another room in the school, and provide blank paper, colored markers or pencils, tempera paint, brushes, drop cloths, old newspapers, and masking tape.

2. Begin this activity by asking a student to read Rom 7.14–25 aloud to the class. Have another student read the article "Our Inner Struggle" from the *CYB*.

3. If you are using the song "In the Light," play it for the class. Direct the students to write a reflection about what the song says to them.

4. Tell the students that they will each design a picture of the "inner war" described in the song and of the freedom that can be found in Jesus, and paint that picture on a window. Identify the windows that the class will be using, noting their size and shape and assigning each student a window or part of a window. Explain that the students will each sketch their idea on blank paper and show it to you for approval. Once you have approved their design, they will use tempera paint to transfer it to their assigned window.

If the windows are in another area of the school, move to that area. Protect carpeting and other items near the windows using drop cloths, old newspapers, and masking tape. Caution the students to be careful with their paint, and supervise their work.

5. Invite the students to discuss their finished windows and insights, as they are comfortable. Point out that the presence of spiritual struggle in our lives does not mean that we are not trying to follow God. Note that it is important, however, not to face temptation on our own but to reach out to God and others for support.

Variations. If painting directly on the school windows is not a good option for your class, provide transparency sheets, pieces of clear plastic, old windows, or even newsprint for this project, and hang the results in the windows.

Instead of having the students work individually, assign the painting as a mural, guiding the class to work cooperatively. The mural might be done in tempera paint on a large window, or on butcher paper taped to a wall.

God's Grace and Human Hope

Artistic Reflections on Hope
Romans, chapter 8
"Hope," Rom 8.18–30, CYB

This activity encourages the students to draw on different sources in creating an artistic interpretation of hope.

1. Before this activity, ask the students to bring in some items from home that symbolize hope for them. They may bring pictures, song lyrics, poems, symbolic objects, and so on.

2. To begin this activity, call one student to read Rom 8.18–30 aloud to the class and another student to read the article "Hope" from the *CYB*.

3. Give the students blank paper and ask them each to create a visual depiction of hope. Explain the assignment as follows, in your own words:

- Use the item you brought from home for ideas or incorporate that item in your artwork; for example, if you brought in song lyrics, you might copy and illustrate those lyrics. You may use color, images, words, photos, and so on, to convey your understanding of hope. Also write a short reflection that explains your art and connects your understanding of hope with some of the verses in the passage from Romans.

4. Invite the students to share their completed visual and written interpretations of hope. Discuss the centrality of hope for Paul and for all who risk living the Christian message.

Rapping with Paul
Romans, chapter 8

Creating a cheer or rap leads the students to explore aspects of the powerful message in Romans, chapter 8.

1. Have the students read Rom 8.28–39.

2. Ask the students to write five different phrases from the reading that particularly strike them.

3. Form groups and direct them each to use the phrases written by their members to create a rap or a cheer. Explain that the phrases may be rewritten or used as-is, and the rap or cheer is to be written out and then performed for the class.

4. After the groups' performances, discuss the passage's meaning and its form of witness and exhortation.

Living the Christian Life

The Christian Team
Romans, chapter 12
"A Great Team," Rom 12.1–8, CYB

The metaphor of a football game helps the students to assess how they participate in the Christian life.

1. Prepare for this exercise by bringing in props to use for creating the experience of a football game in the classroom. You might use a ball to signify a player, a pom-pom for a cheerleader, a clipboard for a coach, a whistle for the referee, a microphone for the announcer, and so on.

2. Ask one student to read Rom 12.1–8 aloud to the class and another to read the article "A Great Team" from the *CYB*. Point out that everyone has a special role to play in the image of Christianity portrayed in the readings.

3. Move the students' desks or tables to the outside of the room and use them for the stands in a football stadium. Also use the props you have brought

to create the sense of a football game in the classroom, placing them around the room as appropriate—for example, you might set a whistle somewhere along the edge of the room, indicating the spot where the referee would stand.

4. Explain your football stadium setup to the students and suggest that the experience of a football game can be a parallel to the Christian life. Instruct the students to choose for themselves a place in the stadium that represents where they fit into the Christian life. You might want to help them by asking, for instance, if they are in the midst of the action, calling the shots, cheering others on, or watching from the stands.

5. As the students select their spots, invite them to share with those near to them the reasons for their choices. Then invite the whole class to listen as individuals explain why they have chosen their spots. Make observations and ask follow-up questions as you go. When everyone has contributed, ask, "Do Christians give as much attention to the Christian life as they do to sports?"

6. Revisit Rom 12.1–8 and compare the "one body" image Paul uses to describe the Christian community with the football stadium model. Lead a discussion focusing on these questions:
  ■ Are all the roles in the stadium model equally as helpful?
  ■ Are people in the stands contributing to the Christian community like Paul imagined? Why or why not?
  ■ Are you satisfied with where you currently place yourself? Would you like to participate in a different way?
  ■ Why is the body a good image for the Christian community?

(This exercise is based on the activity "Football Stadium," from *Get 'Em Talking,* by Mike Yaconelli and Scott Koenigsaecker, p. 45.)

Children's Books
Romans, chapter 12

The students read Romans, chapter 12, and collaborate in groups to create children's books on the marks of a true Christian.

1. Bring to class some examples of children's books for the students to look at in step 3.

2. Read Rom 12.9–21 aloud to the class. Point out that that passage names characteristics, or marks, of a true Christian.

3. Divide the class into groups and ask the groups each to make a list of the qualities identified in the Scripture passage. Then explain that each group should create a book that is based on the passage and aimed specifically at children of a certain age-group
Brainstorm the types of children's books that exist—ABC books, picture books, storybooks, puzzle books, and so on. Show the students the examples that you have brought in, and instruct the groups each to pick a type of book and a targeted age-group.
Distribute blank paper and other supplies (or use a desktop publishing program), and allow time for the groups to create their books. Challenge the groups to think of the interests and questions common to children of their

targeted age-group, and then to present the qualities they have listed in light of the needs of the audience.

4. Invite the groups to read their finished books to the class, explaining their approach and rationale for choosing specific types of presentation. Note the interpretations that the groups have made about Paul's message through this process.

5. Arrange for the students to read their books to children in the targeted age-groups, and consider donating the books to the children.

Stumbling Blocks
Romans, chapter 14
"Respecting Difference," Rom 14.1–23, CYB

Paul's argument for respecting differences motivates the students to reflect on the "stumbling blocks" in their lives and how they put such blocks in the way of others.

1. In preparation for this activity, ask the students to bring boxes into class, or provide some yourself. You will need boxes in various sizes, about one for every two students.

2. Begin this activity by asking the students to think about the stumbling blocks that human beings place in one another's way, knowingly or unknowingly, as a student reads Rom 14.13–23 aloud to the class. Explain the context of Paul's argument, referring to the article "Respecting Differences" in the *CYB*.

3. Form groups of six to eight students, give each group three or four of the boxes that have been brought to class, and direct the groups each to use their boxes to create three-dimensional representations of the blocks that get in the way of living out our faith. Explain that, for example, jealousy often gets in the way in our relationships, and that a group could paint a box green and label it "Jealousy."

4. When the groups have completed their blocks, instruct them each to develop a "real-life" skit, applicable to teens today, that portrays how its blocks keep us from living out our faith. The actual boxes must somehow appear in the skit as visual reminders of the things that cause us to stumble.

5. As the groups perform their skits, discuss the stumbling blocks that are presented and the themes that emerge.

Read the following contemporary letters and answer the questions below them:

Dear Mom,

How are things at home? I wanted to say something more about our conversation the other night. I think stealing is OK even though you talk a lot about risk. I can really help everyone out if I steal and don't get caught. Of course, when I do get caught, I become really afraid of what everyone will think. A few times when I have arrived back at the dorm, I could tell that the others knew what I had done and thought it was a big mistake. That's a terrible feeling. Talk to you soon.

Pete

Dear Karen,

Hi! How are your classes going, and did you have fun the other night at the game? I can't believe that Sarah dropped Randall. What a fool! Randall doesn't know me from anyone else, but if Randall thought half as much of me as of her, I would stick it out to the end no matter what kind of effort I had to put into it. Some people just don't have the eyes to see a good thing when it happens!

I am still planning to meet you for coffee tomorrow—call me if you can't make it.

Alicia

Questions

1. What is the subject matter of each letter?

2. What is your initial impression of the authors of the letters, Pete and Alicia? Do the letters give clues to their values or concerns?

3. Do you have any sense of the recipients of the letters, Pete's mother and Karen?

4. Would Pete's mother and Karen have a better chance of understanding their letter than we do? Why or why not? What kind of information helps a reader best understand the contents of a letter?

• • • • • • • • • • • • • ▶ The Nature of Paul's Travels

The following quotes describe traveling conditions that Paul likely encountered during his journeys:

A normal day's journey for those traveling by carriage was from inn to inn, roughly 25 Roman miles or 22 modern miles. Those who walked, as Paul did, would have had to extend themselves to cover this distance. It is unlikely that Paul could have maintained such an average for long periods, particularly when the road was hilly. (Pages 40–41)

If Paul says that he was "in hunger and thirst, often without food, in cold and exposure" (2 Corinthians 11:27), it is obvious that on occasion he found himself far from human habitation at nightfall. He may have failed to reach shelter because of weather conditions; an unusually hot day may have sapped his endurance; mountain passes may have been blocked by unseasonably early or late snowfalls; spring floods may have made sections of the road impassable . . . ; or fierce hail-storms may have forced him to take refuge. The average height of the Anatolian plateau (present day central Turkey) is 3,000 feet above sea-level, but great sections of it rise to double that and extreme variations of temperature are the rule. (Page 41)

When Paul made it to an inn, he could not look forward to a night of total repose. The average inn was no more than a courtyard surrounded by rooms. Baggage was piled in the open space, where animals were also tethered for the night. The drivers sat around noxious little fires fueled by dried dung, or slept on the ground wrapped in their cloaks. (Page 42)

Those who could afford better rented beds in the rooms. The snorting and stamping of the animals outside was sometimes drowned out by the snores of others who shared the room, any one of whom might be a thief. Paul's anxiety that he might lose the tools of his trade was hardly conducive to a sound night's sleep. And sound sleep was made infinitely more difficult by that perennial occupant of all inns, the bed-bug. (Page 42)

In the countryside the road was a *via glarea strata,* an unsealed or grav-el road. On these roads, the danger from flying stones thrown up by passing vehicles was a menace the walking traveler had to live with. (Page 45)

Wild animals were another danger. . . . Apuleius refers explicitly to bears, wolves and wild boar. Travelers in this story are armed with throwing-spears, heavy hunting-spears, bows and clubs. (Page 45)

Several segments of Paul's second missionary journey were by sea. . . .
. . . Storms blew regularly in winter; the violence of these winter storms is well documented. . . .
Storms were not the only reason the seas were usually closed in winter. Sailors plotted a course by the sun and stars, as well as by land-marks. In winter, fog or heavy cloud cover would cut off their naviga-tional guides, easily leading to shipwreck. (Page 45)

268   **Handout Rom–B:** Permission to reproduce this handout for classroom use is granted.

Since passengers were nothing more than an incidental benefit to the owner, the ship provided water, but neither food nor services. Passengers were expected to furnish their own provisions, other than water, for the duration of the voyage. They had to cook for themselves, which meant taking turns, after the crew had been fed, at the hearth in the galley. (Page 46)

Passengers had to live on deck; there were no cabins on the average coastal vessel. Apart from a little shade thrown by the mainsail, no shelter was provided. (Page 46)

Some of the areas through which Paul passed are spectacularly beautiful; yet this seems not to have influenced him in any way. On the other hand, his experiences as a lonely traveler almost certainly affected his theology. His pessimistic view of human nature may have been born of the ethos of his age, but it was surely reinforced by what he encountered at the inns and seaports of Greece and Asia Minor. His own poverty forced him to rub shoulders with the most downtrodden and brutalized elements in society. He no doubt felt the impact of the forces that made these elements of society what they were. He himself felt the force of a value system that the poorer elements of society could not escape. His own struggle against the insidious miasma of egocentricity would have sharpened his consciousness of sin and at the same time strengthened his dedication to the salvation of its victims. "Who is weak, and I am not weak? Who is made to fall, and I do not burn with anger?" (2 Corinthians 11:29). (Jerome Murphy-O'Connor, OP, "On the Road and on the Sea with St. Paul: Traveling Conditions in the First Century," in *Bible Review,* volume 1, number 2, summer 1985, page 47. Copyright © 1985 by the Biblical Archaeology Society.)

1 Corinthians

The Mystery of the Death and Resurrection of Jesus

The Paradox of the Cross
1 Corinthians, chapter 1
"God's Wisdom and Ours," 1 Cor 1.18–31, CYB

Portraying Jesus' death by execution in a modern way allows the students to revisit the horror of his death and to see why Paul's "message about the cross is foolishness" (1 Cor 1.18).

1. Read 1 Cor 1.18–25 aloud and ask a student to read the article "God's Wisdom and Ours" from the *CYB*. Discuss the meaning of the term *paradox*, which is "an apparently contradictory statement that is, in fact, true." Apply that term to Paul's interpretation of the meaning of Jesus' death on the cross. Summarize this discussion as follows, using your own words:
   - Although Jesus' death on the cross was an apparent failure, it really revealed the power of God. Christians can become so familiar with the image of the crucified Jesus that they no longer are shocked at it. We may forget that the cross was a painful and demeaning method of execution that killed its victims slowly by suffocation.

2. Form small groups and assign each group one of these methods of capital punishment used today:
   - lethal injection
   - the gas chamber
   - the firing squad
   - electrocution
   - the gallows
Instruct the groups each to draw a picture of Jesus being killed by their assigned procedure. Mention that their portrayal of Jesus on that modern cross may be literal or symbolic. Distribute blank paper and other art supplies for the drawings.

3. Invite the groups to share their pictures with the class. Discuss the pictures with the students, asking them whether Jesus would have suffered the same fate if he had come into the world today.

4. Direct the students to write personal reflections on Jesus' death with the new eyes they have gained through the groups' drawings and 1 Cor 1.18–25.

Variation. Have the groups research the use and frequency of their assigned procedure before drawing their picture in step 2. They might use the Internet, the school media center, the community library, or other resources for their research.

Deeply Held Hopes
1 Corinthians, chapter 2

This activity invites the students to give shape, color, symbol, and form to hopes held deeply in their hearts.

1. For this activity, consider using a recording of Marty Haugen's "Eye Has Not Seen," on the album *Anthology 1: 1980–1984* (GIA Publications, 1999). You will also need these art supplies: white and colored construction paper, crayons, colored markers or pencils, glue, glitter, scissors, pieces of fabric, old magazines, and so on.

2. Consider playing the song "Eye Has Not Seen" while the students listen quietly. Then direct the students to read 1 Cor 2.6–16 carefully to themselves.

3. Ask the students to write a journal entry about the hopes that they hold in their hearts and to try to imagine what good things God has prepared for them.

4. Invite the students each to give shape, color, symbol, and form to the hopes and dreams they have written about, using the art supplies you have provided. Explain that their expressions should be nonverbal, using images exclusively.

5. Display the completed visual expressions in the classroom and allow the students to view them quietly. Invite the students to explain their creations if they wish, and encourage discussion about the hopes and dreams of teenagers today.

Seed Packages
1 Corinthians, chapter 3

This activity challenges the students to design a seed packet that reflects the growth process described in 1 Corinthians, chapter 3.

1. Prepare for this activity by creating small, blank "seed packages" or finding small envelopes to use as seed packets. Also collect some actual seed packets to use as examples.

2. Begin this activity by requesting the students to read 1 Cor 3.1–9. Talk about how seeds work with the soil, water, and light to grow into plants. Compare this to how we humans work with nature, people, and God to grow into the beings we were created to be.

3. Show the students the seed packages you have collected as examples, and review the graphics and information presented in their design.

4. Hand out the blank seed packages you have prepared, and colored markers or pencils. Direct the students each to design a seed package representing themselves. Present the following instructions in your own words:

- On the front, put a drawing of the seed (yourself in the beginning), a name for the plant (your own name or an epithet), and a description or illustration of what the plant (you) will look like full-grown. On the back, include a list of what will help the plant grow, how long it will take to mature, when the best growing season is, and so on. Also include part of the Scripture passage on the package.

5. Invite the students to share their finished packets and discuss the insights about spiritual growth that emerged from this activity.

The Bases of Our Lives

Personal Foundations
1 Corinthians, chapter 3
"From the Bottom Up," 1 Cor 3.10–17, CYB

Items from home help the students reflect on the foundations on which they would like to build their lives.

1. Call one student to read 1 Cor 3.10–17 aloud to the class and another to read the article "From the Bottom Up" from the *CYB*. Note the different types of materials mentioned in verse 12 of the Scripture reading, and discuss why those items would make a strong or weak foundation as defined in the reading.

2. For the next class, ask the students to bring from home three to five items that reflect the kind of foundation that they would like to lay for themselves in life. Explain that the items should be not building materials but rather objects that reflect spiritual qualities or values that they think are important. Direct the students to write a brief explanation of each item's significance.

3. When the students bring in their completed homework, invite them to share their symbols in groups, and then conduct a class discussion based on the foundations that the students have chosen and the qualities of those items.

Advice on Living the Christian Message

Paul and Our Sexualized Culture
1 Corinthians, chapter 5

Skits allow the students to reflect on the First Corinthians passage regarding sexual immorality, and relate Paul's thoughts to the sexualized culture in which we live today.
Note: This activity covers sensitive material in a unique way. It would be good to send a letter to parents beforehand, outlining the topic and procedure.

1. Read 1 Cor 5.9–13 aloud to the class in a strong, dramatic manner. Discuss with the students why Paul would address the topic of sexuality with the Corinthians and why he called the early Christians to a purer way of life.

2. Form small groups, and have each group prepare a skit in which Paul is a character, guest, or commentator. Provide the following instructions in your own words:

- In the skit, bring Paul evidence of the sexual immorality in our world—such as television, music, or video clips, and magazine advertisements. The key part of the skit is Paul's response. Address the question What challenges would he give our society?

Make sure to set clear guidelines about the nature of the examples the students are to provide; note that those examples need only point to the general values of the particular medium and should not be the most graphic examples of the medium. Consider previewing the examples before the skits are performed. Allow the students a day or two to bring in examples and prepare their skits.

3. After the skits have been presented, discuss Paul's point about the danger of exposing oneself to people and situations with values contrary to the Christian message. Ask, "To what extent does our environment end up shaping the kind of values that we have?"

A Rhythm Chant
1 Corinthians, chapters 10–11

The students join the teacher in a finger-snapping rhythm chant based on the scriptural verse "Be imitators of me, as I am of Christ" (1 Cor 11.1).

1. Prepare for this exercise by writing the adapted passage in step 3 on an overhead or computer transparency, on the board, or on a handout. Also read the leader's verses in step 3 several times to find a rhythm that works for you.

2. Begin this exercise by having the students read 1 Cor 10.23—11.1 to themselves.

3. Note Paul's statement in 1 Cor 11.1, "Be imitators of me, as I am of Christ." Begin a finger-snapping rhythm that the students imitate. Point out the following scriptural adaptation on a transparency, on the board, or on a handout. Invite the students to join you in chanting the verses to the rhythm you have established, with you reading the calls, marked "Leader," and the students reading the response, marked "All."

All. Imitate me, as I imitate Christ.

Leader. Nothing's forbidden, but not everything does good. Nothing's forbidden, but not everything helps build.
All. Imitate me, as I imitate Christ.

Leader. Do not look to yourself, but look out for the other. The butcher's meat's good; do not feel guilty about it.
All. Imitate me, as I imitate Christ.

Leader. If you're at a pagan's house, eat what is served.
All. Imitate me, as I imitate Christ.

Leader. But if someone says, "This was offered to a god," then out of respect, say, "No thanks, okay?" (For the other person's concern, not yours, you see?)
All. Imitate me, as I imitate Christ.

Leader. Whatever you eat, whatever you drink, whatever you do, let it be for the glory of God.
All. Imitate me, as I imitate Christ.

Leader. Never offend a Jew or a Greek. Never offend the church of God.
All. Imitate me, as I imitate Christ.

Leader. Just try to be helpful to everyone at all times so that everyone may be saved for the glory of God.
All. Imitate me, as I imitate Christ.

Invite the students to add to the chant ways that they could imitate Christ. Give them a few moments to think of something to contribute. Then continue the chant by going from student to student for a call. For example, a student might say, "Always forgive when you have been hurt." The students would then respond in unison with, "Imitate me, as I imitate Christ."

4. Discuss the advice that Paul gives in the Bible passage, in addition to qualities that the students suggest make Christ's presence visible in our lives today.

Living in Love Together

The Face and Body of Christ
1 Corinthians, chapter 12

Creating a collage of faces to depict the face of Christ allows the students to reflect on the meaning of the Body of Christ.

1. In preparation for this activity, find a simple drawing of Jesus' face, or sketch one yourself, or invite an artistic student to create one, and make an overhead or computer transparency of it. Bring in butcher paper or newsprint, a collection of photocopied pages from a school yearbook, and a pile of documents that represent school life (memos, bulletins, announcements, newsletters, etc.).

2. Begin this activity by calling several students to take turns reading 1 Cor 12.1–30 aloud, and discuss the analogy of the church as the Body of Christ.

3. Hang a large piece of butcher paper or newsprint on the wall, and project onto it the transparency of Jesus' face that you have prepared. Tell a student to outline or shade the projected image of Jesus.

4. Take the image off the wall and lay it on the floor. Pass out the copies of yearbook pages that you have brought in, the pile of school documents that you have collected, scissors, and glue. Assign some students to cut out faces from the yearbook pages and fit them into the face of Jesus, so that it appears to be a collage of many faces. Direct the other students to cut apart the school documents and use them to fill in the background of the collage. Encourage students with artistic gifts to guide the assembling of faces and background material to heighten the effects of the collage.

5. Once the collage is finished, hang it up. Invite the students to contemplate the various people who make up the Body of Christ at their school, as you read the Scripture verses again. Then ask, "Do we often see the face of Jesus in our midst? Why or why not?"

6. Consider also using the finished collage for a prayer service with other members of the school community.

(Rick Keller-Scholz and Julie Campbell, of Bellarmine Preparatory School, Tacoma, Washington, contributed this activity.)

Agape Cards
1 Corinthians, chapter 13
"God's Love," 1 Corinthians, chapter 13, CYB

This activity guides the students to create cards based on the images of love presented in 1 Corinthians, chapter 13.

1. Bring in some examples of greeting cards that communicate different kinds of love: romantic, familial, and friendship. Discuss the various ways that love manifests itself and ways that the cards portray those different types of love.

2. Ask one student to read 1 Corinthians, chapter 13, aloud to the class, and another student to read the article "God's Love" from the *CYB*. Discuss agape love and see if the students have witnessed that type of love in their own life experience.

3. Distribute blank paper and colored markers or pencils, and direct the students to use them to create greeting cards that express agape love. Allow them to choose from various genres, including birthday, sympathy, and holiday (such as Valentine's Day).

4. Invite the students to share their finished cards. Point out that all types of love can grow toward agape love if the parties involved are in touch with God.

The Mission of Love
1 Corinthians, chapter 13

This activity invites the students to reflect on the traits of love found in 1 Corinthians, chapter 13, using a clip from the movie *The Mission,* and then collaborate on booklets or pamphlets that would help various audiences live out that vision of love.

1. Before this activity, obtain a copy of the video *The Mission* (Warner Bros. Goldcrest, Kingsmere Productions, and Enigma, 1987, 125 min., rated PG) and find the following segment:
Robert De Niro's character, Mendoza, confesses to Jeremy Irons's character, Father Gabriel, that he wants to change but does not know how to live. Father

Gabriel gives a Bible to Mendoza, who reads the passage from 1 Corinthians, chapter 13, as he "sees" the mission he has been called to and the Guarani (the Tupi-Guaranian people of Bolivia, Paraguay, and southern Brazil) for the first time.

This clip is about 40 to 50 minutes into the movie, and lasts around 5 minutes. Set the tape at the beginning of the clip, so that it is ready to show the students. Also prepare a brief introduction for the clip, explaining the context and characters.

2. Begin this activity by asking the students to raise their hand as soon as they recognize the Scripture passage that you read aloud. Proceed to read 1 Corinthians, chapter 13, to the class. Ask the students why it is a memorable passage. Solicit any memories they have of hearing the passage in other settings.

3. Introduce the video clip from *The Mission* that you have prepared, and then show it to the students.

4. Form small groups, and direct them each to produce a booklet or pamphlet with instructions on how to live out the vision of love expressed in 1 Corinthians. Note that the materials the students create must give specific, authentic, and meaningful suggestions on how to love. Assign each group one of the following audiences to address, and distribute art supplies as needed:
- young children
- teens
- parents
- employees
- older people

5. Invite the groups to share their booklets or pamphlets and to discuss the various approaches they took in presenting to a particular audience 1 Corinthians' powerful message about the gift of love.

Variation. Instead of directing the groups to design and create booklets or pamphlets, have them each produce an infomercial that sells such a publication.

Creedal Statements

Student Creeds
1 Corinthians, chapter 15
"The First Creed and a Contemporary Creed!" 1 Cor 15.3–11, CYB

This activity invites the students to write creeds reflecting their own faith experiences, using the Apostles' Creed and the Nicene Creed as a guide.

1. Before this activity, make copies of the Apostles' Creed or the Nicene Creed, or both. Also prepare five statements of personal belief and corresponding experiences to use as examples.

Note: The Apostles' Creed and the Nicene Creed are listed in the *Catechism,* at the end of part 1, "The Profession of Faith" (see appendix A).

2. Begin this activity by asking one student to read 1 Cor 15.1–11 aloud to the class and another student to read the article "The First Creed and a Contemporary Creed!" from the *CYB*. Discuss the passage and article, offering this explanation in your own words:

■ A creed is a collection of short statements of faith that originate from faith experiences that real people have had. This is shown by the creedal statements from the Third Encuentro Nacional Hispano de Pastoral in the *CYB* article. Those statements of belief arose out of the experiences of Hispanics, just as Paul's statements of belief came from the experiences of the earliest Christians.

3. Provide the students with copies of the Apostles' Creed or the Nicene Creed, or both. Depending on your schedule, spend time discussing the meaning of one or both creeds.

4. Ask the students each to write their own creed consisting of five belief statements. Explain that they may take some or all of those statements from the church creeds, or make them up completely. Add that after each statement, they should describe what in their own life has shaped that belief. Present your prepared examples of your own statements of belief and corresponding experiences.

5. Invite the students to share their completed creedal statements in pairs and then with the rest of the class. Support the students as they examine how traditional creeds relate to their own experiences of faith.

2 Corinthians

The Inner Life

Poetry Treasures
2 Corinthians, chapter 4
"Christ in Us," 2 Cor 4.5–10, CYB

After reading 2 Corinthians, chapter 4, the students write a haiku poem based on the image of treasure in clay jars.

1. Call a student to read 2 Corinthians, chapter 4, aloud. Encourage the class to pay special attention to the mention of clay jars in the reading.
    Request a student to read the article "Christ in Us" from the *CYB* aloud to the class. Ask the students to reflect on the article and Bible passage, and to give real-life examples that illustrate the major points.

2. Invite the students to consider what treasure they hold within their own clay jars. Have them each write a haiku poem based on that image. Explain that a haiku poem has three lines, usually with five, seven, and five syllables, respectively. Direct the students to transfer their poem to a large piece of construction paper and decorate it. Distribute construction paper and other art supplies.

3. Display the students' completed artwork in the classroom or hallways. Point to the visual and poetic imagery used in that artwork as you discuss the way we carry Christ within us.

Ads for Inner Needs
2 Corinthians, chapter 5
"It's What's Inside That Counts," 2 Cor 5.1–5, CYB

This exercise challenges the students to transform advertisements for the ideal body into advertisements that invite perfection for the soul.

1. Have one student read 2 Cor 5.1–5 aloud to the class and another read the article "It's What's Inside That Counts" from the *CYB*. Discuss the contents of the *CYB* article. Say something such as this in your own words:
    - The false and unrealistic messages that advertising gives about beauty can lead to spiritual anorexia as well as physical eating disorders. Just as physical anorexia deceives people into seeing themselves as overweight and unattractive, spiritual anorexia can distort people's inner sense of themselves, filling them with the need to conform internally to society's norms.

- The more that people feel entrapped by false and unrealistic expectations, the more they starve spiritually, denying themselves the opportunity to pray and nurture their souls; and they lose the ability to notice that their spiritual selves are wasting away.

2. Distribute popular magazines (fashion magazines for men and women will work well here). Ask the students to choose a magazine ad that somehow encourages the development of a person's physical appearance, and have them transform it into an ad that develops a person's spiritual or inner life as discussed in the *CYB* article. Provide art supplies such as blank paper, colored markers and pens, scissors, and glue.

3. Invite the students to share their finished advertisements and the insights they have gained from reading the article and completing the exercise.

How Strong Is Our Faith?

Walking by Faith
2 Corinthians, chapter 5

The students listen to a contemporary interpretation of 2 Corinthians, chapter 5, and discuss the implications of charting one's life course with God's guidance.

1. In preparation for this activity, try to bring in a recording of the song "Walk by Faith," by Out of the Grey, on the album *Remember This: The Out of the Grey Collection* (Emd/Sparrow, 1998). (It is possible to complete this activity without the song if it is unavailable.) Also bring in enough blindfolds for half of the class.

2. Begin the activity by asking a student to read 2 Cor 5.6–10 aloud to the class. If possible, play the song "Walk by Faith."

3. Explain that the students will now participate in a simulation of blindness. Instruct all the students to mill around the classroom, navigating around desks and tables, to become familiar with objects that could be obstacles to someone who is blind.
   Observe the students for a minute or two, then ask one half of the class to put on the blindfolds you brought in, and the other half to lead the blindfolded students around the room. Caution the leaders to be sure that their partner does not get hurt.
   After a few minutes, have the students switch roles as blindfolded ones and guides. Make sure all the students experience "walking by faith."
   Note: You may want to do this part of the activity in small groups, depending on the size of your room, or take the students to another space in your building or on the grounds.

4. Invite the students to share their experiences of blindness and guiding. Ask them some of the following questions in your own words:
   - Would you prefer to be blindfolded or nonblindfolded as you negotiate your life here at school?

- If your guide would do a better and safer job of leading you around the school than your own eyes, would you choose to rely on the guide or on your own vision? Why?
- In many cases, we can choose whether to rely on God or on our own wisdom. Do you trust God's wisdom over your own insight? Why or why not?
- Have you observed times in your own life or in the lives of others when it was necessary or attractive to trust God's wisdom?

Invite the students to explore other questions related to trusting God's wisdom, such as, "How can one recognize God's guidance?" Also discuss how the song played at the beginning of the activity ties in with their experience of walking blind versus walking with sight.

Tough-Love Letters
2 Corinthians, chapter 7

This exercise allows the students to examine a biblical example of tough love and apply the concept of tough love to a variety of scenarios.

1. To prepare for this exercise, copy examples of advice column letters from the newspaper.

2. To begin this exercise, explain to the students that Paul was deeply concerned with the attitudes and behaviors of the Christian community in Corinth and that that interest drove him to write 1 Corinthians. Have the students skim 1 Corinthians and identify three complaints Paul had against the people in Corinth. List those complaints on the board.

3. Call a student to read 2 Cor 7.5–13 aloud to the class. Point out that Paul feels that his tough words were ultimately helpful to the spiritual well-being of the community. Explain that that is an example of tough love. Note that the most honest and loving thing one can do in some cases is to tell another person the truth, even if it hurts. Add that that allows the other person to see the error of her or his ways.

4. Divide the class into six groups. Direct the groups each to write a letter to Paul in the genre of an advice column. Distribute the copies of advice column letters that you have copied from the newspaper, and have the students review them in order to get a sense of how to write their own. The groups' letters should seek advice about problem situations.

5. After the groups are done writing, direct them to swap letters, take on the persona of Paul as an advice columnist, and compose a tough-love response to the letter they received in the swap.

6. When the groups have finished their responses, gather the students and discuss the letters requesting advice and the return letters. From the letters and further discussion, assess when tough love is a necessary response to a situation.

The Christ-Within Test
2 Corinthians, chapter 13

The students work together in groups to create a "test" for teens today that will evaluate whether they realize Christ is within them.

1. Read 2 Cor 13.5–10 aloud, emphasizing verse 5.

2. Divide the class into groups to develop tests that will assess whether the students are living the faith and recognizing Christ's presence within them. Each group should type its test, which may be any format, such as true-and-false, multiple-choice, short-answer, or essay. Some type of scoring key or scale should be created along with the test.
Tell the groups that the tests are meant to be positive tools for growth. Ask them each to consider how the results of their test can affirm, support, and challenge the one who takes it.

3. Allow class time for the groups each to administer their completed test to either the entire class or another group. Discuss the contents and results of the tests, as a way of exploring Paul's message and identifying the essence of living in companionship with Christ.

Galatians

Different Types of Spirit

A Fiery Sermon
Galatians, chapter 3

The students work in groups to prepare a "fiery sermon" modeled on Gal 3.1–5.

1. Discuss with the class the types of sermons that they often hear at church. Ask, "What style, language, and tone are used?" Consider inviting a few students up to the front of the class to imitate the variety of homiletic styles that they have heard. The class should then act out the congregation's response to different types of preaching.

2. Have a student read Gal 3.1–5 aloud to the class. Comment that there are strong lessons in the Scriptures, as in that passage, and many times, preachers use a bold, fiery style to get those points across. Ask a few volunteers to read the same passage aloud in a fiery style.

3. Divide the class into groups and direct the groups each to paraphrase the Scripture passage into modern language, retaining its message and tone. Instruct the groups each to select one person to deliver their modern short sermon to the class.

4. After the sermons, discuss the effectiveness of the different styles presented. Ask, "Why are some styles more or less effective for different audiences?"

Guess the Virtue or Vice
Galatians, chapter 5
"Our Inner Struggle," Rom 7.20, CYB

A game introduces to the students the works of the flesh and fruit of the Spirit named in Gal 5.16–26.

1. Prepare for this activity by listing the works of the flesh from Gal 5.19–21 on one index card, and the fruit of the Spirit from Gal 5.22–23 on another index card. Label the first card "Vices" and the second card "Virtues." Also make sure you have a clock or watch that indicates seconds, so that you can keep track of time during the game in step 3.

2. Begin this activity by calling a student to read Gal 5.16–26 aloud. Explain Paul's use of the terms *Spirit* and *flesh*. Read or review the article "Our Inner Struggle" from the *CYB,* to help clarify the difference between the Spirit and the flesh.

3. Divide the class into two teams. Explain that the qualities in the Scripture passage will become the items for a game similar to Taboo, in which one player on each team has a list of words and calls out synonyms for those words, while another player on the same team tries to guess the words themselves. Then give the following guidelines for the game in your own words:

- In this version of the game, one person from each team receives a card listing either virtues or vices. Those people begin by giving another player on their team synonyms for the first word listed on their card. They must be careful not to give the word itself, to give only synonyms. As soon as the other player guesses the first word, the reader starts giving synonyms for the second word, and so on. After 30 seconds, the first person stops guessing and another person on the team begins guessing. The play continues in this manner until one team has guessed all its words. That team is the winner.

Distribute the index cards and tell the teams to begin. Call time every 30 seconds. After the game, congratulate the winner.

4. Discuss the nature of the works of the flesh and the fruit of the Spirit, and help the students identify situations from their own lives in which elements of either appeared. Ask, "How might these virtues and vices be indicators to help Christians make decisions?"

The Nature of Competition
Galatians, chapter 5

The students discuss how competition can be a positive or destructive force in their lives and in our society, and develop role-plays that show how competition plays out in real life.

1. Read Gal 5.22–26 aloud, emphasizing verse 26, "Let us not become conceited, competing against one another, envying one another."

2. Lead the students in a discussion of the difference between healthy and unhealthy competition.

3. Form small groups, and tell the groups each to develop a role-play that reflects the competition in the students' lives. Encourage the groups to make their role-plays as realistic as possible, but discourage any scenarios that too closely resemble actual events or name names.

4. Invite the groups to present their role-plays to the class. After each role-play, discuss how the spirit of the Scripture passage can challenge us to live differently in situations like the one presented. Conclude the activity by asking, "How might you now describe the line between healthy and unhealthy forms of competition?"

Ephesians

How Are We Saved?

Faith-Versus-Works Debate
Ephesians, chapter 2
"Faith Versus Good Works," Eph 2.1–10, CYB

This activity involves the students in a debate about Paul's theology of salvation by grace rather than works.

1. Consider beginning this activity with a classroom simulation, using academic success as a parallel to salvation. In this simulation, a genuine interest in the Scriptures will resemble "grace," and hard work in the class (completing homework, studying for tests, etc.) will be "works." Hand back an assignment with randomly assigned grades that do not necessarily correspond to the work completed. When questioned, explain that you decided to assess the assignment based on the students' interest in the class rather than the quality of the work—a new approach. (A poker face is helpful here.) Try to reason with the students, explaining that it seems that real engagement in the material is much more important than completed homework, and so on.

2. After revealing that the students have just taken part in a simulation, talk about the relation between interest in a subject and performance in it, addressing questions like these:
- How often is success in a class based solely on hard work?
- Is it possible to learn material without doing most or all of the homework and studying for the tests?
- How does interest in a subject encourage or discourage hard work?

3. Ask one student to read Eph 2.1–10 and another to read the article "Faith Versus Good Works" from the *CYB*.

4. Using the length of your classroom, create a continuum with "God," at one end and "People" at the other. Direct the students each to place themselves along the continuum, choosing a spot that reflects their understanding of how much a person's salvation depends on God and how much on the human being's effort. Point out that the middle spot reflects an equal partnership.

5. Divide the class into several groups based on where they stand, and invite the groups to reflect on how the salvation process works. Have them create mind maps—simple visual presentations—showing the relation between God, the human being, faith, and works as they see it.

6. After the groups share their visual presentations with the class, discuss the complexity of understanding how God works in us. Pose these questions:

- If faith is God's gift, is it given equally?
- Where does free will fit into the picture?

Christian Unity

Puzzle Prayer
Ephesians, chapter 4
"Weave for Us a Garment," Eph 4.1–6, CYB

A prayer service allows the students to reflect on their individual gifts and talents and see them in the context of "one body" (Eph 4.6).

1. In preparation for this activity, obtain music for use during a short prayer service, such as a recording of "We Are Many Parts," by Marty Haugen, from the album *Anthology 1: 1980–1984* (GIA Publications, 1999). Also trace or draw an outline of a life-size body on butcher paper and hang it on the wall. Create a second outline of the same body and cut puzzle pieces out of it, one piece for each student in the class.

2. Plan and lead a short prayer service that includes Eph 4.1–16 and the article "Weave for Us a Garment" from the *CYB*. Play appropriate music, such as "We Are Many Parts."

3. Give the students each a puzzle piece that you have prepared, and invite them to write one of their gifts or talents on it. Provide glue or tape, and have the students collaborate and put together the puzzle pieces that make up the "one body" hanging on the wall.

4. Display the body puzzle in the classroom as a visual reminder of the prayer and Scripture passage. Ask the students what comes to mind as they look at the image. Discuss whether they experience themselves as a single body or as individual units, when they work together as a class or school.

Advice for Christian Living

Practical Relationship Advice
Ephesians, chapter 4

This activity encourages the students to discuss the practicality of the advice for good relationships offered in Eph 4.25–32, and look at how they could apply it to their lives.

1. Request a student to read Eph 4.25–32 aloud to the class. Then tell the students to focus on two lines from the passage: "Do not let the sun go down on your anger" (verse 26) and "Let no evil talk come out of your mouths, but only what is useful for building up" (verse 29).

2. Form small groups, and have the students discuss in them how practical the advice for good relationships in Eph 4.26,29 is. Request that they provide specific examples as part of the discussion.

3. Direct the groups each to decide how they can best apply the advice from the Scripture reading in their own lives and to plan a demonstration of that application for the class in the form of a role-play.

4. Invite the groups to present their role-plays to the class. Then discuss the various ways that the students found the two sayings from Ephesians to be relevant.

A Modern Letter from Paul
Ephesians, chapters 5–6
"Family Relationships," Eph 5.21—6.4, CYB; *"The Christian Family,"*
    Col 3.18—4.1, CYB

The students reflect on the cultural influences that might have led Paul to write Ephesians, chapters 5–6, in his time, as well as explore what he would say today.

1. Invite a student to read Eph 5.21—6.4 aloud to the class. Discuss with the students why that passage upsets many people today.
    Call a student to read the article "Family Relationships" from the *CYB*, and the article "The Christian Family" cross-referenced within it. Talk about Paul's message in light of this new information.

2. Form small groups, and instruct them each to write a letter that Paul might write to Christians today on the topic of the Christian household. Encourage the groups to explore the language he would use and what he would say to husbands, wives, and children.

3. Request each group to read its finished letter aloud to the class. After all the groups have done so, identify similarities and differences between the letters, and discuss the ways that the students have adapted something of Paul's approach to modern situations.

Philippians

Modern Examples of Biblical Virtue

Biblical Bookmarks
Philippians, chapter 1

This activity invites the students to make bookmarks for important people in their lives, using verses from the first chapter of Philippians.

    1. For this activity, you will need blank 5-by-8-inch index cards; art supplies such as colored markers or pencils, crayons, glitter, glue, and stickers; and clear contact paper and scissors.

    2. To begin this activity, with soft instrumental music playing in the background, invite the students to think of important people in their lives. Tell the students to hold those people in their hearts as you read Phil 1.2–11. Then read the passage slowly and clearly.

    3. Provide the index cards and art supplies you have gathered for this activity. Instruct the students each to pull out verses from the Scripture passage and use them to create decorated bookmarks for some of the important people they remembered during the reading. Supply clear contact paper for covering the bookmarks.

    4. When the bookmarks are done, discuss the verses most often chosen for this activity. Ask, "Why are they so appealing?"

Humility Today
Philippians, chapter 2
"Divine Humility, Cosmic Glory," Phil 2.1–11, CYB

The students reflect on the virtue of humility and discuss the presence of that virtue in our world today.

    1. Ask one student to read Phil 2.1–11 aloud to the class and another to read the article "Divine Humility, Cosmic Glory" from the *CYB*. Help the students to define humility and offer examples.

    2. Divide the class into groups and challenge the groups each to find music, videos, literature, and movie and television clips that clearly demonstrate the virtue of humility or that display a blatant lack of humility. Note that it might be easier for the groups to find the latter, but that they should also obtain at least one example of the former. Give the groups several days to find and bring in their examples.

3. Select a few of the groups' examples to show or play for the class. Discuss how the themes, characters, and story lines support the qualities in the Scripture passage. Reflect on these questions with the class:

- What enabled Jesus to be humble in his greatness?
- What invites us to humility today?
- What is the difference between humility and low self-esteem?

Variation. Help the students to choose one of the videos brought in, and to host a movie night for their families, their peers, or younger students. Guide them in arranging a space to show the video, providing refreshments, and handling invitations and publicity. Encourage them to lead a discussion of humility after the movie, incorporating the Scripture reading and article used in class.

Christian Music: Then and Now

Modern Hymns
Philippians, chapter 2

An examination of an ancient Christian song leads the students to a review of modern Christian music.

1. Prepare for this activity by directing the students to listen to some current Christian rock music on their own time. Ask them to write down some of the themes that they hear in the music and to bring their notes to class for this activity. Also suggest that the students bring in some Christian or Catholic liturgical music of their own choosing, or provide some yourself.

2. Begin this activity by reading Phil 2.1–11 aloud. Discuss the themes present in that early Christian song.

3. Play the Christian or Catholic liturgical music brought in by the students or you. Discuss the messages presented through the music as well as the genre of the music.

4. Invite the students to discuss the power of music to communicate spiritual themes. Encourage them to refer to the notes they took in preparation for this activity. Ask, "Does the genre of music used to talk about God affect your own interest in the music? Why or why not?"

Variations. To extend this activity, help the class arrange a concert of Christian music for their peers. Guide the students in brainstorming a list of Christian music groups that perform locally, and also check with local youth ministry leaders to identify such groups. Then lead the students in selecting a group, arranging a time and place for the concert, promoting the concert, and hosting the performance. If you are not comfortable with those tasks, consider recruiting an adult who has experience, to help you advise the class.

Another option is to help the students plan and provide music for an upcoming Mass.

The Christian's Goal

Prized Bulletin Board
Philippians, chapter 3
"Commitment to Your Goal," Phil 3.13–16, CYB

This exercise asks the students to create a bulletin board that is based on Phil 3.12–21.

    1. Ask a student to read Phil 3.12–21 aloud to the class. Have the students read the *CYB* article "Commitment to Your Goal" to themselves and think about goal setting and maturity.

    2. Divide the class into groups and direct the groups to submit designs for a bulletin board that would best stress verse 14 of the Scripture reading: "I press on toward the goal for the prize of the heavenly call of God in Christ Jesus."

    3. Have the class vote on the best design or combine the favorite features from several. Then invite all the students to collaborate on putting up the bulletin board. Provide art supplies such as construction paper, stencils, colored markers, magazines that can be cut up, scissors, and glue. Note the cooperation involved in completing this project. Ask, "How do God and the presence of other people help us attain the goals and promises God has for us?"

LETTERS

Colossians

Sources of Strength and Deception

Roots
Colossians, chapter 2
"Where Are Your Roots?" Col 2.6–7, CYB

The image of a tree helps the students assess what nourishes them and reflect on the life that the nourishment brings.

1. Ask one student to read Col 2.6–7 aloud to the class and another student to read the article "Where Are Your Roots?" from the *CYB*.

2. On the board, draw a picture of a tree with its roots, designating it as a representation of the people to whom Paul or his disciple was speaking. Label the roots "Jesus."

3. Give the students sheets of blank paper and appropriate art supplies, and direct them each to design a tree representing themselves. For the roots, they should identify persons, experiences, activities, and beliefs that nourish them. For the branches, they should name the results of that kind of nourishment in their lives.

4. Invite the students to share aspects of their finished drawings. Return to the picture on the board and ask them to identify what signs of life should come from a life based in Jesus. Note the following points in your own words:
- There is a clear parallel between the health of a tree and the health of a human being. Roots nourished by healthy sources produce strong branches and healthy leaves, and nourishment from healthy sources in our own lives produces physical, mental, and spiritual health.

Empty Promises
Colossians, chapter 2

The students brainstorm examples of "philosophy and empty deceit" (Col 2.8) in today's world and create warning labels that advise teens today to avoid empty promises.

1. Request a student to read Col 2.8–23 aloud. Emphasize verse 8. Discuss with the students what philosophies and empty deceits may be dangerous in today's world.

2. Form small groups, and have the groups each make a warning label or sign that advises teens today to avoid the empty promises the class has identified. Distribute blank paper or poster board, colored markers or pens, and other art supplies.

3. Display the completed visuals in the classroom and discuss effective ways of warning teenagers about various types of deceptions. Address questions such as these:
- What faulty philosophies are most threatening?
- Are there groups of people trying to warn young people about them? If so, how is that working?

The Christian Family

A Christian Family Conference
Colossians, chapters 3–4
"The Christian Family," Col 3.18—4.1, CYB

The students write short sermons addressing the contemporary Christian family and discuss how faith affects the success of family life.

1. Call one student to read Col 3.18—4.1 aloud to the class and another to read the article "The Christian Family" from the *CYB*.

2. Invite the students each to prepare an outline for a brief "sermon," or talk, that they might give at a conference about the Christian family. The title should be "Characteristics of the Christian Family," and the talk should contain simple pieces of advice to family members based on the students' observations of their own and other families. The students may think of songs or movie clips to complement their talks, and note those at the appropriate spots in their outline.

3. When the students have finished their outlines, divide the class into groups and have the students share some of their ideas in their groups. Direct the groups each to devise a single sermon, or talk, based on the insights shared. Note that the sermon may use brief clips from different media.

4. Allow the groups to present their talks at a miniconference on the Christian family right in your classroom. Discuss the different insights that arise. Ask, "To what extent does faith affect the success of family life?"

Variation. In step 4, invite the students' families, and other students and their families, to attend the conference.

1 Thessalonians

The Challenge of Acting Like Jesus
1 Thessalonians, chapter 2
"Doing the Right Thing," 1 Thess 2.1–2, CYB

This activity asks the students to pick realistic and challenging situations that they might face, and look for creative ways to respond as Jesus might have.

1. Invite one student to read 1 Thess 2.1–2 aloud and another to read the article "Doing the Right Thing" from the *CYB*.

2. Divide the class into small groups and ask the groups each to create a realistic and challenging situation that teens might encounter, one that would require some moral courage. Have the groups write down their detailed scenario. Collect the finished scenarios and make enough copies for each group.

3. The next day, pass the scenarios out to the class and have each group address each of the various situations with a creative response that applies the teachings and actions of Jesus.

4. When the groups have completed their responses, direct them to pass each situation and its response to the group that wrote the situation. Then instruct the groups each to do for the class a brief role-play that shows the different ways that their situation could be handled. Invite discussion about each of the responses.

5. After all the situations have been presented, invite student reflection about how one develops the ability to discern what Jesus would do in different situations. Pose questions similar to these:
   - How does one find the moral courage to carry out a particular response?
   - What kind of relationship must a person have with Jesus in order for him or her to do what Jesus would do?
   - Does God ask us to do exactly what Jesus would do in each situation, or might God have a more specific request for each of us?

Paul as a Minister Today
1 Thessalonians, chapter 2

This activity invites the students to reflect on how Paul's abilities as a minister would serve the church today.

1. Ask the students to imagine their parish priest or minister saying the words of 1 Thessalonians, chapter 2, to them as you read the passage aloud.

2. Form small groups, and give them each the following directions in your own words:

- Make a checklist of what you see as desirable qualities in a minister, priest, or preacher. Think about the many ministry roles in the church today, including those of religious educator, youth minister, liturgical director, pastor, altar server, musician, and pastoral minister—both female and male. Compare your completed list with Paul's description of how he believed he ministered to the people in Thessalonica. Then decide how you would rate Paul (on a scale of 1 to 10) as a minister.

3. Gather the class and ask the students whether they would want Paul in their church today as a minister. Discuss the students' insights, noting the similarities and differences between what made a good minister in the early church and what makes a good one today. Ask what new demands modern ministers face.

4. Encourage the students to explore how ministers are chosen or hired in their churches, and to offer their time and interest in the interview processes.

Variation. In step 3, if the students know enough about Paul, suggest that they conduct mock interviews to explore the issue of whether they would want Paul as a minister. Tell them to begin by preparing a short list of interview questions based on their group's rating criteria, and then interview someone representing Paul. You might act as Paul in the interviews, or a student might. After the interviews, lead the discussion described in step 3.

"Made in Thessalonica"
1 Thessalonians, chapter 5

The students design greeting cards or other products for the Thessalonians, based on the Scripture passage.

1. Invite a student to read 1 Thess 5.1–28 aloud to the class.

2. Ask the students to identify verses from the Scripture passage that they find inspirational or interesting. Provide art supplies for the students: white construction paper, colored paper, glitter, colored markers, glue, and so on. Invite the students to design greeting cards or other items—such as bumper stickers, posters, bookmarks, and T-shirts—for the Thessalonians, based on the passage. The artwork should be upbeat, inspirational, colorful, and creative.

3. Invite the students to share their finished pieces of art with one another. Discuss the verses chosen, and the interpretations given by the students through their choice of medium and verse.

2 Thessalonians

Wanted Posters
2 Thessalonians, chapter 2

Designing wanted posters and television clips helps the students visualize the person of lawlessness described in 2 Thessalonians, chapter 2.

   1. Ask the students to visualize the person described as the lawless one while you read 2 Thessalonians, chapter 2, aloud in a dramatic, bold manner.

   2. Divide the class into groups and have the groups each design a wanted poster for the person of lawlessness described in the passage. The design should be done on poster board and should be large enough to display in the classroom. Distribute poster board and art supplies such as colored markers or pencils.
   Also direct the groups each to create a television spot that will air during the *Most Wanted* show in Thessalonica. Their poster should be featured in the spot.

   3. Present the *Most Wanted* show in class and discuss how similar and different the wanted people are. Raise the question, "To what extent have you encountered characteristics of the 'lawless one' in real people or in movies and other media?" Have a student read 2 Thess 2.13–15, and emphasize the contrast between the "lawless one" and those who follow Jesus. Ask, "Have you encountered people who resemble the description in this second passage?"

My Final Days
2 Thessalonians, chapters 1–2
"The Parousia," 2 Thess 1.5—2.17, CYB

Creating a chart that shows how they would spend their time in the final week before the Parousia helps the students understand and interpret the end time as it is described in 2 Thessalonians.

   1. Before this exercise, prepare a handout with a chart that lists seven days and indicates time periods—such as morning, afternoon, evening, and night—for each day.

   2. To begin this exercise, invite several students to read 2 Thess 1.5—2.17 aloud to the class and another to read the article "The Parousia" from the *CYB*.

   3. Call the students to imagine that they know the end of the world is coming in a week. Note that this exercise hopefully will elicit some of their own values, God imagery, and sense of what God expects of them. Point out that the Catholic church claims that the end of the world could come at any moment, and does not believe that human beings will have any precise indicators of when it will come (*Catechism,* nos. 673–677, 1038–1050 [see appendix A]).

Invite the students to reflect on the type of end time portrayed in 2 Thessalonians, chapter 2, and ask if that description makes sense to them. Remind them that the end time is under the control of the loving, merciful, and just God.

4. Distribute the handout you have prepared. Give the students some quiet time to jot down on the chart what they would do in their last seven days if they knew that the Parousia lay ahead. After a while, invite the students to share aspects of their chart with another student.

5. As a class, discuss the approaches the students took to their last week. Help the students identify, from the examples they share, the characteristics of their image of God and their values. To close the discussion, invite the students to write a reflection about how they might incorporate aspects of their hypothetical last week into their daily lives.

Project Motivation
2 Thessalonians, chapter 3
"Laziness," 2 Thess 3.6–13, CYB

The students plan a motivational speech or video or song for the people in Thessalonica, and for any teens today who are slipping into a life of idleness.

1. Ask a student to read 2 Thess 3.6–13 aloud, emphasizing verses 11–12. Have a second student read the article "Laziness" from the *CYB.*

2. Help the students define idleness and describe what its forms look like today.

3. Divide the class into groups and tell the groups each to plan a motivational video, speech, or song for people who are slipping into a life of idleness. Note that their creations should be aimed at both the people in Thessalonica and teens today.

4. Invite the groups to perform their creations in class and discuss how inspirational and necessary the messages are. Use questions like these to guide your discussion:
- Does high school life inspire idleness or too much busyness?
- What different kinds of inspirational messages would be necessary for different types of teenagers, depending on their commitments and stress?

Pastoral Letters

1 Timothy

Advice Columns
1 Timothy

The students compose letters asking advice that matches that actually given in the Second Letter to the Thessalonians.

    1. Prepare for this activity by copying advice column letters and their responses from the newspaper. Also request the students to read 1 Timothy as homework the night before, or begin the activity with that assignment in class.

    2. Begin this activity by asking the students each to write down eight pieces of advice that Paul offers Timothy about various topics. Tell the students that the letters written by Paul suggest that the recipients had problems that they brought to Paul or that came to his attention through reports from others. Note that because of that, Paul resembles an advice columnist.

    3. Pass out the copies of advice column letters and their responses that you have prepared. Tell the students each to create a letter to Paul seeking advice that Paul actually gives in the reading. Suggest that they address a piece of advice from the list they created earlier. Note that they are also to write a response to the Dear Paul letter.

    4. Invite the students to share some of their completed letters and responses. Note the incredible variety of issues that Paul addresses in the Second Letter to the Thessalonians. Explain that though his main calling may have been to share the message of Jesus, he had to do so in the complicated realities of people's lives. Discuss what variety of issues a modern Paul might identify as important in the lives of contemporary Catholics.

Résumés for Members of the Early Church
1 Timothy, chapters 3, 5

This activity challenges the students to create résumés for various members of the early church community, in response to the qualifications given for different positions in 1 Timothy.

    1. Prepare for this activity by bringing in examples of good résumés.

    2. Begin this activity by inviting several students to take turns reading 1 Tim 3.1–13 and 5.3–16.

3. Give the students the examples of good résumés that you have brought in. Explain that when people write résumés for jobs, they take a job description and then try to show how their own experience and background qualifies them for the position.

4. Form the class into six groups. Assign each of three groups to draft a résumé for one of the following positions in the early church:
- bishop (1 Tim 3.1–7)
- deacon (1 Tim 3.8–13)
- widow (1 Tim 5.3–16)

Explain that the groups should feel free to be creative and add information based on their study of Paul, using names and places that might be appropriate, and so on.

Assign the other three groups each one of the same three positions. Instruct those groups each to draft job interview questions for their position, based on the information provided in the reading.

5. Pair up the applicant groups and interview groups by position. Allow each pair to conduct an interview before the class. In each interview, the candidate group should share its résumé with the prospective-employer group and answer the employer group's questions. The employer group should then have a brief conference to select its bishop, deacon, or widow, and explain the choice to the rest of the class.

6. After all the interviews have been completed, discuss with the class the standards used to identify bishops and deacons and the qualifications for the status of widow. Note the number of fairly personal issues that the First Letter to Timothy suggests. Solicit responses to questions like these:
- How many of the same issues should be considered when hiring church ministers?
- Are other qualities equally as important or more important for such ministers today?

2 Timothy

Symbols of Faith
2 Timothy, chapter 2

Household utensils and other items help the students describe an aspect of their relationship with God.

1. Prepare for this activity by choosing a household utensil or other item for use as a demonstration in step 3. For example, you might select a can opener, and bring it and a can to class. Also gather a variety of old household utensils and other items, at least one for each student; heavy wire; and duct tape.

2. Start this activity by asking a student to read 2 Tim 2.20–26 aloud to the class. Note the use of utensils as images for believers. Ask the students why a utensil is a helpful image for a faith-filled Christian.

3. Present the item you chose for an example and demonstrate its use. For instance, if you brought in a can opener, use it to open a can. Then say something like this about your item:

- I feel that just like I use a can opener to open a can, God calls me to open the Scriptures. God wants to share God's word with you and invites me to help open up the Scriptures for you, so that you can receive God's loving invitation of companionship and forgiveness.

4. Display your collection of old household utensils and other items, and direct the students each to choose one item that reflects their sense of how they can best serve God at this time in their life. Give them a few minutes to jot down why they chose that item. Then invite them to share their items in small groups, explaining the items' significance.

5. Call some of the students to explain their items to the class as a whole. Listen carefully to the students' sharing, asking follow-up questions as appropriate and affirming the ideas given. Summarize the students' input at the end. Revisit the Bible passage, and compare Paul's analogy with the ones that the students have made.

6. Help the students create a sculpture using the items they have chosen, heavy wire, and duct tape. Ask one or two students to make a label for the sculpture using the words from 2 Tim 2.20. Display the sculpture in the classroom or in another room in the school, such as the cafeteria or media center.

Timothy's Prayer for Paul
2 Timothy, chapters 3–4

The students compose a prayer that Timothy might have offered for Paul, given the experiences that are shared in the Scripture passage.

1. Ask the students to read 2 Tim 3.1—4.18 to themselves.

2. Have the students identify five concerns or ideas that Paul expresses in the reading. Direct the students to compose a short prayer that Timothy might say for Paul based on those five items, citing the appropriate chapter and verse for each item.

3. Ask the students to share their prayers, first in threes and then with the whole class. Listen carefully to the images of God, perceptions of Paul, and sense of solidarity or friendship expressed by Timothy in the prayers. Use your observations as a basis for a discussion of ways that the students can support one another in prayer.

Titus

Christmas Cards
Titus, chapters 2–3

Passages from Titus inspire the students to create appropriate cards for the Christmas season.

1. Prepare for this exercise by gathering construction paper, colored markers or pencils, and old Christmas cards or other decorations that may be used in an art project.

2. Begin this exercise by having the students read Titus 2.11–14 and 3.4–8 to themselves. Point out that those verses are read at different Christmas liturgies.

3. Provide the materials you have gathered for this art project, and direct the students each to make a Christmas card that includes one of the texts from Titus and that conveys something of the text's meaning in the context of the season.

4. Discuss the completed cards, the use of the readings from Titus during the Christmas season, and the nature of the season as a whole. Arrange for the students to deliver their cards to people in care facilities or others who might appreciate a Christmas message.

Philemon

The Reunion

A Dialog: Philemon and Onesimus
Philemon

This exercise guides the students to create dialogs that explore the relationship between Philemon and Onesimus after the two are reunited.

   1. Call the students to read the Letter to Philemon aloud. Discuss why Onesimus may have run away in the first place. Explore why Paul is sending him back to Philemon.

   2. Form groups, and direct the groups each to create a skit portraying an imaginary dialog between Philemon and Onesimus. Explain that the skit should have at least five conversation interchanges and should address concerns such as these:
   - What will their relationship and lives be like now?
   - What changes will have occurred?

   3. When all the skits have been performed, discuss the insights that arise from them. Examine the request for forgiveness that Paul makes and the way that he does it. Note the particular challenge to reconciliation that the imbalance of power between Philemon and Onesimus brings. Address questions like the ones that follow:
   - What kind of trust did Onesimus need to have in Paul and in Philemon, in order for Philemon to return?
   - What does the Letter to Philemon suggest about the power of God's grace for reconciliation?

Hebrews

Attentiveness to God's Presence

Attention Rap!
Hebrews, chapter 2

The students create rap songs based on Heb 2.1–4 and discuss the need to pay attention to God's word.

1. Divide the class into groups. Direct the groups each to read Heb 2.1–4 and then discuss why the Hebrews needed a call to pay attention.

2. Ask the groups each to write a rap song based on the passage. Encourage them to consider the tone, mood, volume, and beat carefully as they attempt to capture the message of the passage.

3. After the raps are performed, discuss the need to pay attention to God's word today, and the many distractions that can interfere with our ability to be attentive.

Symbols of Promise
Hebrews, chapter 6

The students create three-dimensional symbols, both biblical and personal, of God's promise to us.

1. For this activity, you will need to gather art materials such as paper, glue, glitter, shoe boxes, magazines, modeling clay, felt, pipe cleaners, and aluminum foil.

2. To begin this activity, invite a student to read Heb 6.13–20 aloud. Encourage the students to focus on the themes of hope and promise during the reading, and help them work through the passage, explaining the various references.

3. Ask for definitions for *promise* and *symbol*. Explore the nature of symbols, giving examples.

4. Provide the art materials you have gathered for the students. Tell the students to work individually or in pairs to create three-dimensional symbols of God's promise to us. Explain that those may be actual biblical symbols (such as a rainbow, an olive branch, and an anchor), interpretations based on the Scriptures, or personal symbols.

5. Invite the students to present and explain their finished symbols. Ask them to reflect on the relation between God's promise and our faith. Remind them that even when our faith in God's promise is weak, God's promise and faithfulness are constant.

The Nature of Sacrifice

Sacrifice: A Literary Interpretation
Hebrews, chapter 10
"The Perfect Sacrifice," Heb 10.1–18, CYB

C. S. Lewis's novel *The Lion, the Witch, and the Wardrobe* helps the students explore the meaning of sacrifice.

1. For this activity, you will need a copy of C. S. Lewis's *The Lion, the Witch, and the Wardrobe: A Story for Children* (New York: Macmillan, 1950; also widely available from other publishers).

2. Begin this activity by instructing the students to read Heb 10.1–25 silently. Then go through the passage again slowly, explaining the contrast that Paul is drawing between Jesus as high priest and the high priest of Judaism. Ask a second student to read the article "The Perfect Sacrifice" from the *CYB*.

3. Discuss the meaning of the word *sacrifice* in a literal and symbolic way. Note that its literal meaning is "to make holy." Help the students to connect the general way that the word is understood with that meaning. Encourage the students to give examples of sacrifice from their own lives or the lives of others.

4. Read chapters 13 to 15 of C. S. Lewis's *The Lion, the Witch, and the Wardrobe*. Discuss these questions:
- What is the meaning of sacrifice in this text?
- How does Aslan explain the meaning of his sacrifice?
- How is this text comparable to the text from Hebrews?

The Personal Meaning of Faith

The Faith of One's Life Journey
Hebrews, chapter 11
"How Do You Spell Faith?" Heb 11.1–3, CYB

The image of a car offers a creative way for the students to explore how their own faith is part of their life journey.

1. Ask one student to read Heb 11.1–3 aloud to the class and another student to read the article "How Do You Spell Faith?" from the *CYB*.

2. Invite the students to "spell the meaning of faith" following the format used in the article. Then ask them each to sketch a car that can carry at least four passengers. Provide the following instructions in your own words:

- The car should represent the way that you "travel" through life, so design it accordingly. Put yourself in the car and also put God and faith in it. You may add other people or things to represent what you use to guide your way (such as a steering wheel) or fuel your journey (such as gas).

3. Direct the students to share their finished pictures in small groups and then as a class. Listen carefully and ask follow-up questions to help the students explore their sense of God and faith. Consider inviting the students to respond to these two summation questions, either verbally or in writing:

- Where is your car going?
- What route is it taking?

"Cloud of Witnesses" Talk Show
Hebrews, chapters 11–12

Presenting faith-filled individuals from the Old Testament as guests on a talk show allows the students to reflect on the meaning of faith.

1. Invite several students to read Heb 11.1—12.2 aloud to the class. Discuss the similarities between the different people's experiences of faith in that passage.

2. Assign different Old Testament characters or groups from the Bible passage to different individuals or small groups. Have the students list what the passage says about their assigned character and add any other elements of the character's life that they can recall. Note that the students might go back to some of the relevant passages from the Old Testament to refresh their memory.

3. Create a talk show featuring the "cloud of witnesses" (Heb 12.1) and include all the characters remembered for their faith. A moderator should invite the different characters to explain what the word *faith* means to them and how they kept their faith. The students may reflect on the definition that Paul offers in Heb 11.1–2, from their character's perspective or their own.

4. Note common characteristics of faith that emerge from the testimonies of the witnesses. Compare those with faith experiences from the students' own lives.

Angels

Entertaining Angels
Hebrews, chapter 3

The students reflect on the importance of service in different aspects their lives, including the family, school, and parish.

1. Read Heb 13.1–3 aloud to the class. Ask the students to define *service* and to examine the interpretation of service given by the Scripture passage.

2. Call the students' attention to Jesus' statement in Mt 25.40, "Truly I tell you, just as you did it to one of the least of these who are members of my family, you did it to me." Ask them to relate the subject of that verse to the concept of angels in Heb 13.1–3. Also note that *The New Oxford Annotated Bible with the Apocryphal/Deuterocanonical Books,* new revised standard version, edited by Bruce M. Metzger and Roland E. Murphy (New York: Oxford University Press, 1994), page 330, suggests that the phrase "entertained angels" in Heb 13.2 refers to Gen 18.1–8 and 19.1–3, and instruct the students to explore those passages.

3. Prompt the students to brainstorm a list of angels in their midst, such as the local food shelf, crisis hot line, and drop-in youth center. Encourage the students to bring in names, addresses, phone numbers, and brief descriptions of those angels. Guide them in putting that information into a booklet that they and others can use. (Consider using a desktop publishing program to produce the booklet.)

4. Invite the students to make note of the many opportunities available for service, and help them become involved if they indicate an interest in doing so. Also help them make their booklet available to others who might be able to use it, perhaps by giving copies to the school media center and community library.

Variation. Invite one or more representatives of the agencies listed in the booklet to speak to the class about their work.

Exegetical Tools: The Concordance—the Nature of Angels
Hebrews, chapter 13
"Entertaining Angels," Heb 13.1–5, CYB

The students reflect on the reality of angels from both the religious and secular perspectives.

1. Before this activity, look up "angels" in a biblical concordance (see appendix A) and note the Bible references listed there. Decide how many references you would like to assign to each small group in step 3, and how to divide up the Bible so that you have about that number of references in each section. Also make sure you have enough concordances for the groups, or information from the relevant pages of a concordance.

2. To start this activity, request one student to read Heb 13.1–2 aloud and another to read the article "Entertaining Angels" from the *CYB*.

3. If necessary, introduce or review the process for using a biblical concordance (refer to "Exegetical Tools: The Concordance and Wisdom Themes," on pages 111–112 of this manual, for an explanation of that tool). Then divide the class into small groups, and distribute concordances or the information you have gathered from a concordance. Assign each group one of the sections of the Bible that you have identified. Tell the groups each to find the references to angels in their section of the Bible.

4. Invite the groups to report their findings to the class and discuss their insights. Then ask the students to bring to the next class items that portray or refer to angels: literature, pictures, statues, music, video clips, and so on. Bring in some different items yourself. Preparing some clips from recent movies that feature angels would be fun for the class. Also provide some traditional Catholic prayers about angels, and information about angels from the *Catechism*, numbers 328 to 336 (see appendix A).

5. At the next class, invite the students to share their angel items, and share your own as well. Help the students explore what their items communicate about different perspectives of the presence and role of angels in our everyday lives. Compare the culture's understanding of angels with the Catholic church's tradition about angels and the biblical presentation of angels.

The Unchanging Jesus

Signs for Jesus
Hebrews, chapter 13

The students create a sandpainting to emphasize the meaning of Heb 13.8.

1. For this activity, you will need colored sand (available from art and craft supply stores), and surfaces on which to create sandpaintings, such as pieces of heavy paper, cardboard, wood, or buckskin.

2. Begin this activity by asking a student to read Heb 13.1–16 as a way of providing a context for verse 8: "Jesus Christ is the same yesterday and today and forever."

3. Tell the students that they will now work in groups to create sandpaintings that capture the meaning of that slogan about Jesus. Offer a brief description of the art of sandpainting, such as this:
- The Navajo and Pueblo Indians use sandpainting in religious ceremonies. They create designs of colored sand on a flat surface of sand or buckskin, using symbols and colors that have special meanings for them.

4. Divide the class into groups of four or five. Explain that each group's sandpainting should include images of Jesus as he was and is and will be. Suggest that the groups use symbols and colors that have special meaning for the students as Christians. Distribute blank paper, colored markers or pencils, colored sand, and surfaces for the paintings. Suggest that the groups sketch their design on paper first, then transfer it to the sand.

5. Invite the groups to share their finished sandpaintings and to explain their use of images and colors. Discuss the insights that arise.
Afterward, ask the students what will now happen to the paintings. As they realize that their artwork is not permanent and cannot be preserved or hung for display, point out that just as the sandpaintings will be brushed away but will remain in their memories, Jesus disappeared from the earth but remains in our hearts and minds.

Variation. Instead of creating sandpaintings, the students could draw designs outside using sidewalk chalk. The follow-up discussion could again close with reflection on the temporary nature of the artwork and of Jesus' earthly body.

James

The Power of the Word

James's Puppet Show
James
Introduction to James, CYB

The students create simple puppets and then present some of James's message through a puppet show.

1. Bring to class materials for puppet making, or ask the students to do so. Sock puppets with faces created by markers, or small cardboard figures on sticks would work well.

2. Introduce the Letter of James by inviting a student to read the introduction to it from the *CYB*.

3. Divide the class into four groups and assign one of the following themes to each group. The students should read their assigned passages aloud in their groups, and then each group should design a cast of puppet characters to deliver the Scripture message and illustrate its meaning for the class.
■ Wealthy and poor Christians (Jas 2.1–9; 4.13—5.6)
■ The tongue (Jas 3.1–12)
■ Disunity among believers (Jas 3.13–18; 4.1–3)
■ Resisting temptation (Jas 1.12–18; 4.7–10)

4. Arrange for the groups each to give their puppet play to a group of younger kids, or to videotape it for use by a primary class teacher. Afterward, discuss James's messages and the various ways that the students chose to present them. Ask the students how those ideas are relevant to our lives today.

The Power of Speech
James, chapter 3
"The Tongue: Friend or Foe?" Jas 3.1–12, CYB

A simple affirmation exercise allows the students to explore the ways that speech can be used to hurt and heal.

1. Ask one student to read Jas 3.1–12 aloud to the class, and have another student read the article "The Tongue: Friend or Foe?" from the *CYB*.

2. Lead the students to brainstorm first about the different ways that the tongue can hurt others, and then about the different ways that the spoken word can heal or help others. List their insights on the board.

307

3. Divide the class into groups of three or four. Give each person a piece of paper and a pen or pencil, and direct the groups each to complete an affirmation exercise as follows:

- The youngest person in the group sits with her or his back to the group, and the remaining group members take turns each listing three things that they like about the person. The person being affirmed writes those positive things down as they are named. Then the next-youngest person takes a turn listening to positive statements, and so on, until everyone in the group has been affirmed.

Emphasize that the students are to be positive and affirming in this exercise. Caution them to avoid saying anything that might embarrass or hurt someone.

4. After everyone has been affirmed, invite the students each to write a brief paragraph describing how it felt to listen to the positive comments of their peers. Also suggest that they think about past experiences in which people said things that were hurtful to them or others.

5. Gather the students and invite them to share their reflections. In summary, lead the class to suggest some general guidelines that might help teens use the gift of speech well.

Prayer Aids

Prayer Kits
James, chapter 5

This exercise invites the students to create prayer kits based on James's sayings on prayer and on their own experience.

1. Invite a student to read Jas 5.13–16 aloud to the class. Have the students list the prayer advice that James gives to readers.

2. Form small groups, and have them each devise a prayer kit based on the ideas in the reading and on their own understanding of the power of prayer. Suggest that the students copy the passage from James, other meaningful Scripture passages, and inspirational prayers; create bookmarks and prayer cards; make rosaries; collect votive candles, incense, and icons; and so on. Note that one student in each group should also bring a box or other container.

3. At the next class, invite the groups to assemble their prayer kits, and then share them with the class and explain the choices of items. Note the different occasions for prayer mentioned in the Scripture passage. Discuss these questions:

- Does one often require material items in order to pray?
- What spiritual things does one need in order to pray?

Afterward, arrange to donate the prayer kits to a prison, nursing home, homeless shelter, or other institution.

LETTERS

1 Peter

Building Up a Spiritual House
1 Peter, chapter 2

Building a small structure with bricks helps the students explore the significance of the spiritual house mentioned in 1 Peter, chapter 2.

   1. Prepare for this activity by bringing in actual bricks of some sort, or creating cardboard or paper ones. You need enough for each student to have one brick. The students should be able to write on the bricks, either directly or by attaching a piece of paper to them. Also bring in or create a cornerstone with Jesus' name on it.

   2. Begin this activity by asking a student to read 1 Pet 2.4–8 aloud to the class. Discuss the meaning of the passage.

   3. Provide the bricks you have brought in. Note that the living stones of 1 Pet 2.4 are "chosen and precious in God's sight." Give the students some quiet time to ponder how God shows them they are chosen and precious.

   4. Direct the students to write on their brick their name and one thing that they think God appreciates about them. Then, after placing the cornerstone with Jesus' name somewhere on the floor, ask the students to add their bricks and construct a small structure with them.

   5. Lead the students in a discussion of what it means to be part of the structure they have just built, which symbolizes the spiritual house referred to in verse 5. Address questions such as these:
- How could this structure be a stumbling block to some?
- What is powerful about a community that recognizes the gifts within it?

Variation. Extend this activity by arranging for the students to participate in a Habitat for Humanity project, or in a local volunteer program for building or repairing structures such as homes, playgrounds, or hiking trails.

Reflections on Suffering
1 Peter, chapters 3–4
"Shout for Joy!" 1 Pet 4.12–19, CYB

Music offers the students a way of discussing the meaning of suffering.

   1. Ask some students to read 1 Pet 3.13–17 and 4.12–17, and the article "Shout for Joy!" from the *CYB.*

2. Invite the students to reflect on the mystery of suffering as expressed in music. Tell them each to pick a piece of music (with lyrics or instrumental) that portrays an aspect of the experience or meaning of suffering. As a homework assignment for the next class, have them write a short reflection on their choice of music, including key lyrics if applicable.

3. In the next class, ask the students to share their selections and insights in small groups, and then invite a few students to play their music and talk about it.

4. Revisit the passages from 1 Peter, chapters 3–4. Ask the students to discuss the meaning of 1 Pet 3.17, using the following questions or others like them:

- What are some concrete examples of times we could choose to suffer for doing good rather than suffer for doing evil?
- At times, it is within our power to decide how to suffer. What kind of challenge does that present a Christian?
- What does it mean to connect suffering with God's will? Is it God's will that we suffer, or does the author of the Bible passage mean that God would want us to embrace suffering if it came with doing good?

2 Peter

The Day of the Lord
2 Peter, chapter 3

This exercise invites the students to explore their own understanding of the Day of the Lord and their image of "new heavens and a new earth" (2 Pet 3.13).

1. Ask a student to read 2 Pet 3.1–13 aloud to the class.

2. Have the students individually create a list that answers this question: "If the Day of the Lord came today, what twenty-five things would you really miss or really be thankful for?"

3. Invite the students to share their completed list with a partner and then have them offer some of their thoughts to the whole class.

4. Direct the students to work with a partner again, this time to draw up a time chart that reflects the title "A Day in My Life in the 'New Heavens and a New Earth.'" As the pairs present their hypothetical days to the class, discuss what would be new and different about the era following the Day of the Lord.

5. Given the ideas that have surfaced from this exercise, share as a class how a Christian might best live out the rest of her or his life here on earth. Ask the students, "Do you agree with the advice given in the Second Letter of Peter? Why or why not?"

1, 2, and 3 John

1 John

Discerning Spirits
1 John, chapter 4
"Testing the Spirits," 1 Jn 4.1–21, CYB

This exercise encourages the students to reflect on indicators of the presence and absence of God.

1. You might want to prepare for the discussion in step 3 by consulting and then summarizing for the students Saint Ignatius's "Rules for the Discernment of Spirits," in *The Spiritual Exercises of St. Ignatius: Based on Studies in the Language of the Autograph,* translated by Louis J. Puhl (Chicago: Loyola University Press, 1951), numbers 314 to 336.

2. Begin this exercise by inviting one student to read 1 John, chapter 4, aloud to the class and another to read the article "Testing Spirits" from the *CYB.*

3. Discuss the method of discernment used in the Scripture passage, offering your summary of Saint Ignatius's rules if you have prepared one. Then encourage the students to call out other signs that a person might look for that indicate the presence or absence of God in a spirit, mood, or decision. List their responses on the board and ask the students to copy them.

4. Assign the students to watch a TV drama or movie within the following week, and ask them to assess the ways that the characters in it make decisions. Direct them to write a short reflection that addresses these questions:
   - From what you can tell, do the characters make decisions based on the spirit of God or on spirits opposed to God? Why?
   - Can you think of times you made a decision following one spirit or another? Describe those times generally.
   - In what types of situations might the guidelines presented in 1 John be helpful?

5. Ask the students to bring their reflections to class, and then discuss both the kind of decision making portrayed in the media and the value of that kind of decision making.

Exegetical Tools: The Concordance—a Study of Love
1 John, chapter 4
"Understanding Love," 1 Jn 4.7–21, CYB

The students use the Scriptures, the modern culture, and their own experience to explore the superficial and real qualities of love.

1. Before class, decide whether to assign the collage in step 6 as homework or class work, and bring in the necessary art supplies if you choose the latter.

2. To begin class, ask one student to read 1 Jn 4.7–21 aloud to the class and another student to read the article "Understanding Love" from the *CYB*.

3. Discuss the thoughts that the First Letter of John offers about love and list them on the board. Note that the term *love* is often used and described casually and generally in our culture, and that the reading from 1 John unpacks the real meaning of love.

4. Introduce or review the use of a biblical concordance (refer to "Exegetical Tools: The Concordance and Wisdom Themes," on pages 111–112 of this manual, for an explanation of that tool). Then provide copies of a concordance, or information from concordance articles that deal with love in the New Testament (see appendix A for a recommended concordance). Instruct the students to look up three New Testament passages that discuss love and to write down what those passages say about love.

5. Direct the students to find references to love in three different modern media (literature, music, comics, proverbs, movies, etc.). Explain that they should spend some time absorbing the different interpretations and deciding what they themselves think is most essential about the mystery of love. Give the students about a week to work on this.

6. After a week, tell the students each to create a collage that presents the New Testament references to love, the media interpretations of love, and their own interpretation of love. The collage should somehow present both superficial descriptions of love and a deeper, true meaning. For example, the students could put around the outside of a piece of poster board lyrics or comic strips that show love as portrayed by the modern culture, and then write words, quotes, or biblical verses within to show the "essence" of love. Either assign the collage as homework, or supply a variety of art materials and set aside time for the students to create their collage in class.

7. Invite the students to share their finished collages in groups, and then discuss, as a class, the insights that emerge. Address these questions:
   - How does God's love enable us to love other human beings at a deeper level?
   - Do some of the images of love in our modern culture confuse us about how to relate to God and others?

2 and 3 John

Anti-Deception Posters
2 John
"Unwelcome Guests," in 2 John, CYB

This activity asks the students to create posters that challenge cultural messages that they perceive are false.

1. Invite one student to read 2 John aloud to the class and another to read the article "Unwelcome Guests" from the *CYB*. Discuss the notion of a "deceiver" as discussed in the Scripture passage. Note the parallels about deceptive messages made by the *CYB* article.

2. Divide the class into small groups and have the groups discuss some deceptive messages that the students encounter in the world around them. Ask the groups each to identify media "guests" that visit their homes and to list the positive and negative values and behaviors introduced by those guests, as suggested in the article.

3. Direct the students, in groups or as individuals, to pick one of the guests they listed in step 2 and create a counterpoint to it in the same media. For example, if they identified a Web page that sells extremely expensive designer clothes, they might design a Web page that collects clothing for needy people or that gives suggestions for dressing nicely on a limited budget.

4. Invite the students to share their media counterpoints. Discuss why the messages of the corresponding media guests are false, and how the counterpoints counteract those messages. Ask questions like these:
   - Who gives the negative messages?
   - What needs do the messages claim to meet?
   - How do the students' counterpoints address those needs?

Footprints of Truth
2 and 3 John

Making and labeling paper footprints helps the students explore the meaning of "walking in the truth."

1. Have the students read 2 and 3 John, paying special attention to the author's focus on "walking in the truth."

2. Provide some large sheets of butcher paper, markers, and scissors. Tell the students each to trace one of their feet on butcher paper and cut out the footprint. They should then pair up. On one partner's footprint, they should write statements from 2 and 3 John that explain the concept of walking in the truth, and on the other partner's footprint, they should write their own interpretation of that concept.

3. Place the completed footprints on the floor or wall as though they were following a path. Let the students look at the prints and discuss the various interpretations that are presented on them. Discuss the challenges and rewards of looking for "the truth." Ask, "How can we recognize the truth?"

Jude

A Modern Christian Letter

Modern Letter Writing
Jude
Introduction to Jude, CYB

Composing a modern letter styled after Jude's letter leads the students to examine the issues facing the early church and the church today.

    1. Invite the students to take turns reading the Letter of Jude aloud to the class. Have one person read the introduction to that book from the *CYB*.

    2. Talk about the format of the letter, noting the introduction (salutation) and the interesting prayer that is used at the closing. Point out that the author encourages, warns, and ultimately blesses the congregation.

    3. Direct the students each to write a letter that parallels Jude's format. Tell them to address a modern Christian audience and use encouragement, warning, and blessing in their writing. Ask them to imitate the style of the introduction and conclusion as well.

    4. Call the students to share excerpts of their finished letters and to discuss the issues that they raised and the way they chose to present those issues.

Revelation

An Overview of Revelation

Coded Language
Revelation
Introduction to the Letters and Revelation

Reflecting on their own use of coded language helps the students understand the veiled language used by the author of the Book of Revelation.

  1. Ask a student to read the introduction to the Letters and Revelation from the *CYB*. Note the reason why John used coded language in the Book of Revelation.

  2. Direct the students to skim the Book of Revelation to find some examples of coded language. Tell them to jot down the examples they find, including cites. Then invite them to share the passages or verses with the class, and note the questions and ideas that surface.

  3. Form pairs, and ask them each to come up with examples of language used by teens that others might have a hard time understanding. Have the pairs create a few sentences to illustrate those words or phrases.

  4. Gather the class and discuss the use of language particular to teens or to members of other age-groups. Address these questions:
  ■ How does the language develop?
  ■ Does the group intend to disguise the meaning of its words, as did the author of Revelation?

A Revelation Catalog
Revelation

As an overview of Revelation, the students skim the book and create a catalog of various items found within it.

  1. Divide the class into groups. Ask the groups each to skim the Book of Revelation and create an illustrated sales catalog that showcases some of the interesting items found in the book. Explain that the groups may include as many items as time in the class period allows.

  2. Invite the groups to share some aspects of their completed catalogs and to offer other observations that they made as they examined the Book of Revelation. Ask, "What was the most interesting item that you found in the book?"

Apocalyptic Literature

Exegetical Tools: Form Criticism—Apocalyptic Literature
Revelation
"Apocalyptic Literature," Daniel, chapters 7–10, CYB; "Symbolic Numbers and Colors," Rev 4.1—7.17, CYB; "The Seven Seals and Seven Trumpets," Revelation, chapters 6–9, CYB; "The Woman and the Dragon," Rev 12.1–17, CYB; "The Number of the Beast," Revelation, chapter 13, CYB; "The Sins of Empires," Revelation, chapter 17, CYB

This activity exposes the students to apocalyptic literature as a literary form in the Bible and challenges them to write some of their own.

1. A biblical commentary will be helpful for this activity (see the activity "Exegetical Tools: Form Criticism and the Biblical Commentary," on page 171 of this manual, for an example of how to use biblical commentaries, and see appendix A for recommended biblical commentaries).

2. Introduce form criticism as outlined in the activity "Exegetical Tools: Form Criticism—the Saga," on page 59 of this manual, or refresh the students' understanding of that scholarly approach. Have a student read the *CYB* article "Apocalyptic Literature" as an example of that type of literature.

3. Ask the students to take turns reading Revelation, chapter 4, aloud to the class. Discuss the nature of that passage by identifying some of the symbolism in it. Then call a student to read the article "Symbolic Numbers and Colors" from the *CYB*.

4. Divide the class into four groups and assign each group one of the following passages and associated articles from the *CYB*. Tell the groups to read their assigned material and to prepare a short presentation of excerpts from the passage and a summary of what they have learned, to share with the class.
- Rev 6.1—7.19; "The Seven Seals and Seven Trumpets"
- Rev 12.1–17; "The Woman and the Dragon"
- Rev 13.1–18; "The Number of the Beast"
- Rev 17.1–18; "The Sins of Empires"

5. For homework, ask the students to create a short piece of apocalyptic literature that uses symbolic language to describe the present time. They should attach to the essay a key that explains the symbolism they have chosen.

6. Invite the students each to read their finished piece of apocalyptic literature in class, and to ask the other students to guess the issues it addresses. Discuss the insights that arise from this sharing.

Painting the Picture
Revelation, chapter 1

This exercise invites the students to work in groups to "paint a picture" of Rev 1.12–20 with words and gestures.

1. Have the students read Rev 1.12–20, and ask them to notice the vivid language and highly descriptive verses.

2. Form small groups, and tell the groups each to plan a dramatic reading of the Scripture passage, accompanied by actions. Encourage the students to proclaim the passage with emotion, emphasize important aspects of the description, and use body movements or gestures that help "paint the picture." Note that in some respects, this is similar to a game of charades played reverently and with words.

3. Allow the groups to present their dramatizations in class and discuss the unique movements and gestures used.

Symbolic Numbers of Revelation
Revelation
"Symbolic Numbers and Colors," Rev 4.1—7.17, CYB

This activity introduces the symbolic numbers found in the Book of Revelation, by asking the students to create tally sheets, and charts or graphs, based on those numbers.

1. Direct the students to work in pairs to create a tally sheet and a chart or graph that reflect how many times the numbers 1 to 12, 144, and 1,000 are used throughout the Book of Revelation. Allow the groups to pick from various types of charts or graphs (including pie graphs, bar graphs, and pictographs), aiming for a variety of representations among the groups. Encourage the use of computer graphics for this activity if possible. Provide a biblical concordance (see appendix A) to help the students quickly find the numbers.

2. After the pairs are done working, ask a student to read the article "Symbolic Numbers and Colors" from the *CYB*. Discuss the effectiveness of using the symbolic numbers mentioned in the article.

3. Display the completed charts and graphs in class, and refer to them in the context of other lessons throughout the study of Revelation.

Songs of Glory and Majesty
Revelation, chapter 7
"Sing God's Glory," Rev 7.10–17, CYB

The students create music that expresses their sense of the power and majesty of God.

1. In preparation for this exercise, invite the students each to bring in a different musical instrument, such as a harmonica, kazoo, flute, guitar, or trumpet. Encourage them to be creative, noting that a comb covered with tissue paper makes a fine instrument. Also ask those who have special musical talents to be prepared to share them. Consider moving the class to a room with a piano in order to make that instrument available as well.

L
E
T
T
E
R
S

2. To begin this exercise, ask one student to read Rev 7.10–17 aloud and another to read the article "Sing God's Glory" from the *CYB*. Examine the other passages mentioned in the article.

3. Invite the students to remember a place or time when they experienced the grandeur of God. Give them some examples (like great cathedrals, special liturgical occasions such as the Christmas midnight Mass or Confirmation, and profound scenes in nature) to trigger their memories. Ask the students to share a few of their memories.

4. Encourage the students to recall a piece of music that they think expresses something of God's "power and might" as praised by the angels in the Scripture passage. The music may be instrumental, or it may have lyrics. The students should write a paragraph explaining their choice.

5. Divide the class into groups of four or five, and challenge the groups each to write a song of praise and glory to God. Provide the following instructions in your own words:
- You may develop your own lyrics and melody from scratch, or base either or both on a familiar tune. Incorporate the musical instruments you have brought to class, and include a refrain or other opportunity for audience participation. Make copies or transparencies of your lyrics so that the class can follow along when you present your song.

6. When the groups are ready, invite them to take turns performing their songs, encouraging participation and enthusiasm. Afterward, call for student reactions. Instruct the students to consider why music has a special ability to capture our feelings about God. Ask, "Why has much of the music written in the Western world been religious?"

Travel Brochures
Revelation, chapters 20–22
"The New Jerusalem," Rev 20.1—22.5, CYB

This activity asks the students to pretend they are travel agents and sales representatives for the destination of "a new heaven and a new earth" (Rev 20.1).

1. Invite the students to read Rev 20.1—22.5 to themselves. Then read Rev 21.1–8 aloud in a dramatic and bold way. Ask a student to read the article "The New Jerusalem" from the *CYB*.

2. Ask the students to describe what the new heaven and new earth mentioned in the Bible passage might be like.

3. Form small groups, and have the groups each create a brochure for the new heaven and new earth. They should pretend they are travel agents or sales representatives for this new destination, and create a brochure that would capture people's attention and encourage them to go to it. Provide the necessary art supplies, or, if possible, encourage the students to develop their brochures on a computer.

4. Display the groups' finished brochures and ask the students to identify what is appealing about them. Discuss the following questions:

- Do you think that many people would want to travel to this place?
- What might still attract people to the "old" earth?

The Fruit of Revelation
Revelation, chapter 22

The students illustrate and name the "twelve kinds of fruit" on the tree of life (Rev 22.2).

1. Bring in a tree that can be decorated with ornaments, such as a potted Norfolk pine or an artificial Christmas tree or a bare branch anchored in a pail of sand. Also supply art materials for creating paper fruits in step 3.

2. Ask a student to read Rev 22.1–7 aloud to the class. Invite the students to consider the image of the "twelve kinds of fruit" on the tree of life. Discuss the symbolic nature of fruit in the reading.

3. Have the students discuss, in small groups, what the fruits on the tree of life might be. Encourage them to think of "fruits" that they have found to be life-giving and healing in their reading of the New Testament. Explain that they should be prepared to explain why they chose the fruits they did, and to provide evidence from the Scriptures that each is indeed a spiritual fruit for the Christian soul.

Point out the tree you brought to class and explain that the students will decorate this tree with the fruits of life. Distribute art materials and direct the groups to create a paper representation of each fruit of life they identified.

4. Call the groups to present their paper fruits to the class by hanging them on the tree. Discuss the variety of fruits chosen and the Scripture passages cited. Note whether there are some fruits that are consistently mentioned, and ask the students to reflect on the most obvious characteristics of the spiritual life.

Appendices

APPENDIX A

For Further Reading

General Resources on the Scriptures

Achtemeier, Paul J., ed. *The HarperCollins Bible Dictionary*. San Francisco: HarperSanFrancisco, 1996.

Alter, Robert. *The Art of Biblical Narrative*. New York: Basic Books, 1981.

Bergant, Dianne, and Robert J. Karris, gen. eds. *The Collegeville Bible Commentary*. Collegeville, MN: Liturgical Press, 1989.

Brown, Raymond E. *An Introduction to the New Testament*. New York: Doubleday, 1997.

———. *Responses to 101 Questions on the Bible*. New York: Paulist Press, 1990.

Brown, Raymond E., Joseph A. Fitzmyer, and Roland E. Murphy, eds. *The New Jerome Biblical Commentary*. Englewood Cliffs, NJ: Prentice-Hall, 1990.

Brown, Robert McAfee. *Unexpected News: Reading the Bible with Third World Eyes*. Philadelphia: Westminster Press, 1984.

Brueggemann, Walter. *The Bible Makes Sense*. Rev. ed. Winona, MN: Saint Mary's Press, 1997.

Charpentier, Etienne. *How to Read the Old Testament*. New York: Crossroad, 1982.

Frank, Harry Thomas, ed. *Atlas of the Bible Lands*. Maplewood, NJ: Hammond, 1977.

Gardner, Joseph L., ed. *Reader's Digest Atlas of the Bible: An Illustrated Guide to the Holy Land*. Pleasantville, NY: Reader's Digest Association, 1981.

Gilles, Anthony E. *The People of the Book: The Story Behind the Old Testament*. Cincinnati: St. Anthony Messenger Press, 1983.

———. *The People of the Way: The Story Behind the New Testament*. Cincinnati: St. Anthony Messenger Press, 1984.

Hiesberger, Jean Marie, ed. *The Catholic Bible: Personal Study Edition*. New York: Oxford University Press, 1995. Includes five hundred pages of excellent, easy-to-understand background on each book of the Bible; New American Bible translation.

Holladay, William Lee. *Long Ago, God Spoke: How Christians May Hear the Old Testament Today*. Minneapolis: Fortress Press, 1995.

Hollyday, Joyce. *Clothed with the Sun: Biblical Women, Social Justice, and Us*. Louisville, KY: Westminster/John Knox Press, 1994.

Kohlenberger, John R., III, ed. *The Concise Concordance to the New Revised Standard Version*. New York: Oxford University Press, 1993.

Libreria Editrice Vaticana. *Catechism of the Catholic Church*. Trans. United States Catholic Conference (USCC). Washington, DC: USCC, 1994.

McKenna, Megan, and Tony Cowan. *Keepers of the Story: Oral Traditions in Religion*. Maryknoll, NY: Orbis Books, 1997.

McKenzie, John L. *Dictionary of the Bible*. New York: Macmillan, 1965.

The New Jerome Biblical Handbook. Collegeville, MN: Liturgical Press, 1992.

Newland, Mary Reed. *A Popular Guide Through the Old Testament*. Winona, MN: Saint Mary's Press, 1999.

———. *Written on Our Hearts: The Old Testament Story of God's Love.* Rev. Barbara Allaire. Winona, MN: Saint Mary's Press, 1999.

Perkins, Pheme. *Reading the New Testament: An Introduction.* Rev. ed. New York: Paulist Press, 1988.

Ralph, Margaret Nutting. *"And God Said What?" An Introduction to Biblical Literary Forms for Bible Lovers.* New York: Paulist Press, 1986.

———. *The Bible and the End of the World: Should We Be Afraid?* New York: Paulist Press, 1997.

———. *Discovering the Gospels: Four Accounts of the Good News.* New York: Paulist Press, 1990.

———. *Discovering Old Testament Origins: The Books of Genesis, Exodus, and Samuel.* New York: Paulist Press, 1992.

Rohr, Richard, and Joseph Martos. *The Great Themes of Scripture: New Testament.* Cincinnati: St. Anthony Messenger Press, 1988.

———. *The Great Themes of Scripture: Old Testament.* Cincinnati: St. Anthony Messenger Press, 1987.

Schatz, Larry, Dee Bernhardt, and Laurie Ziliak. *Good News, Day by Day.* Winona, MN: Saint Mary's Press, 1999.

Scripture from Scratch. Cincinnati: St. Anthony Messenger Press. For more information about this four-page monthly periodical covering topics on the Scriptures, and a list of available articles, call 800-488-0488.

Senior, Donald, ed. *The Catholic Study Bible.* New York: Oxford University Press, 1990.

Vatican Council II. *Dogmatic Constitution on Divine Revelation (Dei Verbum).* Council document, 18 November 1965.

Witherup, Ronald D. *The Bible Companion: A Handbook for Beginners.* New York: Crossroad, 1998.

Zanzig, Thomas. *Jesus of History, Christ of Faith.* Winona, MN: Saint Mary's Press, 1999.

Scripture Resources for Ministry with Teenagers

Ayer, Jane E. *Guided Meditations on Images of God: Mother, Potter, Compassion, Love.* Winona, MN: Saint Mary's Press, 1999.

———. *Guided Meditations on the Paschal Mystery: Consequences, Idolatry, Revelation, Reconciliation.* Winona, MN: Saint Mary's Press, 1999. CDs and cassette recordings of the guided meditations are also available.

Calderone-Stewart, Lisa-Marie. *In Touch with the Word.* Winona, MN: Saint Mary's Press. Published in four separate volumes with the subtitles *Lectionary-Based Prayer Reflections, Advent, Christmas, Lent, and Easter* (1996); *Lectionary-Based Prayer Reflections, Cycle A for Ordinary Time* (1998); *Lectionary-Based Prayer Reflections, Cycle B for Ordinary Time* (1999); and *Lectionary-Based Prayer Reflections, Cycle C for Ordinary Time* (1997).

Haas, David. *Prayers Before an Awesome God: The Psalms for Teenagers.* Winona, MN: Saint Mary's Press, 1998.

Hakowski, Maryann. *Sharing the Sunday Scriptures with Youth.* Winona, MN: Saint Mary's Press. Published in three separate volumes with the subtitles *Cycle A* (1998), *Cycle B* (1996), and *Cycle C* (1997).

Koch, Carl, ed. *You Give Me the Sun: Biblical Prayers by Teens.* Winona, MN: Saint Mary's Press, 2000.

O'Connell-Roussell, Sheila, and Terri Vorndran Nichols. *Lectionary-Based Gospel Dramas for Advent, Christmas, and Epiphany.* Winona, MN: Saint Mary's Press, 1997.

O'Connell-Roussell, Sheila, and Therese Vorndran Nichols. *Lectionary-Based Gospel Dramas for Lent and the Easter Triduum.* Winona, MN: Saint Mary's Press, 1999.

Singer-Towns, Brian. *The Bible: Power and Promise.* Winona, MN: Saint Mary's Press, 1997. An active-learning minicourse from the Horizons Program, a senior high parish religious education series.

Singer-Towns, Brian, gen. ed. *The Catholic Youth Bible.* Winona, MN: Saint Mary's Press, 1999.

Theisen, Michael, and Nora Bradbury-Haehl. *ScriptureWalk Senior High.* Winona, MN: Saint Mary's Press, 2000.

APPENDIX B

Audiovisual and Interactive Recommendations

The Bible Library for Catholics (Liguori Publications, 1996): CD-ROM for Windows and DOS, $99.95.

This is a great reference tool for teachers. It contains three complete translations of the Bible (New American Bible, New Revised Standard Version: Catholic Edition, and Revised Standard Version with Apocrypha) plus these valuable study aids: Greek and Hebrew definitions, Nave's topical index, Barclay's *Daily Study Bible Series: New Testament,* and Windows and DOS versions of the Bible on Disk program.

Available from Liguori Publications, One Liguori Drive, Liguori, MO 63057-9999; phone 314-464-2500; web site *http://www.liguori.org.*

Bible timeline (Crossways International, 1997): wall chart, $14.50; transparency, $8.75; laminated foldout version, $3.75; the booklet *The Bible's Big Story: Our Story,* with a copy of the timeline inside, $9.00.

A good, accurate Bible timeline.

Available from Crossways International, 7930 Computer Avenue South, Minneapolis, MN 55435-5415; phone 800-257-7308 or 612-832-5454; fax 612-832-5553; web site *http://www.crossways.org.*

***The Blood of the Martyrs,* volume 1 of the *Passion of the Saints* series** (The Learning Channel, 1996): 50-minute videotape, $19.99.

This historical documentary explores the lives of remarkable saints who devoted themselves totally to God, even sacrificing their own lives. Viewers witness the rise of "martyrdom" and the bloody hand of Roman cruelty, which ironically propelled Christianity to new heights. Beginning with Stephen, the first Christian martyr, they see the great sacrifices men and women made for their faith throughout the ages. From the familiar stories of Joan of Arc and Thomas Becket to little-known tales of martyrs such as the twentieth-century priest Maximillian Kolbe, they behold how good triumphs over evil, time and time again.

Available from Discovery Channel Video, 700 Wisconsin Avenue, Bethesda, MD 20814; phone 301-986-0444 or 800-889-9950; fax 301-986-4826; web site *http://www.discovery.com.* Also available from Gateway Films/Vision Videos, P.O. Box 540, Worcester, PA 19490; phone 610-584-3500; web site *http://www. gatewayfilms.com.*

An Empire Conquered (Marca-Relli Productions, 1991): 52-minute videotape with study guide, $19.99.

This moving docudrama filmed in Rome brings to life the intriguing days of the early Christians when followers of Christ were cruelly persecuted and martyred for their beliefs. The film looks at five Christians who lived during those turbulent years—Augustus, Clement, Cecilia, Apollonius, and Agnes. It is narrated by the Emmy Award–winning actor Joseph Campanella.

Available from Gateway Films/Vision Videos (see *The Blood of the Martyrs* above).

***The Gospel of Luke* series** (Genesis Project, 1979): set of four videotapes, 50 to 75 minutes each; $59.95 for the set.

Some of the footage from these videos was used in the series *Jesus and His Times* (see below). Teachers may find this version of the Gospel of Luke more advantageous for Scripture study because the biblical text is narrated word for word over well-done re-enactments. You can hear the actors speaking in languages of the times under the narrative. This portrayal of Jesus is about as convincing and inspiring as one could imagine.

The set of four videos divides the Gospel of Luke into four parts—*Christmas, Early Ministry, Parables,* and *Easter*—with each part containing more than its title suggests.

Available from Rated G Films, a distributor for Bridgestone Multimedia Group, 300 North McKemy Avenue, Chandler, AZ 85226; phone 800-523-0988; web site *http://www.bridgestonemultimedia.com.*

***Jesus and His Times* series** (Reader's Digest Association, 1991): set of three 60-minute videotapes; $44.85 for the set, $14.95 for each video.

This series on Jesus reflects impressive biblical scholarship as well as superior writing, photography, music, acting, and production values. The videos dramatize events from the Gospels and also reveal fascinating background for those events—historical, cultural, geographical, archaeological, and so on. Despite their emphasis on accurately portraying the times, the videos do not lose anything in inspirational value.

The titles in the series are *The Story Begins,* which covers the time around Jesus' birth to his visit to the Temple at age twelve; *Among the People,* which relates the ministry of Jesus from his baptism to his time of preaching and healing in Galilee; and *The Final Days,* which follows Jesus into Jerusalem and to his death and Resurrection.

Available from Saint Mary's Press, 702 Terrace Heights, Winona, MN 55987-1320; phone 800-533-8095; web site *http://www.smp.org.*

Jesus of Nazareth (1992): 390-minute (6½-hour) film, $59.95.

This is a classic feature-length film directed by Franco Zeffirelli, packaged in a three-video set.

Available for rental at video stores or for purchase from Rated G Films, a distributor for Bridgestone Multimedia Group (see *The Gospel of Luke* above).

Judaism: The Religion of a People (Delphi Productions, 1994): 24-minute videotape with discussion guide, $195.00.

This documentary presents an overview of the practices, beliefs, rituals, and history of Judaism. It uses live footage and descriptive details to cover topics such as the Torah, worship, festivals, and bar and bat mitzvahs. The strength of the Jewish faith is illustrated through continuous persecution and struggles, including the Diaspora, the Holocaust, and the establishment of the state of Israel.

Available from AGC/United Learning, 1560 Sherman Avenue, Suite 100, Evanston, IL 60201; phone 800-323-9084; web site *http://www.unitedlearning.com.*

Out of the Tombs (American Bible Society): CD-ROM for Windows, $29.95.

This CD-ROM offers a compelling way for young people to explore the word of God. Packed with information, it includes videos, music, maps, and interactive features. Inspired by Mark's story of the healing of the Gerasene demoniac, this award-winning computer program tells of a man who lives in fear and is feared by all—until he encounters Jesus.

Available from the American Bible Society, 1865 Broadway, New York, NY 10023-7505; phone 212-408-1200; web site *http://www.americanbible.org.*

The Passover Celebration: A Haggadah for the Seder (Liturgy Training Publications, 1980): pamphlet, $2.95; 30-minute companion audiocassette, titled *Songs for the Seder Meal,* $5.95.

Available from Liturgy Training Publications, 1800 North Hermitage Avenue, Chicago, IL 60622-1101; phone 800-933-1800; web site *http://www.ltp.org.*

Peter and Paul (MCA Home Video, 1981): 194-minute videotape with study guide, $39.99.

This video chronicles the ministries of Paul and Peter until their deaths in Rome.

Available from Gateway Films/Vision Videos (see *The Blood of the Martyrs* above).

'Shua: The Human Jesus (ACTA Publications, 1987): 60-minute videotape with sixteen-page discussion guide, $39.95; book version, $8.95.

This unusual, intriguing videotape was created by Fr. William Burke, a master storyteller. To convey the humanity of Jesus, Burke has invented a boyhood friend of Jesus', who calls Jesus 'Shua. This character, played by Burke in contemporary dress, tells stories of his childhood, adolescence, and young adulthood with 'Shua in Galilee. Although he has heard about Jesus' ministry and Crucifixion, he speaks not as someone who believes in Jesus as the Messiah but as someone who has been profoundly affected by Jesus' friendship.

Though well grounded in scholarship about the Holy Land and the culture of Jesus' time, the incidents relayed in the video *are* fictional, and viewers must keep that in mind. The stories are quite plausible, and they give marvelous insight into how the Jesus we know from the Gospels could have developed and formed his convictions through the experiences of his youth.

Available from ACTA Publications, 4848 North Clark Street, Chicago, IL 60640; phone 800-397-2282.

Voyage Through the Bible: New Testament, and Voyage Through the Bible: Old Testament (Jones Digital Century, 1995): CD-ROMs for both IBM-compatible and Macintosh computers, $39.95 each.

Actor Charlton Heston is the host for these remarkable interactive, multimedia journeys featuring key stories from the Bible. The CD-ROMs combine video of historical sites, three-dimensional animation, interactive maps and timelines, and more.

Available from JEC Knowledge Store; phone 888-757-8673; web site *http://www.jec.edu.*

***We Are Fire: Companion Songs for* The Catholic Youth Bible** (Comet Records, 1999): audio CD, $15.95.

A variety of Catholic musicians—both contemporary and liturgical—gathered to create this CD of original songs that parallel the major themes in *The Catholic Youth Bible,* which is published by Saint Mary's Press

Available by calling 800-759-5805 or logging on to the web site *http://www.davidkauffman.com,* and from Saint Mary's Press (see *Jesus and His Times* above).

APPENDIX C

Prayer Services

Prayer Service 1: "Let There Be Light!"

Genesis, chapter 1; John, chapters 1, 8, 12; 1 Thessalonians, chapter 5; James, chapter 1; 1 John, chapter 1

In this prayer service, the students examine how God brought light to the world and what it means for them to be light for the world.

Preparation

Gather the following materials:
- ☐ copies of handout App C–1, "Let There Be Light!" one for each student
- ☐ a refrain from a familiar song about light (optional)
- ☐ seven candles and matches
- ☐ a tub of sand (or a mirror)
- ☐ music and lyrics for the song "Christ Be Our Light," by Robert C. Moore, from *Breaking Bread Hymnal* (Portland, OR: OCP Publications, 1992), or another song that centers on light (optional)

Create a prayer space in the center of the meeting room.

Choose seven students and assign each a reading. Give the readers each a candle and matches, and relay the following instructions to them in your own words:
- As we gather for the service, spread out to the far corners and edges of the room. Just before reading your assigned passage, light your candle. When you finish your reading, bring your candle to the center of the room and stick it in the tub of sand [or on the mirror], and then return to your seat with the rest of the group.

Opening Words

Handout App C–1

If possible, begin the prayer service in darkness or semidarkness. Distribute copies of handout App C–1. Then begin with the following invitation:

Leader. Let us remember that we are in the holy presence of God.

Teach the students a refrain to sing or proclaim after each reading. You might choose a refrain from a familiar song about light, or use the words, "You are the Light of the World!"

Readings

Reader 1.

In the beginning, when God created the heavens and the earth, the earth was a formless void and darkness covered the face of the deep, while a wind from God swept over the face of the waters. Then God said, "Let there be light"; and there was light. And God saw that the light was good. (Gen 1.1–4) . . . *[Refrain]*

Reader 2.

In the beginning was the Word, and the Word was with God, and the Word was God. He was in the beginning with God. All things came into being through him, and without him not one thing came into being. What has come into being in him was life, and the life was the light of all people. The light shines in the darkness, and the darkness did not overcome it. (Jn 1.1–5) . . . *[Refrain]*

Reader 3.

You yourselves know very well that the day of the Lord will come like a thief in the night. . . . But you, beloved, are not in darkness, for that day to surprise you like a thief; for you are all children of light and children of the day; we are not of the night or of darkness. (1 Thess 5.2–5) . . . *[Refrain]*

Reader 4.

Do not be deceived, my beloved.

Every generous act of giving, with every perfect gift, is from above, coming down from the Father of lights, with whom there is no variation or shadow due to change. (Jas 1.16–17) . . . *[Refrain]*

Reader 5.

The light is with you for a little longer. Walk while you have the light, so that the darkness may not overtake you. If you walk in the darkness, you do not know where you are going. While you have the light, believe in the light, so that you may become children of the light. (Jn 12.35–36) . . . *[Refrain]*

Reader 6.

We declare to you what we have seen and heard so that you also may have fellowship with us; and truly our fellowship is with the Father and his Son Jesus Christ. We are writing these things so that our joy may be complete.

This is the message we have heard from him and proclaim to you, that God is light and in [God] there is no darkness at all. (1 Jn 1.3–5) . . . *[Refrain]*

Reader 7.

Again Jesus spoke to them, saying, "I am the light of the world. Whoever follows me will never walk in darkness but will have the light of life." (Jn 8.12) . . . *[Refrain]*

Sharing and Closing Prayer

Leader. At this time, I invite each of you to identify someone who has served as a light in your life. You may give either a name or a description, such as "a teacher." If you would like, you may briefly explain how he or she has been a light for you.

After everyone has shared, lead them in this response:

All. Dear God, you are the source of all the real light in our lives. We thank you for all the people who have been light for us, and have revealed your love through their concern for us. Thank you for illuminating our lives and showing us the way. Let us learn to be light for one another. May each of us reflect the light of Christ to our weary world. We ask this through Christ, our light, our brother, and our Lord. Amen.

Lead the class in singing "Christ Be Our Light" or another song that centers on light, if you so desire.

(This prayer service is from Br. Larry Schatz, FSC, formerly campus minister at Saint Mary's University, Winona, Minnesota.)

Prayer Service 2: Sin and Temptation
Genesis, chapter 3; Matthew, chapter 4

In this prayer service, the students explore the issues of sin and temptation, good and evil. They examine the historical origin of sin, possible responses to temptations in society today, and God's presence and support in the face of temptation.

This prayer service is especially suited for use during Lent, but may easily be adapted for use during any liturgical season.

Preparation

Gather the following materials:
- [ ] copies of handout App C–2, "Sin and Temptation," one for each student
- [ ] a recording of the song "My Life Is in Your Hands," by Kirk Franklin, from Franklin's album *God's Property* (Uni/Interscope, 1997) (optional)
- [ ] a tape or CD player (optional)
- [ ] two signs, one labeled "Good" and the other labeled "Evil"
- [ ] a large rope, at least 15 feet long
- [ ] simple props (optional; see the directions following this list)
- [ ] music and lyrics for the song "Were You There?" (a popular, traditional hymn that can be found in many Catholic songbooks) (optional for Lent)

Decide if you will use the suggested music for this prayer service. If you are not conducting the service during Lent, you may want to omit the closing song "Were You There?" or substitute another song.

Read the first three skits in this plan, and decide if they are all appropriate for your class and whether you want to present all three. Also determine if the students will present the skits, or if you will recruit other adults, or teens from outside the class, to assume some or all of the roles in the skits. You will need as many as twenty-four actors if everyone plays a separate role, or as few as six if each actor plays a role in all four skits. You might want to assign roles before the service, or wait and ask for volunteers during the prayer service itself, depending on how your class handles spontaneity and role-playing. Consider providing simple props, such as a Northface or other popular jacket.

Gathering Song

Handout **App C–2**

Distribute copies of handout App C–2, and play the song "My Life Is in Your Hands" if you so desire.

Opening Words and Reading

Leader. God created Adam and Eve in God's image, and created the Garden of Eden to supply all their needs on earth. Adam and Eve were happy in the garden. They lived without clothes and were not ashamed to be naked. Then one day, a serpent approached Eve and tempted her to disobey one of God's commands.

Reader.

Now the serpent . . . said to the woman, "Did God say, 'You shall not eat from any tree in the garden'?" The woman said to the serpent, "We may eat of the fruit of the trees in the garden; but God said, 'You shall not eat of the fruit of the tree that is in the middle of the garden, nor shall you touch it, or you shall die.'" But the serpent said to the woman, "You will not die; for God knows that when you eat of it your eyes will be opened, and you will be like God, knowing good and evil." So when the woman saw that the tree was good for food, and that it was a delight to the eyes, and that the tree was to be desired to make one wise, she took of its fruit and ate; and she also gave some to her husband, who was with her, and he ate. Then the eyes of both were opened, and they knew that they were naked; and they sewed fig leaves together and made loincloths for themselves. (Gen 3.1–7)

Leader. When Adam and Eve disobeyed God, they broke their relationship of trust with God. Once that relationship was broken, sin became a part of the human story. Ever since that moment, human beings have faced temptations that pull them away from God's love and grace.

Litany

Divide the class in half and assign each half to read one side of the following litany:

Side 1. We are sometimes torn between the voice that calls us to love . . .
Side 2. and the voice that calls us to hate.
Side 1. We are sometimes torn between the voice that calls us to do good . . .
Side 2. and the voice that calls us to do evil.
Side 1. We are sometimes torn between the voice that draws us to God . . .
Side 2. and the voice that wants to block God out of our lives.

Skit 1: Stealing

You will need six people to perform the following skit. Assign each person a part. Give the person playing the role of Good a sign labeled "Good," and the person playing the role of Evil a sign labeled "Evil." Position these two at opposite sides of the staging area. Tie a large rope around the waist of a third person, leaving at least 6 feet on each end, and position this person in the middle of the staging area. Give the fourth and fifth persons each an end of the rope. Position one rope holder near the person holding the "Good" sign, and the other near the person holding the "Evil" sign. Tell the rope holders to pull gently and firmly on their end each time the actor near them reads his or her part, so that the middle person is forced to move toward the "Good" sign when the "Good" parts are read, and vice versa. Position the narrator to one side, so that the class can see what is happening during the skit. If another brand of jacket is more popular than The Northface with your class, suggest that the narrator use its brand name rather than *Northface.*

Narrator. Brian got a new Northface jacket and has been proudly showing it off to everyone. All his friends admire it—except for Jordan. Jordan wanted the jacket, and Brian bought it first. This makes Jordan mad. Now Jordan is contemplating the situation.

Good. It's such a cool jacket. I've had my eye on it forever. But Jordan's got it, and it looks good on him.

Evil. But he stabbed me in the back. I wanted that jacket, and he knew that. It's not right. It's just not right.

Good. Brian had a right to buy it. He wanted it just as badly as I did.

Evil. Who cares? That jacket is hot. So hot that I'm going to steal it.

Good. No. I can't steal it. Brian is my friend. He paid for the jacket with his own money. Besides, who I am is much more important than what I wear. And I'm no thief.

Skit 2: Drugs

Assign roles and set the stage as you did for skit 1.

Narrator. Delia is at a party on a Saturday night. It is the party of the year, and she is having the time of her life, sitting around with a really cool crowd. In fact, she is sitting right next to Michael, a guy she really likes. Suddenly, Michael hands her a marijuana joint.

Good. Pot? You've got to be kidding! I can't smoke that. It'll mess me up.

Evil. One joint can't hurt. I can stop anytime I want, especially after just one.

Good. Or can I? What am I thinking? It's pot! What about its long-term effects? It destroys brain cells. It harms chromosomes. What about the children I want to have in the future? Will they be okay?

Evil. But it's Michael offering it to me. I like Michael. Maybe he will like me if I smoke. It can't be so bad. Everyone else is smoking. What'll they all think if I don't join them?

Good. Forget it. If Michael doesn't like me for who I am, he doesn't deserve me. And if the others laugh at me, they're not real friends. I can deal with that. This is my decision and my life. And my choice is to pass.

Skit 3: Sex

Assign parts and set the stage as you did for skits 1 and 2.

Narrator. Jorge and his girlfriend, Tiffany, are in his house alone. They are kissing, and their feelings for each other are becoming stronger and stronger.

Evil. I want to make love. We're both responsible. We have protection, so we don't have to worry about a baby. Neither of us has been with anyone else, so we don't have to worry about AIDS or STDs.

Good. Yes, we have both been responsible people so far. We don't have to worry about AIDS or STDs. But no method of protection is 100 percent effective. There's always a chance that if we have sex, we could bring a baby into the world. Neither of us is ready for that kind of responsibility yet.

Evil. Sure, there's always a chance we could have a baby. But the chance is slim. We have been going together for a while. Sharing sex will bring us closer.

Good. Sounds good, but let's not fool ourselves. Sex is no shortcut to real intimacy, to real, deep friendship. Communication, honesty, care for each other's well-being—those are the things that will bring us closer. Not sex.

Evil. We would not be just having sex. We love each other. Love makes it right.

Good. We do love each other. But how much? Are we ready and able to make a life together, to love each other always and forever? To be honest, neither of us is ready for that kind of love. We both have school to finish, careers to start, people to meet, and goals to achieve before we're ready for that kind of unconditional, always-and-forever love. Let's swear to each other never to make promises to each other that we can't keep. We will wait until we are ready and able to love each other always and forever.

Skit 4: Jesus in the Desert

Assign parts and set the stage as you did for skits 1, 2, and 3.

Narrator. Because Jesus was human, he too experienced temptation and sin. In the weeks before Jesus died, the Spirit led him out into the desert, and he remained there for forty days and forty nights. Afterward, he was hungry, and the tempter approached him.

Evil. If you are the Son of God, turn these stones into loaves of bread.

Good. People need more than bread to live; they need the Word of God.

Narrator. The evil tempter took Jesus to the top of the Temple in Jerusalem.

Evil. If you are the Son of God, throw yourself down from the top of this Temple and let your angels minister to you.

Good. You should not put the Lord your God to the test.

Narrator. The devil took Jesus to the top of a mountain and pointed out all the nations below it.

Evil. All these countries I will give you if you throw yourself down at my feet and worship me.

Good. Get away from me, Satan, for it is written, "The Lord your God should you worship, and God alone shall you serve."

(This skit is adapted from Mt 4.1–10.)

Reflection

Regather the students and invite them to sit in a relaxed position, with their hands in their lap and their eyes closed, and to breathe slowly and deeply for a moment. Then ask them to open their eyes and reflect on some questions that you will ask. Pause briefly after each question, to allow time for the students to think.

- When is the last time you were tempted to do the wrong thing?
- How did you respond?
- Were you able to feel God's presence during this experience? If so, was that a source of support for you? If not, why not?

Closing Prayer

Leader.

> Give me the courage to do right
> in the face of wrong.
> Instill in my heart
> a set of values that prompts me
> to think of others
> instead of just myself.
> Give me the willingness to
> stand up for what I believe in—
> not following the crowd.
> Give me the strength to
> look evil in the eye
> and withstand it.
> Because I know
> with you at my side
> all things are possible.
> (Theresa Vonderwell, in Carl Koch, ed., *More Dreams Alive,* p. 28)

Closing Song

Lead the group in singing the traditional spiritual "Were You There?" or another song, if you wish.

(This prayer service is adapted from one conceived and written by Helen Wolf and others, both adults and students, at Bishop Loughlin Memorial High School, Brooklyn, New York.)

Prayer Service 3: A Rainbow of Hope and Peace
Genesis, chapter 9

This prayer service leads the students to consider God's promise to bring the glory of heaven to earth, and their responsibility to reach out in peace, as Jesus did, to bring hope to the world.

Preparation

Gather the following materials:
- ☐ a communities-of-hope rainbow outline (see the directions following this list)
- ☐ copies of handout App C–3, "A Rainbow of Hope and Peace," one for each student
- ☐ a pillar candle and matches
- ☐ newsprint and a marker
- ☐ pens or pencils
- ☐ strips of red, blue, yellow, and orange paper, one of each color for each student
- ☐ tape
- ☐ music and lyrics for the song "Let There Be Peace on Earth" (available in many hymnals) (optional)

Create a communities-of-hope rainbow outline by painting a rainbow on several sheets of newsprint or butcher paper taped together, or by painting one on an old sheet, and post it on a wall in the prayer space. Or attach strips of colored fabric or paper directly to the wall in a rainbow shape. Place a pillar candle near the rainbow.

Read the group names listed for the reflection activity, and decide if you want to add, delete, or substitute terms to reflect the interests and activities of your particular students and community.

Handout **App C–3**

Opening Prayer and Reading

Gather in front of the communities-of-hope rainbow outline you have posted in the prayer space, and distribute copies of handout App C–3. Light a pillar candle and call a volunteer to begin with the Scripture reading.

Reader.

> God said, "This is the sign of the covenant that I make between me and you and every living creature that is with you, for all future generations: I have set my bow in the clouds, and it shall be a sign of the covenant between me and the earth. When I bring clouds over the earth and the bow is seen in the clouds, I will remember my covenant that is between me and you and every living creature of all flesh; and the waters shall never again become a flood to destroy all flesh. When the bow is in the clouds, I will see it and remember the everlasting covenant between God and every living creature of all flesh that is on the earth." God said to Noah, "This is the sign of the covenant that I have established between me and all flesh that is on the earth." (Gen 9.12–17)

Leader. God sends the rainbow to remind us of God's promise to grant the glory of heaven to all who believe in God. The rainbow is thus a symbol of hope. In spite of all the violence in the world, God gives us hope through Jesus Christ, who is the source of all peace. When we believe in God, we love God and strive to do God's will by reaching out to serve others in peace, as Jesus did, trusting in God's grace.

Reflection Activity

Invite the students to think about the various groups of people that they belong to. Explain that you will read a list of groups, and that you would like them to stand for 2 seconds when you call out the name of a group they belong to. Then read the following list, or one you prepared specifically for your students, pausing for 2 seconds after each group name:

- a soccer team
- a youth group
- a Bible study group
- a family
- the Air Force
- [your community]
- a secret spy club
- a chess team
- a cheerleading squad
- [schools in your area]
- [parishes in your area, if the students may come from more than one]
- the people who live in the United States
- 4-H
- a wrestling team
- people who live in Europe
- the Girl Scouts
- Future Farmers of America
- a volleyball team
- a book or record club
- the Boy Scouts
- people who live in the Milky Way Galaxy
- a basketball team

Ask everyone to sit, and make the following comments in your own words:

- A community is defined as a group of people with a "common unity."
- Human life is basically communal. We are made in the image of God. The doctrine of the Trinity tells us that this God is a communion of love. We are called to live out the communion of love that is God.
- Further, we are the Body of Christ, which means that we are members of the universal church community—not just separate individuals. We belong to one another and therefore must strive for the common good.
- A community of hope is one based on our common unity in Christ. Our hope comes from trust in Christ's promises, and relies not on our own strength but on the grace of the Holy Spirit.
- Violence is any action or response that is destructive or disrespectful of human life.
- Violence is sometimes the product of a disagreement, sometimes the product of frustration, and sometimes the product of irrational behavior.
- A victim is a person whose quality of life is impinged by violence.
- Conflict resolution is a process that seeks to clear up a dispute through an alternative that does not include violence. As people of hope, we can make a difference in our communities by learning the skills of this process. [If there is time, share the story of a saint or of someone who has made a difference in your community.]

Mention that we all belong to four communities: family, school, parish, and civic. Brainstorm with the students definitions of those communities and write the definitions on newsprint.

Divide the class into four groups and assign each group one of the four communities you have just defined. Direct the groups each to discuss their assigned community by answering the following questions:

- How have I experienced the peace of Jesus in this community?
- How does this community give hope and produce solutions to violence? What people in this community of hope are part of the solution?
- What steps can I take to become an instrument of peace in this community of hope?

Closing Prayer

Distribute pens or pencils and give each student four different-colored slips of paper. Note that each color represents one of the communities of hope:
- red for home
- blue for school
- yellow for parish
- orange for civic

Direct the students to write on each slip one thing that they can do in that community to share the peace of Jesus.

Lead the students in saying the Peace Prayer of Saint Francis of Assisi together:

All.

> Loving God, make me an instrument of your peace.
> Where there is hatred, let me sow love;
> Where there is injury, pardon;
> Where there is doubt, faith;
> Where there is despair, hope;
> Where there is darkness, light;
> And where there is sadness, joy.
> O, Divine Teacher, grant that I may not so much seek to be consoled as
> to console;
> To be understood as to understand;
> To be loved as to love;
> For it is in giving that we receive;
> It is in pardoning that we are pardoned;
> And it is in dying that we are born to eternal life.
> (Joseph M. Stoutzenberger and John D. Bohrer,
> *Praying with Francis of Assisi,* p. 54)

Invite the students to tape each of their colored slips in the corresponding section of the rainbow—for example, red strips go in the red section of the rainbow. Depending on the class and on the mood you desire, ask that this be done in silence, or call the young people to share what they have written.

Close by singing "Let There Be Peace on Earth" or sharing a sign of peace.

(This prayer service is from Clare vanBrandwijk, campus minister, Bishop O+Gorman High School, Sioux Falls, South Dakota.)

Prayer Service 4:
"Be Still, and Know That I Am God!"
Psalm 46

In this prayer service, the students open themselves to God's presence and reflect on the magnitude of God's support and love.

Preparation

Gather the following materials:
- [ ] copies of handout App C–4, "'Be Still, and Know That I Am God!'" one for each student
- [ ] a recording of instrumental music
- [ ] a tape or CD player
- [ ] a pillar candle and matches
- [ ] a recording of the song "You Are Mine," by David Haas, from the album *You Are Mine: The Best of David Haas* (GIA Publications, 1995) (optional)

Opening Words

Handout App C–4

Divide the class into two approximately equal sides and distribute handout App C–4. Play soft instrumental music in the background. Light a pillar candle and invite the students to close their eyes and focus on their breathing. Tell them to imagine breathing in Christ's love and peace, and breathing out stress and negativity. Allow for several minutes of quiet.

Reading and Litany

Leader. A reading from Psalm 46:

> God is our refuge and strength,
>   a very present help in trouble.
> Therefore we will not fear, though the earth should change,
>   though the mountains shake in the heart of the sea;
> though its waters roar and foam,
>   though the mountains tremble with its tumult.

(Verses 1–3)

> "Be still, and know that I am God!"

(Verse 10)

Side 1. When the loud alarm goes off in the morning . . .
All. "Be still, and know that I am God!"
Side 2. In the routines of dressing and getting off to school . . .
All. "Be still, and know that I am God!"
Side 1. In the comings and goings throughout the school day . . .
All. "Be still, and know that I am God!"
Side 2. In the mundane tasks of going to the locker and walking in the halls . . .
All. "Be still, and know that I am God!"
Side 1. In the frenzied pace of the cafeteria . . .
All. "Be still, and know that I am God!"

Side 2. In the stacks of books and pages of homework . . .
All. "Be still, and know that I am God!"
Side 1. In the quiet of night and stillness of sleep . . .
All. "Be still, and know that I am God!"

Quiet Reflection

If you wish, play the song "You Are Mine."

Closing Prayer

All. Loving God, you come to us in the silence and in the laughter, in the moments of joy and sorrow. The busy-ness of our lives sometimes keeps us from taking the time to be quiet, to be still, and to rest in your love. Let us open ourselves to the enfolding grace of your presence this day. Let us be still and know that you hold us in your heart and that we are your cherished children. Let us be still and know that you are our God, our loving creator and friend. We ask this in Jesus' name. Amen.

Prayer Service 5: Being a Humble Servant
Sirach, chapter 3; Micah, chapter 6; Matthew, chapter 18; John, chapter 13

This prayer service allows the students to consider the meaning of humility, and the need to gather with other Christians and open themselves to God so that they may help bring about the Reign of God.

Preparation

Gather the following materials:
☐ copies of handout App C–5, "Being a Humble Servant," one for each student
☐ a pillar candle and matches
☐ a recording of the song "Servant Song," by Bobby Fisher, from the album *Spirit of Malia* (GIA Publications, 1999) (optional)
☐ a tape or CD player (optional)

Opening Words

Handout **App C–5**

Divide the class into two approximately equal sides and distribute copies of handout App C–5. Then light a pillar candle and invite the students to prayer.

Leader. Jesus said to his disciples, "For where two or three are gathered in my name, I am there among them" (Mt 18.20). As we gather today, in Jesus' name, let us come together quietly and reverently to be with our loving Creator, whose spirit fills us and makes us whole.

Allow a few minutes of quiet.

Litany and Reading

Leader. All wisdom is from God. We need to listen and learn.
Side 1. Open our hearts so that these words become branded on our hearts.
Side 2. Open our minds so that our intellect can be challenged.
Side 1. Open our eyes to the beauty of creation.
Side 2. Open our hands so that we can work to bring forth the Reign!
Leader. A reading from the Book of Sirach:

> My child, perform your tasks with humility;
> > then you will be loved by those whom God accepts.
> The greater you are, the more you must humble yourself;
> > so you will find favor in the sight of the Lord.
> For great is the might of the Lord;
> > but by the humble he is glorified.

> (3.17–20)

Side 1. When I find myself bragging about all I can do . . .
All. Let me remember that all wisdom is from God, and I should be humble.
Side 2. When I find myself thinking I am better than someone else . . .
All. Let me remember that all wisdom is from God, and I should be humble.
Leader. Jesus gave us a powerful example—washing the feet of the Apostles. Listen to his explanation from the Gospel of John: "For I have set you an example, that you also should do as I have done to you. Very truly, I tell you, servants are not greater than their master, nor are messengers greater than the one who sent them. If you know these things, you are blessed if you do them" (13.15–17).
All. We know these things. We must live them out. We know what the Lord God asks of us—only this: that we act justly, love tenderly, and walk humbly with our God (adapted from Mic 6.8).

Quiet Reflection

Play "Servant Song," if you wish.

Prayers

Leader. As we strive to be merciful and true, let us bring our needs to our God.

Mention that the sides will now take turns offering prayers. Note that after each prayer, everyone is to respond, "Lord, hear our needs."

Side 1. For peace in our world, and justice in our land, we pray . . .
Side 2. For courage in decisions, and compassion in our actions, we pray . . .
Side 1. For lonely hearts, and empty hands, we pray . . .
Side 2. For our individual needs, we pray . . . *[Encourage the students to share their own needs aloud or to ponder them in silence.]*
Leader. We thank you, God, for all you have given us, and we know that you hear our prayers. We ask that you bless us and remember us as we pray the words you taught us:
All. Our Father . . . *[Lead the class in saying the Lord's Prayer.]*

Prayer Service 6:
Do Not Be Afraid—a Service for Advent
Isaiah, chapter 41

This prayer service encourages the students to focus on the presence and love of God as they prepare to celebrate the coming of Jesus.

Preparation

Gather the following materials:
- ☐ a fireplace or candles or an outdoor bonfire, and matches
- ☐ music and lyrics for the hymn "O Come, O Come, Emmanuel" (found in many traditional hymnals)
- ☐ copies of the reading and the reflection, one of each for those who will present those pieces

Opening Words

Gather the students in a circle around a glowing fireplace, an arrangement of burning candles, or an outdoor bonfire. If you are inside and you can, dim all other lighting. Call for two readers, and give one a copy of the reading and the other a copy of the reflection.

Leader. The season of Advent invites us to huddle together against the cold and harsh realities of life and to face the darkness courageously. We light candles that suggest glimmers of hope, and tell the stories of faith that make us one. As church, we wait in joyful hope. As companions, we do not wait alone. When we were little, we were afraid of the dark. The reassuring presence of someone we trusted helped us know that morning would come. Jesus, the morning star, scattered the darkness of sin and division forever. Jesus, the prince of peace, comforts us in our fear. Jesus said: "Do not be afraid. I am with you always." With confidence, we pray, "Come, Lord Jesus, come!"

Song

Lead the class in singing "O Come, O Come, Emmanuel."

Reading

Reader.

> For I, the LORD your God,
>   hold your right hand;
> it is I who say to you, "Do not fear,
>   I will help you."

(Isa 41.13)

Reflection

Read the following story yourself, or invite a student to do so:

> I was seven at the time. Small, frail, and scared of almost anything. I was taking swimming lessons at the community pool down the road from my house. It was a hot, stuffy day in August. I had improved my swimming greatly in the past week, so my instructor, Frostie, wanted my group and me to try something different. Frostie said she wanted us to jump off the diving board and swim to the side of the pool and get out.
>
> We all got in line in front of the diving board, and I was last. Everyone else jumped off ahead of me and said it was a piece of cake. For me, it was a piece of rotten cake that had sat in the fridge for two weeks and was hard to swallow.
>
> It was my turn. I stepped up on the ladder, feeling sick to my stomach. I walked to the edge of the board, feeling my knees grow weak, and my palms were all sweaty. I looked down into the deep water. It looked cold and frightening. I looked up at Frostie, who was encouraging me to jump. I was too scared to even hear her. I looked down at the water that lay beneath me again—shimmering, crystal blue. The diving board was moving because of my shaking. I looked up at Frostie again. Her eyes were full of encouragement. They were saying: "You can do it. You know you can." Suddenly, I realized that Frostie was right. I took a deep breath, clenched my teeth, held my nose, and jumped. I fell into the sparkling water, rose to the surface, and swam excitedly to the edge of the pool. Frostie was waiting there for me. I thanked her for helping me. I felt like the proudest person in the world.
>
> Frostie taught me a lot that sunny August day. I learned that I can trust other people and look to them for guidance and support. I learned that taking risks is part of growing up. I learned that to conquer fear, I must do both—trust and risk. On that August day when I was seven, I also learned to trust in God. Jesus came among us to show us how to live. He trusted his Father and invites us to do the same. I learned that whatever God does, it is for the best.
>
> I've grown up a lot since I was seven. I've learned to confide in my family and friends more, and I have found out it is perfectly fine to take risks. Courage is not being without fear. It is learning to face my fears with confidence.
>
> During this season of Advent, perhaps we can reflect on what keeps us standing on the edge of the diving board, afraid of the deep. Jesus, like Frostie, stands at the edge of our fears and says to us: "You can do it. You know you can." It's up to us, though. He does not push. He invites. I know I can risk more today because Frostie taught me to believe in myself. (Stephanie Piraino, class of 2001, submitted by Michelle France, Academy of Notre Dame de Namur, Villanova, Pennsylvania)

Closing Prayers

Leader. With confidence in God, let us pray together the words Jesus gave us: Our Father . . . *[Lead the class in the Lord's Prayer.]*

Leader. Let us pray, in this Advent time, for hearts that are steadfast and trusting:

> God of day and God of darkness,
> draw near to us this day.
> May the fears that hold us bound
> be dispelled in your holy light.

May you strengthen our hands for service
and bless our longing hearts
that we may be ready to welcome you anew
this Christmas once again. Amen.

Leader. Let us offer one another a sign of peace.

(This prayer service is from Michelle France, Academy of Notre Dame de Namur, Villanova, Pennsylvania.)

Prayer Service 7: We Are All Precious in God's Sight
Isaiah, chapters 43, 49

In this prayer service, the students explore cultural diversity, their own personal uniqueness, and how all people and peoples are precious to God.

Preparation

Gather the following materials:
- ☐ objects symbolic of Christian worship, such as a pillar candle and a cross
- ☐ recordings of soft instrumental music (optional)
- ☐ a tape or CD player (optional)
- ☐ a copy of the reading
- ☐ a large basket or tray of leaves—more than one leaf for each student

Place objects symbolic of Christian worship, and a basket or tray of leaves, at the center of your prayer space.

Opening Prayer and Reading

Gather the students in a circle in the prayer space. Encourage silence, or play soft instrumental music. Call a volunteer to present the reading, and provide a copy of the words.

Leader. In the name of our glorious Creator God, whose imagination dreamed up the beauty of our trees, bushes, and plants, I welcome you to this time of worship. We turn to this wonderful, affectionate God to hear words of comfort and love.

Reader.

Do not fear, for I have redeemed you;
I have called you by name, you are mine.

. . . .

Because you are precious in my sight,
and honored, and I love you.

. . . .

Do not fear, for I am with you.

. . . .

I will say . . .

. . . . . .

"bring my sons from far away
and my daughters from the end of the earth—

everyone who is called by my name,
    whom I created for my glory,
    whom I formed and made."

(43.1–7)

    . . . I will not forget you.
See, I have inscribed you on the palms of my hands.

(Isa 49.15–16)

Leaf Ritual

Begin with this introduction:

- God knows each of us as a precious, unique, individual child who is loved, honored, and cherished.

  There are billions of people in the world, and God knows each of us by name.

  And the world includes many different people—so much diversity. There are Africans, Asians, Europeans, South Americans, and Native Americans. There are married people, single people, and divorced people. There are stepsisters, half brothers, godmothers, and grandfathers. There are heterosexuals and homosexuals. There are infants, schoolchildren, teenageers, twenty-somethings, and thirty-fourty-fifty-sixty-seventy-eighty-ninety-somethings. How does God keep track?

  Each of us is a precious, unique, individual child of God who is loved, honored, and cherished.

  This basket contains a lot of leaves. The world is full of different leaves—so much diversity. There are maples, oaks, elms, chestnuts, firs, pines, spruces, and palms. There are tropical, woodland, and mountain trees. There are coniferous and deciduous trees. How can we keep track?

  Each leaf in this basket is a unique creation of God.

  We will be passing the leaves around the circle. When the basket comes to you, select one leaf and hold on to it.

Pass the basket around. Be ready to encourage individuals to move more quickly if they are taking too long trying to find the "perfect leaf." When the basket comes back to you, remove the remaining leaves. Continue leading the participants through the process with these or similar words:

- Examine your leaf; look for its unique traits. Look over its color, the shape of its edges, the length of its stem, the pattern of its veins. Get to know your leaf as an individual creation of God.

  I will pass the basket around again. When it comes to you, put your leaf back. The basket will come around one more time after that, and you will be asked to find your own leaf again—the one you originally held in your hand and examined, the one whose uniquenesss you discovered the first time the basket was passed.

Pass the empty basket around the circle so that everyone can put their leaf in it. When the basket returns to you, gently scramble the leaves so that their order is no longer the same. But be careful not to damage any of the leaves. Pass the basket in the same direction again, so that the first person to have placed his or her leaf into the basket is also the first person to remove his or her leaf from the basket. Continue the process with these or similar words:

- As you looked through the leaves, you might have discovered that no leaf is perfect. Every leaf is beautiful, but each one has imperfections. Some are torn, some are uneven, some have holes, some are bent, some are colored with blotches. But all of them are wonderful. I think God wants us to understand that we do not have to be perfect in order to be wonderful.

Together all the leaves on a tree can do what the tree needs to have done. Together all of us can do what our group needs to have done. Sometimes it helps the group if we all see the unique traits of each member. So we're going to take the opportunity now to conduct a brief group sharing.

As we go around the circle, please tell us one thing you can offer the group—a gift or talent you have. Also tell us one thing you need from the group—an area in which you are not so strong. And as we hear about the gifts and needs of our group, let us remember that we do not need to be perfect in order to be wonderful.

Begin the sharing yourself, as an example for the group. Be brief. After everyone has shared, move on to the blessing.

Blessing

Read this story, which contains the blessing:

- A legend in the Sioux tradition explains why leaves turn color in the autumn.

Many, many moons ago, when the world was young, the grass and flower folk were enjoying the beautiful summer weather. But as the days went by, the weather became colder and colder.

The grass and flowers grew sad, for they had nothing to protect them from the sharp cold. Just when it seemed that there was no hope for living, the Holy One who created all things came to their aid. The leaves of the trees were told to fall to the ground and spread a soft, warm blanket over the tender roots that were about to freeze. To repay the leaves for their kindness, the Creator gave them one last bright array of beauty.

That is why the trees take on their pretty farewell colors of red, gold, and brown each year during Indian summer. Then the leaves turn to their task of covering the earth with a thick rug of warmth.

Most people want to be useful. Like the leaves in this old Sioux legend, they want to be of service. (Adapted from R. L. Gowan, ed., *Inspiration from Indian Legends, Proverbs, and Psalms,* p. 59)

May God bless our group as we follow the example of the leaves, looking for ways to be useful and to serve those created by the Holy One. Amen.

(This prayer service is adapted slightly from the long prayer of set 1, "Leaves," in *Prayer Works for Teens,* book 2, by Lisa-Marie Calderone-Stewart, pp. 20–23.)

Prayer Service 8: Called to Serve
Matthew, chapter 5

In this prayer service, the students examine God's call to serve, consider the many forms it takes, and identify specific ways that they can carry it out in their own lives. The service includes a unique ritual for blessing and sharing bread as a sign of the students' faith in God, the power of love, and the mystery of God's call.

Preparation

Gather the following materials:

- [ ] copies of handout App C–6, "Called to Serve," one for each student
- [ ] a pillar candle and matches
- [ ] copies of the hymnal *Gather Comprehensive,* edited by Robert J. Batastini and Michael A. Cymbala (Chicago: GIA Publications, 1994) (optional)
- [ ] music and lyrics for the hymn "Blest Are They" (in *Gather Comprehensive*) (optional)
- [ ] slips of blank paper, one for each student
- [ ] pens or pencils
- [ ] a service collage or other service visual (see the directions that follow this list)
- [ ] a basket
- [ ] votive candles, one for each student
- [ ] music and lyrics for the song "Here I Am, Lord," by Dan Schutte (in *Gather Comprehensive*) (optional)
- [ ] a plate or bowl of saltine crackers
- [ ] a plate or bowl of shortbread
- [ ] a plate or bowl of cornbread
- [ ] a plate or bowl of nut bread
- [ ] music and lyrics for the song "For the Life of the World" (in *Gather Comprehensive*) (optional)

If you would like to, create a collage of service acts by cutting pictures and headlines from used magazines and newspapers, and gluing them onto a piece of poster board. Include a wide variety of acts of kindness involving the family, parish, school, community, state, nation, and world. Post this collage in the prayer space where all can see it. (If you are using this prayer service as a follow-up to an activity in which the students created a visual about service, such as the activity "Personal Idols: Reflections of God?" you might want to display their visuals instead.)

If you have a small class, combine some of the reader roles as necessary. If your students would benefit from more leadership, recruit another adult to help supervise the candle lighting in the reflection and to play the reader roles in the blessing of the breads.

Opening Words

Handout **App C–6**

Gather the students in the prayer space and distribute copies of handout App C–6. Light a pillar candle and invite everyone to be still and quiet.

Leader. Let us remember that we are in the holy presence of God.

Light a pillar candle.

Leader. We are gathered to give witness to the enduring realities of life.
All. We have come to affirm that life is a gift, that the gift is good, and that it comes from God.
Leader. We are gathered to renew our hope in Jesus Christ, as we travel life's long journey.
All. We find God in the paths of our present and our past, and we also trust in God's love in our future.

Leader. The same God guides us all the way, every day of our lives, and beyond life.

All. Let us praise God with our whole hearts, and entrust our lives to God's hands. Amen.

Opening Song

Lead the class in singing the hymn "Blest Are They," if you choose to.

Reading

Divide the class into two sides, and lead the sides in reading the Beatitudes (Mt 5.3–10) responsively, as follows:

Leader. Let us now listen to the word of God, which reminds us of the preciousness of human life, and of our responsibility to one another.

Side 1. "Blessed are the poor in spirit . . ."

Side 2. "for theirs is the kingdom of heaven."

Side 1. "Blessed are those who mourn . . ."

Side 2. "for they will be comforted."

Side 1. "Blessed are the meek . . ."

Side 2. "for they will inherit the earth."

Side 1. "Blessed are those who hunger and thirst for righteousness . . ."

Side 2. "for they will be filled."

Side 1. "Blessed are the merciful . . ."

Side 2. "for they will receive mercy."

Side 1. "Blessed are the pure in heart . . ."

Side 2. "for they will see God."

Side 1. "Blessed are the peacemakers . . ."

Side 2. "for they will be called children of God."

Leader. Loving Creator, we ask for wholeness for ourselves and for your church. Do not allow fear, ignorance, or pride to limit the action of your Spirit, do not allow mere custom to prevent the divine creativity within us from bearing fruit.

All.
We ask for insight to understand
the needs of people today,
that we might grasp the complexity of the situations that face us
and the absolute simplicity of human need:
the poor have a right to hear the Gospel,
the hungry a right to food,
the oppressed a right to freedom.

Reflection Activity

Pass out slips of paper, and pens or pencils. Point out the collage of service acts if you posted one in the prayer space (or any other service visual you have displayed), and briefly mention a variety of ways that young people can serve in their home, parish, school, and community. Invite the students each to write on their slip of paper one act of service that they will perform in the next week.

When everyone is finished writing, ask the students to fold their slip of paper and bring it with them as they are called to the front or center. Then call each student in turn to come up, drop their paper in a basket near the burning candle, use a taper to light a votive candle, and form a circle around the prayer space. (If your group is large, you may want to ask the students to return to their seat after lighting the candle, rather than forming a circle.) When everyone has joined the circle, hold up the basket of service slips and lead the students in the following prayer:

All. We light these candles and ask, God, that you enable us to be enthusiastic disciples in your ministry, contagious in our love and eager to be among your people as ones who serve. Be with us as we carry out the acts of service we have pledged this week, and other acts of love and kindness throughout our lives. This we ask through Jesus Christ, who came as brother and servant to us all.

Lead the class in singing "Here I Am, Lord," if you so desire.

Presentation of the Bread

Reader 1. We have shared bread many times in our lives, in many places, for many reasons. Just as there is no single symbol of the church, there is no single bread that can feed our hunger.

Reader 2. And so we bless many kinds of breads today, as a sign that our church savors the taste and feel of a variety of foods, and savors the variety of women and men who make up our community.

All. May our acceptance of these various breads be a sign of our faith in the unending goodness of a God who journeys with us, in the power of love to remove any barrier among us, and in the mystery of the call given to each of us, to make bread and life in beauty available to everyone.

Leader. Let us share this bread as Jesus taught us, knowing that our lives are forever changed by this, and every, breaking of the bread.

Blessing and Sharing of the Bread

Reader 3. *[Holding up a plate or bowl of saltine crackers]* Let saltines represent the elderly, and women who have been battered or abused—"the salty ones":
> those who have endured
> those who have learned wisdom
> those who are fragile
> those forgotten in our society

Leader. This bread has been presented and blessed. *[Reader 3 raises the bread.]* Take and eat, knowing that our lives are forever changed by this, and every, breaking of the bread. *[The reader passes the bread around the group as the next presentation begins, and the students each take a portion and eat it as it comes to them.]*

Reader 4. *[Holding up a plate or bowl of shortbread]* Shortbread brings to mind children and youth. Let this bread signify
> boys and girls who suffer physical and sexual abuse
> boys and girls who carry the heavy burden of family separations
> troubled teenagers who have no safe places left to go

Leader. This bread has been presented and blessed. *[Reader 4 raises the bread.]* Take and eat, knowing that our lives are forever changed by this, and every, breaking of the bread. *[The bread is passed and eaten.]*

Reader 5. *[Holding up a plate or bowl of cornbread]* Let cornbread signify our African American, Hispanic and Latino, Native American, Asian American, Appalachian, and homosexual sisters and brothers who have suffered and continue to suffer discrimination, racism, and oppression.

Let it remind us of the past from which they have come and the struggle they continue to this day.

Let us not forget the equality, fairness, freedom, and dignity that are the right of each individual not only in this country but throughout the world.

Leader. This bread has been presented and blessed. *[Reader 5 raises the bread.]* Take and eat, knowing that our lives are forever changed by this, and every, breaking of the bread. *[The bread is passed and eaten.]*

Reader 6. *[Holding up a plate or bowl of nut bread]* Nut bread represents women and men who are considered crazy in our society because they are incomprehensible to most people:

those who are homeless
those who are mentally ill
those who suffer addiction or AIDS
the dreamers, the visionaries, the prophets among us

Leader. This bread has been presented and blessed. *[Reader 6 raises the bread.]* Take and eat, knowing that our lives are forever changed by this, and every, breaking of the bread. *[The bread is passed and eaten.]*

Closing Prayers

Reader 7.

We pray, then, good and gracious God,
that we might recognize you in this bread today.
It is the bread of heaven,
the bread of the poor,
the bread of our lives.

Reader 8.

We are here to give ourselves to you and your people.
It is through what we are and do
that others come to know you.

Reader 9.

We are here to bring peace to a broken people,
and healing to those in need.

Reader 10.

We are here to witness to the world
that we live in response to a desperate society,
seeking truth, equality, and freedom.

Reader 11.

We are called to stand together,
sharing our many gifts.
And so, let us join together
in prayer.

All.

God of the poor and oppressed, we ask for your help.
Teach us to become eyes for those who are blind,
ears for those who are deaf to your Word,
and hands for those who refuse to work at building the Reign of God.
We pray all this in your name and for your honor and glory.
Amen.

Charge and Blessing

Leader.

God of all justice,
we thank you for the gifts you have given each of us.
We pray that we may always be mindful
of all your people who are in need,
and share our gifts with them.
We ask this through Christ our Lord. Amen.

Closing Song

Perhaps lead the class in singing "For the Life of the World."

(This prayer service is adapted from one by Laurie Ziliak, campus minister, Saint Mary's University.)

Prayer Service 9: Fourteen Courageous Steps— the Stations of the Cross for Lent
Matthew, chapter 27; Mark, chapters 14–15; Luke, chapter 23

This prayer service leads the students through the fourteen stations of the cross and invites them to examine their personal responses to each station.

Preparation

Gather the following materials:
☐ copies of handout App C–7, "Fourteen Courageous Steps—The Stations of the Cross," one for each student or each reader
☐ music and lyrics for the song "Were You There?" (a popular, traditional hymn that can be found in many Catholic songbooks) (optional)
☐ the stations of the cross

Arrange for the class to encounter the stations of the cross during this prayer service. Depending on your class, the time you have available, and the needs and desires of you and your students, you may choose to make this service very simple or quite elaborate. Here are some suggestions:
- Post images of the fourteen stations around the walls of the prayer space, and move just yourself or the entire class from one image to the next as you proceed through the stations.
- Project photos or pictures of the stations on a screen or wall, switching images as you progress through the stations. If you use this option, you might dim the lights and use candles to set a prayerful mood.
- Take the class to a church that displays the stations, and process through the stations as you conduct the service.
- Celebrate the service at an outdoor stations of the cross, either an existing facility or one that you create.

For background information, including student illustrations of the stations, refer to *Stations for Teens: Meditations on the Death and Resurrection of Jesus,* by Gary Egeberg (Winona, MN: Saint Mary's Press, 2000).

Note: If you completed the activity "The Stations of the Cross," in which the students build their own stations representing Mark's Passion account, you can use a prayer service similar to this as a follow-up and visit the students' own creations on display. You will need to create a new handout listing the readings used for that activity, and write new leader parts directed at the content of those passages.

Opening Song

Handout **App C–7**   Distribute copies of handout App C–7, and lead the class in singing a few verses of "Were You There?" if you so desire.

Station 1: Jesus Was Condemned to Death

Reader 1. Jesus was arrested and taken before the council, where many people testified against him.

Then the high priest stood up before them and asked Jesus, "Have you no answer? What is it that they testify against you?" But he was silent and did not answer. Again the high priest asked him, "Are you the Messiah, the Son of the Blessed One?" Jesus said, "I am; and

'you will see the Son of Man
seated at the right hand of the Power,'
and 'coming with the clouds of heaven.'"

Then the high priest tore his clothes and said, "Why do we still need witnesses? You have heard his blasphemy! What is your decision?" All of them condemned him as deserving death. Some began to spit on him, to blindfold him, and to strike him, saying to him, "Prophesy!" The guards also took him over and beat him. (Mk 14.60–65)

Leader. Jesus was condemned for something that the high priest did not even understand. Many times, we are criticized, ridiculed, or simply told we are nothing. Think of a time that happened to you. What did you feel like? What did you want to do?

Leader. Lord, have mercy.
All. Lord, have mercy.
Leader. Christ, have mercy.
All. Christ, have mercy.
Leader. Lord, have mercy.
All. Lord, have mercy.

Station 2: Jesus Took Up His Cross

Reader 2.

Then the soldiers led him into the courtyard of the palace (that is, the governor's headquarters); and they called together the whole cohort. And they clothed him in a purple cloak; and after twisting some thorns into a crown, they put it on him. And they began saluting him, "Hail, King of the Jews!" They struck his head with a reed, spat upon him, and knelt down in homage to him. After mocking him, they stripped him of the purple cloak and put his own clothes on him. Then they led him out to crucify him. (Mk 15.16–20)

Leader. Jesus endured great pain even though he was innocent. Have you ever been punished for something you did not do? Remember that time, experience the feelings again, and ask Jesus how he would handle it. We are asked to carry a very light burden compared with Jesus. We carry a sliver of the cross; he carries the remainder.

Leader. Lord, have mercy.
All. Lord, have mercy.
Leader. Christ, have mercy.
All. Christ, have mercy.
Leader. Lord, have mercy.
All. Lord, have mercy.

Station 3: Jesus Fell the First Time

Reader 3. The pressure was too much. Jesus was weak from being beaten, bruised, and whipped. He fell with the weight of the cross. The pain was excruciating, but he got back up and began the seemingly long journey to the Place of the Skull, Golgotha.

Leader. What drains you of energy and brings you to the ground? Is it a lack of patience, courage, or understanding? Like Jesus, we need to rise from our downtrodden state.

Leader. Lord, have mercy.
All. Lord, have mercy.
Leader. Christ, have mercy.
All. Christ, have mercy.
Leader. Lord, have mercy.
All. Lord, have mercy.

Station 4: Jesus Met His Mother

Reader 4. Mary said: "I look into his eyes. There is so much pain. My Son, if I could take away this agony, I would. You still have so much love in your eyes. You are incredible. I love you!"

Leader. How do your parents look at you? What do they see? How do you know they love you? How do you show your love for them?

Leader. Lord, have mercy.
All. Lord, have mercy.
Leader. Christ, have mercy.
All. Christ, have mercy.
Leader. Lord, have mercy.
All. Lord, have mercy.

Station 5: Simon Helped Jesus Carry His Cross

Reader 5. "As [the soldiers] led [Jesus] away, they seized a man, Simon of Cyrene, who was coming from the country, and they laid the cross on him, and made him carry it behind Jesus" (Lk 23.26).

Leader. Who is with you through the good times and the bad times? Who is there to help you carry your cross? How does this person help you? How do you help this person?

Leader. Lord, have mercy.
All. Lord, have mercy.

Leader. Christ, have mercy.
All. Christ, have mercy.
Leader. Lord, have mercy.
All. Lord, have mercy.

Station 6: Veronica Wiped the Face of Jesus

Reader 6. Veronica said: "I see him from a distance. As he comes closer, I see the sweat, blood, and tears. I wipe his face. It is the least I can do. He has done so much for me."
Leader. Compassion is a virtue. To help one another is a gift. How have you been kind to your family, friends, and even strangers? Veronica wiped the face of Jesus with love, compassion, and sorrow. How do we do this for others?
Leader. Lord, have mercy.
All. Lord, have mercy.
Leader. Christ, have mercy.
All. Christ, have mercy.
Leader. Lord, have mercy.
All. Lord, have mercy.

Station 7: Jesus Fell the Second Time

Reader 7. With each step, the cross became heavier. The pain was agonizing. Jesus fell again. The weight was constant, the pressure consistent.
Leader. All of us have continuous sources of stress. These become a heavy burden and may cause fatigue. What are ongoing sources of stress for you?
Leader. Lord, have mercy.
All. Lord, have mercy.
Leader. Christ, have mercy.
All. Christ, have mercy.
Leader. Lord, have mercy.
All. Lord, have mercy.

Station 8: Jesus Met the Women of Jerusalem

Reader 8.

A great number of the people followed [Jesus], and among them were women who were beating their breasts and wailing for him. But Jesus turned to them and said, "Daughters of Jerusalem, do not weep for me, but weep for yourselves and for your children. For the days are surely coming when they will say, 'Blessed are the barren, and the wombs that never bore, and the breasts that never nursed.' Then they will begin to say to the mountains, 'Fall on us'; and to the hills, 'Cover us.' For if they do this when the wood is green, what will happen when it is dry?" (Lk 23.27–31)

Leader. Even when he was racked with pain, Jesus thought of others. Who believes in you and always thinks of you: friends, family members, teachers? What inspiration do they provide?
Leader. Lord, have mercy.
All. Lord, have mercy.
Leader. Christ, have mercy.

All. Christ, have mercy.
Leader. Lord, have mercy.
All. Lord, have mercy.

Station 9: Jesus Fell the Third Time

Reader 9. Once again, the weight was just too much. Jesus fell for the third time. Then he gathered the last bit of strength he had, got up, and carried his cross onward.
Leader. When do you feel exhausted but just keep going? What makes you continue?
Leader. Lord, have mercy.
All. Lord, have mercy.
Leader. Christ, have mercy.
All. Christ, have mercy.
Leader. Lord, have mercy.
All. Lord, have mercy.

Station 10: Jesus Was Stripped of His Garments

Reader 10. When they reached Golgotha, the soldiers stripped Jesus of his garments. They cast lots to split his clothes among themselves.
Leader. Being stripped is a shameful experience and can cause great doubt. When have you felt stripped of your defenses and naked in front of the world?
Leader. Lord, have mercy.
All. Lord, have mercy.
Leader. Christ, have mercy.
All. Christ, have mercy.
Leader. Lord, have mercy.
All. Lord, have mercy.

Station 11: Jesus Was Nailed to the Cross

Reader 11. The soldiers laid Jesus on the cross, spread his arms, and drove a stake through each of his wrists. The first stake sent waves of excruciating pain up and down his body. The second was worse. The soldiers raised his knees and crossed his feet and drove a stake through the arch of each foot.
Leader. When Jesus was nailed to the cross, he could no longer move. What holds you stationary? What keeps you from accomplishing your dreams?
Leader. Lord, have mercy.
All. Lord, have mercy.
Leader. Christ, have mercy.
All. Christ, have mercy.
Leader. Lord, have mercy.
All. Lord, have mercy.

Station 12: Jesus Died on the Cross

Reader 12. It was around midday, and the sky became dark. Jesus cried out, "My God, my God, why have you forsaken me?" Jesus uttered a loud cry, and died.

Leader. At times, there seems to be no hope. What hopes, beliefs, ideals, and dreams have died or been lost for you?
Leader. Lord, have mercy.
All. Lord, have mercy.
Leader. Christ, have mercy.
All. Christ, have mercy.
Leader. Lord, have mercy.
All. Lord, have mercy.

Station 13: Jesus Was Taken Off the Cross

Reader 13. The soldiers came to break the legs of those who were not dead. When they saw that Jesus was dead, they pierced his side; blood and water poured out. They took Jesus off the cross. Joseph of Arimathea gathered his body to bury him.
Leader. Think about the people who have been there to pick you up, clean you off, and take care of your needs. How have you felt when they have done that?
Leader. Lord, have mercy.
All. Lord, have mercy.
Leader. Christ, have mercy.
All. Christ, have mercy.
Leader. Lord, have mercy.
All. Lord, have mercy.

Station 14: Jesus Was Laid in a Tomb

Reader 14.

So Joseph took the body and wrapped it in a clean linen cloth and laid it in his own new tomb, which he had hewn in the rock. He then rolled a great stone to the door of the tomb and went away. Mary Magdalene and the other Mary were there, sitting opposite the tomb. (Mt 27.59–60)

Leader. Jesus was put to rest. Where do you go to get rest and to rejuvenate? What is your sacred space like?
Leader. Lord, have mercy.
All. Lord, have mercy.
Leader. Christ, have mercy.
All. Christ, have mercy.
Leader. Lord, have mercy.
All. Lord, have mercy.

Closing Prayer

Leader. Dear Jesus, thank you for taking us on this journey. Many times, we feel troubled, beaten up by life, and just ready to give up hope. Please help us to realize that we can always come to you because you will understand.
    You suffered for us, and you brought us abundant life by your Resurrection. You cried, you died, and you rose.

The class might conclude by singing the remaining verses of "Were You There?"

(This prayer service is from Debra Thorpe, Notre Dame Academy, Los Angeles, California.)

Prayer Service 10: Saying Yes to Jesus
Luke, chapter 6

In this prayer service, the students are invited to commit their life to God and to follow the light and example of Jesus.

Preparation

Gather the following materials:
- [ ] copies of handout App C–8, "Saying Yes to Jesus," one for each student
- [ ] a pillar candle and matches
- [ ] sheets of black and white construction paper, one of each for each student
- [ ] pens or markers
- [ ] a recording of instrumental music
- [ ] a tape or CD player
- [ ] glue sticks
- [ ] a recording of the song "I Say Yes, My Lord," by Donna Peña, from the album *How Excellent: Songs for Teens,* volume 1 (GIA Publications, 1996) (optional)

Opening Words and Readings

Handout **App C–8**

Choose four readers and distribute copies of handout App C–8. Then light a pillar candle and invite the students to quiet and to prayer.

Leader. Jesus has told us that he is the light of the world and that he will dispel the darkness. Today, as we pray together, let us choose light. Let us commit ourselves to living an examined life, one in which we consciously and deliberately choose God.

Reader 1. Why should we choose God? Is there not pain, betrayal, temptation, and persecution when we follow the words of Jesus? That path is not easy, and it may cause rejection.

Reader 2. "Blessed are you when people hate you, and when they exclude you, revile you, and defame you on account of the Son of Man" (Lk 6.22).

Reader 3. "Love your enemies, do good to those who hate you, bless those who curse you, pray for those who abuse you" (Lk 6.27).

All. These words are not ones we hear often. Jesus Christ, be with us now. Open our hearts and give us the courage to say yes to you.

Reflection Activity

Give each student a piece of black construction paper and a pen or marker. Ask everyone to think of all the messages and obstacles that keep them from saying yes to God, and to write those on the piece of paper. Note that the writing will be hard to see, and that that is fine. With instrumental music playing in the background, allow some time for quiet reflection and writing.

Reader 4.

No good tree bears bad fruit, nor again does a bad tree bear good fruit; for each tree is known by its own fruit. . . . The good person out of the good treasure of the heart produces good, and the evil person out of evil treasure produces evil; for it is out of the abundance of the heart that the mouth speaks. (Lk 6.43–45)

All. Teach us to follow the good treasure of the heart and produce good. Let us tear the evil from our lives and choose God again. Let us again say yes to God.

Instruct the students to tear their black paper into pieces approximately 1 inch square. Give out white construction paper and glue sticks. Explain that the students should use their black squares to form the word "YES" on the white paper and glue them down. Then, if you choose, play the song "I Say Yes, My Lord" while the students work.

Prayers of the Faithful

Leader. We bring our needs to you, God.

Invite the students to share their needs as individual petitions. After each petition, lead the class in responding, "Lord, hear our prayer."

Leader. It is a struggle to say yes, but with a firm resolve and the support of this Christian community, we can do it!

All. In all the good times, and all the bad times, we choose your ways, O God. We choose the cross, knowing that with the pain comes the glory of Christ. We choose the good, the light, the whole, the holy. We say yes to you, this day. Amen.

•••••••••••••••••••► "Let There Be Light!"

Opening Words

Leader. Let us remember that we are in the holy presence of God.

Readings

Reader 1.

> In the beginning, when God created the heavens and the earth, the earth was a formless void and darkness covered the face of the deep, while a wind from God swept over the face of the waters. Then God said, 'Let there be light'; and there was light. And God saw that the light was good. (Gen 1.1–4) . . . *[Refrain]*

Reader 2.

> In the beginning was the Word, and the Word was with God, and the Word was God. He was in the beginning with God. All things came into being through him, and without him not one thing came into being. What has come into being in him was life, and the life was the light of all people. The light shines in the darkness, and the darkness did not overcome it. (Jn 1.1–5) . . . *[Refrain]*

Reader 3.

> You yourselves know very well that the day of the Lord will come like a thief in the night. . . . But you, beloved, are not in darkness, for that day to surprise you like a thief; for you are all children of light and children of the day; we are not of the night or of darkness. (1 Thess 5.2–5) . . . *[Refrain]*

Reader 4.

> Do not be deceived, my beloved.
>
> Every generous act of giving, with every perfect gift, is from above, coming down from the Father of lights, with whom there is no variation or shadow due to change. (Jas 1.16–17) . . . *[Refrain]*

Reader 5.

> The light is with you for a little longer. Walk while you have the light, so that the darkness may not overtake you. If you walk in the darkness, you do not know where you are going. While you have the light, believe in the light, so that you may become children of the light. (Jn 12.35–36) . . . *[Refrain]*

Reader 6.

> We declare to you what we have seen and heard so that you also may have fellowship with us; and truly our fellowship is with the Father and his Son Jesus Christ. We are writing these things so that our joy may be complete.
>
> This is the message we have heard from him and proclaim to you, that God is light and in [God] there is no darkness at all. (1 Jn 1.3–5) . . . *[Refrain]*

Reader 7.

Again Jesus spoke to them, saying, "I am the light of the world. Whoever follows me will never walk in darkness but will have the light of life." (Jn 8.12) . . . *[Refrain]*

Sharing and Closing Prayer

Leader. At this time, I invite each of you to identify someone who has served as a light in your life. You may give either a name or a description, such as "a teacher." If you would like, you may briefly explain how he or she has been a light for you.

[After everyone has shared, they respond:]

All. Dear God, you are the source of all the real light in our lives. We thank you for all the people who have been light for us, and have revealed your love through their concern for us. Thank you for illuminating our lives and showing us the way. Let us learn to be light for one another. May each of us reflect the light of Christ to our weary world. We ask this through Christ, our light, our brother, and our Lord. Amen.

[The class may sing "Christ Be Our Light."]

(This prayer service is from Br. Larry Schatz, FSC, formerly campus minister at Saint Mary's University, Winona, Minnesota.)

► Sin and Temptation

Gathering Song

[The class may listen to the song "My Life Is in Your Hands."]

Opening Words

Leader. God created Adam and Eve in God's image, and created the Garden of Eden to supply all their needs on earth. Adam and Eve were happy in the garden. They lived without clothes and were not ashamed to be naked. Then one day a serpent approached Eve and tempted her to disobey one of God's commands.

Reader.

Now the serpent . . . said to the woman, "Did God say, 'You shall not eat from any tree in the garden'?" The woman said to the serpent, "We may eat of the fruit of the trees in the garden; but God said, 'You shall not eat of the fruit of the tree that is in the middle of the garden, nor shall you touch it, or you shall die.'" But the serpent said to the woman, "You will not die; for God knows that when you eat of it your eyes will be opened, and you will be like God, knowing good and evil." So when the woman saw that the tree was good for food, and that it was a delight to the eyes, and that the tree was to be desired to make one wise, she took of its fruit and ate; and she also gave some to her husband, who was with her, and he ate. Then the eyes of both were opened, and they knew that they were naked; and they sewed fig leaves together and made loincloths for themselves. (Gen 3.1–7)

Leader. When Adam and Eve disobeyed God, they broke their relationship of trust with God. Once that relationship was broken, sin became a part of the human story. Ever since that moment, human beings have faced temptations that pull them away from God's love and grace.

Litany

Side 1. We are sometimes torn between the voice that calls us to love . . .

Side 2. and the voice that calls us to hate.

Side 1. We are sometimes torn between the voice that calls us to do good . . .

Side 2. and the voice that calls us to do evil.

Side 1. We are sometimes torn between the voice that draws us to God . . .

Side 2. and the voice that wants to block God out of our lives.

Skit 1: Stealing

[The person reading the role of Good stands to one side of the staging area, holding a sign labeled "Good." The person reading the role of Evil stands to the opposite side of the staging area, holding a sign labeled "Evil." A person with a large rope tied around her or his waist stands between them. A fifth person holds one end of the rope and stands near the "Good" sign, and a sixth person holds the other end of the rope and stands near the "Evil" sign. The narrator stands off to the side so that the audience can see all the actors.]

Narrator. Brian got a new Northface jacket and has been proudly showing it off to everyone. All his friends admire it—except for Jordan. Jordan wanted the jacket, and Brian bought it first. This makes Jordan mad. Now Jordan is contemplating the situation.

Good. It's such a cool jacket. I've had my eye on it forever. But Jordan's got it, and it looks good on him.

Evil. But he stabbed me in the back. I wanted that jacket, and he knew that. It's not right. It's just not right.

Good. Brian had a right to buy it. He wanted it just as badly as I did.

Evil. Who cares? That Northface is hot. So hot that I'm going to steal it.

Good. No. I can't steal it. Brian is my friend. He paid for the jacket with his own money. Besides, who I am is much more important than what I wear. And I'm no thief.

Skit 2: Drugs

[The scene is staged as for skit 1.]

Narrator. Delia is at a party on a Saturday night. It is the party of the year, and she is having the time of her life, sitting around with a really cool crowd. In fact, she is sitting right next to Michael, a guy she really likes. Suddenly, Michael hands her a marijuana joint.

Good. Marijuana? You've got to be kidding! I can't smoke that. It'll mess me up.

Evil. One joint can't hurt. I can stop anytime I want, especially after just one.

Good. Or can I? What am I thinking? It's weed! What about its long-term effects? It destroys brain cells. It harms chromosomes. What about the children I want to have in the future? Will they be okay?

Evil. But it's Michael offering it to me. I like Michael. Maybe he will like me if I smoke. It can't be so bad. Everyone else is smoking. What'll they all think if I don't join them?

Good. Forget it. If Michael doesn't like me for who I am, he doesn't deserve me. And if the others laugh at me, they're not real friends. I can deal with that. This is my decision and my life. And my choice is to pass.

Skit 3: Sex

[The scene is staged as for skits 1 and 2.]

Narrator. Jorge and his girlfriend, Tiffany, are in his house alone. They are kissing, and their feelings for each other are becoming stronger and stronger.

Evil. I want to make love. We're both responsible. We have protection, so we don't have to worry about a baby. Neither of us has been with anyone else, so we don't have to worry about AIDS or STDs.

Good. Yes, we have both been responsible people so far. We don't have to worry about AIDS or STDs. But no method of protection is 100 percent effective. There's always a chance that if we share sex, we could bring a baby into the world. Neither of us is ready for that kind of responsibility yet.

Evil. Sure, there's always a chance we could have a baby. But the chance is slim. We have been going together for a while. Sharing sex will bring us closer.

Good. Sounds good, but let's not fool ourselves. Sharing sex is no shortcut to real intimacy, to real, deep friendship. Communication, honesty, care for each other's well-being—those are the things that will bring us closer. Not sex.

Evil. We would not be just having sex. We love each other. Love makes it right.

Good. We do love each other. But how much? Are we ready and able to make a life together, to love each other always and forever? To be honest, neither of us is ready for that kind of love. We both have school to finish, careers to start, people to meet, and goals to achieve before we're ready for that kind of unconditional, always-and-forever love. Let's swear to each other never to make promises to each other that we can't keep. We will wait until we are ready and able to love each other always and forever.

Skit 4: Jesus in the Desert

[The scene is staged as for skits 1, 2, and 3.]

Narrator. Because Jesus was human, he too experienced temptation and sin. In the weeks before Jesus died, the Spirit led him out into the desert, and he remained there for forty days and forty nights. Afterward, he was hungry, and the tempter approached him.

Evil. If you are the Son of God, turn these stones into loaves of bread.

Good. People need more than bread to live; they need the Word of God.

Narrator. The evil tempter took Jesus to the top of the Temple in Jerusalem.

Evil. If you are the Son of God, throw yourself down from the top of this Temple and let your angels minister to you.

Good. You should not put the Lord your God to the test.

Narrator. The devil took Jesus to the top of a mountain and pointed out all the nations below it.

Evil. All these countries I will give you if you throw yourself down at my feet and worship me.

Good. Get away from me, Satan, for it is written, "The Lord your God should you worship, and God alone shall you serve."

(This skit is adapted from Mt 4.1–10.)

Reflection

[Everyone reflects on several questions posed by the leader.]

Closing Prayer

Leader.

Give me the courage to do right
in the face of wrong.
Instill in my heart
a set of values that prompts me
to think of others
instead of just myself.

Give me the willingness to
stand up for what I believe in—
not following the crowd.
Give me the strength to
look evil in the eye
and withstand it.
Because I know
with you at my side
all things are possible.
(Theresa Vonderwell, in *More Dreams Alive: Prayers by Teenagers,* edited by Carl Koch [Winona, MN: Saint Mary's Press, 1995], page 28. Copyright © 1995 by Saint Mary's Press. All rights reserved.)

Closing Song

[The group may sing the traditional spiritual "Were You There?"]

(This prayer service is adapted from one conceived and written by Helen Wolf and others, both adults and students, at Bishop Loughlin Memorial High School, Brooklyn, New York.)

••••••••••▶ A Rainbow of Hope and Peace

Opening Prayer and Reading

Reader.

God said, "This is the sign of the covenant that I make between me and you and every living creature that is with you, for all future generations: I have set my bow in the clouds, and it shall be a sign of the covenant between me and the earth. When I bring clouds over the earth and the bow is seen in the clouds, I will remember my covenant that is between me and you and every living creature of all flesh; and the waters shall never again become a flood to destroy all flesh. When the bow is in the clouds, I will see it and remember the everlasting covenant between God and every living creature of all flesh that is on the earth." God said to Noah, "This is the sign of the covenant that I have established between me and all flesh that is on the earth." (Gen 9.12–17)

Leader. God sends the rainbow to remind us of God's promise to grant the glory of heaven to all who love God and do God's will. The rainbow is thus a symbol of hope. In spite of all the violence in the world, God gives us hope through Jesus Christ, who is the source of all peace. We love God and do God's will when we reach out to serve others in peace, as Jesus did, trusting in God's grace.

Reflection Activity

[Everyone identifies groups they belong to. The leader explains what it means to belong to a community of hope. Small groups discuss their personal experiences of peace in a community of hope.]

Closing Prayer

[Each person gets four colored strips of paper, representing four communities of hope, and writes on each strip one thing he or she can do in that community to share the peace of Jesus. Then everyone says the Peace Prayer of Saint Francis of Assisi together:]

All.

Loving God, make me an instrument of your
   peace.
Where there is hatred, let me sow love;
Where there is injury, pardon;
Where there is doubt, faith;
Where there is despair, hope;
Where there is darkness, light;
And where there is sadness, joy.
O, Divine Teacher, grant that I may not so
   much seek to be consoled as to console;
To be understood as to understand;
To be loved as to love;
For it is in giving that we receive;
It is in pardoning that we are pardoned;
And it is in dying that we are born to eternal
   life.
   (Joseph M. Stoutzenberger and John D.
      Bohrer, *Praying with Francis of Assisi*
   [Winona, MN: Saint Mary's Press, 1989],
         page 54. Copyright © 1989 by
   Saint Mary's Press. All rights reserved.)

[Each person tapes each of her or his colored strips in the corresponding section of the community-of-hope rainbow. Everyone sings "Let There Be Peace on Earth" or shares a sign of peace.]

(This prayer service is from Clare vanBrandwijk, campus minister, Bishop O+Gorman High School, Sioux Falls, South Dakota.)

Handout App C–3: Permission to reproduce this handout for classroom use is granted.

......▶ "Be Still, and Know That I Am God!"

Opening Words

Reading and Litany

Leader. A reading from Psalm 46:

God is our refuge and strength,
>   a very present help in trouble.
Therefore we will not fear, though the earth should change,
>   though the mountains shake in the heart of the sea;
though its waters roar and foam,
>   though the mountains tremble with its tumult.

(Verses 1–3)

"Be still, and know that I am God!"

(Verse 10)

Side 1. When the loud alarm goes off in the morning . . .
All. "Be still, and know that I am God!"
Side 2. In the routines of dressing and getting off to school . . .
All. "Be still, and know that I am God!"
Side 1. In the comings and goings throughout the school day . . .
All. "Be still, and know that I am God!"
Side 2. In the mundane tasks of going to the locker and walking in the halls . . .
All. "Be still, and know that I am God!"
Side 1. In the frenzied pace of the cafeteria . . .
All. "Be still, and know that I am God!"
Side 2. In the stacks of books and pages of homework . . .
All. "Be still, and know that I am God!"
Side 1. In the quiet of night and stillness of sleep . . .
All. "Be still, and know that I am God!"

Quiet Reflection

[The class may listen to the song "You Are Mine."]

Closing Prayer

All. Loving God, you come to us in the silence and in the laughter, in the moments of joy and sorrow. The busy-ness of our lives sometimes keeps us from taking the time to be quiet, to be still, and to rest in your love. Let us open ourselves to the enfolding grace of your presence this day. Let us be still and know that you hold us in your heart and that we are your cherished children. Let us be still and know that you are our God, our loving creator and friend. We ask this in Jesus' name. Amen.

Handout App C–4: Permission to reproduce this handout for classroom use is granted.

367

▶ Being a Humble Servant

Opening Words

Leader. Jesus said to his disciples, "For where two or three are gathered in my name, I am there among them" (Mt 18.20). As we gather today, in Jesus' name, let us come together quietly and reverently to be with our loving Creator, whose spirit fills us and makes us whole.

Litany and Reading

Leader. All wisdom is from God. We need to listen and learn.

Side 1. Open our hearts so that these words become branded on our hearts.

Side 2. Open our minds so that our intellect can be challenged.

Side 1. Open our eyes to the beauty of creation.

Side 2. Open our hands so that we can work to bring forth the Reign!

Leader. A reading from the Book of Sirach:

My child, perform your tasks with humility;
then you will be loved by those whom
God accepts.
The greater you are, the more you must
humble yourself;
so you will find favor in the sight of the
Lord.
For great is the might of the Lord;
but by the humble he is glorified.

(3.17–20)

Side 1. When I find myself bragging about all I can do . . .

All. Let me remember that all wisdom is from God, and I should be humble.

Side 2. When I find myself thinking I am better than someone else . . .

All. Let me remember that all wisdom is from God, and I should be humble.

Leader. Jesus gave us a powerful example—washing the feet of the Apostles. Listen to his explanation from the Gospel of John: "For I have set you an example, that you also should do as I have done to you. Very truly, I tell you, servants are not greater than their master, nor are messengers greater than the one who sent them. If you know these things, you are blessed if you do them" (13.15–17).

All. We know these things. We must live them out. We know what the Lord God asks of us—only this: that we act justly, love tenderly, and walk humbly with our God (adapted from Mic 6.8).

Quiet Reflection

[The class may listen to "Servant Song."]

Prayers

Leader. As we strive to be merciful and true, let us bring our needs to our God.

[The sides take turns offering prayers. After each prayer, everyone responds, "Lord, hear our needs."]

Side 1. For peace in our world, and justice in our land, we pray . . .

Side 2. For courage in decisions, and compassion in our actions, we pray . . .

Side 1. For lonely hearts, and empty hands, we pray . . .

Side 2. For our individual needs, we pray . . . *[Everyone shares their own needs aloud or ponders them in silence.]*

Leader. We thank you, God, for all you have given us, and we know that you hear our prayers. We ask that you bless us and remember us as we pray the words you taught us:

All. Our Father . . . *[Everyone says the Lord's Prayer.]*

Handout App C–5: Permission to reproduce this handout for classroom use is granted.

Opening Words

Leader. Let us remember that we are in the holy presence of God.

[The leader lights a pillar candle.]

Leader. We are gathered to give witness to the enduring realities of life.

All. We have come to affirm that life is a gift, that the gift is good, and that it comes from God.

Leader. We are gathered to renew our hope in Jesus Christ, as we travel life's long journey.

All. We find God in the paths of our present and our past, but we also trust in God's love in our future.

Leader. The same God guides us all the way, every day of our lives, and beyond life.

All. Let us praise God with our whole hearts, and entrust our lives to God's hands. Amen.

Opening Song

[The class may sing the hymn "Blest Are They."]

Reading

[The class is divided into two sides and reads the Beatitudes (Mt 5.3–10) responsively, as follows:]

Leader. Let us now listen to the word of God, which reminds us of the preciousness of human life, and of our responsibility to one another.

Side 1. "Blessed are the poor in spirit . . ."

Side 2. "for theirs is the kingdom of heaven."

Side 1. "Blessed are those who mourn . . ."

Side 2. "for they will be comforted."

Side 1. "Blessed are the meek . . ."

Side 2. "for they will inherit the earth."

Side 1. "Blessed are those who hunger and thirst for righteousness . . ."

Side 2. "for they will be filled."

Side 1. "Blessed are the merciful . . ."

Side 2. "for they will receive mercy."

Side 1. "Blessed are the pure in heart . . ."

Side 2. "for they will see God."

Side 1. "Blessed are the peacemakers . . ."

Side 2. "for they will be called children of God."

Leader. Loving Creator, we ask for wholeness for ourselves and for your church. Do not allow fear, ignorance, or pride to limit the action of your Spirit, do not allow mere custom to prevent the divine creativity within us from bearing fruit.

All.
We ask for insight to understand
the needs of people today,
that we might grasp the complexity of the
   situations that face us
and the absolute simplicity of human need:
the poor have a right to hear the Gospel,
the hungry a right to food,
the oppressed a right to freedom.

Reflection Activity

[Everyone writes on a slip of paper one act of service that they will perform in the next week, puts the paper in a basket, uses a taper to light a votive candle, forms a circle around the prayer space, and then says the following prayer:]

All. We light these candles and ask, God, that you enable us to be enthusiastic disciples in your ministry, contagious in our love and eager to be among your people as ones who serve. Be with us as we carry out the acts of service we have pledged this week, and other acts of love and kindness throughout our lives. This we ask through Jesus Christ, who came as brother and servant to us all.

[The class may sing "Here I Am, Lord."]

Presentation of the Bread

Reader 1. We have shared bread many times in our lives, in many places, for many reasons. Just as there is no single symbol of the church, there is no single bread that can feed our hunger.

Reader 2. And so we bless many kinds of breads today as a sign that our church savors the taste and feel of a variety of foods, and savors the variety of women and men who make up our community.

All. May our acceptance of these various breads be a sign of our faith in the unending goodness of a God who journeys with us, in the power of love to remove any barrier among us, and in the mystery of the call given to each one of us, to make bread and life in beauty available to everyone.

Leader. Let us share this bread as Jesus taught us, knowing that our lives are forever changed by this, and every, breaking of the bread.

Blessing and Sharing of the Bread

Reader 3. *[Holding up a plate or bowl of saltine crackers]* Let saltines represent the elderly, and women who have been battered or abused— "the salty ones":

> those who have endured
> those who have learned wisdom
> those who are fragile
> those forgotten in our society

Leader. This bread has been presented and blessed. *[Reader 3 raises the bread.]* Take and eat, knowing that our lives are forever changed by this, and every, breaking of the bread. *[The reader passes the bread around the group as the next presentation begins, and the students each take a portion and eat it as it comes to them.]*

Reader 4. *[Holding up a plate or bowl of shortbread]* Shortbread brings to mind children and youth. Let this bread signify

> boys and girls who suffer physical and sexual abuse
> boys and girls who carry the heavy burden of family separations
> troubled teenagers who have no safe places left to go

Leader. This bread has been presented and blessed. *[Reader 4 raises the bread.]* Take and eat, knowing that our lives are forever changed by this, and every, breaking of the bread. *[The bread is passed and eaten.]*

Reader 5. *[Holding up a plate or bowl of cornbread]* Let cornbread signify our African American, Hispanic and Latino, Native American, Asian American, Appalachian, and homosexual sisters and brothers who have suffered and continue to suffer discrimination, racism, and oppression.

> Let it remind us of the past from which they have come and the struggle they continue to this day.

> Let us not forget the equality, fairness, freedom, and dignity that are the right of each individual not only in this country but throughout the world.

Leader. This bread has been presented and blessed. *[Reader 5 raises the bread.]* Take and eat, knowing that our lives are forever changed by this, and every, breaking of the bread. *[The bread is passed and eaten.]*

Reader 6. *[Holding up a plate or bowl of nut bread]* Nut bread represents women and men who are considered crazy in our society because they are incomprehensible to most people:

> those who are homeless
> those who are mentally ill
> those who suffer addiction or AIDS
> the dreamers, the visionaries, the prophets among us

Leader. This bread has been presented and blessed. *[Reader 6 raises the bread.]* Take and eat, knowing that our lives are forever changed by this, and every, breaking of the bread. *[The bread is passed and eaten.]*

Closing Prayers

Reader 7.

We pray, then, good and gracious God,
that we might recognize you in this bread
today.
It is the bread of heaven,
the bread of the poor,
the bread of our lives.

Reader 8.

We are here to give ourselves to you and
your people.
It is through what we are and do
that others come to know you.

Reader 9.

We are here to bring peace to a broken
people,
and healing to those in need.

Reader 10.

We are here to witness to the world
that we live in response to a desperate
society,
seeking truth, equality, and freedom.

Reader 11.

We are called to stand together,
sharing our many gifts.
And so, let us join together
in prayer.

All.

God of the poor and oppressed, we ask for
your help.
Teach us to become eyes for those who are
blind,
ears for those who are deaf to your Word,
and hands for those who refuse to work at
building the Reign of God.
We pray all this in your name and for your
honor and glory.
Amen.

Charge and Blessing

Leader.

God of all justice,
we thank you for the gifts you have given
each of us.
We pray that we may always be mindful
of all your people who are in need,
and share our gifts with them.
We ask this through Christ our Lord. Amen.

Closing Song

[The class may sing "For the Life of the World."]

(This prayer service is adapted from one by
Laurie Ziliak, campus minister, Saint Mary's University.)

••••••••••▶ Fourteen Courageous Steps— the Stations of the Cross

Opening Song

[The class may sing a few verses of "Were You There?"]

Station 1: Jesus Was Condemned to Death

Reader 1. Jesus was arrested and taken before the council, where many people testified against him.

Then the high priest stood up before them and asked Jesus, "Have you no answer? What is it that they testify against you?" But he was silent and did not answer. Again the high priest asked him, "Are you the Messiah, the Son of the Blessed One?" Jesus said, "I am; and

> 'you will see the Son of Man
> seated at the right hand of the Power,'
> and 'coming with the clouds of heaven.'"

Then the high priest tore his clothes and said, "Why do we still need witnesses? You have heard his blasphemy! What is your decision?" All of them condemned him as deserving death. Some began to spit on him, to blindfold him, and to strike him, saying to him, "Prophesy!" The guards also took him over and beat him. (Mk 14.60–65)

Leader. Jesus was condemned for something that the high priest did not even understand. Many times, we are criticized, ridiculed, or simply told we are nothing. Think of a time that happened to you. What did you feel like? What did you want to do?

Leader. Lord, have mercy.
All. Lord, have mercy.
Leader. Christ, have mercy.
All. Christ, have mercy.
Leader. Lord, have mercy.
All. Lord, have mercy.

Station 2: Jesus Took Up His Cross

Reader 2.

Then the soldiers led him into the courtyard of the palace (that is, the governor's headquarters); and they called together the whole cohort. And they clothed him in a purple cloak; and after twisting some thorns into a crown, they put it on him. And they began saluting him, "Hail, King of the Jews!" They struck his head with a reed, spat upon him, and knelt down in homage to him. After mocking him, they stripped him of the purple cloak and put his own clothes on him. Then they led him out to crucify him. (Mk 15.16–20)

Leader. Jesus endured great pain even though he was innocent. Have you ever been punished for something you did not do? Remember that time, experience the feelings again, and ask Jesus how he would handle it. We are asked to carry a very light burden compared with Jesus. We carry a sliver of the cross; he carries the remainder.

Leader. Lord, have mercy.
All. Lord, have mercy.
Leader. Christ, have mercy.
All. Christ, have mercy.
Leader. Lord, have mercy.
All. Lord, have mercy.

Handout App C–7: Permission to reproduce this handout for classroom use is granted.

Station 3: Jesus Fell the First Time

Reader 3. The pressure was too much. Jesus was weak from being beaten, bruised, and whipped. He fell with the weight of the cross. The pain was excruciating, but he got back up and began the seemingly long journey to the Place of the Skull, Golgotha.

Leader. What drains you of energy and brings you to the ground? Is it a lack of patience, courage, or understanding? Like Jesus, we need to rise from our downtrodden state.

Leader. Lord, have mercy.
All. Lord, have mercy.
Leader. Christ, have mercy.
All. Christ, have mercy.
Leader. Lord, have mercy.
All. Lord, have mercy.

Station 4: Jesus Met His Mother

Reader 4. Mary said: "I look into his eyes. There is so much pain. My Son, if I could take away this agony, I would. You still have so much love in your eyes. You are incredible. I love you!"

Leader. How do your parents look at you? What do they see? How do you know they love you? How do you show your love for them?

Leader. Lord, have mercy.
All. Lord, have mercy.
Leader. Christ, have mercy.
All. Christ, have mercy.
Leader. Lord, have mercy.
All. Lord, have mercy.

Station 5: Simon Helped Jesus Carry His Cross

Reader 5. "As [the soldiers] led [Jesus] away, they seized a man, Simon of Cyrene, who was coming from the country, and they laid the cross on him, and made him carry it behind Jesus" (Lk 23.26).

Leader. Who is with you through the good times and the bad times? Who is there to help you carry your cross? How does this person help you? How do you help this person?

Leader. Lord, have mercy.
All. Lord, have mercy.
Leader. Christ, have mercy.
All. Christ, have mercy.
Leader. Lord, have mercy.
All. Lord, have mercy.

Station 6: Veronica Wiped the Face of Jesus

Reader 6. Veronica said: "I see him from a distance. As he comes closer, I see the sweat, blood, and tears. I wipe his face. It is the least I can do. He has done so much for me."

Leader. Compassion is a virtue. To help one another is a gift. How have you been kind to your family, friends, and even strangers? Veronica wiped the face of Jesus with love, compassion, and sorrow. How do we do this for others?

Leader. Lord, have mercy.
All. Lord, have mercy.
Leader. Christ, have mercy.
All. Christ, have mercy.
Leader. Lord, have mercy.
All. Lord, have mercy.

Station 7: Jesus Fell the Second Time

Reader 7. With each step, the cross became heavier. The pain was agonizing. Jesus fell again. The weight was constant, the pressure consistent.

Leader. All of us have continuous sources of stress. These become a heavy burden and may cause fatigue. What are ongoing sources of stress for you?

Leader. Lord, have mercy.
All. Lord, have mercy.
Leader. Christ, have mercy.
All. Christ, have mercy.
Leader. Lord, have mercy.
All. Lord, have mercy.

Station 8:
Jesus Met the Women of Jerusalem

Reader 8.

A great number of the people followed [Jesus], and among them were women who were beating their breasts and wailing for him. But Jesus turned to them and said, "Daughters of Jerusalem, do not weep for me, but weep for yourselves and for your children. For the days are surely coming when they will say, 'Blessed are the barren, and the wombs that never bore, and the breasts that never nursed.' Then they will begin to say to the mountains, 'Fall on us'; and to the hills, 'Cover us.' For if they do this when the wood is green, what will happen when it is dry?" (Lk 23.27–31)

Leader. Even when he was wracked with pain, Jesus thought of others. Who believes in you and always thinks of you: friends, family members, teachers? What inspiration do they provide?
Leader. Lord, have mercy.
All. Lord, have mercy.
Leader. Christ, have mercy.
All. Christ, have mercy.
Leader. Lord, have mercy.
All. Lord, have mercy.

Station 9: Jesus Fell the Third Time

Reader 9. Once again, the weight was just too much. Jesus fell for the third time. Then he gathered the last bit of strength he had, got up, and carried his cross onward.
Leader. When do you feel exhausted but just keep going? What makes you continue?
Leader. Lord, have mercy.
All. Lord, have mercy.
Leader. Christ, have mercy.
All. Christ, have mercy.
Leader. Lord, have mercy.
All. Lord, have mercy.

Station 10:
Jesus Was Stripped of His Garments

Reader 10. When they reached Golgotha, the soldiers stripped Jesus of his garments. They cast lots to split his clothes among themselves.
Leader. Being stripped is a shameful experience and can cause great doubt. When have you felt stripped of your defenses and naked in front of the world?
Leader. Lord, have mercy.
All. Lord, have mercy.
Leader. Christ, have mercy.
All. Christ, have mercy.
Leader. Lord, have mercy.
All. Lord, have mercy.

Station 11: Jesus Was Nailed to the Cross

Reader 11. The soldiers laid Jesus on the cross, spread his arms, and drove a stake through each of his wrists. The first stake sent waves of excruciating pain up and down his body. The second was worse. The soldiers raised his knees and crossed his feet and drove a stake through the arch of each foot.
Leader. When Jesus was nailed to the cross, he could no longer move. What holds you stationary? What keeps you from accomplishing your dreams?
Leader. Lord, have mercy.
All. Lord, have mercy.
Leader. Christ, have mercy.
All. Christ, have mercy.
Leader. Lord, have mercy.
All. Lord, have mercy.

Station 12: Jesus Died on the Cross

Reader 12. It was around midday, and the sky became dark. Jesus cried out, "My God, my God, why have you forsaken me?" Jesus uttered a loud cry, and died.

Leader. At times, there seems to be no hope. What hopes, beliefs, ideals, and dreams have died or been lost for you?

Leader. Lord, have mercy.

All. Lord, have mercy.

Leader. Christ, have mercy.

All. Christ, have mercy.

Leader. Lord, have mercy.

All. Lord, have mercy.

Station 13: Jesus Was Taken Off the Cross

Reader 13. The soldiers came to break the legs of those who were not dead. When they saw that Jesus was dead, they pierced his side; blood and water poured out. They took Jesus off the cross. Joseph of Arimathea gathered his body to bury him.

Leader. Think about the people who have been there to pick you up, clean you off, and take care of your needs. How have you felt when they have done that?

Leader. Lord, have mercy.

All. Lord, have mercy.

Leader. Christ, have mercy.

All. Christ, have mercy.

Leader. Lord, have mercy.

All. Lord, have mercy.

Station 14: Jesus Was Laid in a Tomb

Reader 14.

So Joseph took the body and wrapped it in a clean linen cloth and laid it in his own new tomb, which he had hewn in the rock. He then rolled a great stone to the door of the tomb and went away. Mary Magdalene and the other Mary were there, sitting opposite the tomb. (Mt 27.59–60)

Leader. Jesus was put to rest. Where do you go to get rest and to rejuvenate? What is your sacred space like?

Leader. Lord, have mercy.

All. Lord, have mercy.

Leader. Christ, have mercy.

All. Christ, have mercy.

Leader. Lord, have mercy.

All. Lord, have mercy.

Closing Prayer

Leader. Dear Jesus, thank you for taking us on this journey. Many times, we feel troubled, beaten up by life, and just ready to give up hope. Please help us to realize that we can always come to you because you will understand.

You suffered for us, and you brought us abundant life by your Resurrection. You cried, you died, and you rose.

[The class might sing the remaining verses of "Were You There?"]

(This prayer service is from Debra Thorpe, Notre Dame Academy, Los Angeles, California.)

Opening Words and Readings

Leader. Jesus has told us that he is the light of the world and that he will dispel the darkness. Today, as we pray together, let us choose light. Let us commit ourselves to living an examined life, one in which we consciously and deliberately choose God.

Reader 1. Why should we choose God? Is there not pain, betrayal, temptation, and persecution when we follow the words of Jesus? That path is not easy, and it may cause rejection.

Reader 2. "Blessed are you when people hate you, and when they exclude you, revile you, and defame you on account of the Son of Man" (Lk 6.22).

Reader 3. "Love your enemies, do good to those who hate you, bless those who curse you, pray for those who abuse you" (Lk 6.27).

All. These words are not ones we hear often. Jesus Christ, be with us now. Open our hearts and give us the courage to say yes to you.

Reflection Activity

[Everyone thinks of all the messages and obstacles that keep them from saying yes to God, and writes those on a piece of black paper.]

Reader 4.

No good tree bears bad fruit, nor again does a bad tree bear good fruit; for each tree is known by its own fruit. . . . The good person out of the good treasure of the heart produces good, and the evil person out of evil treasure produces evil; for it is out of the abundance of the heart that the mouth speaks. (Lk 6.43–45)

All. Teach us to follow the good treasure of the heart and produce good. Let us tear the evil from our lives and choose God again. Let us again say yes to God.

[Everyone tears their black paper into pieces and uses the pieces to form the word "YES" on a piece of white paper.]

Prayers of the Faithful

Leader. We bring our needs to you, God.

[Everyone shares their individual needs. After each petition, the class responds, "Lord, hear our prayer."]

Leader. It is a struggle to say yes, but with a firm resolve and the support of this Christian community, we can do it!

All. In all the good times, and all the bad times, we choose your ways, O God. We choose the cross, knowing that with the pain comes the glory of Christ. We choose the good, the light, the whole, the holy. We say yes to you, this day. Amen.

Retreat Outlines

Retreat 1: A Day of Reflection on Creation

This mini-retreat is a roughly 5½-hour experience and can take place on or off campus. The focus is a prayerful interpretation of and reflection on each day of Creation. Arranging for students and other adults and teens to present some of the readings and talks can enhance the retreat experience. Before you conduct the retreat, recruit people to help you with those activities.

Preparation

Gather the following materials:
- [ ] paper
- [ ] pens or pencils
- [ ] newsprint and markers
- [ ] tape
- [ ] a tape or CD player
- [ ] a sound recording of instrumental music
- [ ] a pillar candle and matches
- [ ] small candles, one for each person (see the suggestion that follows this list)
- [ ] tapers
- [ ] Bibles
- [ ] symbolic objects for the prayer space, such as flowers and a crucifix (optional)
- [ ] copies of the hymnal *Gather Comprehensive,* edited by Robert J. Batastini and Michael A. Cymbala (Chicago: GIA Publications, 1994) (optional)
- [ ] music and lyrics for the song "This Little Light of Mine" (in *Gather Comprehensive*) or another song about being a light for Christ
- [ ] a television and VCR
- [ ] the videotape *A Universe Drama in Three Acts* (Maryknoll World Productions, 1996, 15 min.)
- [ ] a sound recording of water with instrumental music
- [ ] a sound recording of "Song Over the Waters," by Marty Haugen, from Haugen's album *Anthology 2: 1985–1989* (GIA Publications, 1999) (optional)
- [ ] a bowl of water
- [ ] pictures or slides of beautiful vegetation, and any necessary projection equipment
- [ ] clay pots, one for each student
- [ ] paint and brushes
- [ ] potting soil
- [ ] seeds
- [ ] a sound recording of "The Sower," by Marty Haugen, from the album *The Song of Mark* (GIA Publications), or a similar song (optional)

☐ a sound recording of "We Praise You," by the Dameans, from the album *Gather,* or another song of praise to God

☐ wire, glue, a hammer and nails, string, and so forth

☐ a sound recording of "Under the Sea," from the soundtrack for Disney's movie *The Little Mermaid* (1997)

☐ a clip from the movie *Dances with Wolves* (Orion Home Video, 1990, 181 min., rated PG-13) or another movie valuing animals

☐ a clip from the movie *The Lion King* (Walt Disney Home Video, 1995, 88 min., rated G) (optional)

☐ a sound recording of a song about God's breathing life into us, how wonderfully we are made, and reverence for life

☐ a sound recording of "All You Works of God," from the album *How Can I Keep from Singing* (GIA Publications, 1997)

☐ butcher paper (optional)

☐ finger paints

☐ a sound recording, or lyrics and music (in *Gather Comprehensive*), for one of the following songs or for another song that celebrates creation:

  ☐ "Canticle of the Sun," by Marty Haugen, from Haugen's album *Instruments of Peace* (GIA Publications, 1996)

  ☐ "Sing Out Earth and Skies," by Tom Conry

  ☐ "Sing to the Mountains," by Bob Dufford

On small slips of paper, write the names of parts of God's creation, such as a willow tree blowing in the wind, an anteater, a snail, waves, and lightning. Put the same item on each of four slips, and make enough slips for everyone in the class. (You might use pictures of the items instead of names.)

List on newsprint the following questions, and post the list where everyone can see it:

- What in nature are you most like? Why?
- Have you ever been deeply touched by or in awe of nature? If so, describe your experience.
- What is the scariest thing about nature (or things in nature) for you?

At the front or center of your prayer space, display a pillar candle, small candles for the students, tapers, and Bibles. You might also want to include symbolic objects such as flowers and a crucifix.

For the small candles the students use in this retreat, you might want to put an inch of sand in the bottom of plastic glasses and then place a votive candle or tea light in each glass. This will eliminate the possibility of dripping, and it will also look nice.

1. Welcome, Icebreaker, and Introduction (20 minutes)

As the students arrive, welcome them and give them each a slip of paper identifying a part of God's creation. Then give everyone the following directions in your own words:

- All of you, at the same time, act out the element of creation written on your slip, without saying its name out loud, and look for others acting out the same element. Once you have found those others, discuss in your small group the questions posted on newsprint.

Allow the groups about 10 minutes to form and discuss.

When time is up, gather the students around the objects you have arranged at the front or center of the prayer space, and explain the general plan for the day. Encourage the young people to be open to the experience and to enter into the reflection, discussion, and other activities in a positive, cooperative spirit.

2. Opening Reading, Talk, and Prayer: Let There Be Light (20 minutes)

Dim the lights in the room and play instrumental music in the background. Read the following verses from Psalm 43 while you light a pillar candle:

> O send out your light and your truth;
>   let them lead me;
> let them bring me to your holy hill
>   and to your dwelling.
> Then I will go to the altar of God,
>   to God my exceeding joy;
> and I will praise you with the harp,
>   O God, my God.

(Verses 3–4)

Read Gen 1.1–5 and talk with the students, sharing thoughts and personal experiences as follows:
- Point out that light and dark were the first things God created.
- Discuss the symbol of light and how even one candle can penetrate the darkness.
- Reflect on how the darkness of negativity, evil, and some world values can cast shadows on our world of light.
- Discuss how we can be "light" to one another.

Give each student a small candle, and invite everyone to come up to the pillar candle and use a taper to light their small candle. Ask the students to take their candle back to their place and reflect on the burning flame and how that little light can represent the burning light of faith within us. (If you are concerned about your students carrying lighted candles back to their seats, ask the young people to light their small candles and leave them in the display.)

After all the candles have been lit, lead the students in singing together "This Little Light of Mine" or another song about being a light for Christ. Then direct the students to blow out their candles and return them to the display.

3. Video Presentation and Discussion, Part 1 (15 minutes)

Show the first act of the video *A Universe Drama in Three Acts*. This is a beautiful video that tells the story of Creation vividly and with a scientific twist.

Discuss with the students their impressions of the video, its filming, and anything that they found interesting or fascinating about it.

4. Reading and Talk: Water (10 minutes)

Ask the students to sit quietly and listen to a Scripture reading while you play background music. Then play a sound recording of water and instrumental music as you read Gen 1.6–8.

Reflect on the following ideas in a short talk, or ask another teacher or a student to do so:
- the role of water and bodies of water (oceans, etc.) in the world
- the role of water in our bodies (We are made up of a lot of water!)
- the role of amniotic fluid in the womb
- our need for water in order to live

- the beauty of rain showers and thunderstorms
- the grandeur of oceans, lakes, and rivers

5. Baptism: A Life-Giving Symbol of Cleansing (5 minutes)

Say a short blessing over a bowl of water, and then invite the students to use the water to bless themselves with the sign of the cross. You might want to play "Song Over the Waters" while the students perform this ritual.

6. Snack Break (10 minutes)

7. Reading and Talk: The Earth and Plants (10 minutes)

Read Gen 1.9–13 aloud. Then show pictures or slides of beautiful vegetation and give a brief talk touching on the following points. (Consider recruiting one or two other people to present this reading and talk.)
- earth, dirt, or soil, and how it makes things grow
- what nutrients must be found in the soil for things to grow well and strong
- what kinds of things we plant ourselves in—positive thinking, good relationships, and so on
- what grows in the garden of our souls

8. Activity: The Sower and the Seeds (30 minutes)

Give each student a small clay pot. Supply paint and brushes, and encourage the young people to decorate their pots with symbols of life. Provide potting soil and seeds, and invite the students to plant the seeds in their pots. While the students work, you might want to play the song "The Sower" or another such piece of music softly in the background.

9. Video Presentation and Discussion, Part 2 (15 minutes)

Show the second act of the video *A Universe Drama in Three Acts*. This illustrates the sin of destroying creation.

Discuss images and impressions from the video. Allow the students to share honestly and to raise questions for one another.

10. Reading and Talk: The Sun, Moon, and Stars (20 minutes)

Read Gen 1.14–19. Then play the song "We Praise You" or another song of praise to God.

Divide the class into small groups and encourage sharing on these questions:

- As a small child, were you amazed with the sun, moon, or stars? Why or why not?
- What do you find most amazing about those heavenly objects now?
- Why do children draw those objects in their pictures?
- Why do people wear jewelry fashioned after them?

11. Lunch Break (30 minutes)

Before breaking for lunch, instruct the students each to go outside during the break and to bring back an item from nature that tells them something about who God is.

12. Nature Sharing (20 minutes)

When the students return after lunch, display a large object from nature, such as a log or rock, and explain what it tells you about God. Invite the young people to take turns sharing the items they found in nature and what those items tell them about God. When everyone is done sharing, help the students attach their items to the large one you have displayed, using tape, wire, glue, a hammer and nails, string, and so forth.

13. Scripture Search: Creatures of the Sea and Air (30 minutes)

Play the song "Under the Sea." Break the class into groups, and give each group paper, pens or pencils, and several Bibles. Direct the groups to find as many references to birds and sea creatures as they can in the Scriptures, and to list those creatures on their paper, including cites.

After 20 minutes, discuss the stories and images with the students.

14. Reading and Talk: Land Creatures (20 minutes)

Read Gen 1.20–25 and talk about what makes animals special. Then show a clip from the movie *Dances with Wolves* or another movie in which animals are valued and appreciated. Possibly also show a clip from Disney's movie *The Lion King* in which the "circle of life" is discussed. Talk about the notion of stewardship and how we are called to live it out. (Consider inviting others to handle part or all of this activity.)

15. Break and Cleanup (10 minutes)

16. Reading and Talk: The Creation of Humans (20 minutes)

Read Gen 1.26–31 and 2.1–7, and discuss the intimate nature of God's creating humans by breathing life into them.

Read Psalm 139 and discuss how "wonderfully made" we are. Note that reverence for life is our responsibility. Play the song "All You Works of God."

17. Art Activity: Creation Murals (40 minutes)

Divide the class into seven groups and give each group a long piece of butcher paper or newsprint. Provide finger paints and assign each group one of the seven days of Creation. Direct the groups each to paint a mural for their day of Creation. When the groups are all done, direct them to clean up and post the murals in order around the room.

18. Closing Prayers, and Video Presentation, Part 3 (30 minutes)

Invite the students to gather together for prayer and to sit with their groups from the mural-painting activity. Assign each group four or five verses from Ps 104.5–34, and call the groups to read their passages aloud in turn.

Show the third act from the video *A Universe Drama in Three Acts*.

Invite the students to take turns offering prayers of thanksgiving for the wonders and marvels of creation. After each prayer, call the student who gave it to come up, use a taper to light his or her small candle from the pillar candle, and then return to his or her seat.

Play or sing "Canticle of the Sun," "Sing Out Earth and Skies," "Sing to the Mountains," or any other appropriate song that celebrates creation.

Pray together the Lord's Prayer and offer one another a sign of peace.

Join in a final "Amen."

Retreat 2: A Day of Reflection Based on the Letter to the Philippians

This is a roughly 5½-hour experience based on the Letter of Paul to the Philippians. It could serve as a day of reflection or mini-retreat within the school day. Arranging for students and other adults and teens to present some of the readings and talks can enhance the retreat experience. Before you conduct the retreat, recruit people to help you with those activities.

Preparation

Gather the following materials:
- [ ] paper
- [ ] pens or pencils
- [ ] pieces of poster board or white drawing paper, one for every two students
- [ ] colored markers
- [ ] used magazines
- [ ] scissors
- [ ] glue
- [ ] tape
- [ ] a bag or bowl of multicolored candies like Skittles or M&Ms
- [ ] newsprint
- [ ] a Bible
- [ ] a pillar candle and matches

☐ symbolic objects for the prayer space, such as flowers and a crucifix (optional)

☐ copies of handout App D–1, "A Day of Reflection Based on the Letter to the Philippians," one for each student

☐ a tape or CD player

☐ copies of the hymnal *Gather Comprehensive,* edited by Robert J. Batastini and Michael A. Cymbala (Chicago: GIA Publications, 1994) (optional)

☐ a sound recording, or music and lyrics (in *Gather Comprehensive*), for "Light of Christ/Exsultet," by Marty Haugen, from *Gather Us In* (GIA Publications, 1987), or for another song with the theme of God's love, light, and peace

☐ a sound recording, or music and lyrics, for a contemporary song of thanks for others

☐ thank-you notes, envelopes, and stamps, one of each for each student

☐ a sound recording, or music and lyrics, for a popular or contemporary song about love

☐ a bag of jelly candy worms (optional)

☐ a sound recording, or music and lyrics, for a popular or contemporary song about humility

☐ a sound recording, or music and lyrics, for a popular or contemporary song about working toward a heavenly goal

☐ a sound recording of soft instrumental music

Count the number of colors in the bag of multicolored candies you obtain, and write on newsprint an equal number of questions like these:

- In the last day or so, who did something nice for you that you're thankful for? What was it like to be the recipient of that act of kindness?
- If you could give any nonmaterial gift to your best friend, what would it be?
- Who can make you really laugh? Why?
- Whose love for you has made a significant difference in your life? Tell a bit about that person and how he or she has influenced you.
- What is one humbling experience that you have had?
- Do you have any heavenly goals—that is, goals that might help bring about the Reign of God? If so, what are they?

Using markers in the same colors as the candies, draw a different-colored dot before each question. For example, if you are using Skittles, write five sentences on the newsprint and mark each sentence with a purple, red, orange, yellow, or green dot.

At the front or center of your prayer space, display a Bible and a pillar candle. You may also include symbolic objects such as flowers and a crucifix.

You might want to invite students to help you select and obtain contemporary music for this retreat.

1. Welcome and Icebreaker (10 minutes)

When everyone has arrived, welcome the students to this retreat experience. Then pass around a bag or bowl of colored candies. Direct the students each to take a candy without looking in the bag. Explain that whatever color candy a student gets, he or she must answer the corresponding question from the list posted on newsprint. Mention that the students need not use names when answering the questions, that they may instead refer to other people by titles such as "a neighbor" and "an aunt." Go around the group two or three times, or as long as the students are engaged in the activity.

2. Introduction (30 minutes)

Pass out paper, and pens or pencils. Ask everyone to think of one word that represents the secret to a fulfilling life for them, and to write that word on their paper. When everyone is done, tell the students to find one other person who wrote down the same word or a synonym—for example, if they wrote *happiness,* they should find someone who wrote *happy, joy, smile,* or something like that. Help any students who have trouble—and get creative about connecting words if necessary.

Once everyone has a partner, tell the students that they will now have a wonderful opportunity to share their secrets to a fulfilling life with one another. Provide poster board or large sheets of white drawing paper, colored markers, used magazines, scissors, and glue, and give the following directions:

- Create a slogan for fulfilling Christian living that includes the word or words you wrote on your sheets of paper. The slogan should be ten words or less, original, and creative. Write it on your poster, and decorate your poster with drawings and symbols and pictures.

Give the pairs about 10 minutes to create their posters, then another 10 minutes to clean up, hang their posters in the prayer space, and take a look at one another's work.

Gather the students and make the following comments in your own words:

- Paul wrote the Letter to the Philippians to share his thoughts about the best way to live a fulfilling life in Christ. When he wrote the letter, he was a prisoner on a charge that could have him put to death. Although he was not afraid to die, Paul felt that he would live in order to support the Philippians and the other new churches he had helped to start. His letter urged the Philippians to imitate Christ by keeping a positive attitude, humbling themselves, becoming servants, and being obedient to God.

Explain that this day of reflection centers on the themes found in the Letter to the Philippians. It is primarily a day of thanksgiving, love, and humility. Encourage the students to be open to the experience.

3. Opening Prayer (10 minutes)

Handout **App D–1**

Invite the students to prayer by lighting a pillar candle and asking them to place themselves in the presence of Christ. Pass out copies of handout App D–1 and begin the prayer as follows:

Leader. "Grace to you and peace from God our Father and the Lord Jesus Christ" (Phil 1.2).
All. And also with you.

Play or sing the introduction and refrain from the song "Light of Christ/Exsultet" or another song with the theme of God's love, light, and peace.

Leader. Dear God, let your love enfold us as we spend this time together today.
     Let your light shine before us and illuminate the words we will hear spoken.
     Let us find your presence in all we meet and do today. We ask this in Christ's name.
All. Amen

Extinguish the candle.

4. Reading and Talk: Thanks to You (20 minutes)

Read Phil 1.3–5:

> I thank my God every time I remember you, constantly praying with joy in every one of my prayers for all of you, because of your sharing in the gospel from the first day until now.

Using those Scripture verses, give a talk that addresses the following points:
- Define thanks.
- Pose these questions:
    - What people are you thankful for?
    - Why do you thank God for them?
    - What have they taught you?
- Share a specific, personal story, and invite the students to do so as well. Play or sing a contemporary song that sums up the points of this talk.

5. Snack Break (10 minutes)

6. Reflection Activity: Writing Thank-You Notes (20 minutes)

Distribute thank-you notes, envelopes, and stamps, and give the following instructions in your own words:
    - Call to mind a person you are thankful for. Quietly, in your heart, picture that person and thank God for all that she or he has done in your life.
    - Write a thank-you note to that person.
Allow time for the students to write their notes. When everyone is done, direct the young people to address and stamp their envelopes and mail their notes. Note that they may do this at home if they do not know the recipient's address.

7. Reading and Talk: Love One Another (20 minutes)

Read Phil 1.9–10:

> And this is my prayer, that your love may overflow more and more with knowledge and full insight to help you to determine what is best.

Using those Scripture verses, give a talk that touches on the following points:
- Define love.
- Ask, "How does one show love in relationships?"
- Explain that love is a decision, and that according to Jesus, love means actions, not just words.
- Address these questions:
    - How does love help one make right decisions?
    - How does Jesus' view of love help one determine what is best in a situation?
    Play or sing a popular or contemporary song that sums up the points of this talk.

8. Reflection Activity: Creating Musical Jingles (20 minutes)

Divide the class into groups; distribute paper, and pens or pencils; and instruct the groups each to come up with a musical jingle that calls people to live out Jesus' message of love. Explain that the jingles will be performed live for everyone. Encourage the students to add harmony or simple dance steps, or both, to their jingle. Allow 10 minutes for this preparation.

9. Lunch Break (50 minutes)

10. Presentation: Performing the Musical Jingles (15 minutes)

Call each group up to present its jingle. Discuss any interesting points made in the jingles.

11. Reading and Talk: Humble Yourself (20 minutes)

Read Phil 2.3–4:

> Do nothing from selfish ambition or conceit, but in humility regard others as better than yourselves. Let each of you look not to your own interests, but to the interests of others.

Using those Scripture verses, give a talk that touches on the following points:
- Define humility.
- Describe times when you were *not* humble.
- Reflect on why people are boastful.
- Share how being humble is imitating Christ.
- Discuss how Jesus calls us to serve humbly.
  Play or sing a song that reflects the point of this talk.

12. Reflection Activity: Small-Group Discussion (20 minutes)

Divide the class into small groups and direct them each to discuss the following questions:
- What point of the talk on humility affected you the most?
- Is being humble popular in our society? Why or why not?
- Describe some of the most humble people you know. What are they like? Do you admire them?

13. Break and Cleanup (10 minutes)

14. Warm-up Exercise: Humble Worms (10 minutes)

After lunch, help the students form groups of five or six. Then direct the young people to sit on the floor in their groups, all the group members facing forward in a straight line, and to wrap their legs around the person in front of them, forming a worm. Once all the groups have formed their worm, announce that at your signal, the worms are to race, or wiggle, to a designated spot, and whichever group gets there (or there and back) first wins. Give the signal, cheer the contestants, and announce the winners and console the nonwinners. You may want to award the winning group a bag of jelly candy worms.

Give the students a minute or two to settle for the reading and talk that follow.

15. Reading and Talk: A Heavenly Goal (20 minutes)

Read Phil 3.14–15:

> I press on toward the goal for the prize of the heavenly call of God in Christ Jesus. Let those of us then who are mature be of the same mind.

Using those Scripture verses, give a talk that touches on the following points:
- Address these questions:
  - Why should we work toward a heavenly goal?
  - How is such a goal different from the ones often valued in our society?
  - How do the values of being thankful, loving, and humble help us work toward a heavenly goal?
- Personally share how you are striving to live out those values, and invite the students to do the same.
- Motivate the students to press on to the goal.

Play or sing a song that sums up the key points of this talk.

16. Closing Readings, Prayers, and Song (20 minutes)

Place the pillar candle in a central spot near the posters the students created at the beginning of this retreat. Light the candle, and ask the students to quiet themselves and put themselves in God's presence. Play soft instrumental music in the background throughout the closing readings.

Reader 1.

> For God is my witness, how I long for all of you with the compassion of Christ Jesus. And this is my prayer, that your love may overflow more and more with knowledge and full insight to help you to determine what is best, so that in the day of Christ you may be pure and blameless. (Phil 1.8–10)

All. May the light of Christ surround us.
Reader 2.

> Only, live your life in a manner worthy of the gospel of Christ, so that, whether I come and see you or am absent and hear about you, I will know that you are standing firm in one spirit, striving side by side with one mind for the faith of the gospel. (1.27)

All. May the love of Christ enfold us.
Reader 3.

> Beware of the dogs, beware of the evil workers (verse 2). . . .
>
> For many live as enemies of the cross of Christ; I have often told you of them, and now I tell you even with tears. Their end is destruction. (3.18–19)

All. May the power of Christ protect us.

Reader 4.

> Finally, beloved, whatever is true, whatever is honorable, whatever is just, whatever is pure, whatever is pleasing, whatever is commendable, if there is any excellence and if there is anything worthy of praise, think about these things. Keep on doing the things that you have learned and received and heard and seen in me, and the God of peace will be with you. (4.8–9)

All. May the presence of Christ be with us now and always. Amen.

> Ask the students to offer petitions of faith.
> Lead the young people in saying the Lord's Prayer together.

Leader. Greet every saint in Christ Jesus. The friends who are with me greet you. The grace of the Lord Jesus Christ be with your spirit.

All. And also with you.

Leader. Let us offer one another a sign of peace.

Lead the students in sharing a sign of peace.

> Play or sing the rest of the song "Light of Christ/Exsultet" or another song with the theme of God's love, light, and peace.

●●●●●●●●●●●●●●●●●●●▶ A Day of Reflection
Based on the Letter to the Philippians

Opening Prayer

Leader. "Grace to you and peace from God our Father and the Lord Jesus Christ" (Phil 1.2).
All. And also with you.

[The class listens to or sings the introduction and refrain from the song "Light of Christ/Exsultet" or another song with the theme of God's love, light, and peace.]

Leader. Dear God, let your love enfold us as we spend this time together today.

Let your light shine before us and illuminate the words we will hear spoken.

Let us find your presence in all we meet and do today. We ask this in Christ's name.
All. Amen

Closing Readings, Prayers, and Song

[The leader lights the pillar candle and plays soft instrumental music in the background.]

Reader 1.

For God is my witness, how I long for all of you with the compassion of Christ Jesus. And this is my prayer, that your love may overflow more and more with knowledge and full insight to help you to determine what is best, so that in the day of Christ you may be pure and blameless. (Phil 1.8–10)

All. May the light of Christ surround us.
Reader 2.

Only, live your life in a manner worthy of the gospel of Christ, so that, whether I come and see you or am absent and hear about you, I will know that you are standing firm in one spirit, striving side by side with one mind for the faith of the gospel. (1.27)

All. May the love of Christ enfold us.

Reader 3.

Beware of the dogs, beware of the evil workers. (verse 2). . . .

For many live as enemies of the cross of Christ; I have often told you of them, and now I tell you even with tears. Their end is destruction. (3.18–19)

All. May the power of Christ protect us.
Reader 4.

Finally, beloved, whatever is true, whatever is honorable, whatever is just, whatever is pure, whatever is pleasing, whatever is commendable, if there is any excellence and if there is anything worthy of praise, think about these things. Keep on doing the things that you have learned and received and heard and seen in me, and the God of peace will be with you. (4.8–9)

All. May the presence of Christ be with us now and always. Amen.

[Everyone offers petitions of faith.]
[Everyone says the Lord's Prayer together.]

Leader. Greet every saint in Christ Jesus. The friends who are with me greet you. The grace of the Lord Jesus Christ be with your spirit.
All. And also with you.
Leader. Let us offer one another a sign of peace.

[Everyone shares a sign of peace. The class listens to or sings the rest of the song "Light of Christ/ Exsultet" or another song with the theme of God's love, light, and peace.]

Acknowledgments *(continued)*

The scriptural quotations contained herein are from *The Catholic Youth Bible,* by Saint Mary's Press (Winona, MN: Saint Mary's Press, 2000). Copyright © 2000 by Saint Mary's Press. All rights reserved.

The scriptural material described as adapted is freely paraphrased and is not to be used or understood as an official translation of the Bible.

The contents of handout Intro-A are from *Written on Our Hearts: The Old Testament Story of God's Love,* by Mary Reed Newland, revised by Barbara Allaire (Winona, MN: Saint Mary's Press, 1999), pages 13–19. Copyright © 1999 by Saint Mary's Press. All rights reserved.

The extract on page 59 is from *The Catholic Bible: Personal Study Edition,* edited by Jean Marie Hiesberger (New York: Oxford University Press, 1995), page 95. Copyright © 1995 by Oxford University Press.

The extracts on handout Josh–A are from *Aman: The Story of a Somali Girl,* by Virginia Lee Barnes and Janice Boddy (New York: Pantheon Books, 1994), pages 102–109. Copyright © 1994 by Aman and the Estate of Virginia Lee Barnes.

Lord Acton's words on page 82 are quoted from *Familiar Quotations,* by John Bartlett (Boston: Little, Brown and Company, 1980), page 615. Copyright © 1882 by John Bartlett.

Station 1 in the exercise "Seeing Others with God's Eyes," on page 70, is based on the activity "Who Would You Choose?" in *Get 'Em Talking: 104 Great Discussion Starters for Youth Groups,* by Mike Yaconelli and Scott Koenigsaecker ([El Cajon], CA: Youth Specialties; Grand Rapids, MI: Zondervan Publishing House, 1989), page 93. Copyright © 1989 by Youth Specialties.

The extracts on handout 2 Kings–A are from *The Rites of the Catholic Church as Revised by Decree of the Second Vatican Ecumenical Council and Published by Authority of Pope Paul VI,* study edition, by the Catholic Church, English translation prepared by the International Commission on English in the Liturgy (New York: Pueblo Publishing Company, 1990), pages 404 and 161. Copyright © 1976, 1983, 1988, 1990 by Pueblo Publishing Company.

The information about the examen on handout Ps–A comes from *Sleeping with Bread: Holding What Gives You Life,* by Dennis Linn, Sheila Fabricant Linn, and Matthew Linn, SJ (Mahwah, NJ: Paulist Press, 1995), copyright © 1995 by Dennis Linn, Sheila Fabricant Linn, and The Wisconsin Province of the Society of Jesus; and from *The Spiritual Exercises of St. Ignatius: Based on Studies in the Language of the Autograph,* translated by Louis J. Puhl, SJ (Chicago: Loyola University Press, 1951), pages 142–143, copyright © 1951 by The Newman Press. The questions on the handout are adapted from *Sleeping with Bread,* pages 6–7.

The maps on handouts Mt–A and Acts–A are adapted from *The Catholic Youth Bible,* by Saint Mary's Press (Winona, MN: Saint Mary's Press, 2000), pages 1539 and 1540. Copyright © 2000 by Saint Mary's Press. Maps copyright © 2000 by Thomas Nelson, Inc.

The extracts on handout Lk–A are from *The Miracle of Mindfulness: A Manual on Meditation,* revised edition, by Thich Nhat Hanh, translated by Mobi Ho (Boston: Beacon Press, 1987), pages 3–5. Copyright © 1975 by Thich Nhat Hanh. Preface and English translation copyright © 1975 by Mobi Ho. Reprinted by permission of Beacon Press, Boston.

The exercise "The Christian Team" on pages 264–265 is based on the activity "Football Stadium," from *Get 'Em Talking,* by Yaconelli and Koenigsaecker, page 45.

The extracts on handout Rom–B are from "On the Road and on the Sea with St. Paul: Traveling Conditions in the First Century," by Jerome Murphy-O'Connor, OP, in *Bible Review,* volume 1, number 2, summer 1985, pages 38–47. Copyright © 1985 by the Biblical Archaeology Society. Used by permission of the author.

The closing prayer in prayer service 2 and on handout App C–2 is by Theresa Vonderwell, in *More Dreams Alive: Prayers by Teenagers,* edited by Carl Koch (Winona, MN: Saint Mary's Press, 1995), page 28. Copyright © 1995 by Saint Mary's Press. All rights reserved.

The Peace Prayer of Saint Francis of Assisi in prayer service 3 and on handout App C–3 is quoted from *Praying with Francis of Assisi,* by Joseph M. Stoutzenberger and John D. Bohrer (Winona, MN: Saint Mary's Press, 1989), page 54. Copyright © 1989 by Saint Mary's Press. All rights reserved.

The reflection story in prayer service 6 is by Stephanie Piraino and was submitted by Michelle France, Academy of Notre Dame de Namur, Villanova, PA. Copyright by Stephanie Piraino. Permission applied for.

Prayer service 7 is adapted slightly from the long prayer of set 1, "Leaves," in *Prayer Works for Teens,* book 2, by Lisa-Marie Calderone-Stewart (Winona, MN: Saint Mary's Press, 1997), pages 20–23. Copyright © 1997 by Saint Mary's Press. All rights reserved.

The legend in the blessing for prayer service 7 is adapted from *Inspiration from Indian Legends, Proverbs, and Psalms,* page 59, compiled and edited by R. L. Gowan. To order, contact Ray or Marian Gowan, P.O. Box 1526, Rapid City, South Dakota 57709.

Handout Masters

List of Handout Masters

Intro–A A Sprint Through Salvation History

Gen–A The Ups and Downs of Trust

Josh–A Exegetical Tools: What Is Exegesis?
1 Sam–A Jealousy: Saul and Teens Today
2 Kings–A The Presentation of the Lighted Candle
2 Kings–B Disposition and the Path Toward God
2 Kings–C Leadership Report Card

Ps–A The Jesuit Examen: A Simple Form

Isa–A Images of God in Isaiah
Jer–A Jeremiah and Jesus Match
Bar–A Christianity and the Media

Mt–A A Map of First-Century Palestine
Mt–B Characters in Matthew's Passion Narrative
Lk–A The Practice of Mindfulness
Lk–B The *Palestinian Times:* The Good News Edition
Acts–A Paul's Missionary Journeys

Rom–A Contemporary Letters
Rom–B The Nature of Paul's Travels

App C–1 "Let There Be Light!"
App C–2 Sin and Temptation
App C–3 A Rainbow of Hope and Peace
App C–4 "Be Still, and Know That I Am God!"
App C–5 Being a Humble Servant
App C–6 Called to Serve
App C–7 Fourteen Courageous Steps—the Stations of the Cross
App C–8 Saying Yes to Jesus

App D–1 A Day of Reflection Based on the Letter to the Philippians

••••••▶ A Sprint Through Salvation History

The God revealed in the Old Testament is not aloof or distant from human affairs; this God acts within human history. The Story of God's actions and the people's responses over many centuries is called **salvation history.**

It will help to keep the big picture of that history in mind as we set out to discover the meaning of the Old Testament because the history and the Scriptures of ancient Israel were intertwined. . . . Do not be concerned about memorizing names and events at this point; they will come up again many times in this course. Instead, simply try to recognize the broad pattern of history.

First, referring to the timelines on pages [1542 to 1545 of the *CYB*], note the time period in which the biblical events happened. As you can see, humankind existed for many thousands of years before the biblical era; most of that time is called prehistory because no historical records of those ancient peoples exist. (The time period of the Creation and the earliest stories of humankind appearing in the Old Testament fall into the category of prehistory.) About 3000 [B.C.], history as we know it began, with the development of early forms of writing. The biblical period—from the beginnings of Israel as a people through the time of Jesus and the earliest years of the church—went from about 1850 [B.C.] until about [A.D.] 100 It lasted almost two thousand years. And that is about the same amount of time as has elapsed from the time of Jesus until today.

What follows is a brief overview of the events of the biblical period. You may also refer to the [maps on pages 1535 to 1541 of the *CYB*].

The Founders and the Promise

The history and the religion of the Israelites began with Abraham. Abraham was a wandering herdsman, or nomad, who lived in the region now called Iraq, around 1850 [B.C.] According to the Book of Genesis, God made an agreement with Abraham. God promised to make Abraham's descendants a blessing to the world and to give them the land of Canaan, later known as Palestine. The Promise, as this is called, was that Abraham's descendants would reveal the one God to the world. Christians believe that this Promise reached its fulfillment in the coming of Christ.

Abraham's descendants and their families inherited the Promise. Abraham, his son Isaac, and grandson Jacob would be called the patriarchs, or founders, of the Jewish faith. Their wives—Sarah, Rebekah, and Rachel—would be called the matriarchs.

The Exodus of the Israelites and the Covenant

At the close of the Book of Genesis, the descendants of Abraham are living in Egypt, having traveled there from Canaan in order to survive a famine. Yet as the Book of Exodus opens, we find them enslaved by the Egyptians. Practically nothing is known about the Israelites in Egypt from about 1700 to 1290 [B.C.]

Moses, the main character in the story of the Exodus, was one of the greatest religious leaders in history. About 1290 [B.C.], the understanding that one God was above all other gods came to Moses when God revealed God's name—Yahweh, meaning "I am the One who is always present." With God's power the Israelites, led by Moses, made a daring escape from Pharaoh's army through the sea—the Exodus—and were thus freed from slavery.

After a dramatic encounter between Moses and God on Mount Sinai, a covenant, or agreement, between Yahweh and the Israelites was confirmed. The Israelites' part of the Covenant was to keep the Ten Commandments, which God had presented to Moses. God's part was to make the Israelites "the people of God" and to be with them as long as they kept the Covenant. Once again God promised that they would be given the land of Canaan. But before they entered Canaan, they wandered for forty years in the desert as they learned to trust God's care for them.

Taking Over the Promised Land

After Moses' time the Israelites, led by Joshua, entered Canaan. Over the next centuries—from about 1250 to 1000 [B.C.]—they fought against the people who lived in that region. In these battles the Israelites were led by military leaders called judges. During this time the Israelites abandoned their nomadic ways for the more settled agricultural life that was native to the region.

The Nation and the Temple

Around 1000 [B.C.] Israel became recognized as a nation, with David as its anointed king and Jerusalem as its capital city. God made a promise to David that his royal line would endure forever. (Later Jews put their hopes in a descendant of David to save them from oppression.)

David's son Solomon built the Temple in Jerusalem, and it became the principal place of worship for the nation. As both a political and a religious capital, Jerusalem became a great and holy city.

The Kings and the Prophets

After Solomon's death in 922 [B.C.], the nation divided, with the kingdom of Israel in the north and the kingdom of Judah in the south. Heavy taxes and forced service in both kingdoms created hardships for the people. In addition, the kings often practiced idolatry—the worship of idols (images of other gods).

Prophets spoke out against both kingdoms' injustices to the people and infidelity to God. They questioned the behavior of the kings and called them and their people back to the Covenant. Yet the kingdoms continued to oppress the poor and worship pagan gods until eventually both kingdoms were crushed by powerful conquerors. The Assyrians obliterated the northern kingdom of Israel in 721 [B.C.] and took its people into exile. In 587 [B.C.] the Babylonians destroyed Judah, including the city of Jerusalem, and took its people to Babylon as captives.

The Babylonian Exile and the Jewish Disperson

While the people were exiled in Babylon, still other prophets encouraged them to repent of their sins and turn back to God. During this time the prophet known as Second Isaiah proclaimed that God was the one and only God. Monotheism, the belief in one God, was now the revelation of this people to the world, their blessing to the nations.

After fifty years in Babylon, the exiles were released from captivity by the conquering Persians and allowed to return home. Judah, no longer a politically independent kingdom, had become a district within the Persian Empire, and the returned exiles became known as Jews, from the word *Judah.* They rebuilt the Temple, and under Ezra and Nehemiah, they re-established the Law and restored Jerusalem. That city became the religious capital for the Jews who had resettled all over the world—that is, the Jews of the Dispersion.

During the exile the Jewish leaders had begun collecting and reflecting on their ancestral writings, forming the core of what would later become their Bible, known to Christians as the Old Testament.

More Oppressors

The Persian Empire was conquered in 330 [B.C.] by the armies of Alexander the Great, leader of the Greek Empire. This made the Greeks overlords of the Jews for nearly three hundred years, with the exception of a brief period of independence after a revolt led by the Maccabees family. The Greeks were followed by the Romans, who captured Jerusalem in 63 [B.C.] Although tolerant of other cultures and religions, the Roman Empire severely punished its subjects for revolts.

It was a dark time for the people of the Promise, who longed for release from oppression and for the day when all their hopes for a good and peaceful life would be fulfilled. Many Jews looked toward the coming of a messiah, one sent by God to save them; some expected this messiah to be from the family line of David.

It is at this point in the history of Israel that the Old Testament accounts end. . . .

Jesus, the Savior

Into a situation of defeat and darkness for the people of Israel, Jesus was born, one of the house, or family line, of David. Christians see Jesus as the long-awaited Messiah—the fulfillment of all God's promises to Israel and the Savior of the world. With his death and Resurrection, Jesus' followers recognized that he was the Son of God. The community of believers began to grow, first among Jews but later among Gentiles, or non-Jews. The story of Jesus and the growth of the early church is told in the New Testament.

••••••••••••••►The Ups and Downs of Trust

Read or review the Bible stories about Abraham listed below. Then assess Abraham's level of trust in God in each account (high, medium, or low) and mark a dot at that level on the scale below the Bible cite. When you have assessed the trust level in all the accounts, connect the dots and make a graph. Below the graph, in a different color ink, write some important events in your own life and graph your own level of trust in God during those events. Compare the two graphs.

Abraham's life	Gen 12.1–9	Gen 12.10–20	Gen 15.1–6	Gen 16.1–6	Genesis, chapter 17	Gen 18.22–23	Gen 22.1–19

High --

Medium --

Low --

My own life							

High --

Medium --

Low --

▶ Exegetical Tools: What Is Exegesis?

Read the following passage and write some conclusions you can draw about the speaker:

> After three weeks we decided to get married. He spent a night in our town with my uncle so he could pick me up in the morning. I stopped by the night before to make the arrangements. . . . I went straight to see my niece, who was like a sister to me. I told her I would need her the next morning. It took me about two hours to explain to her what was going on, but finally she understood and she agreed to go with me. I went home and had dinner with Mama. . . . I took the dress I wanted to wear with me and went back to my niece's house. (Virginia Lee Barnes and Janice Boddy, *Aman: The Story of a Somali Girl* [New York: Pantheon Books, 1994], pages 107–108. Copyright © 1994 by Aman and the Estate of Virginia Lee Barnes.)

Conclusions you can draw about the speaker:

_____

_____

_____

_____

_____

- ✂

Read the following statements by the same speaker, and then write some observations about these thoughts and the previous statement:

> I remember I was thirteen years and seven months old when I was married. (Page 102)

> We had a great, great dinner, and then I asked her if I could spend the night over at my niece's because it was Ramadan and there would be feasting and reading of the Qur'an over there. (Page 108)

> In the car, about halfway back, I told him he had to give me some money. I wanted to go to Mogadishu. (Virginia Lee Barnes and Janice Boddy, *Aman: The Story of a Somali Girl* [New York: Pantheon Books, 1994], page 109. Copyright © 1994 by Aman and the Estate of Virginia Lee Barnes.)

Your observations about the thoughts listed here and about the previous statement:

_____

_____

_____

_____

_____

•••••••••••▶ Jealousy: Saul and Teens Today

Jealousy is a very powerful and familiar human emotion. All people experience some level of jealousy. At times jealousy can be quite strong. Occasionally, jealousy leads a person to do dangerous or damaging things. Read 1 Samuel, chapters 18–19, and rate the following examples of Saul's jealousy of David as Normal, Strong, or Dangerous by checking the appropriate column. Then think of examples of Normal, Strong, and Dangerous jealousy that you observe in the lives of teens and write them out in the proper column. Conclude by giving advice to Saul and your peers about how to deal with jealousy.

Examples from the life of Saul	Normal jealousy	Strong jealousy	Dangerous jealousy
1 Sam 18.8–9			
1 Sam 18.10–11			
1 Sam 18.12–13			
1 Sam 18.17–19			
1 Sam 18.20–29			
1 Sam 19.8–10			
1 Sam 19.11–17			
Examples from the lives of teens today	Normal jealousy	Strong jealousy	Dangerous jealousy

What advice would you give to Saul to ease his jealousy? What helps teens deal successfully with jealousy?

Read the following passages from the baptismal rites for children and adults. Note that Elisha's call by Elijah shares characteristics with a new Christian's call by Christ.

Number 100 from the Rite of Baptism for Children
Parents and godparent (or godparents), this light is entrusted to you to be kept burning brightly. This child of yours has been enlightened by Christ. He (she) is to walk always as a child of the light. May he (she) keep the flame of faith alive in his (her) heart. When the Lord comes, may he (she) go out to meet him with all the saints in the heavenly kingdom. (Page 404)

Number 230 from the Rite of Christian Initiation of Adults
You have been enlightened by Christ.
Walk always as children of the light
and keep the flame of faith alive in your hearts.
When the Lord comes, may you go out to meet him
with all the saints in the heavenly kingdom.

(*The Rites of the Catholic Church as Revised by Decree of the Second Vatican Ecumenical Council and Published by Authority of Pope Paul VI,* study edition, by the Catholic Church, English translation prepared by the International Commission on English in the Liturgy [New York: Pueblo Publishing Company, 1990], page 161. Copyright © 1976, 1983, 1988, 1990 by Pueblo Publishing Company.)

.... ▶ Disposition and the Path Toward God

Finish the sentences in column 1 from your own perspective, putting down the first thing that comes to your mind. Your teacher will explain how to fill out the rest of the chart.

My own disposition	The disposition of characters in 2 Kings, chapter 5	Did the character in column 2 help or hinder God's will?	Do my dispositions help or hinder God's will?
I suffer . . .	Suffering Character: Verse:		
I help . . .	Helping Character: Verse:		
I fear . . .	Fearing Character: Verse:		
I am confident . . .	Confident Character: Verse:		
I am arrogant . . .	Arrogant Character: Verse:		
I am grateful . . .	Grateful Character: Verse:		
I am generous . . .	Generous Character: Verse:		
I am selfless . . .	Selfless Character: Verse:		
I am greedy . . .	Greedy Character: Verse:		
I deceive . . .	Deceiving Character: Verse:		

•••••••••••••••••••► Leadership Report Card

For each of the following biblical kings, read the Scripture passage listed and give the king a traditional letter grade (A to F). Then list three modern leaders and grade them as well. Write a comment about each leader in the space provided—either an affirmation for good work or a critique for areas that need improvement. Finally, answer the reflection question below the chart.

Grading period: Ancient Judah	Grading period: Present-day leaders
King Jehoram (2 Kings 8.16–24) Grade: Comments:	Name: Grade: Comments:
King Hezekiah (2 Kings, chapters 18–20) Grade: Comments:	Name: Grade: Comments:
King Manasseh (2 Kings 21.1–18) Grade: Comments:	Name: Grade: Comments:

In what ways does your assessment of current leaders resemble the assessment of Jewish leaders found in 2 Kings?

•••••• ► The Jesuit Examen: A Simple Form

Saint Ignatius of Loyola believed that daily experiences of faith, hope, joy, and love for which we are grateful are signs of God's presence, and that we should try to repeat and emphasize them. He further believed that experiences that regularly make us feel sad, hopeless, doubtful, and lonely may be areas in need of God's love and grace. To help us identify and reflect on both types of experiences, he created a prayer exercise called the examen, which he described in his guide *The Spiritual Exercises.* This handout presents a simple form of the exercise that is a prayerful means of reviewing your day, week, year, and so on. It can be done alone or with others.

1. Before going to sleep, quiet yourself and imagine God's love for you.

2. Together with God, look over your day and ask yourself this pair of questions:
   - For what experience today am I most grateful?
   - For what experience today am I least grateful?

   Also reflect on these questions if you wish to:
   - When today did I give and receive the most love? When today did I give and receive the least love?
   - When today did I feel the most alive? When today did I feel the most drained of life?
   - When today did I have the greatest sense of belonging to myself, others, God, and the universe? When today did I have the least sense of belonging?
   - When today was I happiest? When today was I saddest?
   - What was today's high point? What was today's low point?

3. Thank God for the whole day and especially the part that made you feel grateful. Ask God's help for dealing with difficult experiences.

(This information about the examen comes from Dennis Linn, Sheila Fabricant Linn, and Matthew Linn, SJ, *Sleeping with Bread: Holding What Gives You Life* [Mahwah, NJ: Paulist Press, 1995], copyright © 1995 by Dennis Linn, Sheila Fabricant Linn, and The Wisconsin Province of the Society of Jesus; and from *The Spiritual Exercises of St. Ignatius: Based on Studies in the Language of the Autograph,* translated by Louis J. Puhl, SJ [Chicago: Loyola University Press, 1951], pages 142–143, copyright © 1951 by The Newman Press. The questions are adapted from *Sleeping with Bread,* pages 6–7.)

Isa 8.13	Isa 41.10
Isa 8.14	Isa 43.25
Isa 10.18	Isa 44.24
Isa 12.2	Isa 45.7
Isa 13.9	Isa 47.3
Isa 24.1	Isa 49.15
Isa 25.1	Isa 51.12
Isa 25.8	Isa 54.10
Isa 26.4	Isa 55.8–9
Isa 30.18	Isa 62.5
Isa 40.1	Isa 64.8
Isa 40.11	Isa 65.17
Isa 40.28	Isa 66.13

···········► Jeremiah and Jesus Match

Jeremiah and Jesus shared some common experiences during their lifetimes. Look up the following passages for those two men. Decide which experience from column 2 is discussed in each passage, and put the proper letter in the space.

JEREMIAH	Common experiences	**JESUS**
1. Jer 12.6 _____	a. Both are touched by God in the womb of their mother.	1. Lk 4.16–29 _____
2. Jer 31.31–34 _____	b. Both are rejected by friends from home.	2. Lk 22.20 _____
3. Jer 37.17–21 _____	c. Both mourn about the condition of their homeland.	3. Lk 19.28,41–44 _____
4. Jer 8.18–22 _____	d. Both refer to the Temple as a "den of robbers."	4. Jn 3.1–21 _____
5. Jer 1.5 _____	e. Both are consulted fearfully and secretly by believers.	5. Lk 1.26–38 _____
6. Jer 7.11 _____	f. Both speak of the New Covenant.	6. Mt 21.12–13 _____

Reflection Question

Was Jesus a prophet? Why or why not?

·············► Christianity and the Media

Baruch shows that the Jews experienced some conflicts between their own beliefs and the values that they encountered in other cultures while in exile. U.S. Christians sometimes find their beliefs supported by their culture and other times find their values in opposition to their culture. As a class, choose five values that you believe are central to Christianity and list them in the chart below. Then watch a television drama or situation comedy to see how one aspect of U.S. culture reflects U.S. values. Name and describe the show in the spaces provided above the chart, assess the TV show's treatment of each listed Christian value by marking the appropriate box in the chart, and write a short reflection about the show in the space provided below the chart.

Name of TV show:

Date and time watched:

Short plot summary:

Five important Christian values	Treatment of the five important Christian values in the TV show				
	Strongly supported	Supported	Treated neutrally or not addressed	Opposed	Strongly opposed
1.					
2.					
3.					
4.					
5.					

Overall, to what extent did this show support or oppose Christian values? Why?

........► A Map of First-Century Palestine

A Map of First-Century Palestine. Locations shown include Sidon, Damascus, Zarephath, Phoenicia, Mt. Lebanon (11,000), Mt. Hermon (9,200), Iturea, Tyre, Panias (Caesarea Philippi), Trachonitis, Ptolemais, Galilee, Chorazin, Bethsaida?, Capernaum, Gennesarat, Magdala (Magadan), Sea of Galilee, Gergesa, Cana, Tiberias, Mediterranean Sea, Nazareth, Mt. Tabor (1,843), Gadara?, Nain, R. Yarmuk, Esdraelon, R. Jezreel, Caesarea, Scythopolis, Mt. Gilboa (1,696), Decapolis, Samaria, Gerasa, Sychar, R. Jabbok, Mt. Gerizim (2,890), Antipatris, Joppa, Perea, River Jordan, Mt. Carmel (1,742), R. Kishon.

Key: (1,742) Elevation, in feet; ? Exact location questionable. Scale of Miles: 0 10 20.

Adapted. © Thomas Nelson, Inc., 2000

*According to a footnote for Mt 15.39 in *The New Oxford Annotated Bible with the Apocryphal/Deuterocanonical Books,* new revised standard version, edited by Bruce M. Metzger and Roland E. Murphy (New York: Oxford University Press, 1994), the site of Magadan is not known for certain but was apparently on the west side of the Sea of Galilee.

▶ Characters in Matthew's Passion Narrative

Caiaphas (26.3)	Barabbas (27.16)
A woman with ointment (26.7)	Pilate's wife (27.19)
Judas Iscariot (26.14)	A member of the crowd (27.20)*
The man who owns the house used for Jesus' Passover with the Apostles (26.18)	A soldier (27.27)*
Peter (26.33)	Simon of Cyrene (27.32)
A son of Zebedee (26.37)*	A bandit (27.38)*
A person with a sword or club (26.47)*	A passerby (27.39)*
The high priest's slave who lost an ear (26.51)	A bystander with wine (27.48)
Jesus' follower who cuts off the slave's ear (26.51)	A person to whom a risen saint appears (27.53)*
A scribe (26.57)*	The centurion (27.54)
An elder (26.57)*	Mary Magdalene (27.56)
A false witness (26.60)*	Mary the mother of James and Joseph (27.56)
Pilate (27.2)	The mother of the sons of Zebedee (27.56)

While washing the dishes one should only be washing the dishes, which means that while washing the dishes one should be completely aware of the fact that one is washing the dishes. At first glance, that might seem a little silly: why put so much stress on a simple thing? But that's precisely the point. The fact that I am standing there and washing these bowls is a wondrous reality. I'm being completely myself, following my breath, conscious of my presence, and conscious of my thoughts and actions. There's no way I can be tossed around mindlessly like a bottle slapped here and there on the waves. (Pages 3–4)

If while washing dishes, we think only of the cup of tea that awaits us, thus hurrying to get the dishes out of the way as if they were a nuisance, then we are not "washing the dishes to wash the dishes." What's more, we are not alive during the time we are washing the dishes. In fact we are completely incapable of realizing the miracle of life while standing at the sink. If we can't wash the dishes, the chances are we won't be able to drink our tea either. While drinking the cup of tea, we will only be thinking of other things, barely aware of the cup in our hands. Thus we are sucked away into the future—and we are incapable of actually living one minute of life. (Thich Nhat Hanh, *The Miracle of Mindfulness: A Manual on Meditation,* revised edition, translated by Mobi Ho [Boston: Beacon Press, 1987], pages 4–5. Copyright © 1975, 1976 by Thich Nhat Hanh. Preface and English translation copyright © 1975, 1976, 1987 by Mobi Ho.)

Exercise

In two fifteen-minute blocks, explore the Buddhist practice of mindfulness by completely focusing on the activity that you are doing—riding the bus, eating, listening to music, running, or whatever. Be sensitive to the sights, sounds, smells, and feel of the activity. Then, in the spaces below, describe your experiences and reflect on the values, challenges, and results of this exercise.

■ My description of the first experience:

■ My description of the second experience:

■ My reflections on the value and challenges of mindfulness:

■ How mindfulness might help people become more aware of the good things in their lives and be less anxious:

•••••••••••••••••••• ► The *Palestinian Times:* The Good News Edition

Read Lk 19.28—24.53 and any other materials provided by your teacher. Using those sources, create a four-page newspaper that includes the following nine items. For each item, cite the chapters and verses from Luke, and the titles and page numbers of other sources that supplied information.

1. **Feature article.** Using major headlines, create a main story around the torture, death, and Resurrection of Jesus (Luke, chapters 22–24).

2. **Letters to the editor.** Write reactions to the news that Jesus rose from the dead, from the positions of two of the following characters:
   - a male or female disciple of Jesus
   - Pontius Pilate
   - a Pharisee, Sadducee, chief priest, or scribe
   - a Zealot

3. **Interview.** Choose one of the following passages and report an interview with the main character or characters. The interview should have at least four questions and answers.
   - Simon Peter's betrayal and forgiveness (Lk 22.31–34,54–62)
   - Joseph of Arimathea and the burial of Jesus (Lk 23.50–56)
   - The Roman soldier at the cross (Lk 23.44–49)
   - The disciples walking to Emmaus (Lk 24.13–35)

4. **Financial article.** Create a finance question-and-answer article based on at least two of the following passages:
   - Lk 19.45–47
   - Lk 20.20–26
   - Lk 21.1–4

5. **Guest editorials.** Write a guest editorial by Jesus entitled "Why I Don't Get Along with the Pharisees, Sadducees, Chief Priests, and Scribes," and then a rebuttal by one of those groups, entitled "Why We Don't Get Along with Jesus." For background, use two of the following passages in which Jesus and the Pharisees or Sadducees are arguing. Under each headline, give the corresponding side's view of the issue and related feelings.
   - Lk 19.45–48
   - Lk 20.1–8
   - Lk 20.9–19
   - Lk 20.27–40
   - Lk 20.45–47

6. **Horoscope.** List Jesus' predictions about the future, which can be found in these and other passages:
   - Lk 19.41–44
   - Lk 21.5–6
   - Lk 21.7–19
   - Lk 21.20–24
   - Lk 21.25–28
   - Lk 21.29–33

7. **Picture.** Provide one picture that relates to one of the news items listed above, and write a caption for the picture.

8. **Advertisement.** Create one advertisement for an item related to something in Luke, chapters 19–24.

9. **One additional article.** Create an article for a section such as weather, gardening, kids, comics, puzzles, sports, or want ads.

● ● ● ● ● ● ● ● ● ● ▶ Paul's Missionary Journeys

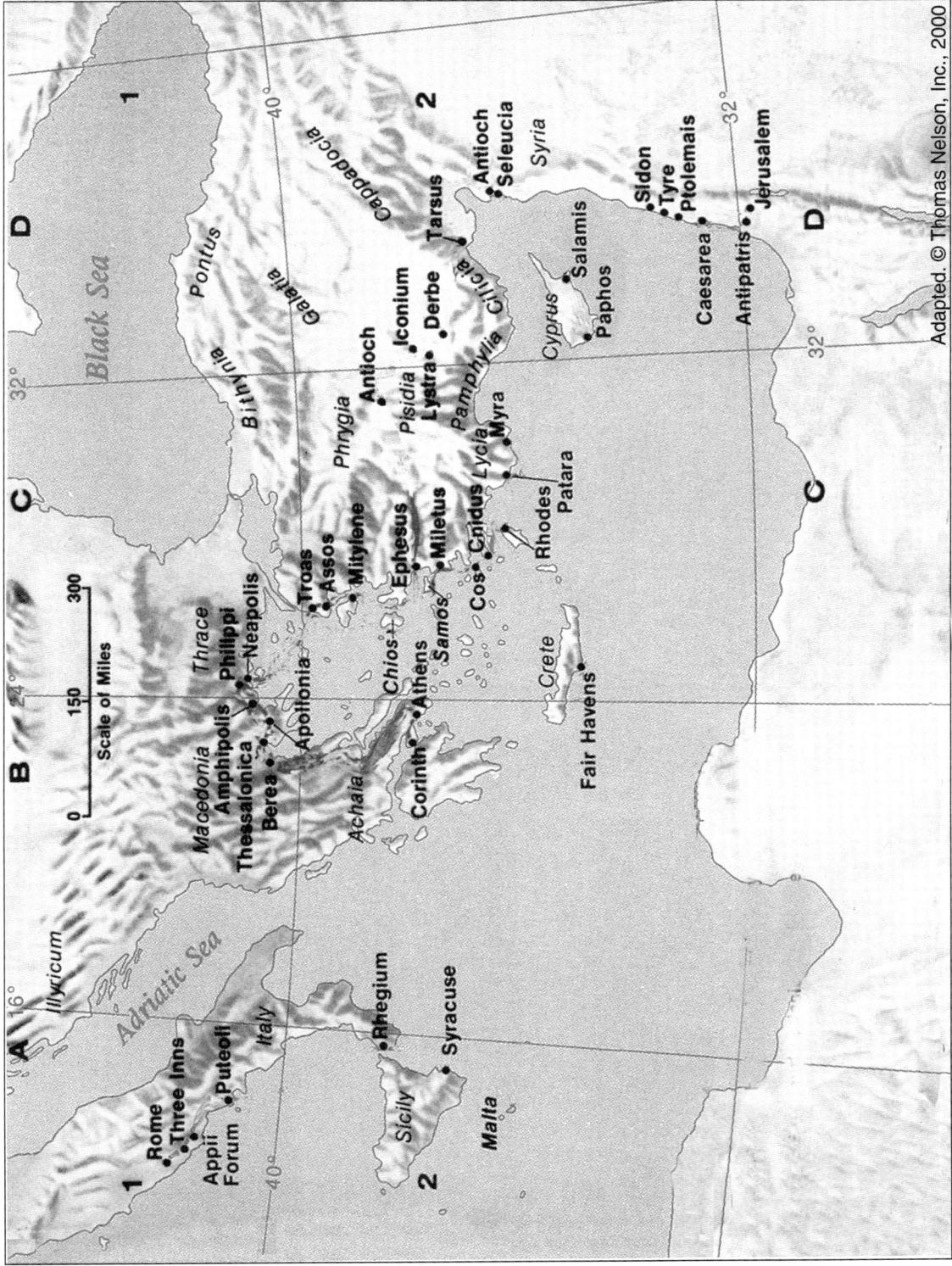

Read the following contemporary letters and answer the questions below them:

Dear Mom,

How are things at home? I wanted to say something more about our conversation the other night. I think stealing is OK even though you talk a lot about risk. I can really help everyone out if I steal and don't get caught. Of course, when I do get caught, I become really afraid of what everyone will think. A few times when I have arrived back at the dorm, I could tell that the others knew what I had done and thought it was a big mistake. That's a terrible feeling. Talk to you soon.

Pete

Dear Karen,

Hi! How are your classes going, and did you have fun the other night at the game? I can't believe that Sarah dropped Randall. What a fool! Randall doesn't know me from anyone else, but if Randall thought half as much of me as of her, I would stick it out to the end no matter what kind of effort I had to put into it. Some people just don't have the eyes to see a good thing when it happens!

I am still planning to meet you for coffee tomorrow—call me if you can't make it.

Alicia

Questions

1. What is the subject matter of each letter?

2. What is your initial impression of the authors of the letters, Pete and Alicia? Do the letters give clues to their values or concerns?

3. Do you have any sense of the recipients of the letters, Pete's mother and Karen?

4. Would Pete's mother and Karen have a better chance of understanding their letter than we do? Why or why not? What kind of information helps a reader best understand the contents of a letter?

.... ▶ The Nature of Paul's Travels

The following quotes describe traveling conditions that Paul likely encountered during his journeys:

A normal day's journey for those traveling by carriage was from inn to inn, roughly 25 Roman miles or 22 modern miles. Those who walked, as Paul did, would have had to extend themselves to cover this distance. It is unlikely that Paul could have maintained such an average for long periods, particularly when the road was hilly. (Pages 40–41)

If Paul says that he was "in hunger and thirst, often without food, in cold and exposure" (2 Corinthians 11:27), it is obvious that on occasion he found himself far from human habitation at nightfall. He may have failed to reach shelter because of weather conditions; an unusually hot day may have sapped his endurance; mountain passes may have been blocked by unseasonably early or late snowfalls; spring floods may have made sections of the road impassable . . . ; or fierce hailstorms may have forced him to take refuge. The average height of the Anatolian plateau (present day central Turkey) is 3,000 feet above sea-level, but great sections of it rise to double that and extreme variations of temperature are the rule. (Page 41)

When Paul made it to an inn, he could not look forward to a night of total repose. The average inn was no more than a courtyard surrounded by rooms. Baggage was piled in the open space, where animals were also tethered for the night. The drivers sat around noxious little fires fueled by dried dung, or slept on the ground wrapped in their cloaks. (Page 42)

Those who could afford better rented beds in the rooms. The snorting and stamping of the animals outside was sometimes drowned out by the snores of others who shared the room, any one of whom might be a thief. Paul's anxiety that he might lose the tools of his trade was hardly conducive to a sound night's sleep. And sound sleep was made infinitely more difficult by that perennial occupant of all inns, the bed-bug. (Page 42)

In the countryside the road was a *via glarea strata,* an unsealed or gravel road. On these roads, the danger from flying stones thrown up by passing vehicles was a menace the walking traveler had to live with. (Page 45)

Wild animals were another danger. . . . Apuleius refers explicitly to bears, wolves and wild boar. Travelers in this story are armed with throwing-spears, heavy hunting-spears, bows and clubs. (Page 45)

Several segments of Paul's second missionary journey were by sea. . . .
 . . . Storms blew regularly in winter; the violence of these winter storms is well documented. . . .
 Storms were not the only reason the seas were usually closed in winter. Sailors plotted a course by the sun and stars, as well as by landmarks. In winter, fog or heavy cloud cover would cut off their navigational guides, easily leading to shipwreck. (Page 45)

Since passengers were nothing more than an incidental benefit to the owner, the ship provided water, but neither food nor services. Passengers were expected to furnish their own provisions, other than water, for the duration of the voyage. They had to cook for themselves, which meant taking turns, after the crew had been fed, at the hearth in the galley. (Page 46)

Passengers had to live on deck; there were no cabins on the average coastal vessel. Apart from a little shade thrown by the mainsail, no shelter was provided. (Page 46)

Some of the areas through which Paul passed are spectacularly beautiful; yet this seems not to have influenced him in any way. On the other hand, his experiences as a lonely traveler almost certainly affected his theology. His pessimistic view of human nature may have been born of the ethos of his age, but it was surely reinforced by what he encountered at the inns and seaports of Greece and Asia Minor. His own poverty forced him to rub shoulders with the most downtrodden and brutalized elements in society. He no doubt felt the impact of the forces that made these elements of society what they were. He himself felt the force of a value system that the poorer elements of society could not escape. His own struggle against the insidious miasma of egocentricity would have sharpened his consciousness of sin and at the same time strengthened his dedication to the salvation of its victims. "Who is weak, and I am not weak? Who is made to fall, and I do not burn with anger?" (2 Corinthians 11:29). (Jerome Murphy-O'Connor, OP, "On the Road and on the Sea with St. Paul: Traveling Conditions in the First Century," in *Bible Review,* volume 1, number 2, summer 1985, page 47. Copyright © 1985 by the Biblical Archaeology Society.)

••••••••••••••••••••▶ "Let There Be Light!"

Opening Words

Leader. Let us remember that we are in the holy presence of God.

Readings

Reader 1.

> In the beginning, when God created the heavens and the earth, the earth was a formless void and darkness covered the face of the deep, while a wind from God swept over the face of the waters. Then God said, 'Let there be light'; and there was light. And God saw that the light was good. (Gen 1.1–4) . . . *[Refrain]*

Reader 2.

> In the beginning was the Word, and the Word was with God, and the Word was God. He was in the beginning with God. All things came into being through him, and without him not one thing came into being. What has come into being in him was life, and the life was the light of all people. The light shines in the darkness, and the darkness did not overcome it. (Jn 1.1–5) . . . *[Refrain]*

Reader 3.

> You yourselves know very well that the day of the Lord will come like a thief in the night. . . . But you, beloved, are not in darkness, for that day to surprise you like a thief; for you are all children of light and children of the day; we are not of the night or of darkness. (1 Thess 5.2–5) . . . *[Refrain]*

Reader 4.

> Do not be deceived, my beloved.
> Every generous act of giving, with every perfect gift, is from above, coming down from the Father of lights, with whom there is no variation or shadow due to change. (Jas 1.16–17) . . . *[Refrain]*

Reader 5.

> The light is with you for a little longer. Walk while you have the light, so that the darkness may not overtake you. If you walk in the darkness, you do not know where you are going. While you have the light, believe in the light, so that you may become children of the light. (Jn 12.35–36) . . . *[Refrain]*

Reader 6.

> We declare to you what we have seen and heard so that you also may have fellowship with us; and truly our fellowship is with the Father and his Son Jesus Christ. We are writing these things so that our joy may be complete.
> This is the message we have heard from him and proclaim to you, that God is light and in [God] there is no darkness at all. (1 Jn 1.3–5) . . . *[Refrain]*

Reader 7.

Again Jesus spoke to them, saying, "I am the light of the world. Whoever follows me will never walk in darkness but will have the light of life." (Jn 8.12) . . . *[Refrain]*

Sharing and Closing Prayer

Leader. At this time, I invite each of you to identify someone who has served as a light in your life. You may give either a name or a description, such as "a teacher." If you would like, you may briefly explain how he or she has been a light for you.

[After everyone has shared, they respond:]

All. Dear God, you are the source of all the real light in our lives. We thank you for all the people who have been light for us, and have revealed your love through their concern for us. Thank you for illuminating our lives and showing us the way. Let us learn to be light for one another. May each of us reflect the light of Christ to our weary world. We ask this through Christ, our light, our brother, and our Lord. Amen.

[The class may sing "Christ Be Our Light."]

(This prayer service is from Br. Larry Schatz, FSC, formerly campus minister at Saint Mary's University, Winona, Minnesota.)

Gathering Song

[The class may listen to the song "My Life Is in Your Hands."]

Opening Words

Leader. God created Adam and Eve in God's image, and created the Garden of Eden to supply all their needs on earth. Adam and Eve were happy in the garden. They lived without clothes and were not ashamed to be naked. Then one day a serpent approached Eve and tempted her to disobey one of God's commands.

Reader.

Now the serpent . . . said to the woman, "Did God say, 'You shall not eat from any tree in the garden'?" The woman said to the serpent, "We may eat of the fruit of the trees in the garden; but God said, 'You shall not eat of the fruit of the tree that is in the middle of the garden, nor shall you touch it, or you shall die.'" But the serpent said to the woman, "You will not die; for God knows that when you eat of it your eyes will be opened, and you will be like God, knowing good and evil." So when the woman saw that the tree was good for food, and that it was a delight to the eyes, and that the tree was to be desired to make one wise, she took of its fruit and ate; and she also gave some to her husband, who was with her, and he ate. Then the eyes of both were opened, and they knew that they were naked; and they sewed fig leaves together and made loincloths for themselves. (Gen 3.1–7)

Leader. When Adam and Eve disobeyed God, they broke their relationship of trust with God. Once that relationship was broken, sin became a part of the human story. Ever since that moment, human beings have faced temptations that pull them away from God's love and grace.

Litany

Side 1. We are sometimes torn between the voice that calls us to love . . .
Side 2. and the voice that calls us to hate.
Side 1. We are sometimes torn between the voice that calls us to do good . . .
Side 2. and the voice that calls us to do evil.
Side 1. We are sometimes torn between the voice that draws us to God . . .
Side 2. and the voice that wants to block God out of our lives.

Skit 1: Stealing

[The person reading the role of Good stands to one side of the staging area, holding a sign labeled "Good." The person reading the role of Evil stands to the opposite side of the staging area, holding a sign labeled "Evil." A person with a large rope tied around her or his waist stands between them. A fifth person holds one end of the rope and stands near the "Good" sign, and a sixth person holds the other end of the rope and stands near the "Evil" sign. The narrator stands off to the side so that the audience can see all the actors.]

Narrator. Brian got a new Northface jacket and has been proudly showing it off to everyone. All his friends admire it—except for Jordan. Jordan wanted the jacket, and Brian bought it first. This makes Jordan mad. Now Jordan is contemplating the situation.
Good. It's such a cool jacket. I've had my eye on it forever. But Jordan's got it, and it looks good on him.
Evil. But he stabbed me in the back. I wanted that jacket, and he knew that. It's not right. It's just not right.
Good. Brian had a right to buy it. He wanted it just as badly as I did.
Evil. Who cares? That Northface is hot. So hot that I'm going to steal it.
Good. No. I can't steal it. Brian is my friend. He paid for the jacket with his own money. Besides, who I am is much more important than what I wear. And I'm no thief.

Skit 2: Drugs

[The scene is staged as for skit 1.]

Narrator. Delia is at a party on a Saturday night. It is the party of the year, and she is having the time of her life, sitting around with a really cool crowd. In fact, she is sitting right next to Michael, a guy she really likes. Suddenly, Michael hands her a marijuana joint.

Good. Marijuana? You've got to be kidding! I can't smoke that. It'll mess me up.

Evil. One joint can't hurt. I can stop anytime I want, especially after just one.

Good. Or can I? What am I thinking? It's weed! What about its long-term effects? It destroys brain cells. It harms chromosomes. What about the children I want to have in the future? Will they be okay?

Evil. But it's Michael offering it to me. I like Michael. Maybe he will like me if I smoke. It can't be so bad. Everyone else is smoking. What'll they all think if I don't join them?

Good. Forget it. If Michael doesn't like me for who I am, he doesn't deserve me. And if the others laugh at me, they're not real friends. I can deal with that. This is my decision and my life. And my choice is to pass.

Skit 3: Sex

[The scene is staged as for skits 1 and 2.]

Narrator. Jorge and his girlfriend, Tiffany, are in his house alone. They are kissing, and their feelings for each other are becoming stronger and stronger.

Evil. I want to make love. We're both responsible. We have protection, so we don't have to worry about a baby. Neither of us has been with anyone else, so we don't have to worry about AIDS or STDs.

Good. Yes, we have both been responsible people so far. We don't have to worry about AIDS or STDs. But no method of protection is 100 percent effective. There's always a chance that if we share sex, we could bring a baby into the world. Neither of us is ready for that kind of responsibility yet.

Evil. Sure, there's always a chance we could have a baby. But the chance is slim. We have been going together for a while. Sharing sex will bring us closer.

Good. Sounds good, but let's not fool ourselves. Sharing sex is no shortcut to real intimacy, to real, deep friendship. Communication, honesty, care for each other's well-being—those are the things that will bring us closer. Not sex.

Evil. We would not be just having sex. We love each other. Love makes it right.

Good. We do love each other. But how much? Are we ready and able to make a life together, to love each other always and forever? To be honest, neither of us is ready for that kind of love. We both have school to finish, careers to start, people to meet, and goals to achieve before we're ready for that kind of unconditional, always-and-forever love. Let's swear to each other never to make promises to each other that we can't keep. We will wait until we are ready and able to love each other always and forever.

Skit 4: Jesus in the Desert

[The scene is staged as for skits 1, 2, and 3.]

Narrator. Because Jesus was human, he too experienced temptation and sin. In the weeks before Jesus died, the Spirit led him out into the desert, and he remained there for forty days and forty nights. Afterward, he was hungry, and the tempter approached him.

Evil. If you are the Son of God, turn these stones into loaves of bread.

Good. People need more than bread to live; they need the Word of God.

Narrator. The evil tempter took Jesus to the top of the Temple in Jerusalem.

Evil. If you are the Son of God, throw yourself down from the top of this Temple and let your angels minister to you.

Good. You should not put the Lord your God to the test.

Narrator. The devil took Jesus to the top of a mountain and pointed out all the nations below it.

Evil. All these countries I will give you if you throw yourself down at my feet and worship me.

Good. Get away from me, Satan, for it is written, "The Lord your God should you worship, and God alone shall you serve."

(This skit is adapted from Mt 4.1–10.)

Reflection

[Everyone reflects on several questions posed by the leader.]

Closing Prayer

Leader.

Give me the courage to do right
in the face of wrong.
Instill in my heart
a set of values that prompts me
to think of others
instead of just myself.

Give me the willingness to
stand up for what I believe in—
not following the crowd.
Give me the strength to
look evil in the eye
and withstand it.
Because I know
with you at my side
all things are possible.

(Theresa Vonderwell, in *More Dreams Alive: Prayers by Teenagers,* edited by Carl Koch [Winona, MN: Saint Mary's Press, 1995], page 28. Copyright © 1995 by Saint Mary's Press. All rights reserved.)

Closing Song

[The group may sing the traditional spiritual "Were You There?"]

(This prayer service is adapted from one conceived and written by Helen Wolf and others, both adults and students, at Bishop Loughlin Memorial High School, Brooklyn, New York.)

••••••••••► A Rainbow of Hope and Peace

Opening Prayer and Reading

Reader.

God said, "This is the sign of the covenant that I make between me and you and every living creature that is with you, for all future generations: I have set my bow in the clouds, and it shall be a sign of the covenant between me and the earth. When I bring clouds over the earth and the bow is seen in the clouds, I will remember my covenant that is between me and you and every living creature of all flesh; and the waters shall never again become a flood to destroy all flesh. When the bow is in the clouds, I will see it and remember the everlasting covenant between God and every living creature of all flesh that is on the earth." God said to Noah, "This is the sign of the covenant that I have established between me and all flesh that is on the earth." (Gen 9.12–17)

Leader. God sends the rainbow to remind us of God's promise to grant the glory of heaven to all who love God and do God's will. The rainbow is thus a symbol of hope. In spite of all the violence in the world, God gives us hope through Jesus Christ, who is the source of all peace. We love God and do God's will when we reach out to serve others in peace, as Jesus did, trusting in God's grace.

Reflection Activity

[Everyone identifies groups they belong to. The leader explains what it means to belong to a community of hope. Small groups discuss their personal experiences of peace in a community of hope.]

Closing Prayer

[Each person gets four colored strips of paper, representing four communities of hope, and writes on each strip one thing he or she can do in that community to share the peace of Jesus Then everyone says the Peace Prayer of Saint Francis of Assisi together:]

All.

Loving God, make me an instrument of your
  peace.
Where there is hatred, let me sow love;
Where there is injury, pardon;
Where there is doubt, faith;
Where there is despair, hope;
Where there is darkness, light;
And where there is sadness, joy.
O, Divine Teacher, grant that I may not so
  much seek to be consoled as to console;
To be understood as to understand;
To be loved as to love;
For it is in giving that we receive;
It is in pardoning that we are pardoned;
And it is in dying that we are born to eternal
  life.
  (Joseph M. Stoutzenberger and John D.
    Bohrer, *Praying with Francis of Assisi*
    [Winona, MN: Saint Mary's Press, 1989],
      page 54. Copyright © 1989 by
    Saint Mary's Press. All rights reserved.)

[Each person tapes each of her or his colored strips in the corresponding section of the community-of-hope rainbow. Everyone sings "Let There Be Peace on Earth" or shares a sign of peace.]

(This prayer service is from Clare vanBrandwijk, campus minister, Bishop O+Gorman High School, Sioux Falls, South Dakota.)

·····▶ "Be Still, and Know That I Am God!"

Opening Words

Reading and Litany

Leader. A reading from Psalm 46:

> God is our refuge and strength,
> a very present help in trouble.
> Therefore we will not fear, though the earth should change,
> though the mountains shake in the heart of the sea;
> though its waters roar and foam,
> though the mountains tremble with its tumult.
>
> (Verses 1–3)
>
> "Be still, and know that I am God!"
>
> (Verse 10)

Side 1. When the loud alarm goes off in the morning . . .
All. "Be still, and know that I am God!"
Side 2. In the routines of dressing and getting off to school . . .
All. "Be still, and know that I am God!"
Side 1. In the comings and goings throughout the school day . . .
All. "Be still, and know that I am God!"
Side 2. In the mundane tasks of going to the locker and walking in the halls . . .
All. "Be still, and know that I am God!"
Side 1. In the frenzied pace of the cafeteria . . .
All. "Be still, and know that I am God!"
Side 2. In the stacks of books and pages of homework . . .
All. "Be still, and know that I am God!"
Side 1. In the quiet of night and stillness of sleep . . .
All. "Be still, and know that I am God!"

Quiet Reflection

[The class may listen to the song "You Are Mine."]

Closing Prayer

All. Loving God, you come to us in the silence and in the laughter, in the moments of joy and sorrow. The busy-ness of our lives sometimes keeps us from taking the time to be quiet, to be still, and to rest in your love. Let us open ourselves to the enfolding grace of your presence this day. Let us be still and know that you hold us in your heart and that we are your cherished children. Let us be still and know that you are our God, our loving creator and friend. We ask this in Jesus' name. Amen.

Being a Humble Servant

Opening Words

Leader. Jesus said to his disciples, "For where two or three are gathered in my name, I am there among them" (Mt 18.20). As we gather today, in Jesus' name, let us come together quietly and reverently to be with our loving Creator, whose spirit fills us and makes us whole.

Litany and Reading

Leader. All wisdom is from God. We need to listen and learn.

Side 1. Open our hearts so that these words become branded on our hearts.

Side 2. Open our minds so that our intellect can be challenged.

Side 1. Open our eyes to the beauty of creation.

Side 2. Open our hands so that we can work to bring forth the Reign!

Leader. A reading from the Book of Sirach:

My child, perform your tasks with humility;
then you will be loved by those whom
God accepts.
The greater you are, the more you must
humble yourself;
so you will find favor in the sight of the
Lord.
For great is the might of the Lord;
but by the humble he is glorified.

(3.17–20)

Side 1. When I find myself bragging about all I can do . . .

All. Let me remember that all wisdom is from God, and I should be humble.

Side 2. When I find myself thinking I am better than someone else . . .

All. Let me remember that all wisdom is from God, and I should be humble.

Leader. Jesus gave us a powerful example—washing the feet of the Apostles. Listen to his explanation from the Gospel of John: "For I have set you an example, that you also should do as I have done to you. Very truly, I tell you, servants are not greater than their master, nor are messengers greater than the one who sent them. If you know these things, you are blessed if you do them" (13.15–17).

All. We know these things. We must live them out. We know what the Lord God asks of us—only this: that we act justly, love tenderly, and walk humbly with our God (adapted from Mic 6.8).

Quiet Reflection

[The class may listen to "Servant Song."]

Prayers

Leader. As we strive to be merciful and true, let us bring our needs to our God.

[The sides take turns offering prayers. After each prayer, everyone responds, "Lord, hear our needs."]

Side 1. For peace in our world, and justice in our land, we pray . . .

Side 2. For courage in decisions, and compassion in our actions, we pray . . .

Side 1. For lonely hearts, and empty hands, we pray . . .

Side 2. For our individual needs, we pray . . . *[Everyone shares their own needs aloud or ponders them in silence.]*

Leader. We thank you, God, for all you have given us, and we know that you hear our prayers. We ask that you bless us and remember us as we pray the words you taught us:

All. Our Father . . . *[Everyone says the Lord's Prayer.]*

Opening Words

Leader. Let us remember that we are in the holy presence of God.

[The leader lights a pillar candle.]

Leader. We are gathered to give witness to the enduring realities of life.
All. We have come to affirm that life is a gift, that the gift is good, and that it comes from God.
Leader. We are gathered to renew our hope in Jesus Christ, as we travel life's long journey.
All. We find God in the paths of our present and our past, but we also trust in God's love in our future.
Leader. The same God guides us all the way, every day of our lives, and beyond life.
All. Let us praise God with our whole hearts, and entrust our lives to God's hands. Amen.

Opening Song

[The class may sing the hymn "Blest Are They."]

Reading

[The class is divided into two sides and reads the Beatitudes (Mt 5.3–10) responsively, as follows:]

Leader. Let us now listen to the word of God, which reminds us of the preciousness of human life, and of our responsibility to one another.
Side 1. "Blessed are the poor in spirit . . ."
Side 2. "for theirs is the kingdom of heaven."
Side 1. "Blessed are those who mourn . . ."
Side 2. "for they will be comforted."
Side 1. "Blessed are the meek . . ."
Side 2. "for they will inherit the earth."
Side 1. "Blessed are those who hunger and thirst for righteousness . . ."

Side 2. "for they will be filled."
Side 1. "Blessed are the merciful . . ."
Side 2. "for they will receive mercy."
Side 1. "Blessed are the pure in heart . . ."
Side 2. "for they will see God."
Side 1. "Blessed are the peacemakers . . ."
Side 2. "for they will be called children of God."
Leader. Loving Creator, we ask for wholeness for ourselves and for your church. Do not allow fear, ignorance, or pride to limit the action of your Spirit, do not allow mere custom to prevent the divine creativity within us from bearing fruit.
All.
We ask for insight to understand
the needs of people today,
that we might grasp the complexity of the
	situations that face us
and the absolute simplicity of human need:
the poor have a right to hear the Gospel,
the hungry a right to food,
the oppressed a right to freedom.

Reflection Activity

[Everyone writes on a slip of paper one act of service that they will perform in the next week, puts the paper in a basket, uses a taper to light a votive candle, forms a circle around the prayer space, and then says the following prayer:]

All. We light these candles and ask, God, that you enable us to be enthusiastic disciples in your ministry, contagious in our love and eager to be among your people as ones who serve. Be with us as we carry out the acts of service we have pledged this week, and other acts of love and kindness throughout our lives. This we ask through Jesus Christ, who came as brother and servant to us all.

[The class may sing "Here I Am, Lord."]

Presentation of the Bread

Reader 1. We have shared bread many times in our lives, in many places, for many reasons. Just as there is no single symbol of the church, there is no single bread that can feed our hunger.

Reader 2. And so we bless many kinds of breads today as a sign that our church savors the taste and feel of a variety of foods, and savors the variety of women and men who make up our community.

All. May our acceptance of these various breads be a sign of our faith in the unending goodness of a God who journeys with us, in the power of love to remove any barrier among us, and in the mystery of the call given to each one of us, to make bread and life in beauty available to everyone.

Leader. Let us share this bread as Jesus taught us, knowing that our lives are forever changed by this, and every, breaking of the bread.

Blessing and Sharing of the Bread

Reader 3. *[Holding up a plate or bowl of saltine crackers]* Let saltines represent the elderly, and women who have been battered or abused— "the salty ones":

> those who have endured
> those who have learned wisdom
> those who are fragile
> those forgotten in our society

Leader. This bread has been presented and blessed. *[Reader 3 raises the bread.]* Take and eat, knowing that our lives are forever changed by this, and every, breaking of the bread. *[The reader passes the bread around the group as the next presentation begins, and the students each take a portion and eat it as it comes to them.]*

Reader 4. *[Holding up a plate or bowl of shortbread]* Shortbread brings to mind children and youth. Let this bread signify

> boys and girls who suffer physical and sexual abuse
> boys and girls who carry the heavy burden of family separations
> troubled teenagers who have no safe places left to go

Leader. This bread has been presented and blessed. *[Reader 4 raises the bread.]* Take and eat, knowing that our lives are forever changed by this, and every, breaking of the bread. *[The bread is passed and eaten.]*

Reader 5. *[Holding up a plate or bowl of cornbread]* Let cornbread signify our African American, Hispanic and Latino, Native American, Asian American, Appalachian, and homosexual sisters and brothers who have suffered and continue to suffer discrimination, racism, and oppression.

> Let it remind us of the past from which they have come and the struggle they continue to this day.

> Let us not forget the equality, fairness, freedom, and dignity that are the right of each individual not only in this country but throughout the world.

Leader. This bread has been presented and blessed. *[Reader 5 raises the bread.]* Take and eat, knowing that our lives are forever changed by this, and every, breaking of the bread. *[The bread is passed and eaten.]*

Reader 6. *[Holding up a plate or bowl of nut bread]* Nut bread represents women and men who are considered crazy in our society because they are incomprehensible to most people:

> those who are homeless
> those who are mentally ill
> those who suffer addiction or AIDS
> the dreamers, the visionaries, the prophets among us

Leader. This bread has been presented and blessed. *[Reader 6 raises the bread.]* Take and eat, knowing that our lives are forever changed by this, and every, breaking of the bread. *[The bread is passed and eaten.]*

Closing Prayers

Reader 7.

We pray, then, good and gracious God,
that we might recognize you in this bread
today.
It is the bread of heaven,
the bread of the poor,
the bread of our lives.

Reader 8.

We are here to give ourselves to you and
your people.
It is through what we are and do
that others come to know you.

Reader 9.

We are here to bring peace to a broken
people,
and healing to those in need.

Reader 10.

We are here to witness to the world
that we live in response to a desperate
society,
seeking truth, equality, and freedom.

Reader 11.

We are called to stand together,
sharing our many gifts.
And so, let us join together
in prayer.

All.

God of the poor and oppressed, we ask for
your help.
Teach us to become eyes for those who are
blind,
ears for those who are deaf to your Word,
and hands for those who refuse to work at
building the Reign of God.
We pray all this in your name and for your
honor and glory.
Amen.

Charge and Blessing

Leader.

God of all justice,
we thank you for the gifts you have given
each of us.
We pray that we may always be mindful
of all your people who are in need,
and share our gifts with them.
We ask this through Christ our Lord. Amen.

Closing Song

[The class may sing "For the Life of the World."]

(This prayer service is adapted from one by
Laurie Ziliak, campus minister, Saint Mary's University.)

Fourteen Courageous Steps— the Stations of the Cross

Opening Song

[The class may sing a few verses of "Were You There?"]

Station 1: Jesus Was Condemned to Death

Reader 1. Jesus was arrested and taken before the council, where many people testified against him.

Then the high priest stood up before them and asked Jesus, "Have you no answer? What is it that they testify against you?" But he was silent and did not answer. Again the high priest asked him, "Are you the Messiah, the Son of the Blessed One?" Jesus said, "I am; and

'you will see the Son of Man
seated at the right hand of the Power,'
and 'coming with the clouds of heaven.'"
Then the high priest tore his clothes and said, "Why do we still need witnesses? You have heard his blasphemy! What is your decision?" All of them condemned him as deserving death. Some began to spit on him, to blindfold him, and to strike him, saying to him, "Prophesy!" The guards also took him over and beat him. (Mk 14.60–65)

Leader. Jesus was condemned for something that the high priest did not even understand. Many times, we are criticized, ridiculed, or simply told we are nothing. Think of a time that happened to you. What did you feel like? What did you want to do?

Leader. Lord, have mercy.
All. Lord, have mercy.
Leader. Christ, have mercy.
All. Christ, have mercy.
Leader. Lord, have mercy.
All. Lord, have mercy.

Station 2: Jesus Took Up His Cross

Reader 2.

Then the soldiers led him into the courtyard of the palace (that is, the governor's headquarters); and they called together the whole cohort. And they clothed him in a purple cloak; and after twisting some thorns into a crown, they put it on him. And they began saluting him, "Hail, King of the Jews!" They struck his head with a reed, spat upon him, and knelt down in homage to him. After mocking him, they stripped him of the purple cloak and put his own clothes on him. Then they led him out to crucify him. (Mk 15.16–20)

Leader. Jesus endured great pain even though he was innocent. Have you ever been punished for something you did not do? Remember that time, experience the feelings again, and ask Jesus how he would handle it. We are asked to carry a very light burden compared with Jesus. We carry a sliver of the cross; he carries the remainder.

Leader. Lord, have mercy.
All. Lord, have mercy.
Leader. Christ, have mercy.
All. Christ, have mercy.
Leader. Lord, have mercy.
All. Lord, have mercy.

Station 3: Jesus Fell the First Time

Reader 3. The pressure was too much. Jesus was weak from being beaten, bruised, and whipped. He fell with the weight of the cross. The pain was excruciating, but he got back up and began the seemingly long journey to the Place of the Skull, Golgotha.

Leader. What drains you of energy and brings you to the ground? Is it a lack of patience, courage, or understanding? Like Jesus, we need to rise from our downtrodden state.

Leader. Lord, have mercy.
All. Lord, have mercy.
Leader. Christ, have mercy.
All. Christ, have mercy.
Leader. Lord, have mercy.
All. Lord, have mercy.

Station 4: Jesus Met His Mother

Reader 4. Mary said: "I look into his eyes. There is so much pain. My Son, if I could take away this agony, I would. You still have so much love in your eyes. You are incredible. I love you!"

Leader. How do your parents look at you? What do they see? How do you know they love you? How do you show your love for them?

Leader. Lord, have mercy.
All. Lord, have mercy.
Leader. Christ, have mercy.
All. Christ, have mercy.
Leader. Lord, have mercy.
All. Lord, have mercy.

Station 5: Simon Helped Jesus Carry His Cross

Reader 5. "As [the soldiers] led [Jesus] away, they seized a man, Simon of Cyrene, who was coming from the country, and they laid the cross on him, and made him carry it behind Jesus" (Lk 23.26).

Leader. Who is with you through the good times and the bad times? Who is there to help you carry your cross? How does this person help you? How do you help this person?

Leader. Lord, have mercy.
All. Lord, have mercy.
Leader. Christ, have mercy.
All. Christ, have mercy.
Leader. Lord, have mercy.
All. Lord, have mercy.

Station 6: Veronica Wiped the Face of Jesus

Reader 6. Veronica said: "I see him from a distance. As he comes closer, I see the sweat, blood, and tears. I wipe his face. It is the least I can do. He has done so much for me."

Leader. Compassion is a virtue. To help one another is a gift. How have you been kind to your family, friends, and even strangers? Veronica wiped the face of Jesus with love, compassion, and sorrow. How do we do this for others?

Leader. Lord, have mercy.
All. Lord, have mercy.
Leader. Christ, have mercy.
All. Christ, have mercy.
Leader. Lord, have mercy.
All. Lord, have mercy.

Station 7: Jesus Fell the Second Time

Reader 7. With each step, the cross became heavier. The pain was agonizing. Jesus fell again. The weight was constant, the pressure consistent.

Leader. All of us have continuous sources of stress. These become a heavy burden and may cause fatigue. What are ongoing sources of stress for you?

Leader. Lord, have mercy.
All. Lord, have mercy.
Leader. Christ, have mercy.
All. Christ, have mercy.
Leader. Lord, have mercy.
All. Lord, have mercy.

Station 8:
Jesus Met the Women of Jerusalem

Reader 8.

A great number of the people followed [Jesus], and among them were women who were beating their breasts and wailing for him. But Jesus turned to them and said, "Daughters of Jerusalem, do not weep for me, but weep for yourselves and for your children. For the days are surely coming when they will say, 'Blessed are the barren, and the wombs that never bore, and the breasts that never nursed.' Then they will begin to say to the mountains, 'Fall on us'; and to the hills, 'Cover us.' For if they do this when the wood is green, what will happen when it is dry?" (Lk 23.27–31)

Leader. Even when he was wracked with pain, Jesus thought of others. Who believes in you and always thinks of you: friends, family members, teachers? What inspiration do they provide?

Leader. Lord, have mercy.
All. Lord, have mercy.
Leader. Christ, have mercy.
All. Christ, have mercy.
Leader. Lord, have mercy.
All. Lord, have mercy.

Station 9: Jesus Fell the Third Time

Reader 9. Once again, the weight was just too much. Jesus fell for the third time. Then he gathered the last bit of strength he had, got up, and carried his cross onward.

Leader. When do you feel exhausted but just keep going? What makes you continue?

Leader. Lord, have mercy.
All. Lord, have mercy.
Leader. Christ, have mercy.
All. Christ, have mercy.
Leader. Lord, have mercy.
All. Lord, have mercy.

Station 10:
Jesus Was Stripped of His Garments

Reader 10. When they reached Golgotha, the soldiers stripped Jesus of his garments. They cast lots to split his clothes among themselves.

Leader. Being stripped is a shameful experience and can cause great doubt. When have you felt stripped of your defenses and naked in front of the world?

Leader. Lord, have mercy.
All. Lord, have mercy.
Leader. Christ, have mercy.
All. Christ, have mercy.
Leader. Lord, have mercy.
All. Lord, have mercy.

Station 11: Jesus Was Nailed to the Cross

Reader 11. The soldiers laid Jesus on the cross, spread his arms, and drove a stake through each of his wrists. The first stake sent waves of excruciating pain up and down his body. The second was worse. The soldiers raised his knees and crossed his feet and drove a stake through the arch of each foot.

Leader. When Jesus was nailed to the cross, he could no longer move. What holds you stationary? What keeps you from accomplishing your dreams?

Leader. Lord, have mercy.
All. Lord, have mercy.
Leader. Christ, have mercy.
All. Christ, have mercy.
Leader. Lord, have mercy.
All. Lord, have mercy.

Station 12: Jesus Died on the Cross

Reader 12. It was around midday, and the sky became dark. Jesus cried out, "My God, my God, why have you forsaken me?" Jesus uttered a loud cry, and died.

Leader. At times, there seems to be no hope. What hopes, beliefs, ideals, and dreams have died or been lost for you?

Leader. Lord, have mercy.
All. Lord, have mercy.
Leader. Christ, have mercy.
All. Christ, have mercy.
Leader. Lord, have mercy.
All. Lord, have mercy.

Station 13: Jesus Was Taken Off the Cross

Reader 13. The soldiers came to break the legs of those who were not dead. When they saw that Jesus was dead, they pierced his side; blood and water poured out. They took Jesus off the cross. Joseph of Arimathea gathered his body to bury him.

Leader. Think about the people who have been there to pick you up, clean you off, and take care of your needs. How have you felt when they have done that?

Leader. Lord, have mercy.
All. Lord, have mercy.
Leader. Christ, have mercy.
All. Christ, have mercy.
Leader. Lord, have mercy.
All. Lord, have mercy.

Station 14: Jesus Was Laid in a Tomb

Reader 14.

So Joseph took the body and wrapped it in a clean linen cloth and laid it in his own new tomb, which he had hewn in the rock. He then rolled a great stone to the door of the tomb and went away. Mary Magdalene and the other Mary were there, sitting opposite the tomb. (Mt 27.59–60)

Leader. Jesus was put to rest. Where do you go to get rest and to rejuvenate? What is your sacred space like?

Leader. Lord, have mercy.
All. Lord, have mercy.
Leader. Christ, have mercy.
All. Christ, have mercy.
Leader. Lord, have mercy.
All. Lord, have mercy.

Closing Prayer

Leader. Dear Jesus, thank you for taking us on this journey. Many times, we feel troubled, beaten up by life, and just ready to give up hope. Please help us to realize that we can always come to you because you will understand.

You suffered for us, and you brought us abundant life by your Resurrection. You cried, you died, and you rose.

[The class might sing the remaining verses of "Were You There?"]

(This prayer service is from Debra Thorpe, Notre Dame Academy, Los Angeles, California.)

Opening Words and Readings

Leader. Jesus has told us that he is the light of the world and that he will dispel the darkness. Today, as we pray together, let us choose light. Let us commit ourselves to living an examined life, one in which we consciously and deliberately choose God.

Reader 1. Why should we choose God? Is there not pain, betrayal, temptation, and persecution when we follow the words of Jesus? That path is not easy, and it may cause rejection.

Reader 2. "Blessed are you when people hate you, and when they exclude you, revile you, and defame you on account of the Son of Man" (Lk 6.22).

Reader 3. "Love your enemies, do good to those who hate you, bless those who curse you, pray for those who abuse you" (Lk 6.27).

All. These words are not ones we hear often. Jesus Christ, be with us now. Open our hearts and give us the courage to say yes to you.

Reflection Activity

[Everyone thinks of all the messages and obstacles that keep them from saying yes to God, and writes those on a piece of black paper.]

Reader 4.

No good tree bears bad fruit, nor again does a bad tree bear good fruit; for each tree is known by its own fruit. . . . The good person out of the good treasure of the heart produces good, and the evil person out of evil treasure produces evil; for it is out of the abundance of the heart that the mouth speaks. (Lk 6.43–45)

All. Teach us to follow the good treasure of the heart and produce good. Let us tear the evil from our lives and choose God again. Let us again say yes to God.

[Everyone tears their black paper into pieces and uses the pieces to form the word "YES" on a piece of white paper.]

Prayers of the Faithful

Leader. We bring our needs to you, God.

[Everyone shares their individual needs. After each petition, the class responds, "Lord, hear our prayer."]

Leader. It is a struggle to say yes, but with a firm resolve and the support of this Christian community, we can do it!

All. In all the good times, and all the bad times, we choose your ways, O God. We choose the cross, knowing that with the pain comes the glory of Christ. We choose the good, the light, the whole, the holy. We say yes to you, this day. Amen.

A Day of Reflection Based on the Letter to the Philippians

Opening Prayer

Leader. "Grace to you and peace from God our Father and the Lord Jesus Christ" (Phil 1.2).
All. And also with you.

[The class listens to or sings the introduction and refrain from the song "Light of Christ/Exsultet" or another song with the theme of God's love, light, and peace.]

Leader. Dear God, let your love enfold us as we spend this time together today.

Let your light shine before us and illuminate the words we will hear spoken.

Let us find your presence in all we meet and do today. We ask this in Christ's name.
All. Amen

Closing Readings, Prayers, and Song

[The leader lights the pillar candle and plays soft instrumental music in the background.]

Reader 1.

For God is my witness, how I long for all of you with the compassion of Christ Jesus. And this is my prayer, that your love may overflow more and more with knowledge and full insight to help you to determine what is best, so that in the day of Christ you may be pure and blameless. (Phil 1.8–10)

All. May the light of Christ surround us.
Reader 2.

Only, live your life in a manner worthy of the gospel of Christ, so that, whether I come and see you or am absent and hear about you, I will know that you are standing firm in one spirit, striving side by side with one mind for the faith of the gospel. (1.27)

All. May the love of Christ enfold us.

Reader 3.

Beware of the dogs, beware of the evil workers. (verse 2). . . .

For many live as enemies of the cross of Christ; I have often told you of them, and now I tell you even with tears. Their end is destruction. (3.18–19)

All. May the power of Christ protect us.
Reader 4.

Finally, beloved, whatever is true, whatever is honorable, whatever is just, whatever is pure, whatever is pleasing, whatever is commendable, if there is any excellence and if there is anything worthy of praise, think about these things. Keep on doing the things that you have learned and received and heard and seen in me, and the God of peace will be with you. (4.8–9)

All. May the presence of Christ be with us now and always. Amen.

[Everyone offers petitions of faith.]
[Everyone says the Lord's Prayer together.]

Leader. Greet every saint in Christ Jesus. The friends who are with me greet you. The grace of the Lord Jesus Christ be with your spirit.
All. And also with you.
Leader. Let us offer one another a sign of peace.

[Everyone shares a sign of peace. The class listens to or sings the rest of the song "Light of Christ/ Exsultet" or another song with the theme of God's love, light, and peace.]